RELIGIOUS THOUGHT IN
THE NINETEENTH CENTURY

RELIGIOUS THOUGHT
IN THE
NINETEENTH CENTURY

ILLUSTRATED FROM
WRITERS OF THE PERIOD

BERNARD M.G.REARDON

Head of the Department of Religious Studies
University of Newcastle upon Tyne

CAMBRIDGE UNIVERSITY PRESS

CAMBRIDGE

LONDON · NEW YORK · MELBOURNE

Published by the Syndics of the Cambridge University Press
The Pitt Building, Trumpington Street, Cambridge CB2 1RP
Bentley House, 200 Euston Road, London NW1 2DB
32 East 57th Street, New York, NY 10022, USA
296 Beaconsfield Parade, Middle Park, Melbourne 3206, Australia

Library of Congress catalogue card number: 66-10542

ISBN 0 521 06049 4 hard covers
ISBN 0 521 09386 4 paperback

First published 1966
Reprinted 1978

Printed in Great Britain at the
University Press, Cambridge

PREFACE

The present volume is designed as a sequel to that on the religious thought of the eighteenth century by the late Professor J. M. Creed and Mr J. S. Boys Smith, now Master of St John's College, Cambridge. Their purpose—to illustrate changes and developments in religious thinking during a selected period by means of passages chosen from representative writers—has been mine too, but the method pursued differs. The authors of *Religious Thought in the Eighteenth Century* (Cambridge University Press, 1934) judged—rightly, I think—that the importance of the age from their point of view lay in the nature of the problems, as they considered, then definitely raised for the first time, more than in the individual greatness of the writers. Their scheme of arrangement therefore was by subject-matter, and they applied it to a very useful end. For my part, however, I have found this procedure to be impracticable, for what is striking about the nineteenth century is undoubtedly the individuality, as in numerous instances also the undeniable greatness, of the writers themselves. Thus their approach to the problem of religious, and in particular, Christian belief, although in most cases they have much in common, differs as between one and another of them to such a degree that any attempt to assemble excerpts from their writings under a few general headings would hardly be very enlightening. Nineteenth-century attitudes, though readily identifiable, are less easily definable and classifiable than are those of the century preceding. Moreover, recognition of the strong individuality of these thinkers is a necessary factor in a just appreciation of their views. It would be as absurd to try to obscure the idiosyncrasy of, say, a Kierkegaard or a Coleridge or a Newman by forcing disparate opinions into an arbitrary synthesis as to underline it by a pointlessly antithetical *sic et non*. I have, accordingly, taken my authors in an order determined merely by geography and chronology. European thought is here more liberally represented than in the book by Creed and Mr Boys Smith, whilst the views of British writers are supplemented by others from across the Atlantic.

In any such enterprise as this the question of whom and what to omit is the most vexing, and the nineteenth century provides an embarrassingly rich field of choice. Some reasonably clear principle of

v

selection had to be adopted, with, in consequence, unavoidable if regrettable omissions. My aim has been to illustrate what may fairly be claimed as characteristic of the age; and this assumes on the whole the form of reflective thought *about* religion, its nature and its significance. Hence beliefs widely, indeed generally, held—traditional dogmatics, I mean, either Catholic or Protestant—are not represented. To mention English divines only, Pusey on baptismal regeneration, for example, or Liddon on the incarnation, or Dale on the atonement, finds no place. On the other hand, I have felt bound to exclude writers who would not usually be regarded as having treated theological issues as a matter of specific concern. To draw the line with an unfaltering hand has not, all the same, been a simple matter. I have included Matthew Arnold but not Carlyle, Kierkegaard but not Nietzsche. In any event one's judgement must, in the final resort, remain personal and something from which the critical reader may well see fit to dissent. Further —a harshly practical consideration—the book had to be of manageable bulk; but since my intention was to produce a collection of texts rather than an anthology of snippets it could easily have been twice the size.

Writers cited in translation, with one exception, are given in versions already published. I have not undertaken to make any new ones of my own.

Acknowledgements

Thanks are due to the following for permission to print extracts from the books mentioned: T. & T. Clark for H. R. Mackintosh and J. S. Stewart's translation of Schleiermacher's *The Christian Faith* (Part 1, no. 1: II); Ernest Benn Ltd for E. B. Saunders' translation of Harnack's *What is Christianity?* (Part 1, no. 7); Princeton University Press for D. F. Swenson's translation of Kierkegaard's *Philosophical Fragments* (Part 1, no. 8); International Universities Press for P. P. Zouboff's translation of Solovyov's *Lectures on Godmanhood* (Part 1, no. 12); John Murray Ltd for Scott Holland's contributions to *Lux Mundi* (Part 2, no. 8); and the Clarendon Press, Oxford, for Bradley's *Appearance and Reality* (Part 2, no. 9: III).

I should also like to thank The staff of The Cambridge University Press for the great care they have bestowed on the production of the book.

B. M. G. R.

Newcastle upon Tyne

CONTENTS

Preface   *page* v

Introduction   1

PART I

EUROPEAN

1 Schleiermacher   39
   I   What Religion Is   42
   II Religious Language   51

2 Hegel   61
   The Absolute Religion   65

3 Feuerbach   82
   Man and Religion   85

4 D. F. Strauss   113
   I   Myth in the New Testament   116
   II Definition and Characteristics of the Gospel Myth   123

5 Lotze   125
   The Divine Personality   127

6 Ritschl   138
   I   God and Metaphysics   141
   II The Special Character of Religious Knowledge   141
   III Value-Judgements   147

7 Harnack   149
   I   Jesus' Essential Teaching   152
   II Protestantism   158

CONTENTS

8   Kierkegaard   *page* 166
     Faith and Reason   170

9   Lamennais   184
     Authority in Religion   187

10   Auguste Comte   196
     The Law of the Three States   199

11   Auguste Sabatier   208
     What Is a Dogma?   211

12   Solovyov   218
     Godmanhood   221

PART II

BRITISH AND AMERICAN

1   Coleridge   239
     I   Reason and Understanding   242
     II   Faith   244
     III The Authority of Scripture   251

2   F. D. Maurice   254
     I   What Is Revelation?   257
     II   The Creeds   262

3   Newman   269
     I   Faith and Reason   273
     II   Belief in God   274
     III Development in Ideas   284

4   Mansel   288
     The Nature and Purpose of Theological Truths   290

5   J. S. Mill   297
     Theism   300

CONTENTS

6 Benjamin Jowett and *Essays and Reviews*   *page* 309
   The Interpretation of Scripture   312

7 Matthew Arnold   324
   Christianity   328

8 Scott Holland and *Lux Mundi*   338
   I   What Is Faith?   341
   II Dogma   349

9 The British Hegelians   352
   I   John Caird: Religion and Philosophy   355
   II Edward Caird: Religion and the Human
       Consciousness   363
   III F. H. Bradley: Faith, God and the Absolute   369

10 Emerson   374
   The Soul and Revelation   377

11 Josiah Royce   381
   Religion as a Moral Code and as a Theory   384

12 William James   392
   The Will to Believe   395

Index of Works Cited   405

INTRODUCTION

I

If the eighteenth century can be summarily characterized as the Age of
Reason its successor is less amenable to facile generalization: the tendencies and developments of which the historian has to take note are
more numerous, diverse and complex. In particular the nineteenth
century, far more obviously than its predecessor, was an era of change.
Again, a large measure of the appeal which the latter has for the modern
mind lies not only in its comparative simplicity of aspect but in its
remoteness: to study it is to encounter, as it were, a prepossessing
stranger. With the nineteenth century, however, we are aware of a
closer affinity, so that it has for us the sometimes tiresome familiarity
of a kinsman. Yet the student of religion is likelier to find it of much
greater interest. Its forerunner represents a time when the religious
spirit blew but fitfully; convention, decorum and prudence were the
usually accepted marks of a right-thinking man, and faith itself admitted
reason as its better part. By contrast the century which began with
revolution and general war, and whose early temper was displayed in
the emotional and imaginative vagaries of the Romantic movement,
turned to religion with a new concern, as to something holding the
key, it might be, to the interpretation of man's historic life itself, a
belief fostered and stimulated by a growing knowledge and appreciation
of the phases through which that life had actually passed. If man has
in his hands the means of shaping his own terrestrial destiny—as in
this century it was increasingly realized that he had—it was because,
nevertheless, he himself was the product of an historical evolution no
part of which was irrelevant to the self-comprehension to which he
aspired. His life might be many-sided, intricate and devious—far more
so than the rationalists of an earlier day had supposed—but it might
also be possible to detect a purpose within it which gave confident
hope—and as the century advanced this expectation swelled—of a
richer, ampler future. If, then, one does venture to epitomize the epoch
in a phrase one might call it the Age of Progress. It is not surprising
that religion itself should have both reflected and promoted the current
forward-looking idealism.

This at least is true of Protestantism, for Catholicism remained to all showing obdurately committed to the past. The former, more amorphous than its ancient rival, was less resistant to the pressure of change, and although a residuum of the old Protestant orthodoxy, on the European continent, in Britain and in America, survived the rigour of a growingly adverse intellectual climate, Protestant thought generally, if in varying degree, felt the need of coming to terms in one way or another with an age in which science, technology and social revolution had together led to what was fast becoming a universal reassessment of inherited values. As between the diverse Christian traditions the old lines of difference seemed to have less point or meaning. The result is that the type of Christian thinking which seems representative of the period is, broadly speaking, liberal, anti-dogmatic and humanistic. Further, the paradox—as it would appear—that the opposition which these trends provoked was itself but a feature of the new outlook is really none at all. Reaction too is a form of action and can be explained only by reference to the forces against which it contends. Newman— to cite the most striking example of this—was as much the child of his times as, say, J. S. Mill or Matthew Arnold. Mill indeed, earnest rationalist that he was, is in some ways more of a hark-back to an older world. But to take the true measure of our period we must return for a moment to the great disruption of western Christendom in the sixteenth century.

The Protestant Reformation, as well as its Catholic counterpart, was as a religious movement not so much the beginning of a new era as a temporary infusion of fresh life into the old. Medieval and even ancient modes of thought persisted. The watchword was Back! rather than Forward! The distant past, it was believed, possessed a truth which later generations had corrupted or obscured. Its repository was the Scriptures, as interpreted by the early Fathers and—now—the champions of reform. Life was at any rate still conceived primarily in theological terms and to its problems, men assumed, religion alone had the answer. Occasionally no doubt the great reformers themselves expressed ideas and insights which afterwards bore fruit; in the immediate aftermath of ecclesiastical revolution, however, these were forgotten or suppressed. Thus the Reformation, in impulse if not in its ultimate character, was a counter-stroke to what is called, however loosely, the Renaissance. Yet without the intellectual ferment which preceded it the religious revival would have been the less effective: Luther owed more to Erasmus than he ever wished to acknowledge. For the reformers were able to take advantage of conditions which, when revolt came, brought down the immemorial religious edifice in ruins, though Roman Catholicism had in truth imbibed more of the humanist spirit than had Protestantism, within which the reassertion of Renaissance aims was long delayed.

In its basic orthodoxy, an inheritance from Christian antiquity which it in the main never questioned, Reformation Protestantism was at one with Catholicism. Indeed the reformers themselves were unmistakable products of the Middle Ages and shared most of their opponents' presuppositions. In substance their respective conceptions of revelation, inspiration, authority and salvation were the same. The issues on which they differed were clear-cut. Where teaching arose which undermined their shared positions they vied with one another in their zeal to repress it. It is no exaggeration to say, therefore, that despite the great doctrinal cleavage of the sixteenth century and the bitter theological controversies to which it gave rise, the fundamental unity of Christian thought in the west continued unimpaired until the latter part of the eighteenth century. But by that time it was becoming evident that the dogmatic tradition in both its Catholic and Protestant forms would have to meet the incursion of intellectual forces tending increasingly to isolate it from the prevailing outlook. Unless faith were to fall back on the stronghold of an absolute authority it must somehow endeavour to compromise with the new conditions. During the nineteenth century Catholicism, as we have said, chose the former alternative and matched it with an appropriate ecclesiastical policy. Protestantism, if with much misgiving, found the latter on the whole unavoidable.

For the sceptical rationalism of the eighteenth century the very idea of a special divine revelation presented difficulty. But the difficulty arose from the fact that the conception of revelation as a publication of divine truths beyond reach of the human intellect was one which it shared with orthodox Christianity. Such truths might belong to the realm of authority and faith, but, as Hume insisted, because they could not be attained neither could they truly be possessed by the reason. Revelation that was rational and hence alone fitted to the proper nature of man had been known to him, in effect, since his first essays in reasoning. 'If', argued the English deist, Matthew Tindal, 'all own, that God, at no Time, cou'd have any Motive to give Laws to Mankind, but for their Good; and that he is, at all Times, equally good, and, at all Times, acts upon the same Motives; must they not own with me, except they

3

are inconsistent with themselves, that his Laws, at all Times, must be the Same?' It was to be concluded that all religions, in their essential teaching, were at one and that there must be an 'exact agreement' between natural and revealed. The further inference, it need hardly be stressed, was that the differential doctrines of Christianity, in which it claimed to preserve a special and all-important revelation, could be disregarded by any reasonable man. The appearance of such doctrines was to be attributed to credulity and priestcraft.

That the criterion so applied to the phenomena of positive religion was shallow and inadequate the nineteenth-century thinkers very soon discerned. If man is not a discarnate intelligence but a creature of time and place, if, that is, his life is historically determined, then his apprehension even of ultimate truth must be subject to historical conditions. Although in course of the ages the knowledge of truth will be both broadened and deepened, no single phase of the process, however partial its understanding, should be discounted. History accordingly is a significant study in its own right and infinitely more than a copy-book of moral examples and awful warnings. Nay, the vista of things long past acquires in the perspective of time an enchantment by comparison with which the present seems only humdrum and commonplace. Nostalgia of this sort, voiced at first in the literature of the time, lessened with the cooling of Romantic enthusiasms, but the historical sense, to which Hegelianism gave metaphysical lustre, was perhaps above all else the nineteenth century's most characteristic development. It provided the impulse whereby historiography was established not as the pastime of literary amateurs but as a science. Ancient documents simply as such became the objects of searching investigation and canons of historico-literary criticism, inspired though they might be by current philosophy, gained widespread academic acceptance. Religious writings, and through them religion itself as an important aspect of human culture, could gain no immunity from similar inquiry; and indeed the Bible, since it offered so sharp a challenge to the critical intelligence, was itself a major stimulus to the more rigorous application of the new methods. The brash procedures of the eighteenth-century rationalists might thus be shown to rest largely on ignorance and misconception. On the other hand, the historical study of the Scriptures quickly suggested that traditional ideas concerning revelation and inspiration, as well as the customary style of literalist exegesis, were due for revision. If historical study could so easily discredit deist assumptions it yet pointed to consequences hardly less encouraging to the orthodox appeal to rational 'evidences'.

This scientific approach to man's understanding of his own past had for background an increasingly elaborate systematized knowledge of the universe in which his life is set. The beginnings of modern natural science no doubt long antedated the age of Darwin, but the theory of evolution imparted to the idea of nature a depth and consistency which hitherto it had for the most part lacked. Man himself was now seen unmistakably to be a part of nature; and if 'natural' in his physical constitution why not also in his mental and moral, so that even his highest cultural achievements may in the last resort be seen as homogeneous with what they rest upon and to be subject to laws analogous, in their fashion, with those which the natural scientist so confidently formulates for the primary levels of experienced reality? Voices soon were heard which had no doubt of an affirmative answer. Thus science, it appeared, could be identified not only with a growing corpus of factual knowledge but with a philosophy claiming the all-sufficiency of such knowledge. For religious thought the menace of positivism lay not merely in its denial of religious truth but in the explanation of it which it plausibly offered. It allowed no 'breaks' in the continuity of man's natural existence, so that if the concept of divine revelation were to retain any meaning at all theology would have to recognize that revelation can occur only through and under the conditions of the natural. The 'supernaturalism' of traditional belief was only a lingering survival of the myth-thinking of a far-off past.

The main philosophical influence was that of Immanuel Kant. The Koenigsberg master cannot himself be described as a Romantic, but he was not unmoved by Rousseau, however distasteful he found Rousseau's sentimentalism, and he later dissociated himself from the rationalist theology of Leibniz and Wolff by which he had been so strongly affected in his student days. The Pietist strain also is evident and the echo of an older Lutheranism is caught in the preface to the *Critique of Pure Reason*, where the author proposes 'to abolish knowledge to make room for faith', which alone, he considers, is religion's proper basis; although the type of faith he envisages—a 'rational faith' (*Vernunfts-glaube*), he calls it—is by no means that of Luther himself, the one work he devotes as a whole to the treatment of the religious problem bearing the very un-Lutheran title of *Religion within the Limits of Reason alone*. Nevertheless, through Schleiermacher and Ritschl, Kantianism was to prove the guiding principle in the religious thought of the succeeding century, Hegelianism being a temporary if powerful interruption. That theology can be founded upon the exercise of speculative reason is a view which few today, other than professed Thomists, would be willing to sustain. But to a more detailed survey of Kant's position we shall return in a moment.

These ideas, although, as we already have pointed out, not entirely unanticipated by Reformation thinking, for the most part transcended the issues by which Christendom had previously been divided. They emerged as a consequence of man's deepening sense of his dependence upon the conditions of his historical existence and growing assurance that his destiny, wherever else it might in the end be achieved, must first be fulfilled upon the historical plane.

II

Religious thought, for the purposes of the present work, should be taken to mean, in the main, thought about religion. The attitude of detachment which makes this kind of approach possible is indeed a mark of modernity. The question is not, initially, whether this or that set of religious beliefs is true or false but the nature and function of religion as an expression of the human consciousness; although in lands where the traditional culture is Christian this must mean, mainly if not exclusively, Christianity. The nineteenth century was thus able, as earlier centuries were not, to view religion in general and Christianity in particular as a subject for historical investigation and critical reflexion. Hence the development within it of such studies as the history of religions, comparative religion and the philosophy of religion. Any attempt to rethink or revalue Christianity is bound therefore to presuppose a phenomenological inquiry. In other words, a religious philosophy, and more specifically a Christian philosophy, could not in the prevailing intellectual climate simply take its basic beliefs, its 'revealed' data, for granted: it first would have to employ critical thought upon them, studying their historical origin and evolution, noting the external influences which have moulded their forms and analysing the psychological and social needs to which they responded. Only on the basis of such pursuits could theological reconstruction be fruitfully tried. Hence also, however, the tentative, apologetic and sometimes negative tone of much nineteenth-century theologizing.

The grounds of belief were shifting and the type of edifice once erected upon them could no longer serve.

The majority of those who contributed most valuably to the religious thinking of the age were themselves Christian, critical though they might be of the inherited orthodoxy. But even those who were not Christian were as a rule deeply concerned with the intellectual and moral problems which Christianity raises. A signal example of this is Feuerbach. He is commonly regarded as an arch-atheist, but the appropriateness of the term depends on the meaning infused into it. His aim, he declared—and of his intense sincerity there can be no question—was 'to make God real and human'. If his work seemed destructive it was, he claimed, only in relation to the unhuman, not the human, elements in religion. The truth that God exists is not to be doubted; but he is a man's own hidden but assured existence, 'the subjectivity of subjects, the personality of persons'. Where, then, Feuerbach's view differs from theism is in its assertion that man himself is the true object of belief and that the idea of a deity has to be humanized before it can properly become the focus of devotion and worship. 'It is not I but religion that worships man, although theology denies it; it is religion itself that says: God is man, man is God.' In translating theology into anthropology Feuerbach's intention is not to destroy religion or dissolve the religious sentiment but rather to revalue and re-establish both by identifying the religious object for what it truly is. Much the same also applies to Matthew Arnold in this country. The Bible, Arnold objected, has been misread. The language of the Pauline letters, for instance, is a literary language, not a technical, but the theologians have used it as though it were scientific. Even more fundamentally, men handle the word of God 'as if it stood for a perfectly definite and ascertained idea, from which we might, without more ado, extract propositions and draw inferences, just as we should from any other definite and ascertained idea'. But can it bear such treatment? The truth is that as used by those for whom it has the vividest meaning it is by no means a term of science or exact knowledge, but one of 'poetry and eloquence, a term thrown out, so to speak, at a not fully grasped object of the speaker's consciousness'. Men mean different things by it as their consciousness differs.

The attitude of both these writers is significant of the spirit of their times. Each from his different background approaches the religious problem with a concern amounting to reverence. Both seek to perpetuate the values of religion by disengaging them from their familiar but false setting, and each discerns in the life of man himself their true ground and object.

The point of view stated with such force and clarity by Feuerbach and Arnold was, however, if in modified guise, increasingly that of liberal theologians. Inevitably the question came to be asked: What is religious dogma? Historical study was of course a principal aid in reaching an answer, in showing how in fact religious beliefs had developed and been formalized. But historical criticism also made it plain that the Scriptures could no more be used as a storehouse of text-materials for the erection of self-consistent doctrinal systems. Theology, like other realms of human thought, belonged to the relativities of time, and no statement of truth could be absolute. The experience behind it might remain in essence the same from one age to another but its expression was bound to change, or, if it did not change, to become obsolete. For doctrine is experience interpreted according to the intellectual norms and standards of the day. The insistence of reason doubtless made the interpretation requisite; clarification and formal definition proved necessary from the exigencies of both teaching and controversy; but the structuralizing of faith, however little it was realized to be so at the time, and whatever weight of traditional authority it might acquire, had no quality of ultimate permanence, and alike in fact and in principle theological doctrine was felt to be open to revision, although opinion might widely differ as to the needful extent of it since general agreement on what constitutes the 'essence' of Christianity has never been reached. Thus the understanding of doctrine varied not simply from denomination to denomination but from individual to individual. Yet what cannot fail to impress the student of this period is the steady growth therein of the conviction that the old teachings could no longer be affirmed in the old way. Some sort of accommodation and compromise was imperative, as even the conservative were obliged to admit.

To return, however, to Kant. The place in modern thought of the author of the two great *Critiques* is one of peculiar ambivalence. In some respects he looks forward to a new age, in others he is the last and most important representative of an earlier one. Neglect this Janus-like quality in him and one fails to weigh his significance adequately. Thus in his treatment of the problem of knowledge he transcends the old dogmatism and rationalism, yet of human experience in its historical dimension he is unappreciative and his conception of reason is of that of the isolated individual. How, therefore, to interpret Kant has ever presented difficulty, for he is not always self-consistent and his thought seems again and again to point beyond itself to further ranges of speculative possibility. But the very fact of its ultimate lack of systematic unity has meant, as often is the way with such thinkers, that it has continued to exercise a vitalizing influence. The manner in which Kant deals with a problem always merits close attention, the breadth and sanity of his viewpoint never but inspire confidence even when the particular conclusions reached appear unacceptable. His many-sidedness was to make of him, despite the abstraction and aridity of his style, a power from which the mind of the ensuing century seemed to have little wish to free itself.

Within the sphere of theology it is Kant's philosophical principles in general rather than his own specifically theological writing that have proved fertile. His treatise on *Religion within the limits of Reason alone*, a work relatively seldom read, is characteristic of the era that closed with his own death in 1804 more than of that which had dawned, but five years earlier, with the *Discourses* of Schleiermacher. It is of interest as illustrating Kant's own ideas and methods rather than for any light it sheds upon the real issues of the religious problem. Where it is of value is in indicating the possibility and need of distinguishing between the essential and the non-essential in religion. The touchstone he applies is the moral consciousness: whatever fails to satisfy this, no matter how insistent its claim to be regarded as divine revelation, cannot be true or important. The substance of religion, through and through, is ethical. 'Everything outside of a good life by which man supposes he can make himself well-pleasing to God is superstition.' The mark of the religious consciousness is that it looks on duties as divine commands. Nevertheless, for all the truth which this moral austerity in Kant's thinking permanently underlines, his sympathy with the religious impulse was narrow and unimaginative. He saw religion as little other than a kind of external complement to morality, and one which, even on his own principles, might be shown to be unnecessary. To introduce God as a means of assuring us that virtue and happiness are finally coincident is a device whose artificiality is evident the moment we turn aside to consider how in fact religion arises. No doubt Kant would have replied that he here is treating of the logic of the reason and not the psychology of the religious consciousness, but the fault lies in the actual intention more than in the omission, and what he gives us is morality, not religion. To the demands of the former he was ever vividly awake; to the appeal of the latter he remained curiously insensitive.

Kant's main contribution to religious thought was in the field of epistemology, and in particular through his determination of the limits of scientific knowledge. There is, he held, no 'external' world which merely imposes itself upon the mind. Experience of space and time is made possible by the synthetic unity of self-consciousness, which through its several 'categories' has a constitutive activity of its own. To suppose that mind can be explained in terms of what, as we know it, is itself dependent on mind, is thus a blatant *petitio principii*. Scientific method, for its own purposes, is entirely valid, but such validity does not extend beyond those purposes. The world cannot be detached from the self, which is the indispensable condition of all knowledge, and to argue that reality is no more than a causal mechanism is to be beguiled by an abstraction. All that science can do is to describe the relations between phenomena, but why phenomena are as they are and whither they tend is not for it to try to answer: teleology lies outside its sphere. The scientist justifiably sets aside what he shows methodologically to be of no concern to him, but it does not follow that what for him can only be an irrelevancy is of no significance in a total view of man. Indeed, later nineteenth-century thinking—in Mach, Poincaré and others—was to contend that recognition of the proper limits of science is bound to undermine the pretensions of naturalism. On the other hand the theologians, among them notably Ritschl and Auguste Sabatier, whilst conceding that teleology has no true place in the understanding of nature, insist upon it as a necessary factor in the interpretation of history. Man, that is, not only subsists in time, he perforce realizes himself only under its conditions. History is the unfolding of his destiny. Hence the symbolical function of the idea of the Kingdom of God, in pointing to the 'end' which history is inwardly directed to achieve. Whereas, then, mere nature is to be represented as a realm simply of 'fact', history is to be seen as one of 'value'. At what point the two realms are to be conceptually united this post-Kantian type of thought is prepared on the whole to leave unstated.

Thus inevitably we come back to Kant's fundamental distinction between the theoretical and practical reason, and so between knowledge and faith. Much has been made of the 'critical' aspect of his philosophy, but important though this is it is subordinate to his aim of establishing the place and rights of the practical reason and through it of human freedom, which for Kant is vital to a proper doctrine of man as a moral entity. For the moral consciousness is something that cannot be bounded by mechanical necessity. Man attains to reality only when he himself is a rational cause. Looking at himself empirically, as it were from without, and viewing himself as a part of the phenomenal world, he discerns no more than a fragment of the truth. As a self-determining *person*, however, he becomes intelligible, and it is this intelligible self which is the presupposition of the empirical. It is the free causative action of the intelligible self which makes possible the secondary or derivative causality experienced under space-time.

The postulates of the practical reason are demands springing from man's inner nature. They are not, Kant tells us, 'theoretical dogmata, but *presuppositions* which have necessarily only practical import'. They do not therefore extend to speculative knowledge but rather give objective reality to the ideas of practical reason *in general*. The ideas, that is, of God, freedom and immortality have 'objects', though not of course such as can be given to perception. They are 'non-phenomenal' and their existence is guaranteed only by our apprehension of the moral law. It would thus be incorrect to think of them as an expression simply of emotional desire: they arise, 'not from the subjective ground of our wishes, but from the objective motive of the will which binds every rational being'. Yet the being of God is something which we cannot prove on theoretical grounds and our knowledge of him is that of a practical relationship alone. It is this practical knowledge which, as we have noted, Kant understands by faith. Knowledge in the strict sense pertains only to phenomena; what faith apperceives is the *noumenal*, the 'real' that lies beyond space and time. Clearly then there are not two 'reasons' but one and the same reason in two distinct but equally necessary aspects. The point to remark, however—for it is here that the Kantian influence has been of decisive importance—is that, for the author of the *Critique of Practical Reason*, faith is not a form of theoretical knowledge for which we have only inconclusive data but a mode of apprehending reality different as to both its origin and the object or objects to which it is directed. The idealist philosophers who followed Kant, dissatisfied with what seemed to them a needless dualism, sought to identify faith with knowledge; yet the disillusionment which followed their grandiose attempt to rationalize all experience within a single framework of thought only meant that writers who were aware of the impossibility of a return to theological dogmatism again looked to Kant for guidance. And where, on the other hand, Kant had shown himself at his weakest—namely, in his inadequate appreciation of the part of the emotions and the imagination in the religious consciousness—he was strengthened by the example of Schleiermacher, a teacher to whom modern theology owes more than to any other, Kant himself alone excepted.

The result has been a heavy emphasis upon faith rather than the rational understanding as the fitting instrument of moral and religious knowledge. Such knowledge is of a different order from the scientific; hence are there two differing modes of certitude and the one cannot be established by the means appropriate only to the other. Science cannot be built on faith, but neither can faith be created by science; and where faith exists 'proof' addressed to anything but the seat of faith—the feeling and willing self—is pointless. Thus the advantage of neo-Kantianism for theology seemed twofold. In the first place it located the ground of religious belief where alone it should be sought, since to base piety on intellectual propositions is to divest it of its true character: science and philosophy are not religion and can afford it no valid sanction. In the second place the religious believer would now be free to pursue inquiry into the history of religion, and in particular the origin and early development of Christianity, without fear that his scientific studies would of necessity imperil faith. Historical criticism could not be ignored, but its place is among the sciences not in theology; essential orthodoxy will look elsewhere—to the religious consciousness itself—for the justification of ideas upon which neither history nor speculative philosophy can rightly pass judgement. The truth of the Christian religion is affirmed by faith, of which its dogmas are the postulates, not by a 'reason' adapted to other and alien purposes.

III

Before passing on to consider the Hegelian solution of the religious problem, the over-confident assertion of which was to lead directly to the neo-Kantian reaction just described, it is worth while to note one more respect in which Kant's influence was to continue to make itself felt: his insistence on the importance of personality, especially as the centre of moral judgement. The place of the self in Kant's epistemology is central: a 'world' exists because of the synthetic activity of the self-conscious subject. But it is in the realm of morals that the personality really exercises its rule. Morality depends on the autonomy of the will; apart from it freedom is meaningless. It is man's glory that so far from his being mechanically determined he determines himself, is a centre of rational causality and hence is a member of an order of being that is truly intelligible. Herein is his peculiar value; he is himself an 'objective end', for which no other can be substituted, and must be treated accordingly. Nature we cannot in the last resort explain, but man, conscious as he is of his inward freedom, is real indeed and knows himself to be so. Hence any attempt on the part of either religion or philosophy to weaken the sense of the individual personality or of moral responsibility finds in Kant an implacable opponent. Neither absolute idealism nor evolutionary naturalism could in this regard have satisfied him, and his inspiration was to be a major factor in securing the resistance of religious thought, in cleaving to the truth of moral freedom and to the imperative of duty, to both these movements.

For Kant's immediate successors, however, it was his failure to impose a systematic unity upon his thinking which called for correction. It seemed to them that he had brought philosophy to a parting of the ways, whilst he himself appeared to stand irresolute as to which of the two should be followed. The one led back to the old empiricism of real —and alone truly real—'things', the other forward to a world constituted purely by thought. The sole alternatives were thus naturalism and idealism, and Fichte (1762–1814), Schelling and Hegel opted for the latter. The Kantian dualism of thought and thing was resolved by the first of these thinkers with a thorough-going assertion of the role in knowledge of the thinking subject. The world appeared to become but the creation of the human mind itself—a doctrine whose evident 'atheism' led to Fichte's dismissal from his professorial chair at Jena. But atheism is not a word capable of easy definition. The constitutive principle of the universe, Fichte went on to maintain, is not man's intelligence but God's. The finite mind exists only in the infinite. All that we are is but a reflexion of what he is, and nothing finally has being except in him. Nature therefore is simply a manifestation or aspect of deity, and mere 'matter', independent of this divine mind, is nonexistent. What Fichte had to offer his generation was a philosophical mysticism. His language, religiously speaking, is pantheistic. But for all its rhetorical extravagance his teaching was to leave its impress upon the theological outlook of the ensuing age.

A moderating tendency showed itself in Fichte's younger contemporary, Schelling (1775–1854). Schelling's concern was to assign an adequate place, within an idealist scheme of thought, to external nature. Nature, he realized, is more than just a background for the self, since the self is demonstrably part of nature. Moreover, nature is intelligible and akin to mind, to which it presents numerous analogues. Indeed it is mind in the making, mind evolving, unfolding, into full personal consciousness. Nature accordingly is not static, a *bloc* of permanently subsisting entities, but is essentially in process, moving from less to more highly organized and intelligible forms, reflecting ever more clearly the intrinsic characteristics of the mind of man, who must himself be regarded as nature's climax and crown. The suggestive idea, then, to which Schelling turns as to the clue to the interpretation of nature as a whole is that of an organism, with its observable growth and development. Science in its several departments may investigate *aspects* of nature or even nature entire; but the world can never remain purely objective: finally, in achieving consciousness in the thinking self, it becomes subject, and the inherent drift and meaning of the whole is at last apparent. Whatever his shortcomings as a thinker—his fancifulness, his sheer lack of relevant knowledge—Schelling is able to supplement Fichte's doctrine both by modifying its subjectivism and by introducing into it a dynamic teleological principle which anticipates the dominant intellectual *motif* of the coming epoch, the theory of evolution. The way was prepared for the full efflorescence of absolute idealism in the commanding genius of Hegel.

Hegel's approach to philosophy may be said to have been prompted by two leading interests—the spectacle of man's historical progress and the intellectual challenge of Christianity. One of his earliest writings (1795) was a *Life of Jesus*, strongly coloured by the moralism of Kant. Its thesis is that the law of man's being is not something external to him, does not impose itself from without, but springs from within him in the shape of a 'reason' whose rights and dominion must be recognized and affirmed. Jesus' teaching, Hegel argues, clearly signifies this. In the Kingdom for whose coming his disciples are bidden to pray all rational creatures will have no other law than that of their moral conscience. Thus ethics and religion are one and the same. But this predominantly Kantian influence was not to continue for long. Hegel soon came to substitute for the categorical imperative an intuitionist morality the principle of which lies in the individual's native sense of right: according with his true inclinations, it takes the form of a non-legalist morality the impulse of which is an expression of love and of freedom. This, Hegel now felt, was the real moral outlook of Jesus and as such constitutes the 'spirit' of Christianity. For what would be the worth of a mere slavish obedience which the soul itself could not receive with joy and which, so far from liberating a man, only thwarted his personal development? The religion of Jesus was a religion of love, life and spirit, his Kingdom a realm of harmony wherein none gives command or is subjected to force. This new view was the outcome of the Romantic enthusiasm to which Hegel, a fellow-student of Schelling's, had now succumbed; though perhaps rather more than a touch of the Romantic attitude, intuitive and mystical, remained with him throughout his life, even when later he became bitingly critical of it.

It was while he was at Jena that Hegel's doctrine matured. The substance of it is already contained in the *Phenomenology* of 1807, in which the differences between Hegel and Schelling clearly emerge. The philosophy of imagination is replaced by that of reflexion. The Romantic thinkers started by positing an Absolute, knowledge of which we possess by intuition. This Hegel denies. The Absolute, he maintains, is not the object of immediate intellectual apprehension but is attainable only as the result of a prolonged and difficult enterprise of the spirit. We reach it by a series of stages in the course of which mind by degrees frees itself from the domination of mere things and becomes self-determining. Consciousness begins with the data of sense-experience, but what is received by the senses, as Heraclitus and Plato long ago had shown, is simply multiplicity and flux, a ceaseless coming-to-be and passing away, which the rational intelligence can never properly grasp. To co-ordinate sensations, to categorize appearances, is the work of the perceiving mind. This is able to detect, under the relations subsisting between one object and another, a deeper truth than shows in the surface. The mere appearances therefore it can disregard and will fasten upon the relations themselves as something of which we may reach an understanding. The next step is from these relationships to the discovery of the laws or forces which, whilst occasioning the changes we observe in phenomena, themselves remain unchanged. In this progressive effort consciousness becomes more and more manifest to itself, realizing that by its activity alone is the chaos of our basic intuitions reduced to order. Thus the very functioning of consciousness enlarges its range and scope and in each succeeding phase of its development it secures a further and fuller self-affirmation. But in the process it seeks to liberate itself from the endlessly varying objects which engage and hold it, and in its failure to gain such liberation entirely it becomes a 'bad conscience'. In revenge it returns to the object in order to conquer it, to absorb it within itself, to explain it in terms of itself. By these means it transforms itself into that sovereign 'reason' which dictates the laws of reality, inasmuch as the essential nature of things is recognized to be identical with that of mind itself. Finally, in taking itself as object, it sees itself as existing in the moral world, the world of the family and society, creating, shaping and developing these universal institutions in the diverse and antagonistic forms whose mutual opposition it nevertheless compels them to transcend in order to approach the Ideal of which it is itself the representation. Under whatever designation—perception, understanding or reason, Spirit or Idea—it is always the Absolute which, in the third part of the *Encyclopaedia of the Philosophical Sciences* (1817), Hegel has in mind and of which he describes the successive phases. Spirit, free and infinite, is revealed in all things, declaring itself ever more certainly and articulately as the grand process of the universe discloses its nature and purpose in man. So, in the *Philosophy of Right* (1821) Hegel is able to demonstrate the real meaning and import of law, art, religion and philosophy.

For Hegel, then, the Absolute is God; one who is not remote from his creation but, on the contrary, wholly immanent in what from beginning to end is the outcome and expression of his own being and act. His transcendence consists only in the extent to which his action is less than his still latent power.

Hegel dealt with the religious problem at length in his lecture-courses at Berlin preserved for us in the posthumous *Philosophy of Religion*. The main question discussed is God's relation to the world, a relation which cannot be stated simply in terms of cause and effect, since neither can be separated from the other. God 'creates' his world as the poet 'creates' his verse. The universe, as his determinate act, is the divine thought realized. He thus dwells in all men, and to live religiously is consciously to place oneself under the divine purpose, to acknowledge the absolute Spirit, to understand that God is in us and we in God. In treating of the various world-religions Hegel discovers the emergence of an increasingly purified spirituality, which in Christianity—and there alone—achieves an absolute utterance. What however flaws his account of the Christian religion is his curious failure to appreciate it in its positive and historic content. For him Christianity is primarily a body of symbolical doctrines, figuring the ideal unity of finite and infinite. It arose from man's sense of the disunity between the world and God; its end is to reconcile them by realizing the Infinite in humanity. Hence the characteristic Hegelian interpretation of the traditional dogmas. The Trinity, the incarnation, redemption are but the symbols of a self-originating, self-determining Absolute, whose particular appearances are continually negatived and transcended with a view to always fuller and profounder disclosures of his eternal being.

Hegel's intention was to support and defend Christianity by rationalizing it. The question is whether, in the attempt, he did not destroy its whole character. Yet his immediate influence was great. The idea that theology portrays religious truth in the guise of representation or figure, whereas the speculative thinker's task is to translate such figures or representations into philosophical concepts, was most resolutely applied by the Swiss theologian A. E. Biedermann (1819–85) and only a little less radically by R. A. Lipsius (1830–90) and Otto Pfleiderer (1839–1908). But the Hegelian stream was soon to be flowing in divergent channels, a right, a left and a centre, with the result that philosophers who alike professed Hegelian principles could be classed either as theists, pantheists and even atheists. Some, like C. H. Weisse, sought to maintain the divine transcendence and to correct the master's system by the aid of Fichte, Schelling or possibly Leibniz; others, like Rosencrantz, remained faithful to the original inspiration and preserved Hegel's distinctive immanentism. But the radical school acquired— from the orthodox—the designation neo-Hegelian, and among them the salient figures were D. F. Strauss and Ludwig Feuerbach. For these latter thinkers the entire notion of a supernatural order is abolished and their attitude towards institutional religion is correspondingly negative. Hegelians nominally, their thinking leans towards the new naturalism. In Feuerbach, as still more patently in Feuerbach's disciple Karl Marx, Hegelianism is turned upside down, the dialectical negation of religion being identified with the materialistic negation of the spiritual world. Feuerbach's materialism provides indeed the very basis of his thought. 'I am a real, a sensuous, a material being,' he declares; 'the body in its totality is my Ego.' Only where 'sensuousness' begins, that is, 'do all doubt and conflict cease'. His own philosophy had for its epistemological principle not abstract 'mind' but the material existant. With his accustomed vigour of expression he confessed his hatred of the idealism which 'tears man out of nature'. Truth accordingly was but the sum of human life and being. Man himself is the *ens realissimum*, and God can be nothing more than man's own inner nature, human nature objectified. But so far from now ceasing to exist God at last becomes real and human. The immanentizing of deity is complete and theology turns into anthropology.

The Hegelian influence was not, however, confined to the philosophers; it deeply affected the critical study of the New Testament and the history of primitive Christianity. This latter inquiry, as a more or less consistent attempt to meet the intellectual problem of the authority of the early Christian scriptures, had already been broached during the preceding century. In the first half of the nineteenth it was resumed with a firmer grasp of what it involved. Thus it acquired scientific status. But initially it suffered from the defect of a sound method and the general treatment tended to be *a priori* and metaphysical. Strauss and the scholars of the Tübingen school, rejecting alike traditional Christian dogma and the naïve rationalism of the older critics, took their guidance from current philosophy. Christian orthodoxy held to the belief that the gospels contain genuine history, whether natural or supernatural, and that miracles were authentic happenings. The rationalists, while dismissing the supernatural element as impossible, contended that it was merely the natural misrepresented; what was needful for 'reasonable' religion was the discovery of the original simple, non-miraculous events, all else being pruned away. Strauss who, in his *Life of Jesus*, also wanted to know whether the gospel history is true and reliable or not, was no less negative in his attitude to miracles than were they—the miraculous he too regarded as an impossibility and the history of Jesus necessarily void of supernatural import—but his understanding of the gospel record as a whole is far more sympathetic and perceptive. Myth, which he considered to have a leading place in it, he claims to be a natural and intelligible way of thinking, since it is the mode of expression which religious enthusiasm spontaneously adopts. To interpret the gospels historically one must allow for their inherently mythical character. Strauss's resulting treatment of the evangelic material is certainly drastic, but he rounds off his massive enterprise with a sincerely motivated reconstruction of Christian belief on typically Hegelian lines. Christ is fundamentally an *idea*, not simply an individual fact; what the age demanded of a Christology was 'to be led to the idea in the fact, to the race in the individual'. His conclusion is that when the mind has 'gone beyond the sensible history and entered into the domain of the absolute, the former ceases to be essential'.

Strauss, it may well be thought, was as much metaphysician as critic and his great work little else than a philosophical speculation disguised as an historical inquiry. F. C. Baur (1792–1860), from the standpoint of New Testament study, is a more considerable magnitude. Strauss had failed, Baur perceived, through lack of the necessary critical equipment. A history of early Christianity could not be undertaken without searching preliminary investigation of the New Testament documents themselves, their date, origin and interrelationship, as well as a knowledge of the conditions of life and thought in the age in which the Christian Church first spread abroad. But Baur, like Strauss, was a Hegelian and his method was developed in accordance with Hegelian principles. Again it is the *idea* which is important, and history is the scene of perpetually conflicting tendencies. Personalities of course play their part, but it is ideas and tendencies which operate through them. Also like Strauss Baur could give no room to the supernatural in the true history of Jesus. The supposed founder of Christianity is himself only a factor in a situation, an element in a process. The growth of the Christian religion must hence be explained in terms of its own dynamism and not by reference to a personality assumed to stand outside it. Briefly, then, the explanation which Baur offers is this. The apostolic age, so far from being one of harmonious and peaceful advance, was in fact a period of conflict between a narrow Ebionite Judaism, incapable of becoming more than a localized sect, and the revolutionary universalism of St Paul. The contest for the mastery was bitter and prolonged and no settlement was achieved during Paul's lifetime. Only after the lapse of a century and a half did historic Catholicism appear as its viable outcome. The surviving relics of the original struggle are the books of the New Testament, in which the four authentic epistles of St Paul (in Baur's view they were no more in number), namely, Galatians, 1 and 2 Corinthians and Romans, are the earliest, the bulk of the New Testament writings dating from the second century. But the theory is based, for all Baur's good intentions, less on a discriminating appraisal of the New Testament evidence itself than on the Hegelian triad of thesis, antithesis and synthesis, the proper application of which to the matter in hand is taken as beyond question. Historical fact is made to fit a prefabricated *schema*.

But although the work which Baur accomplished was thus marred it cannot be denied that in the field of New Testament criticism his name remains among the pre-eminent.

IV

The attempt to rationalize religion in terms of an all-comprehending metaphysic led, however, to a reaction, the leader of which was Albrecht Ritschl of Göttingen, the most influential German theologian of his time. Ritschl, in his antagonism to Hegel, drew inspiration from Kant, though he also learned much from his own contemporary, Hermann Lotze. Yet the sharpest contrast to the Hegelian doctrine had already been provided by Hegel's colleague at Berlin, Friedrich Schleiermacher, the effects of whose thinking—he was at first over-shadowed by the philosopher—were long to outlast the Hegelian vogue and remain potent still. It could reasonably be claimed indeed that his has been the most important voice in theology within the last century and a half. Kant had stressed the moral aspect of faith, Hegel the intellectual. What Schleiermacher emphasized was feeling. His whole teaching, in its domain a characteristic expression of the new Romantic emotionalism, may be said to have been based on recognition of the paramount place of feeling in the religious attitude. He himself possessed a warm and affectionate nature. 'When occupied', he wrote, 'with inward thought, or with observation, or with the enjoyment of what is novel, I need the presence of some loved one, so that on the inner experience there may immediately follow the sharing of it with another.' That his *métier* was that of a theologian not a metaphysician he knew well enough, but the vein of sentiment in him was offset by both strong will-power and a powerful intellect. His significance lies in his having recognized that religion without a deep emotional impulse at its heart cannot be sustained and turns into either rationalism or moralism. It was his conviction that Christian doctrine must, to use his own words, 'be set forth in complete independence of each and every philosophical system'—as certainly that his own faith in Christ did not come from philosophy. In this he is Hegel's opposite. Faith is not imperfect philosophical understanding but something essentially different. It is a feeling of absolute dependence; in the case of Christianity a feeling of absolute dependence upon God in Christ. Primarily it is a matter of individual experience, a personal intuition. It is not, at all events, to be equated with acceptance of theological propositions, for these only follow faith as its consequence and articulation. Faith itself, for the Christian, involves the sense of having been renewed in and by Christ; and this is not the end of any process of cogitation or submission to external judgement. It is simply an inward fact, to be admitted and reckoned with, brought about by confrontation with the historical personality of Jesus as testified by the Scriptures. Every attempt at expressing this experience in the way of rational interpretation, necessary though it may be, is therefore of only relative and temporary value: the ever-renewed experience itself will in time transcend it and render it obsolete. Nevertheless, Schleiermacher does not deny the corporate or communal element in the Christian consciousness. Towards the individualism of Kant, as of the eighteenth century in general, he was unsympathetic: 'In solitude, the springs of my soul dry up, and the course of my thoughts is checked.' The existence of the Church is part of the Christian experience, for its members are dependent, in the life of faith, each upon the rest. Theology itself is a function of this corporate life and its utility has a corporate end. Belief has its necessary outcome in fellowship.

If Schleiermacher was a theologian whose whole approach to the religious problem was radically different from that of Hegel, Albrecht Ritschl, whilst his own position and attitude were in some respects far removed from Schleiermacher's, became the self-declared foe of any attempt at a metaphysical interpretation of Christianity. A zestful controversialist, he had as little use for mysticism, pietism or devotional sentimentalism as he had for speculative rationalism. But it was against the latter that his polemic was mainly directed. All that man can know of God, he contended, is what God himself chooses to make known. 'Every claim to teach something concerning God in himself apart from real revelation on his part felt and perceived on ours is useless.' Natural theology is baseless, since we can reach no valid concept of deity apart from revelation and faith; and revelation is imparted in the unique historical figure of Jesus. What we know of God is what we know of him in Christ. Only in relation to Christ can our idea of the divine receive its full meaning and ethical content. Ritschl follows Kant in distinguishing between 'nature' and 'value' and insists that religion is concerned with the latter alone, for what man there seeks is a solution of the contradiction in which he finds himself as, at once, 'a fact of nature and a spiritual personality claiming to dominate nature'. The aim of religion thus is practical: it is 'the instrument man possesses to free himself from the natural conditions of life'. Our knowledge of God is itself pragmatic, confined to 'his effects on us', so that theological ideas are essentially 'judgements of value', to be clearly differentiated from theoretical propositions. The fact that they are grounded in a historical revelation further means that for Ritschl the historical circumstances themselves assume an overriding importance. Indeed it is to history we must turn if the value-judgement is to be saved from pure subjectivism, whether sentimental or speculative. Hence the great impetus which Ritschlianism gave to New Testament criticism and in particular to the view, so confidently championed by liberal Protestantism generally, that historical research into the origins of Christianity would afford a sure foundation for a religiously valid and effective interpretation of Jesus of Nazareth. One of the most illustrious of Ritschl's followers, Adolf Harnack, argued with force and eloquence that the 'Jesus of history', divested of the metaphysical dogma with which Catholicism had enshrouded him, could alone give to the modern man the religion of his needs. This trust in the historian's ability to authenticate divine revelation implies a degree of historical positivism which was subsequently, however, to be recognized as one of the major weaknesses of Ritschlianism. For what if, after all, the evidence of history should prove to be ambiguous and the 'Jesus of history' less a demonstrable fact than a dubious assumption? Wilhelm Herrmann (1846–1922), Ritschl's closest disciple, allows that the gospels portray their central figure in a way that no longer admits unqualified belief—as, for instance, Jesus' having been miraculously born of a virgin—but he denies that these elements are significant. What strikes us in the gospel pages is, he insists, Jesus' moral character, his inner life, as relevant to our own lives now as to the lives of those who first heard his words. The essence of Christianity is and must be this supreme and imperishable ethical example.

The great value of the Ritschlian teaching lay in its stress on the practical and moral nature of Christianity as against the ever-persisting tendency to obscure it by sacramentalist, dogmatic or speculative interpretations. Religion, it urged, is not science or theory or magic. The same conviction was expressed, with all the resources of a highly original and powerfully dialectical mind, by the Danish thinker Søren Kierkegaard, whose death in 1855 occurred before the appearance of Ritschl's work. Kierkegaard too was moved by his antagonism toward the philosophy of Hegel, but he opposed Hegelianism—for him the symbol of all metaphysical 'objectification' of faith—with the weapons of ironic wit and paradox of which he was so much a master. If Hegel, he declared, had stated in the preface to his *Logic* that the work was intended as an experiment in *thought* 'he would have been the greatest thinker that had ever lived', whereas 'now he is comic'. But it was not only the thought-universe of German metaphysics that Christianity could not accommodate; it was union with philosophy as such which was impossible. 'Christianity', he wrote in his journal, 'will have no dealing with the philosophies, even if they are willing to divide with it the spoils; it cannot endure that the King of Sodom should say, I have made Abraham rich.' Religion transcends even the moral, as the moral transcends the reflective or aesthetic. Faith is not a comfortable assurance intellectually bolstered but a desperate risk; what certainty it has is a 'fighting certainty'. Hence the problem is not that of 'understanding' Christianity in the sense of making it intellectually more amenable—on the contrary, 'Christ enters by closed doors'—but of how to *become a Christian*. No mere intellectual disinterest and objectivity will bring a man to believe, but only an 'infinitely interested' subjectivity. So for all his profoundly Christian concern Kierkegaard in the end hesitated to call himself a Christian. At most he might be on the way to becoming one—which explains his final, bitter embroilment with the established Church of Denmark. The Christianity of official religious organizations he rejected as a travesty of the real thing.

Paradoxically Kierkegaard proved himself to be a thinker only chronologically of his own day; by effective influence he is a contemporary of our own. In this the only other comparable thinkers are Nietzsche and Dostoievsky. It is not an over-heightening of language to describe all three as prophets of an age unborn. Key figures for the future though they were, none can be judged characteristic of his time, in the sense of reflecting and promoting its conscious tendencies and ideals. Thus Nietzsche, especially in his later writings, adopted an attitude hostile not simply to Christian doctrine but to the whole Christian ethic. This he identified with the ascetic ideal and its 'hate of the human, and even more of the animal, and more still of the material', its 'horror of the senses, of reason itself', its 'fear of happiness and beauty'—an ideal signifying only a 'will for Nothingness', a will hostile to life and repudiating its most fundamental conditions. Nevertheless, he insisted that even the will to nothingness remains a will, and Christianity, in demanding not the control but the extirpation of the passions and making even the sex impulse an unclean thing, was itself a perverted manifestation of the universal 'will to power'. Its fault was that essentially it had been the utterance only of the weak and frustrated—a morality for slaves. Because of this it was antagonistic to all excellence, physical or intellectual, preferring the 'soul' to the body and the 'other world' to this. But it should be noted that Nietzsche's rejection of Christian moral values is not the result of any conversion to scientific materialism. Human valuations, he realized, are at once too large and too subtle to be interpreted in terms of a narrowly based naturalism. Man's future—whatever his past may have been—is now dependent upon his own free and responsible choice. He has come of age and the capacity for complete self-transcendence is at last in his hands.

V

But the fact of which traditional religion, as the century advanced, became more and more uncomfortably aware was the rapid growth in both scope and authority of the sciences of nature. The constitution of the universe, as observation and experiment seemed with increasing certainty to indicate, rested on the principle of unchanging law. What room, then, could there be for those breaches of continuity to which religious belief was wont to appeal in support of its assertions? Natural science was creating a cast of mind, a habit of thought, the consequences of which were by no means limited to its own immediate sphere. Science when strictly interpreted may have little to say that has any direct bearing on the problems which most deeply engage the human spirit, but the method and ethos of scientific inquiry were plainly not without influence in the treatment of those problems. Many things appeared incapable any longer of being believed, not necessarily because science had disproved them but because the scientific outlook or disposition had been fatal to the continuance of such belief. The issue of science and religion, their compatibility or otherwise, became as never before a major concern not only to theology but to ordinary piety. It is not easy to point to any single discovery during the period that had an especially revolutionary outcome in this respect, but in England at all events the nature and relevance of the issue became apparent following the publication in 1859 of Charles Darwin's *Origin*

24

of Species, a work the importance of which was less in its being the first enunciation of a guiding principle than in its detailed illustration of that principle, within its author's chosen field of biology, by the patient amassing of factual observations. The principle itself was by no means new. Evolutionism had been a salient feature of the Hegelian philosophy and even in biology Darwin's ideas had been anticipated by Lamarck. (Among British thinkers Herbert Spencer (1820–1903) was an evolutionist before Darwin, although his *First Principles*, which contains the substance of his philosophy, did not appear until 1862.) Upon the controversy which Darwin's work evoked we need not dwell. Not all the hostility, however, came from ecclesiastical quarters; many scientists were critical or dubious and an occasional theologian was to be heard whose words indicated a more considered judgement. All the same, the implications of the ideas of 'natural selection' and of the descent of man from an animal ancestry were a direct and startling challenge to immemorial religious beliefs concerning not only creation and the fall of man—and with it his redemption—but the whole conception of the relations of natural and supernatural. In time the Darwinian theory, or at any rate the evolutionary principles of interpretation in the natural order, was assimilated, more or less. But the effect of the assimilation upon theology was to stress the immanence of deity in the cosmos at the expense of the divine transcendence and magisterial control over that which, in the beginning, had been created *ex nihilo*.

A remarkable if in some ways bizarre attempt to erect science itself into a philosophy with religious trappings is of course associated with the name of Auguste Comte. Comte's aim was to establish a unified and comprehensive science of nature, man and society. His scheme was doctrinaire and over-ambitious, but its significance resides not so much in what it actually was as in what it represented, namely the right of science to exist and advance; for the authority of science was proclaimed to be inherent. Comte's distinction of three stages in reflective thought, the theological, the metaphysical and the positive, had at least the attraction of simplicity, and his classification of the sciences reveals an insight for which he has not always been credited. Yet basically positivism was unsound since it failed to deal in convincing manner with the life of the mind, and contrary to its own principles reintroduced metaphysics in the shape of naturalism. Nevertheless, Comte's far-fetched Religion of Humanity was in itself a notable testimony to the abiding human need of what supernatural religion seeks to offer.

Some of Comte's most eager disciples were to be found in England, and these readily connected his work with the native tradition of philosophical empiricism. Spencer, a leading exponent of scientific agnosticism, denied that he had been influenced by Comte, but he follows Comte in his assurance of the sole validity of scientific knowledge and his concern for total systematization. The upshot was the grandiose Synthetic Philosophy which conferred upon its author a contemporary reputation of which posterity has now largely deprived him. But although Spencer himself is apt to be forgotten and the doctrine of materialism seen to occasion objections no less solid than may be raised against other philosophical attempts to explain the 'ultimate', his teaching, like that of T. H. Huxley, has unquestionably contributed to the growth of that 'scientific outlook' which for multitudes today renders traditional Christian belief not merely unacceptable —for the great majority have never seriously examined it—but irrelevant. This is the hard fact which the teacher of religion must now face and it should not be obscured by a complacent assumption that the 'Victorian' conflict between religion and science is happily at an end. The psychological impact of science continues to make itself felt, with results no more favourable to religious valuations than formerly.

Nevertheless, it would be a falsification to portray orthodox Christianity as simply in headlong retreat during the century with which we are dealing. Not only were theologians and scholars preoccupied with the problem of meeting the difficulties to which new knowledge had given rise but some had no hesitation in declaring war on the very spirit of the age in which Providence had placed them. The Romantic movement was a reaction against the ideals of the Enlightenment and the Revolution, but was itself compounded of many elements and in its way revolutionary. Its imaginative transfiguration of the past was not merely an aesthetic fad but an inspiration to political and social action. With most of its many ramifications we are not here concerned, but its emphasis on historical continuity or the organic and hereditary character of society or on legitimate authority as the principle of civic order was loudly echoed in the ecclesiastical sphere. A fresh sense was to be discerned of the meaning and function of the Church. Chateaubriand's *Génie du Christianisme*, published in 1802, was among the earliest expressions of the new spirit and mood. Its author himself points out how, at that moment, France was emerging from the chaos of revolution. 'The faithful', he claimed, 'believed themselves to be saved by the appearance of a book which answered so well to their inward state of feeling; there was need for a faith, a desire for religious consolation, which came from the very lack of that consolation for so many years. The victims of our troubles...rushed to the altar, just as shipwrecked men cling to the rock on which they hope for safety.' But Chateaubriand's work, for all its moving rhetoric, was superficial in content. A more searching and consistent *rationale* of reaction was offered by such men as Louis de Bonald (1754–1840) and Joseph de Maistre (1753–1821). Both conceived of political power and responsibility in theocentric terms. The former's *Theory of Political and Religious Power in Civil Society* came out as early as 1796 and his later writings do no more than supplement its views. 'The last of the scholastics', he envisages a traditionalist hierarchical society under the supreme authority of the pope. Maistre's *Du Pape* (1819) is an outright assertion of the aims of ultramontanism. Liberty and democracy are of the devil, and the progeny of a godless age; society must be built only on the supernatural and traditional, of which the papacy is the medium and the interpreter. Neither of these writers, however, evinces much of the religious spirit; both are rationalists and political doctrinaires. Lamennais was a man of a different stamp, with a very different career which carried him from the ultramontanism of his early *Essay on Indifference in Matters of Religion*, through the stage of liberal Catholicism, to the passionate radicalism of *Paroles d'un croyant* and the eventual repudiation of the Church altogether. Despite its inner diversity and conflicting objectives this politico-religious movement in France in the first half of the century testified unmistakably to the presence and force of religious revival after the stagnant epoch before the Revolution. Nor was the resuscitation of Catholicism confined to France: to become a Catholic—as among other distinguished intellectuals did Friedrich Schlegel—was almost a mark of the Romantic attitude in Germany. Escapism, flight from the irresistible pressures of rationalism and industrialism—call it what one will—this feeling for the still potent allurements of a traditional and authoritarian faith is a mark of the century which cannot be ignored. It was a reminder to busy utilitarianism that man does not live by bread alone.

The European religious revival had its counterpart in Protestant England in the Tractarian movement and its outcome. In this too we find a reassertion of the principles of tradition and authority and the appeal to antiquity. Its purpose was to reawaken a Church, whose existing conception of its nature and status was Protestant and Erastian, to the implications of its *de facto* Catholic inheritance. The guiding spirit of the movement, until his secession to Rome some twelve years after the date—1833—which he himself regarded as that of its inception, was John Henry Newman, outstanding among religious personalities of his age; and to Newman the enemy to be resisted *à l'outrance* was 'liberalism', which he identified as the 'anti-dogmatic principle', the corrosion of the secular reason. To this he opposed the authority of divine revelation and the Catholic Church. When he discovered that the Church of England could not do this effectively he left it for another, more authoritarian and uncompromising in its witness. But Newman, although a great ecclesiastic, was far from being a mere externalist. The 'inwardness' of his thought, the perpetual interior dialogue upon the nature and demands of belief, his intense moralism— was not conscience the 'aboriginal Vicar of Christ'?—together with the egocentricity of his strangely nuanced temperament, make of him one whose interest to posterity far exceeds that of the active role he may have played—always, it seemed, in despite of himself—in the communion of either his birth or his adoption, although his influence upon both has left an enduring impress. Further, reactionary in his ideals and aims as he supposed himself to be, he was by no means a mere conservator of things past. At its deeper levels his mind was of its own time. He understood, with a sharp perception, the difficulties of religious belief and realized the insufficiency of the old apologetic methods. If faith were to be aroused something more than the assurance of 'evidences' must be its ground, whilst rational argument was inconclusive. 'The works of design in creation', he instructed his hearers from the pulpit of St Mary's, Oxford, 'are beautiful and interesting to a believer in God; but where men have not already recognized God's voice within them ineffective, and this, moreover, from some unsoundness in the intellectual basis of the argument'. The true ground of belief was the experience itself, wherein the primary element— though upon this Tractarian opinion in general was agreed—is the moral consciousness. Newman, so far as we know, never studied Kant, but in this regard the Kantian bias in his outlook is remarkable.

Apart from Newman the Oxford movement contributed little to either the speculative or the interpretative sides of religious thought.

Its leaders, especially Pusey, and many of its adherents were scholarly and learned, but on the whole they did not venture upon possible new aspects of truth. They endeavoured to preserve or restore a heritage rather than enlarge the prospect. In this they were typical of the intellectually isolated and isolationist religious tradition of their country. But with the close of the half century a quickening if also a chilling breeze was to be felt. The theological controversies of the preceding decades had lost much of their urgency and interest and the liberalizing tendencies which religious conservatism had struggled to halt were becoming more overt and self-confident. Social legislation, university reform, a growing trust in scientific meliorism, a stimulating awareness of new cultural influences from the European continent were testimony of a change in the mid-Victorian scene of which religious thinking could not be oblivious. The significant figure in the ecclesiastical world was that of F. D. Maurice, though his originality was less appreciated then than it is today. Maurice's thought ranged widely, and despite a certain inability to express himself with due force and clarity he deepened understanding of any subject to which he turned, whether it related to faith or to society. Yet he was not a 'party' man; more characteristic of the so-called Broad Church attitude were the authors of *Essays and Reviews*, published in 1860, although the hostility which their modest volume incited revealed how little ready the religious public still was for any real qualification of staunchly traditionalist ideas, especially in the matter of biblical study. Yet change was on the way and the next theological symposium to make its appearance, nearly thirty years later, came from the successors of the Tractarian divines. *Lux Mundi*, although less radical than its precursor, admitted the need for a revision of ideas once unquestioned. Historical criticism, Darwin and the Hegelian philosophy—which had at last, in the person of T. H. Green, penetrated to Oxford itself—were all obvious ingredients in the new-style 'liberal' High Anglicanism of which Charles Gore, the book's editor, stood out as the not incautious champion.

Also among the prophets of anti-liberalism—and to none of them could the title of prophet be more fitly applied—looms the portentous figure of Thomas Carlyle (1795–1881). At the end of his life he enjoyed the ripest fruits of contemporary fame. To mid-Victorian England his was a stern and reproving voice, courageously if harshly raised against all insincerity, materialism and shallow-minded optimism. The two primary elements in his make-up were his early Scotch education and his later German culture. The first, it has been said, was in almost all respects his strength; the latter in some respects his weakness. Philosophical idealism, Fichte's in particular, befogged him. His admiration for Goethe may also appear odd in a man of his background and disposition; but he evidently found in the sage of Weimar a spiritual guide and an answer to those 'obstinate questionings' by which any thoughtful man, he would have judged, could not but be troubled. Rationalist negations indeed he detested. At the same time traditional belief was impossible for him. Goethe pointed to a middle way of faith and hope which he found congenial. Religion for Carlyle was the thing a man *practically* believes—'the thing a man does practically lay to heart and know for certain, concerning his vital relation to this mysterious Universe, and his duties and destiny there'. It consists 'not in the many things he is in doubt of and tries to believe, but in the few he is assured of, and has no need of effort for believing'. 'Serene and complete Religion' was the highest aspect of human nature, its opposite, 'serene Cant, or complete No-religion', the lowest. Between them all manner of 'earnest Methodisms, introspections, agonizing inquiries, never so morbid' had or might have their place. Carlyle, however, demanded something more positive, as also potent against the new 'mud-philosophies' of the age, which he held in hearty contempt. A world from which mechanism had ousted God, leaving commercialism and sensuality as the chief ends of man, repelled him utterly. Temperamentally he remained in the grip of the puritan Calvinism of his youth, even if his declared belief veered only towards a neo-Stoic pantheism. The trend of his times—their facile utilitarianism and equation of godliness with prosperity—he felt it his duty to denounce. That today he should seem pompous, irascible and verbally inflated and his Everlasting Yea to have hollow-sounding reverberations ought not to blind us to the genuine power of much that he had to proclaim, even though a later generation than his own left the sermon unheeded.

VI

The attitude of the Roman Catholic Church throughout our period was, as we have observed, one of almost unqualified opposition to liberalizing trends, intellectual or political. This intransigence culminated in Pius IX's *Syllabus of Modern Errors* of 1864 and the decrees of the first Vatican Council. Even so there were sporadic signs that Catholic thinkers and scholars were not unawake to the necessity of change and to the futility of blank antagonism. Besides the already mentioned Liberal Catholic movement in France there was the Catholic school of Tübingen of which J. A. Möhler (1796–1838) was the leader. These theologians, it is of interest to recall, were consciously indebted to Schleiermacher. Like him they sought to transcend the familiar division between revealed religion and natural; all religion, they taught, was in its way a revelation which human reason was capable of receiving. Supernaturalism and rationalism alike misconceived the true nature of man's spiritual life. Dogma was to be understood not merely as a set of abstract propositions to be taken on authority but as the dynamic expression of a spiritual experience. Tradition was not a fixed *depositum* but an evolving process. Moreover, there need be no 'fencing' of truth to shield it from the blasts of historical or philosophical criticism: a vital faith was its own sufficient stay. Regrettably Möhler's ideas were current only within a limited circle and were speedily forgotten until recovered by the Modernists at the end of the century. The historian Ignaz von Döllinger (1799–1890), whose long life nearly spanned the whole period, had in his younger days been a convinced ultramontane, but the actual development of ultramontanism disillusioned him and he became its determined opponent. His refusal to submit to the infallibility decree resulted in his excommunication. But although men like Möhler and Döllinger were little more than isolated instances they at least anticipated the more resolute attempt to expose the Church to contemporary intellectual and cultural influences associated with the published writings and personal example of, notably, such devout laymen as Maurice Blondel (1860–1949) and Baron Friedrich von Hügel (1852–1925), as well as the more radical spirits among whom Alfred Loisy (1857–1940) and George Tyrrell (1861–1909), both of whom were priests, were the recognized protagonists.

To turn from the European to the American scene during the greater part of this century is to move, only too patently, from the centre to the periphery. The dominant characteristic of transatlantic religious thought was, apart from its earnestness—which is unquestionable—its stark provinciality. At the beginning of the period this still raw country was intellectually isolated. It clung tenaciously to its puritan traditions; the theology of the churches, in its narrow fixity, was simply untouched by any exterior cultural force. Methodism had had but slight effect.

The pertinacious questionings of the deists, if not unheard of, were largely ignored. When at length liberal ideas, under the unitarian name, began to obtrude they were as evidently a native growth as was the stolid conservatism which they strove to modify. First among the new thinkers was William Ellery Channing (1780–1842), minister of the Federal Street church in Boston. Although we may safely assume that he had never himself read Schleiermacher, his general viewpoint resembles that of the great German theologian. In his reaction against the dry Calvinism of his day he underlined what he believed to be the natural capacities and terrestrial vocation of man. Free will is the pre-condition of moral responsibility. Conscience is the voice of God. If men are to discover the divine law by which to live let them look within themselves, to their better, or higher, nature. There can be no revelation which is not expressed in terms of human need, capability and understanding, since man's knowledge of God is indissociable from the rational and moral endowment with which the Creator has furnished him. True Christianity has no room for the arbitrary or mechanical—in a word, for the non-moral. That the traditionalist presentation of dogma was, by these criteria, unsatisfactory Channing had no doubt. How far he actually went towards qualifying tradition-alism in his personal interpretations is not perhaps clear. His critics judged him a unitarian. But his Christian humanism, if the term be not inappropriate, was an indication of the path which liberal religious thought was to take.

The best representative of a revised and more supple orthodoxy is Horace Bushnell (1802–76), a teacher whose work has scarcely yet won its due meed of appreciation He was not himself brought up in Calvin-ism—his mother was an Episcopalian—and he disliked Calvinist dogmatism, of which his first book, *Christian Nurture*, is a vigorous critique. The old-fashioned orthodoxy, he argues, gravely miscon-ceived the relationship between man and God; it misunderstood the nature of revelation; and it was crudely individualistic, devoid of any real sense of the corporate character of salvation. In a later work he faced the difficulties of religious language. Such language, he contended, must be of a kind to satisfy the moral conscience; and not only dogma but even the Bible speaks in a way that often offends it. Yet the essential truth of both Bible and dogma is not to be doubted. A problem here calls for solution. Unhappily the remoteness of the American thinker from the intellectual influences that might have led him towards it were lacking. His 1848 addresses at the Divinity Schools of Harvard, Yale and Andover, respectively, are at once challenging and constructive. The first, on the atonement, repudiates the penal theory as a near blasphemy: must God insist on his modicum of suffering? The death of Christ was the expression not of vengeful justice but of love. The Yale address deals with the doctrine of the Trinity, which in orthodox hands had too frequently broken down into tritheism, whereas the essential unity of God points rather to a threefold mode of revelation. Trinitarianism presented as an abstract ontology of the divine merely ends in an intellectual conundrum. The third lecture, at Andover, was more directly concerned with current ecclesiastical issues, but its ironic tone in no way obscures its author's concern for a theology which would be both traditional and humanitarian.

Emerson's ideas took a more radical course and the literary talent with which they were imparted gave them also a wider appeal. Certainly his is the shining personality in the American intellectual scene during the century's first half. But he could hardly be described as a philosopher, and though perhaps a prophet he remains, for all his insight and fervour, provincial. Of a very different stamp are the two thinkers—the second of them especially—who adorn the century's close and whose reputation was international: Royce and William James. Royce was an idealist, one of the last and not the least impressive of the Hegelian succession. But his idealism did not lead him to a strict monism. He understood the world as made up of diverse processes and multiple individualities, each of which has to realize its own pattern of being. The principle which for him would unify this diversity and multiplicity was deity. His teaching therefore can be described as broadly theist, with his own idiosyncratic interpretation of Christianity appended thereto. James' *The Will to Believe* and *Varieties of Religious Experience* offer, on the other hand, a wholly different approach to the religious problem and one avowedly pragmatist. Faith is not, nor is it the product of, any rationalizing or speculative interest. In religion feeling is primary; philosophy, if it have a place at all, but secondary. Its end is practical, to save, not to inform; and the most abstract of theological statements must be morally construed, otherwise it is meaningless.

Can the various trends and developments which nineteenth-century religious thinking discloses be summarized? Its complexity must be recognized. The old clear-cut differences become less distinct because seen in new perspectives. The Protestant tradition, under the impact first of Kant and then of biblical criticism seemed, despite a still-solid core of conservative evangelical belief and observance, to be in process of disintegration; the distance between the liberal outlook and the Reformation confessions to be scarcely bridgeable. Calvinism in particular suffered from the growing anti-dogmatic mood and the humanitarianism of which this was in part at least the expression. The doctrine of election, and especially the corollaries that had been drawn from it, affronted the ideals of human brotherhood and universal justice. Moreover, a critical approach revealed how in fact Christian dogma had taken shape and the sundry and often alien influences to which it had been subjected. The figure of Jesus himself, on the other hand, when released—as was deemed to be possible—from the metaphysical fetters which separated him, more and more obviously and disastrously, from the man of today, now stood out in all the beauty of its ethical appeal. Deity indeed was capable of being defined only in terms of humanity. Man might not himself be God, as Feuerbach had averred, yet the purposes of God were not intelligible except as the fruition of capabilities latent in man from the outset of his historic existence. Thus revelation was to be thought of rather as man's progressive discovery of a divinity always immanent. Religion is essentially a moral education and any given form of it is to be judged according to the way in which it serves that end. It is to be interpreted, that is, with reference more to its unquestionably human subject than to its confessedly divine object. Such views, it is true, were not general, but they gained an increasingly influential currency. The present century has witnessed a reaction against them, though whether this reaction has any power to arrest them permanently has yet to be seen. The signs are that its force is diminishing. In Catholicism, as we have observed, supernaturalist belief was defended in a manner of which the long pontificate of Pius IX is symbolical. Yet here too the spirit of the times was not wholly excluded and the Modernist movement, gathering strength in the century's final decade, was, in its amalgam of immanentist philosophy, radical criticism and political liberalism, in some respects a more typical product of the age than anything Protestantism itself achieved.

The period generally was not, with a very few exceptions, a creative one. It was a time of reflexion, of intellectual stock-taking. Its concern was to understand, explain and defend. The immense growth in knowledge, both scientific and historical, made such tasks necessary. Assuredly it was not an age of indifference in matters of religion. Not only was religious observance still customary but the problem of faith was a live issue for perhaps the majority of educated men. Belief, it had been long assumed, was the precondition of right conduct; but when belief foundered in doubt on what principles if any could action be held to rest? For there were few who were willing, whatever their personal scepticism, openly to discard the moral standards which centuries of Christian teaching had established as beyond question. The voice of a Marx or a Nietzsche registered but an isolated dissent, unheeded or even unheard. The more far-reaching consequences of the decline of faith were thus delayed until a new century, running suddenly upon unexpected and catastrophic events, revealed them with brutal force.

PART I

EUROPEAN

CHAPTER I

SCHLEIERMACHER

Friedrich Ernst Daniel Schleiermacher, born at Breslau in 1768, is aptly described as the father of modern theology. Protestant thought, on the continent of Europe if not in this country, has again and again revealed his influence, whether directly or indirectly. In this he is comparable to Immanuel Kant in the realm of philosophy—Schleiermacher chose always to speak of himself as a theologian—but his characteristic emphasis on the affective or emotional significance of religion marks him out as a portent of the new 'Romantic' age and not as a continuator of the rationalistic principles of the *Aufklärung*, of which Kant himself was in many ways a signal representative. In his lifetime, however, he was overshadowed by the then dominant figure of his colleague Hegel, and it was not until the waning of Hegelianism in Germany that his work made the full impact of its originality.

The son of a Reformed army chaplain, Schleiermacher was educated at the Moravian *Herrenhütter* Brethren's college at Niesky and afterwards at their seminary at Barby. But finding the narrow sectarianism of their teaching oppressive he betook himself in 1787 to the university of Halle, where for the first time he encountered the philosophy of Kant. Three years later he became tutor to a noble family in West Prussia, but on his ordination to the ministry in 1794 he was appointed Reformed preacher at the Charité in Berlin. It was now that he began to sense the appeal of the new Romantic tendencies, especially in the work of Friedrich Schlegel, whose personal acquaintance he had made. His first book, *Reden über die Religion, an die Gebildeten unter ihren Verächtern*, appeared in 1799, to be followed by a second and considerably revised edition in 1806. In it the influence of Spinoza, Leibniz and Kant are all clearly traceable without the novelty of its author's own viewpoint being in any way lessened. In 1800 he brought out his *Monologen*, in which he offered a foretaste of his subsequent opinions on ethics. Nominated professor of theology at Halle in 1804 he returned three years later to Berlin, to become, in 1810, dean of the faculty of theology in the newly founded university. His fame as a preacher also was spreading. From 1819 the task that engrossed the major part of his interest and energy was the preparation of his chief literary undertaking, *Die christliche Glaube*, published 1821–2, in which he elaborated his celebrated definition of religion as a 'feeling of absolute dependence', the fullest and purest expression of which was, he held, to be found in Christian theism, although the actual embodiments of it, whether in a national or an individual form, may and do exhibit a boundless variety. All religions, as manifestations of an abiding and profoundly important aspect of man's nature, must, he urged, be judged to contain a certain substance of truth. Schleiermacher in his last years won for himself much honour and esteem. Happily married, he died in 1834, after a brief illness.

Believing as he did that religion is a fundamental expression of human need, Schleiermacher contended that man's other activities—his science, his art and his moral concepts—are incomplete without it. Further—and Schleiermacher's discernment here is what makes his work a landmark in the history of philosophical theology—it is identifiable with neither knowledge nor morals. Intrinsically it is a matter of feeling (*Gefühl*); in particular, this already mentioned feeling of absolute dependence. Nevertheless, it is an emotion which has within it a cognitive element, in that it presents itself as an immediate consciousness of the finite existing in and through the infinite, as an intuitive sense of the ultimate unity of all things, the principle of which is God. At the same time deity, for Schleiermacher—and in despite of his profound admiration for Spinoza—is not simply the equivalent of the empirical universe; for God is at once the Cause and the End, the real and the ideal, for whom the world, and especially the human souls within it, are the revealing mirror. Yet it is an all too common error to suppose that the starting-point of the religious life is the conception of God as a unique Being 'beyond' or 'behind' the universe: the language of theism is a symbolical language only, a verbal projection of the forms of concrete experience upon the spaces of the unknown; and there is demonstrably more than one kind of such symbolism. Religion, he contended, is a consciousness of divinity which may and does express itself in differing guises but which is independent alike of rational argument and historical tradition. Dogmas, formularies of faith and worship, ecclesiastical institutions, these things are the outcome and manifestation of religion and as such have their due uses; but they are not its ground or its substance. To be religious is not merely to adhere to them but to possess the sense of the Infinite, the risk involved in all adherence to mere forms being the obscuring of that sense. Religion in its historical and institutional embodiment may thus be as much a barrier between man and God as any other human concern and stand in the way of his apprehending that final unity in which all things subsist.

The *Addresses*, appearing at almost the very close of the century of Reason, sought to vindicate the value and necessity of religion by means which its rationalistic detractors had never so much as considered: namely, by appeal not to the logic of propositions but to the complex needs of man's own consciousness. In the process much traditional theologizing had to be cast aside. For the whole familiar apparatus of metaphysical 'proof' and citing of 'evidences' Schleiermacher had no use. Religion could not rest upon such contrivances nor be validated in terms of them. Its true evidence lies in the analysis of its own nature. In other words, the Eternal is to be found only in intuitive contemplation. The strongly mystical character of Schleiermacher's thinking is apparent, and at times the passivity of his attitude—the stress, clear also in his ethical teaching, on the elimination of the self or its absorption into a larger reality—seems more oriental than Christian. Indeed it is his sense of the emotional receptiveness of the human consciousness which leads him to the aestheticism—though the word ought not to be used with any suggestion of the superficial—on account of which he takes his place in the then swelling stream of Romanticism.

In the first edition of the *Addresses* Schleiermacher's conception of deity showed a pantheistic tendency which in later editions, as still more noticeably in *The Christian Faith*, he modifies in a theistic direction. In 1799 he expressed the view that 'piety' rather than any formal idea of God is what matters. The divine may be thought of anthropomorphically, or, alternatively, as beyond anything we can conceive of as personal—as, in truth, 'the universal, productive, connecting necessity of all thought and existence' —and it is idle to charge either the one opinion with idolatry or the other with godlessness. The believer, by equating piety with adherence to an abstract conception, simply misunderstands himself. Subsequently, however, Schleiermacher drew a clearer line between 'God' and man's feelings for him, and the earlier leaning towards pantheism is arrested to the extent that the unity which we apprehend as the ground of all things, both severally and as a whole, is now to be thought of as 'transcendent'. The idea of differing *media* of divine revelation—nature, that is to say, and human history— thus becomes firmer. Yet Schleiermacher's theology never deviates from its principle that God is the object of feeling, not of reasoned understanding, and its account of the divine personality remains fluctuating and hesitant.

As may be expected, Schleiermacher's treatment of Christianity conforms with this basic attitude. A Christian is one who is possessed by the feeling of his dependence upon God as manifested in Jesus Christ. The Christian religion is historical in that we cannot explain it without reference to a series of historical events of which the life and mission of Jesus of Nazareth was the culmination or focal point; but its truth does not lie in the acceptability of the theological propositions, including those which have an historical content, in which Christian piety has found expression. Faith is essentially experience—experience of personal redemption and renewal in and by Christ, and no man does or can merely reason himself into it, just as he may hold it without submitting it to rational judgement. It is something that 'happens' to him and as such is simply to be recognized and acted upon. To equate it with a doctrine is to misconceive its very nature, which is no other than the product of a man's encounter with the historic personality of Jesus as made known to us in the Scriptures. Theology in the shape of rational propositions has its proven utility, if also its dangers, but it can no more be permanent than, of itself, it can ever be sufficient.

The experience of faith, Schleiermacher thinks, is primarily individual: from its intrinsic nature it must be so. But it is not exclusively individual, and in the Christian consciousness there is an element, a disposition, which requires a social embodiment, thus giving to the Christian experience that distinguishable character and continuity by which it is historically identifiable and communally shared. The community of those who do share it is the true Church, and not necessarily assimilable therefore to the body of historic institutions so designated. Schleiermacher's belief is intensely Christocentric. Divine revelation has a scope as wide as man's own awareness of divinity and the non-Christian religions represent, in their several ways and measures, the striving of finite creatures towards the unity of the Whole, a quest, as we must recognize, in which they are not unrewarded. But the Christian religion achieves more in that it acknowledges, within the terms of its special yet potentially universal experience, a singular response on God's part, by which, as between Infinite and finite, Jesus Christ has become the one sufficient Mediator. Man's vocation accordingly is to create in himself, so far as is possible, Christ's own consciousness and character. Only thus will he find deliverance from that domination of 'sense'—his 'fleshly' lower nature—which is the condition of sin.

Bibliographical note

Translations are available of the addresses *On Religion* (by J. Oman, with an introduction by Rudolf Otto, 1958), the *Monologues* (by H. I. Friess, 1926) and *The Christian Faith* (by H. R. Mackintosh, J. S. Stewart and others, 1928). See also G. Cross, *The Theology of Schleiermacher* (1911), J. A. Chapman, *An Introduction to Schleiermacher* (1932), R. B. Brandt, *The Philosophy of Schleiermacher* (1941), F. Flückiger, *Philosophie und Theologie bei Schleiermacher* (1947), H. R. Mackintosh, *Types of Modern Theology* (1937), and Karl Barth, *From Rousseau to Ritschl* (1959).

I. WHAT RELIGION IS

In order to make quite clear to you what is the original and characteristic possession of religion, it resigns, at once, all claims on anything that belongs either to science or morality. Whether it has been borrowed or bestowed it is now returned. What then does your science of being, your natural science, all your theoretical philosophy, in so far as it has to do with the actual world, have for its aim? To know things, I suppose, as they really are; to show the peculiar relations by which each is what it is; to determine for each its place in the Whole, and to distinguish it rightly from all else; to present the whole real world in its mutually conditioned necessity; and to exhibit the oneness of all phenomena with their eternal laws. This is truly beautiful and excellent, and I am not disposed to depreciate. Rather, if this description of mine, so slightly sketched, does not suffice, I will grant the highest and most exhaustive you are able to give.

And yet, however high you go; though you pass from the laws to the Universal Lawgiver, in whom is the unity of all things; though you allege that nature cannot be comprehended without God, I would still maintain that religion has nothing to do with this knowledge, and that, quite apart from it, its nature can be known. Quantity of knowledge is not quantity of piety. Piety can gloriously display itself, both with originality and individuality, in those to whom this kind of knowledge is not original. They may only know it as everybody does, as isolated results known in connexion with other things. The pious man must, in a sense, be a wise man, but he will readily admit, even though you somewhat proudly look down upon him, that, in so far as he is pious, he does not hold his knowledge in the same way as you.

Let me interpret in clear words what most pious persons only guess at and never know how to express. Were you to set God as the apex of your science, as the foundation of all knowing as well as of all knowledge, they would accord praise and honour, but it would not be their way of having and knowing God. From their way, as they would readily grant, and as is easy enough to see, knowledge and science do not proceed.

It is true that religion is essentially contemplative. You would never call anyone pious who went about in impervious stupidity, whose sense is not open for the life of the world. But this contemplation is not turned, as your knowledge of nature is, to the existence of a finite thing, combined with and opposed to another finite thing. It has not even, like your knowledge of God—if for once I might use an old expression—to do with the nature of the first cause, in itself and in its relation to every other cause and operation. The contemplation of the pious is the immediate consciousness of the universal existence of all finite things, in and through the Infinite, and of all temporal things in and through the Eternal. Religion is to seek this and find it in all that lives and moves, in all growth and change, in all doing and suffering. It is to have life and to know life in immediate feeling, only as such an existence in the Infinite and Eternal. Where this is found religion is satisfied, where it hides itself there is for her unrest and anguish, extremity and death. Wherefore it is a life in the infinite nature of the Whole, in the One and in the All, in God, having and possessing all things in God, and God in all. Yet religion is not knowledge and science, either of the world or of God. Without being knowledge, it recognizes knowledge and science. In itself it is an affection, a revelation of the Infinite in the finite, God being seen in it and it in God.

Similarly, what is the object of your ethics, of your science of action? Does it not seek to distinguish precisely each part of human doing and producing, and at the same time to combine them into a whole, according to actual relations? But the pious man confesses that, as pious, he knows nothing about it. He does, indeed, contemplate human action, but it is not the kind of contemplation from which an ethical system takes its rise. Only one thing he seeks out and detects, action from God, God's activity among men. If your ethics are right, and his piety as well, he will not, it is true, acknowledge any action as excellent which is not embraced in your system. But to know and to construct this system is your business, ye learned, not his. If you will not believe, regard the case of women. You ascribe to them religion, not only as an adornment, but you demand of them the finest feeling for distinguishing the things that excel: do you equally expect them to know your ethics as a science?

It is the same, let me say at once, with action itself. The artist fashions what is given him to fashion, by virtue of his special talent. These talents are so different that the one he possesses another lacks; unless someone, against heaven's will, would possess all. But when anyone is praised to you as pious, you are not accustomed to ask which of these gifts dwell in him by virtue of his piety. The citizen—taking the word in the sense of the ancients, not in its present meagre significance— regulates, leads, and influences in virtue of his morality. But this is something different from piety. Piety has also a passive side. While morality always shows itself as manipulating, as self-controlling, piety appears as a surrender, a submission to be moved by the Whole that stands over against man. Morality depends, therefore, entirely on the consciousness of freedom, within the sphere of which all that it produces falls. Piety, on the contrary, is not at all bound to this side of life. In the opposite sphere of necessity, where there is no properly individual action, it is quite as active. Wherefore the two are different. Piety does, indeed, linger with satisfaction on every action that is from God, and every activity that reveals the Infinite in the finite, and yet it is not itself this activity. Only by keeping quite outside the range both of science and of practice can it maintain its proper sphere and character. Only when piety takes its place alongside of science and practice, as a necessary, an indispensable third, as their natural counterpart, not less in worth and splendour than either, will the common field be altogether occupied and human nature on this side complete.

But pray understand me fairly. I do not mean that one could exist without the other, that, for example, a man might have religion and be pious, and at the same time be immoral. That is impossible. But, in my opinion, it is just as impossible to be moral or scientific without being religious. But have I not said that religion can be had without science? Wherefore, I have myself begun the separation. But remember, I only said piety is not the measure of science. Just as one cannot be truly scientific without being pious, the pious man may not know at all, but he cannot know falsely. His proper nature is not of that subordinate kind, which, according to the old adage that like is only known to like, knows nothing except semblance of reality.

His nature is reality which knows reality, and where it encounters nothing it does not suppose it sees something. And what a precious jewel of science, in my view, is ignorance for those who are captive to semblance. If you have not learned it from my Speeches or discovered it for yourselves, go and learn it from your Socrates. Grant me consistency at least. With ignorance your knowledge will ever be mixed, but the true and proper opposite of knowledge is presumption of knowledge. By piety this presumption is most certainly removed, for with it piety cannot exist.

Such a separation of knowledge and piety, and of action and piety, do not accuse me of making. You are only ascribing to me, without my deserving it, your own view and the very confusion, as common as it is unavoidable, which it has been my chief endeavour to show you in the mirror of my Speech. Just because you do not acknowledge religion as the third, knowledge and action are so much apart that you can discover no unity, but believe that right knowing can be had without right acting, and vice versa. I hold that it is only in contemplation that there is division. There, where it is necessary, you despise it, and instead transfer it to life, as if in life itself objects could be found independent one of the other. Consequently you have no living insight into any of these activities. Each is for you a part, a fragment. Because you do not deal with life in a living way, your conception bears the stamp of perishableness, and is altogether meagre. True science is complete vision; true practice is culture and art self-produced; true religion is sense and taste for the Infinite. To wish to have true science or true practice without religion, or to imagine it is possessed, is obstinate, arrogant delusion, and culpable error. It issues from the unholy sense that would rather have a show of possession by cowardly purloining than have secure possession by demanding and waiting. What can man accomplish that is worth speaking of, either in life or in art, that does not arise in his own self from the influence of this sense for the Infinite? Without it, how can anyone wish to comprehend the world scientifically, or if, in some distinct talent, the knowledge is thrust upon him, how should he wish to exercise it? What is all science, if not the existence of things in you, in your reason? what is all art and culture if not your existence in the things to which you give measure, form and order? And how can both come to life in you except in so far as there lives immediately in you the eternal unity of Reason and Nature, the universal existence of all finite things in the Infinite?

Wherefore, you will find every truly learned man devout and pious. Where you see science without religion, be sure it is transferred, learned up from another. It is sickly, if indeed it is not that empty appearance which serves necessity and is no knowledge at all. And what else do you take this deduction and weaving together of ideas to be, which neither live nor correspond to any living thing? Or in ethics, what else is this wretched uniformity that thinks it can grasp the highest human life in a single dead formula? The former arises because there is no fundamental feeling of that living nature which everywhere presents variety and individuality, and the latter because the sense fails to give infinity to the finite by determining its nature and boundaries only from the Infinite. Hence the dominion of the mere notion; hence the mechanical erections of your systems instead of an organic structure; hence the vain juggling with analytical formulas, in which, whether categorical or hypothetical, life will not be fettered. Science is not your calling, if you despise religion and fear to surrender yourself to reverence and aspiration for the primordial. Either science must become as low as your life, or it must be separated and stand alone, a division that precludes success. If man is not one with the Eternal in the unity of intuition and feeling which is immediate, he remains, in the unity of consciousness which is derived, for ever apart.

What, then, shall become of the highest utterance of the speculation of our days, complete rounded idealism, if it do not again sink itself in this unity, if the humility of religion do not suggest to its pride another realism than that which it so boldly and with such perfect right, subordinates to itself? It annihilates the Universe, while it seems to aim at constructing it. It would degrade it to a mere allegory, to a mere phantom of the one-sided limitation of its own empty consciousness. Offer with me reverently a tribute to the manes of the holy, rejected Spinoza. The high World-Spirit pervaded him; the Infinite was his beginning and his end; the Universe was his only and his everlasting love. In holy innocence and in deep humility he beheld himself mirrored in the eternal world, and perceived how he also was its most worthy mirror. He was full of religion, full of the Holy Spirit. Wherefore, he stands there alone and unequalled; master in his art, yet without disciples and without citizenship, sublime above the profane tribe.

Why should I need to show that the same applies to art? Because, from the same causes, you have here also a thousand phantoms, delusions, and mistakes. In place of all else I would point to another example which should be as well known to you all. I would point in silence— for pain that is new and deep has no words. It is that superb youth, who has too early fallen asleep, with whom everything his spirit touched became art. His whole contemplation of the world was forthwith a great poem. Though he had scarce more than struck the first chords, you must associate him with the most opulent poets, with those select spirits who are as profound as they are clear and vivacious. See in him the power of the enthusiasm and the caution of a pious spirit, and acknowledge that when the philosophers shall become religious and seek God like Spinoza, and the artists be pious and love Christ like Novalis, the great resurrection shall be celebrated for both worlds.

But, in order that you may understand what I mean by this unity and difference of religion, science and art, we shall endeavour to descend into the inmost sanctuary of life. There, perhaps, we may find ourselves agreed. There alone you discover the original relation of intuition and

feeling from which alone this identity and difference is to be understood. But I must direct you to your own selves. You must apprehend
a living movement. You must know how to listen to yourselves before
your own consciousness. At least you must be able to reconstruct from
your consciousness your own state. What you are to notice is the rise
of your consciousness and not to reflect upon something already there.
Your thought can only embrace what is sundered. Wherefore as soon
as you have made any given definite activity of your soul an object
of communication or of contemplation, you have already begun to
separate. It is impossible, therefore, to adduce any definite example,
for, as soon as anything is an example, what I wish to indicate is already
past. Only the faintest trace of the original unity could then be shown.
Such as it is, however, I will not despise it, as a preliminary.

Consider how you delineate an object. Is there not both a stimulation
and a determination by the object, at one and the same time, which
for one particular moment forms your existence? The more definite
your image, the more, in this way, you become the object, and the
more you lose yourselves. But just because you can trace the growing
preponderance of one side over the other, both must have been one
and equal in the first, the original moment that has escaped you. Or
sunk in yourselves, you find all that you formerly regarded as a dis-
connected manifold compacted now indivisibly into the one peculiar
content of your being. Yet when you give heed, can you not see as it
disappears, the image of an object, from whose influence, from whose
magical contact this definite consciousness has proceeded? The more
your own state sways you the paler and more unrecognizable your
image becomes. The greater your emotion, the more you are absorbed
in it, the more your whole nature is concerned to retain for the memory
an imperishable trace of what is necessarily fleeting, to carry over to
what you may engage in, its colour and impress, and so unite two
moments into a duration, the less you observe the object that caused it.
But just because it grows pale and vanishes, it must before have been
nearer and clearer. Originally it must have been one and the same
with your feeling. But, as was said, these are mere traces. Unless you
will go back on the first beginning of this consciousness, you can
scarcely understand them.

And suppose you cannot? Then say, weighing it quite generally
and originally, what is every act of your life in itself and without
distinction from other acts. What is it merely as act, as movement? Is

it not the coming into being of something for itself, and at the same time in the Whole? It is an endeavour to return into the Whole, and to exist for oneself at the same time. These are the links from which the whole chain is made. Your whole life is such an existence for self in the Whole. How now are you in the Whole? By your senses. And how are you for yourselves? By the unity of your self-consciousness, which is given chiefly in the possibility of comparing the varying degrees of sensation. How both can only rise together, if both together fashion every act of life, is easy to see. You become sense and the Whole becomes object. Sense and object mingle and unite, then each returns to its place, and the object rent from sense is a perception, and you rent from the object are, for yourselves, a feeling. It is this earlier moment I mean, which you always experience yet never experience. The phenomenon of your life is just the result of its constant departure and return. It is scarcely in time at all, so swiftly it passes; it can scarcely be described, so little does it properly exist. Would that I could hold it fast and refer to it your commonest as well as your highest activities.

Did I venture to compare it, seeing I cannot describe it, I would say it is fleeting and transparent as the vapour which the dew breathes on blossom and fruit, it is bashful and tender as a maiden's kiss, it is holy and fruitful as a bridal embrace. Nor is it merely like, it is all this. It is the first contact of the universal life with an individual. It fills no time and fashions nothing palpable. It is the holy wedlock of the Universe with the incarnated Reason for a creative productive, embrace. It is immediate, raised above all error and misunderstanding. You lie directly on the bosom of the infinite world. In that moment, you are its soul. Through one part of your nature you feel, as your own, all its powers and its endless life. In that moment it is your body, you pervade, as your own, its muscles and members and your thinking and forecasting set its inmost nerves in motion. In this way every living, original movement in your life is first received. Among the rest it is the source of every religious emotion. But it is not, as I said, even a moment. The incoming of existence to us, by this immediate union, at once stops as soon as it reaches consciousness. Either the intuition displays itself more vividly and clearly, like the figure of the vanishing mistress to the eyes of her lover; or feeling issues from your heart and overspreads your whole being, as the blush of shame and love over the face of the maiden. At length your consciousness is finally determined as one or other, as intuition or feeling. Then, even though you have not quite surrendered to this division and lost consciousness of your life as a unity, there remains nothing but the knowledge that they were originally one, that they issued simultaneously from the fundamental relation of your nature. Wherefore, it is in this sense true what an ancient sage has taught you, that all knowledge is recollection. It is recollection of what is outside of all time, and is therefore justly to be placed at the head of all temporal things.

And, as it is with intuition and feeling on the one hand, so it is with knowledge which includes both and with activity on the other. Through the constant play and mutual influence of these opposites, your life expands and has its place in time. Both knowledge and activity are a desire to be identified with the Universe through an object. If the power of the objects preponderates, if, as intuition or feeling, it enters and seeks to draw you into the circle of their existence, it is always a knowledge. If the preponderating power is on your side, so that you give the impress and reflect yourselves in the objects, it is activity in the narrower sense, external working. Yet it is only as you are stimulated and determined that you can communicate yourselves to things. In founding or establishing anything in the world you are only giving back what that original act of fellowship has wrought in you, and similarly everything the world fashions in you must be by the same act. One must mutually stimulate the other. Only in an interchange of knowing and activity can your life consist. A peaceful existence, wherein one side did not stimulate the other, would not be your life. It would be that from which it first developed, and into which it will again disappear.

There then you have the three things about which my Speech has so far turned—perception, feeling and activity, and you now understand what I mean when I say they are not identical and yet are inseparable. Take what belongs to each class and consider it by itself. You will find that those moments in which you exercise power over things and impress yourselves upon them, form what you call your practical, or, in the narrower sense, your moral life; again the contemplative moments, be they few or many, in which things produce themselves in you as intuition, you will doubtless call your scientific life. Now can either series alone form a human life? Would it not be death? If each activity were not stimulated and renewed by the other, would it not be self-consumed? Yet they are not identical. If you would understand your life and speak comprehensibly of it, they must be distinguished.

As it stands with these two in respect of one another, it must stand with the third in respect of both. How then are you to name this third, which is the series of feeling? What life will it form? The religious as I think, and as you will not be able to deny, when you have considered it more closely.

The chief point in my Speech is now uttered. This is the peculiar sphere which I would assign to religion—the whole of it, and nothing more. Unless you grant it, you must either prefer the old confusion to clear analysis, or produce something else, I know not what, new and quite wonderful. Your feeling is piety, in so far as it expresses, in the manner described, the being and life common to you and to the All. Your feeling is piety in so far as it is the result of the operation of God in you by means of the operation of the world upon you. This series is not made up either of perceptions or of objects of perception, either of works or operations or of different spheres of operation, but purely of sensations and the influence of all that lives and moves around, which accompanies them and conditions them. These feelings are exclusively the elements of religion, and none are excluded. There is no sensation that is not pious except it indicate some diseased and impaired state of the life, the influence of which will not be confined to religion. Wherefore, it follows that ideas and principles are all foreign to religion. This truth we here come upon for the second time. If ideas and principles are to be anything, they must belong to knowledge which is a different department of life from religion.

On Religion (1799) (trans. J. Oman)

II. RELIGIOUS LANGUAGE

Christian doctrines are accounts of the Christian religious
affections set forth in speech

1. All religious emotions, to whatever type and level of religion they belong, have this in common with all other modifications of the affective self-consciousness, that as soon as they have reached a certain stage and a certain definiteness they manifest themselves outwardly by mimicry in the most direct and spontaneous way, by means of facial features and movements of voice and gesture, which we regard as their expression. Thus we definitely distinguish the expression of devoutness

from that of a sensuous gladness or sadness, by the analogy of each man's knowledge of himself. Indeed, we can even conceive that, for the purpose of maintaining the religious affections and securing their repetition and propagation (especially if they were common to a number of people), the elements of that natural expression of them might be put together into sacred signs and symbolical acts, without the thought having perceptibly come in between at all. But we can scarcely conceive such a low development of the human spirit, such a defective culture, and such a meagre use of speech, that each person would not, according to the level of reflexion on which he stands, become in his various mental states likewise an object to himself, in order to comprehend them in idea and retain them in the form of thought. Now this endeavour has always directed itself particularly to the religious emotions; and this, considered in its own inward meaning, is what our proposition means by an account of the religious affections. But while thought cannot proceed even inwardly without the use of speech, nevertheless there are, so long as it remains merely inward, fugitive elements in this procedure, which do indeed in some measure indicate the object, but not in such a way that either the formation or the synthesis of concepts (in however wide a sense we take the word 'concept') is sufficiently definite for communication. It is only when this procedure has reached such a point of cultivation as to be able to represent itself outwardly in definite speech, that it produces a real doctrine (*Glaubenssatz*), by means of which the utterances of the religious consciousness come into circulation more surely and with a wider range than is possible through the direct expression. But no matter whether the expression is natural or figurative, whether it indicates its object directly or only by comparison and delimitation, it is still a doctrine.

2. Now Christianity everywhere presupposes that consciousness has reached this stage of development. The whole work of the Redeemer Himself was conditioned by the communicability of His self-consciousness by means of speech, and similarly Christianity has always and everywhere spread itself solely by preaching. Every proposition which can be an element of the Christian preaching (κήρυγμα) is also a doctrine, because it bears witness to the determination of the religious self-consciousness as inward certainty. And every Christian doctrine is also a part of the Christian preaching, because every such doctrine expresses as a certainty the approximation to the state of blessedness which is to

be effected through the means ordained by Christ. But this preaching very soon split up into three different types of speech, which provide as many different forms of doctrine: the poetic, the rhetorical (which is directed partly outwards, as combative and commendatory, and partly inwards, as rather disciplinary and challenging), and finally the descriptively didactic. But the relation of communication through speech to communication through symbolic action varies very much according to time and place, the former having always retreated into the background in the Eastern Church (for when the letter of doctrine has become fixed and unalterable, it is in its effect much nearer to symbolic action than to free speech), and having become ever more prominent in the Western Church. And in the realm of speech it is just the same with these three modes of communication. The relation in which they stand to each other, the general degree of richness, and the amount of living intercourse in which they unfold themselves, as they nourish themselves on one another and pass over into one another—these things testify not so much to the degree or level of piety as rather to the character of the communion or fellowship and its ripeness for reflexion and contemplation. Thus this communication is, on the one hand, something different from the piety itself, though the latter cannot, any more than anything else which is human, be conceived entirely separated from all communication. But, on the other hand, the doctrines in all their forms have their ultimate ground so exclusively in the emotions of the religious self-consciousness, that where these do not exist the doctrines cannot arise.

Dogmatic propositions are doctrines of the descriptively didactic type, in which the highest possible degree of definiteness is aimed at

1. The poetic expression is always based originally upon a moment of exaltation which has come purely from within, a moment of enthusiasm or inspiration; the rhetorical upon a moment whose exaltation has come from without, a moment of stimulated interest which issues in a particular definite result. The former is purely descriptive (*darstellend*), and sets up in general outlines images and forms which each hearer completes for himself in his own peculiar way. The rhetorical is purely stimulative, and has, in its nature, to do for the most part with such elements of speech as, admitting of degrees of signification, can be taken in a wider or narrower sense, content if at the decisive

moment they can accomplish the highest, even though they should exhaust themselves thereby and subsequently appear to lose somewhat of their force. Thus both of these forms possess a different perfection from the logical or dialectical perfection described in our proposition. But, nevertheless, we can think of both as being primary and original in every religious communion, and thus in the Christian Church, in so far as we ascribe to everyone in it a share in the vocation of preaching. For when anyone finds himself in a state of unusually exalted religious self-consciousness, he will feel himself called to poetic description, as that which proceeds from this state most directly. And, on the other hand, when anyone finds himself particularly challenged by insistent or favourable outward circumstances to attempt an act of preaching, the rhetorical form of expression will be the most natural to him for obtaining from the given circumstances the greatest possible advantage. But let us conceive of the comprehension and appropriation of what is given in a direct way in these two forms, as being now also wedded to language and thereby made communicable: then this cannot again take the poetic form, nor yet the rhetorical; but, being independent of that which was the important element in those two forms, and expressing as it does a consciousness which remains self-identical, it becomes, less as preaching than as confession (ὁμολογία), precisely that third form—the didactic—which, with its descriptive instruction, remains distinct from the two others, and is made up of the two put together, as a derivative and secondary form.

2. But let us confine ourselves to Christianity, and think of its distinctive beginning, namely, the self-proclamation of Christ, Who, as subject of the divine revelation, could not contain in Himself any distinction of stronger and weaker emotion, but could only partake in such a diversity through His common life with others. Then we shall not be able to take either the poetic or the rhetorical form of expression as the predominating, or even as the really primary and original, form of His self-proclamation. These have only a subordinate place in parabolic and prophetic discourses. The essential thing in His self-proclamation was that He had to bear witness regarding His ever unvarying self-consciousness out of the depths of its repose, and consequently not in poetic but in strictly reflective form; and thus had to set Himself forth, while at the same time communicating His alone true objective consciousness of the condition and constitution of men in general, thus instructing by description or representation, the instruc-

54

tion being sometimes subordinate to the description, and sometimes vice versa. But this descriptively didactic mode of expression used by Christ is not included in our proposition, and such utterances of the Redeemer will hardly be set up anywhere as dogmatic propositions; they will only, as it were, provide the text for them. For in such essential parts of the self-proclamation of Christ the definiteness was absolute, and it is only the perfection of the apprehension and appropriation which reproduces these, that can be characterized by the endeavour after the greatest possible definiteness. Subordinate to these, however, there do appear genuinely dogmatic propositions in the discourses of Christ, namely, at those points at which He had to start from the partly erroneous and partly confused ideas current among His contemporaries.

3. As regards the poetic and rhetorical forms of expression, it follows directly from what we have said, that they may fall into apparent contradiction both with themselves and with each other, even when the self-consciousness which is indicated by different forms of expression is in itself one and the same. And a solution will only be possible, in the first place, when it is possible in interpreting propositions that are apparently contradictory to take one's bearings from the original utterances of Christ (a thing which can in very few cases be done directly), and, in the second place, when the descriptively didactic expression, which has grown out of those three original forms put together, is entirely or largely free from those apparent contradictions. This, however, will not be possible of achievement so long as the descriptively didactic expression itself keeps vacillating between the emotional and the didactic, in its presentation to the catechumens or the community, and approaches sometimes more to the rhetorical and sometimes more to the figurative. It will only be possible in proportion as the aim indicated in our proposition underlies the further development of the expression and its more definite separation from the rhetorical and the poetic, both of which processes are essentially bound up with the need of settling the conflict. Now, of course, this demand, that the figurative expression be either exchanged for a literal one or transformed into such by being explained, and that definite limits be imposed on the corresponding element in the rhetorical expressions, is unmistakably the interest which science has in the formation of language; and it is mainly with the formation of religious language that we are here concerned. Hence dogmatic propositions develop to any

considerable extent and gain recognition only in such religious communions as have reached a degree of culture in which science is organized as something distinct both from art and from business, and only in proportion as friends of science are found and have influence within the communion itself, so that the dialectical function is brought to bear on the utterances of the religious self-consciousness, and guides the expression of them. Such a union with organized knowledge has had a place in Christianity ever since the earliest ages of the Church, and therefore in no other religious communion has the form of the dogmatic proposition evolved in such strict separation from the other forms, or developed in such fullness.

Postscript. This account of the origin of dogmatic propositions, as having arisen solely out of logically ordered reflexion upon the immediate utterances of the religious self-consciousness, finds its confirmation in the whole of history. The earliest specimens of preaching preserved for us in the New Testament Scriptures already contain such propositions; and on closer consideration we can see in all of them, in the first place, their derivation from the original self-proclamation of Christ, and, in the second place, their affinity to figurative and rhetorical elements which, for permanent circulation, had to approximate more to the strictness of a formula. Similarly in later periods it is clear that the figurative language, which is always poetic in its nature, had the most decided influence upon the dogmatic language, and always preceded its development, and also that the majority of the dogmatic definitions were called forth by contradictions to which the rhetorical expressions had led.

But when the transformation of the original expressions into dogmatic propositions is ascribed to the logical or dialectical interest, this is to be understood as applying only to the form. A proposition which had originally proceeded from the speculative activity, however akin it might be to our propositions in content, would not be a dogmatic proposition. The purely scientific activity, whose task is the contemplation of existence, must, if it is to come to anything, either begin or end with the Supreme Being; and so there may be forms of philosophy containing propositions of speculative import about the Supreme Being which, in spite of the fact that they arose out of the purely scientific interest, are, when taken individually, difficult to distinguish from the corresponding propositions which arose purely out of reflexion upon the religious emotions, but have been worked out dialectically. But when they are considered in their connexions, these two indubitably show differences of the most definite kind. For dogmatic propositions never make their original appearance except in trains of thought which have received their impulse from religious moods of mind; whereas, not only do speculative propositions about the Supreme Being appear for the most part in purely logical or natural-scientific trains of thought, but even when they come in as ethical presuppositions or corollaries, they show an unmistakable leaning towards one or other of those two directions. Moreover, in the dogmatic developments of the earliest centuries, if we discount the quite unecclesiastical Gnostic schools, the influence of speculation upon the content of dogmatic propositions may be placed at zero. At a later time, certainly, when the classical organization of knowledge had fallen into ruins, and the conglomerate philosophy of the Middle Ages took shape within the Christian Church, and at the same time came to exercise its influence upon the formation of dogmatic language, a confusion of the speculative with the dogmatic, and consequently a mingling of the two, was almost inevitable. But this was for both an imperfect condition, from which philosophy freed itself by means of the avowal, growing ever gradually louder, that at that time it had stood under the tutelage of ecclesiastical faith, and therefore under an alien law. Having, however, since then made so many fresh starts in its own proper development, it was able to escape from the wearisome task of inquiring exactly as to what kind of speculative propositions were at that time taken to be dogmatic, and vice versa. For the Christian Church, however, which is not in a position ever and anon to begin the development of its doctrine over again from the start, this separation is of the greatest importance, in order to secure that speculative matter (by which neither the poetic and rhetorical nor the popular expression can consent to be guided) may not continue to be offered to it as dogmatic. The Evangelical (Protestant) Church in particular is unanimous in feeling that the distinctive form of its dogmatic propositions does not depend on any form or school of philosophy, and has not proceeded at all from a speculative interest, but simply from the interest of satisfying the immediate self-consciousness solely through the means ordained by Christ, in their genuine and uncorrupted form. Thus it can consistently adopt as dogmatic propositions of its own no propositions except such as can show this derivation. Our dogmatic theology will not, however, stand on its proper ground and soil with the same assurance with which philosophy has so long stood upon its own, until the separation of the two types of proposition is so complete that, for example, so extraordinary a question as whether the same proposition can be true in philosophy and false in Christian theology, and vice versa, will no longer be asked, for the simple reason that a proposition cannot appear in the one context precisely as it appears in the other: however similar it sounds, a difference must always be assumed. But we are still very far from this goal, so long as people take pains to base or deduce dogmatic propositions in the speculative manner, or even set themselves to work up the products of speculative activity and the results of the study of religious affections into a single whole.

Dogmatic propositions have a twofold value—an ecclesiastical and a scientific; and their degree of perfection is determined by both of these and their relation to each other

1. The ecclesiastical value of a dogmatic proposition consists in its reference to the religious emotions themselves. Every such emotion, regarded singly, is indeed for description an infinite, and all dogmatic concepts, as well as all concepts of psychology, would have to be used to describe one moment of life. But just as in such a moment the religious strain may be the dominant one, so again in every such strain some one relation of the higher self-consciousness stands out as determinative; and it is to this strain, uniformly for all analogous moments of religious emotion, that the dogmatic propositions refer. Thus, in all completely expressed dogmatic propositions, the reference to Christ as Redeemer must appear with the same measure of prominence which it has in the religious consciousness itself. Naturally, however, this is not equally strongly the case in all religious moments, any more than in the life of any civic state the distinctive character of its constitution can appear equally strongly in all moments. Accordingly, the less strongly the reference to Christ is expressed in a dogmatic proposition, as, for example, in the religious emotions mediated by our relation to the external world, the more easily may it resemble a doctrinal proposition of another religious communion, in cases where the distinctive character of that communion too remains for the most part in the background. Now this occurs even within the Christian Church itself, in respect of the various modifications of the Christian consciousness which separate into larger or smaller groups. Now, if a dogmatic

proposition is so formed that it satisfies the Christian consciousness for all alike, then it actually holds good in a larger circle, but it is not calculated to show up differences, which are thus indirectly marked as unimportant or in process of disappearing. If, on the other hand, it has respect only to one of these different modifications, then it holds good only within this smaller compass. Sometimes the former kind of dogma may seem colourless, and the latter be the right kind; at other times the latter may be factious or sectarian, and the former be the right kind. But such differences in dogmatic propositions dealing with the same subject, which do not represent any differences at all in the immediate religious self-consciousness, are of no significance for their ecclesiastical value.

2. The scientific value of a dogmatic proposition depends in the first place upon the definiteness of the concepts which appear in it, and of their connexion with each other. For the more definite these become, the more does the proposition pass out of the indefinite realm of the poetic and rhetorical, and the more certain will it be that the proposition cannot enter into apparent contradiction with other dogmatic propositions belonging to the same form of religious consciousness. But in forming its concepts Dogmatics has not succeeded—indeed, one might say that from the nature of the subject it cannot succeed—in everywhere substituting the exact expression for the figurative; and thus the scientific value of dogmatic propositions depends, from this side, for the most part simply upon the highest possible degree of precision and definiteness in explaining the figurative expressions which occur. And we can the more readily leave it at that, since, even if the exact expression could throughout be substituted for the figurative, the latter is the original, and therefore the identity of the two would have to be shown, which would come to the same thing in the end. In the second place, the scientific value of a dogmatic proposition consists in its fruitfulness, that is to say, its many-sidedness in pointing us towards other kindred ones; and not so much in a heuristic way (since no dogmatic proposition is based on another, and each one can only be discovered from contemplation of the Christian self-consciousness) as in a critical way, because then it can be the more easily tested how well one dogmatic expression harmonizes with others. For it is undeniable that, of a number of dogmatic expressions which are supposed to refer to the same fact of the Christian consciousness, that one will deserve the preference which opens up and enters into com-

bination with the largest range of other expressions referring to kindred facts. And when we find a realm or system of dogmatic language which is closely bound together and forms a self-contained whole, that is an account of the facts which we may presume to be correct.

A proposition which lacks the first of these two properties, and which thus belongs entirely to the poetic or the rhetorical realm of language, has not got the length of being a dogmatic proposition. A proposition which, as regards the second of the two properties, goes beyond the principle we have set up, and seeks to establish anything objectively without going back to the higher self-consciousness, would not be a religious doctrine (*Glaubenssatz*) at all, and would simply not belong to our field.

3. Now since every doctrine of the faith has, as such, an ecclesiastical value, and since these doctrines become dogmatic when they acquire a scientific value, dogmatic propositions are the more perfect the more their scientific character gives them an outstanding ecclesiastical value, and also the more their scientific content bears traces of having proceeded from the ecclesiastical interest.

The Christian Faith (1821–2) (trans. H. R. Mackintosh, J. S. Stewart and others)

CHAPTER 2

HEGEL

Georg Wilhelm Friedrich Hegel was born at Stuttgart in 1770, the son of a minor official in the service of the Duke of Württemberg. After five years at the university of Tübingen, studying philosophy and theology, he began his teaching career as a private tutor at Bern in Switzerland. This post he held from 1793 to 1796 relinquishing it only to take up similar work at Frankfurt-am-Main. In 1801 he was appointed to a lectureship at the university of Jena, but because of the disturbed conditions there following the Prussian defeat by Napoleon in 1806 he retired to Bamberg, where he edited a philosophical journal. Shortly afterwards he moved to Nuremberg to become Rector of the Aegidien Gymnasium, and here, in 1811, he married the daughter of a well-known citizen of the town. He had already in his Frankfurt years devised the ground-plan of his philosophical system, which during the Jena period received further elaboration with the composition of his first major work, the *Phänomenologie des Geistes*, published in 1807. But his principal literary achievement, the *Logik* (1812–16), was the fruit of his sojourn in the old Bavarian city. In 1818, after the brief interval of a professorship at Heidelberg, came the summons to Berlin with the offer of the university chair of philosophy. Here he rapidly acquired a position of European eminence, lecturing to large audiences and gaining many disciples. His published works comprised a general summary of his doctrine—the *Encyclopädie der philosophischen Wissenschaften*—and a treatise on the philosophy of law. His Berlin courses included series on the philosophy of religion, the history of philosophy, aesthetics, and the philosophy of history, all of which, in editions based on his voluminous lecture-notes, were printed posthumously. He died during an outbreak of cholera in 1831. A collection of his letters was published by his son, Karl Hegel, in 1887.

Hegel, although somewhat slow in developing, was a thinker in the grand manner and his system is universal in its scope. His erudition was in his day unsurpassed. But at the root of it all lay his early theological studies, which may be said to have determined both the spirit and the direction of his subsequent teaching. He delighted in the more speculative aspects of Christian doctrine even if the taste so displayed was, in the way he interpreted Christianity, a source rather of weakness than of strength.

Hegel's philosophy cannot be understood except in the light of his relation to Kant, to whom he persistently harks back. Like other post-Kantian idealists he builds on the foundation of the Kantian analysis of reason and knowledge, even when the resulting superstructure involves a complete transformation of Kant's own positions. The Koenigsberg philosopher held that the accessible world is the world as man's native rationality compels him to view it. Something assuredly is 'given' him, but knowledge is no mere impress from without, since the mind itself moulds the shape of it. With this compromise Hegel was not content. The epithet 'accessible' he considered superfluous. What point could there be in talking of a world of 'inaccessible' and 'unknowable' things-in-themselves? The real world is the world of reason and beyond what reason itself requires us to acknowledge there is and can be nothing else. To comprehend what reason is is to comprehend the universe; what is not rational is not real. Whereas then, for Kant, nothing absolute is cognizable, all knowledge being relative, for Hegel the very principles of life and thought—man's own possession—are themselves absolutes. To understand ourselves, therefore, is to understand reality. To the question whether human reason has limits Hegel replies that there are none; for the object of philosophical investigation is not an alien universe which we can explore only gropingly and with but partial success. Rather is it the essential truth of the life we ourselves directly know in the experience of living.

Hegel's *Phenomenology* purports to describe the various stages through which in the course of history the human mind passes in its transition from an unquestioning dependence on the senses to the ultimate state of philosophical reflexion. In his *Logic* he explains how philosophy yields us the categories or successive phases in man's interpretation of absolute truth, a succession determined by a 'dialectical' movement whereby, through an immanent development, the lower are taken up into and transcended in the higher. At this point in the unfolding of his system Hegel intended to elaborate a Philosophy of Nature, but this he never accomplished to his full satisfaction, all he has left us being the relatively brief but brilliant summary in the second part of the *Encyclopaedia*. The whole scheme was to have been completed with a magisterial Philosophy of Mind, comprising in turn psychology and the theory of the relations between nature and mind, ethics and the philosophical theory of the State, aesthetics, and the philosophy of religion. Again the actual achievement was less than its author envisaged and what we have consists only of the *Rechtsphilosophie*, the third section of the *Encyclopaedia* and the posthumous lectures, in which the treatment of their respective subjects, although fragmentary, is often extended.

The dominant features of the Hegelian system are the dialectical method and the theory of the Absolute. According to the former we first acquire truth in the form of 'immediate' experience. This is our necessary starting-point, the primary basis of all knowledge, and as such offers permanent justification of the place of empiricism in philosophy. But philosophy is vastly more than the mere registering of sense-experience, for sense-experience has to be transformed by the activity of reflective thought, the task of which is to divide and classify, to note facts in their distinctive aspects and to frame generalizations. Only thus is knowledge raised to the level of genuine *Gedanken* or theoretical concepts, fixed, abstract and universal. Yet the final scheme implies a range of infinitely various particular truths, and the impulse of the understanding to co-ordinate knowledge in an all-inclusive unity is perpetually countered and thwarted by variety and diversity. The inevitable result is the appearance of contradictions, given the understanding's own paramount concern for formal consistency as the necessary criterion of truth, since in dividing—as for theoretical purposes it must—what is essentially indivisible the understanding substitutes discrete abstractions for the concrete unity of life. We are confronted in fact by the old problem of the One and the Many. We cannot deny the existence of plurality, yet the ideas we form of it are, in their abstractness, as false as are those based on the assumption of a bare monism. Hence for us the way to truth can only be by the road of contradiction; we comprehend it as a synthesis of opposing viewpoints and there can be no synthesis, even though the isolation of a truth must in some degree falsify it, without such opposition. But if knowledge as such is to progress we have to see precisely how it is that a given viewpoint involves contradiction; for the triadic sequence in which one isolated statement (*thesis*) is countered by another (*antithesis*), both being subsequently united and transcended (*aufgehoben*) in a third (*synthesis*), is to be recognized as the pattern of a universal dialectical movement in which all experience and the knowledge founded on it are in the end transformed into a system of truth the elements of which stand revealed in all their necessary connexions. The principle of the method is what Hegel himself called the 'negativity' of thought: perfection of understanding is achieved only through the continuous resolution of imperfection under the pressure of negation.

Such, then, is the dialectic, and the theory of the Absolute is its correlate; for the dialectic not only is a process in the order of knowledge but is constituent of reality itself. Thought indeed is reality, and in man the universe attains to self-consciousness, when Spirit becomes aware of its own developing life. The latter, the ground of the universe, has according to Hegel a life whose manifold forms are those the philosopher has himself attempted to delineate in the *Logic*; and of these the first, as already stated, are the facts of immediate experience. This outer world, which we call Nature, is as it were the concrete manifestation of the primary forms of thought, which have therefore to be seen as more than *mere* forms. In life, and especially in reason, Spirit achieves yet higher expression until it finally becomes one with man's own profoundest insight attained in the course of his historical evolution. The entire world-process is thus to be understood as the developing expression of an immanent rationality which, although its self-consciousness is intrinsic and eternal, appears to us to *achieve* it only in the successive phases of man's temporal existence. The inference is that reality, to become fully self-aware, must await the exposition of the Hegelian metaphysic.

Hegel attaches the highest importance—after philosophy itself—to religion, which for him is essentially the conscious relation of the finite spirit to the Absolute or God—this last an identification which, in the words of the British Hegelian, Edward Caird, involves 'the complete rejection of ordinary supernaturalism', inasmuch as 'the world of intelligence and freedom cannot be different from the world of nature and necessity; it can only be the same world seen in a new light, or subjected to a further interpretation'. But the action of Spirit is necessarily a self-manifestation—in the language of religion, a 'revelation'. Revelation, however, must be understood less as truth *about* God than as knowledge of God *as* truth: he becomes self-conscious in man, as man in turn becomes conscious of God within himself. The achievement of this conscious unity—*Versöhnung*—expresses the vital essence and function of religion. It is an emotional as well as an intellectual awareness, for religious experience, out of which religious belief springs, comprises feeling as well as thought: hence the psychological conviction of God's 'immediacy' and the 'intuitive' character of man's sense of the divine. Nevertheless religious language, being symbolic or figurative only, is inadequate to convey abstract and systematic truth. Its virtue lies in its power to communicate a vivid *personal* apprehension of God's presence to the soul of man. To equate the symbol with the abstract truth is not only an error which critical analysis at once exposes, but one which, mistaking the concrete image (*Vorstellung*) for the speculative idea (*Begriff*), eventually destroys the particular spiritual efficacy of the symbols themselves. Yet philosophy, the final product of the abstract understanding, is necessarily superior to religion as the expression of ultimate truth.

Bibliographical note

The Jubilee Edition of Hegel's *Sämtliche Werke*, edited by H. Glockner, is in course of publication. English translations of individual works include: W. Wallace, *Logic* (2 vols., 1893) and *The Philosophy of Mind* (1894); W. H. Johnston and L. G. Struthers, *The Science of Logic* (2 vols., 1929); J. B. Baillie, *The Phenomenology of Mind* (2nd ed., rev. 1949); and E. B. Speirs and J. B. Sanderson, *The Philosophy of Religion* (3 vols., 1895). See also J. B. Baillie, *Hegel's Logic* (1901); E. Caird, *Hegel* (Blackwood's Philosophical Classics, 1883); W. T. Stace, *The Philosophy of Hegel* (1923); J. N. Findlay, *Hegel: a Reinterpretation* (1958); A. R. M. Murray, *The Philosophy of Hegel* (1960); R. Vancourt, *La pensée religieuse de Hegel* (1965); G. Lasson, *Einführung in Hegels Religionsphilosophie* (1930).

THE ABSOLUTE RELIGION

We have now reached the realized notion or conception of religion, the perfect religion, in which it is the notion itself that is its own object. We defined religion as being in the stricter sense the self-consciousness of God. Self-consciousness in its character as consciousness has an object, and it is conscious of itself in this object; this object is also consciousness, but it is consciousness as object, and is consequently finite consciousness, a consciousness which is distinct from God, from the Absolute. The element of determinateness is present in this form of consciousness, and consequently finitude is present in it; God is self-consciousness, He knows Himself in a consciousness which is distinct from Him, which is potentially the consciousness of God, but is also this actually, since it knows its identity with God, an identity which is, however, mediated by the negation of finitude. It is this notion or conception which constitutes the content of religion. We define God when we say that He distinguishes Himself from Himself, and is an object for Himself, but that in this distinction He is purely identical with Himself, is in fact Spirit. This notion or conception is now realized, consciousness knows this content and knows that it is itself absolutely interwoven with this content; in the Notion which is the process of God, it is itself a moment. Finite consciousness knows God only to the extent to which God knows Himself in it; thus God is Spirit, the Spirit of His Church in fact, i.e., of those who worship Him. This is the perfect religion, the Notion become objective to itself. Here it is revealed what God is; He is no longer a Being above and beyond this world, an Unknown, for He has told men what He is, and this not merely in an outward way in history, but in consciousness. We have here, accordingly, the religion of the manifestation of God, since God knows Himself in the finite spirit. This simply means that God is revealed. Here this is the essential circumstance. What the transition was we discovered when we saw how this knowledge of God as free Spirit was, so far as its substance is concerned, still tinged with finitude and immediacy; this finitude had further to be discarded by the labour of Spirit; it is nothingness, and we saw how this nothingness was revealed to consciousness. The misery, the sorrow of the world, was the condition, the preparation on the subjective side for the consciousness of free Spirit, as the absolutely free and consequently infinite Spirit.

We shall confine ourselves, to begin with (A), to the general aspects of this sphere of thought.

The Absolute Religion is—1. *The Revealed Religion*. Religion is something revealed, it is manifested, only when the notion or conception of religion itself exists for itself; or, to put it differently, religion or the notion of religion has become objective to itself, not in the form of limited finite objectivity, but rather in such a way that it is objective to itself in accordance with its notion.

This can be expressed in a more definite way by saying that religion, according to its general conception or notion, is the consciousness of the absolute Essence. It is the nature, however, of consciousness to distinguish, and thus we have two things, consciousness and absolute Essence. These two at first are in a state of mutual exclusion, standing in a finite relation to each other. We have the empirical consciousness, and the Essence taken in the sense of something different.

They stand in a finite relation to each other, and so far they are themselves both finite, and thus consciousness knows the absolute Essence only as something finite, not as something true. God is Himself consciousness, He distinguishes Himself from Himself within Himself, and as consciousness He gives Himself as object for what we call the side of consciousness.

Here we have always two elements in consciousness, which are related to each other in a finite and external fashion. When, however, as is the case at this stage, religion comes to have a true comprehension of itself, then it is seen that the content and the object of religion are made up of this very Whole, of the consciousness which brings itself into relation with its Essence, the knowledge of itself as the Essence and of the Essence as itself, i.e. Spirit thus becomes the object in religion. We thus have two things, consciousness and the object; in the religion, however, the fulness of which is the fulness of its own nature, in the revealed religion, the religion which comprehends itself, it is religion, the content itself which is the object, and this object, namely, the Essence which knows itself, is Spirit. Here first is Spirit as such the object, the content of religion, and Spirit is only for Spirit. Since it is content and object, as Spirit it is what knows itself, what distinguishes itself from itself, and itself supplies the other side of subjective consciousness, that which appears as finite. It is the religion which derives its fulness from itself, which is complete in itself. This is the abstract characterization of the Idea in this form, or, to put it otherwise, religion is, as a matter of fact, Idea. For Idea in the philosophical sense of the term is the Notion which has itself for object, i.e. it is the Notion which has definite existence, reality, objectivity, and which is no longer anything inner or subjective, but gives itself an objective form. Its objectivity, however, is at the same time its return into itself, or, in so far as we describe the Notion as End, it is the realized, developed End, which is consequently objective.

Religion has just that which it itself is, the consciousness of the Essence, for its object; it gets an objective form in it, it actually *is*, just as, to begin with, it existed as Notion and only as the Notion, or just as at first it was *our* Notion. The absolute religion is the *revealed* religion, the religion which has itself for its content, its fulness.

It is the Christian religion which is the perfect religion, the religion which represents the Being of Spirit in a realized form, or for itself, the religion in which religion has itself become objective in relation to itself. In it the universal Spirit and the particular spirit, the infinite Spirit and the finite spirit, are inseparably connected; it is their absolute identity which constitutes this religion and is its substance or content. The universal Power is the substance which, since it is potentially quite as much subject as substance, now posits this potential being which belongs to it, and in consequence distinguishes itself from itself, communicates itself to knowledge, to the finite spirit; but in so doing, just because it is a moment in its own development, it remains with itself, and in the act of dividing itself up returns undivided to itself.

The object of theology as generally understood is to get to know God as the merely objective God, who is absolutely separated from the subjective consciousness, and is thus an outward object, just as the sun, the sky, etc., are objects of consciousness, and here the object is permanently characterized as an Other, as something external. In contrast to this the Notion of the absolute religion can be so presented as to suggest that what we have got to do with is not anything of this external sort, but religion itself, i.e. the unity of this idea which we call God with the conscious subject.

We may regard this as representing also the standpoint of the present day, inasmuch as people are now concerned with religion, religiousness, and piety, and thus do not occupy themselves with the object in religion. Men have various religions, and the main thing is for them to be pious. We cannot know God as object, or get a real knowledge of Him, and the main thing, what we are really concerned about, is merely the subjective manner of knowing Him and our subjective religious condition. We may recognize this standpoint as described in what has just been said. It is the standpoint of the age, but at the same time it represents a most important advance by which an infinite moment has had its due value recognized, for it involves a recognition of the consciousness of the subject as constituting an absolute moment. The same content is seen to exist in both sides, and it is this potential or true Being of the two sides which is religion. The great advance which marks our time consists in the recognition of subjectivity as an absolute moment, and this is therefore essentially determination or characterization. The whole question, however, turns on how subjectivity is determined or characterized.

On this important advance we have to make the following remarks. When religion is determined from the point of view of consciousness, it is so constituted that the content passes beyond consciousness, and in appearance at least remains something strange or foreign to consciousness. It does not matter what content religion has, this content, regarded solely from the standpoint of consciousness, is something which exists above and outside of consciousness, and even if we add to it the peculiar determination of Revelation, it is nevertheless for us something given and outward. The result of such a conception of religion is that the Divine content is regarded as something given independent of us, as something which cannot be known but is to be received and kept in a merely passive way in faith, and on the other hand it lands us in the subjectivity of the feeling which is the end and the result of the worship of God. The standpoint of consciousness is therefore not the sole and only standpoint. The devout man sinks himself in his object, together with his heart, his devotion, and his will, and when he has attained to this height of devoutness he has got rid of the sense of separation which marks the standpoint of consciousness. It is possible also from the standpoint of consciousness to reach this subjectivity, this feeling that the object is not foreign to consciousness, this absorption of the spirit in those depths which do not represent something distant, but rather absolute nearness and presence.

This doing away with the separation can, however, in turn be conceived of as something foreign to consciousness, as the grace of God, which man has to acquiesce in as something foreign to his own nature, and his relation to which is of a passive sort. It is against this separation that the formula is directed which says that it is with religion as such we have got to do, i.e. with the subjective consciousness which has in itself what God wills. It is in the subject accordingly that the inseparability of subjectivity and of the Other or objectivity exists; or, to put it otherwise, the subject as containing in itself the real relation is an essential element in the whole range of thought. Regarded from this standpoint, the subject is accordingly raised to the rank of an essential characteristic. It is in harmony with the freedom of Spirit that it should thus recover its freedom, that there should be no standpoint at which it is not in company with itself. That it is religion which is objective to itself is a truth which is contained in the notion or conception of the absolute religion, but only in the conception. This conception or notion is one thing, and the consciousness of this notion is another.

Thus in the absolute religion as well the notion may potentially contain the truth referred to, but the consciousness of this is something different. This then is the phase of thought which has reached consciousness and come to the front in the formula which says that it is with religion we have to do. The Notion is itself still one-sided, is taken as merely implicit or potential; and so it appears in this one-sided shape where subjectivity itself is one-sided; it has the characteristic of one of two only, is only infinite form, pure self-consciousness, the pure knowledge of itself, it is potentially without content, because religion as such is conceived of only in its potential character, and is not the religion which is objective to itself, but is only religion in a shape which is not yet real, which has not yet made itself objective or given itself a content. What has no objectivity has no content.

It is one of the rights of truth that knowledge should have in religion the absolute content. Here, however, what we have is not the content in its true form, but only in a stunted form. Thus there must be a content. The content in the present case has, as we have seen, the character of something contingent, finite, empirical, and consequently we have a state of things similar to what existed in Roman times. The times of the Roman Emperors resembled ours in many points. The subject as it actually is, is conceived of as infinite; but as abstract, it changes into the direct opposite, and is merely finite and limited. Its freedom consequently is only of the sort which admits the existence of something beyond the present, an aspiration, a freedom which denies the existence of a distinction in consciousness, and consequently casts aside the essential moment of Spirit, and is thus unspiritual subjectivity, subjectivity without thought.

Religion is the knowledge which Spirit has of itself as Spirit; when it takes the form of pure knowledge it does not know itself as Spirit, and is consequently not substantial but subjective knowledge. The fact, however, that it is nothing more than this, and is therefore limited knowledge, is not apparent to subjectivity in its own form, i.e. in the form or shape of knowledge, but rather it is its immediate potentiality which it finds, to begin with, in itself, and consequently in the knowledge of itself as being simply the infinite, the feeling of its finitude and consequently of its infinitude as well, as a kind of potential Being beyond and above it in contrast to its actual Being, or Being-for-self—the feeling, in short, of longing after something above and beyond it which is unexplained. The Absolute Religion, on the other hand, contains the characteristic, the note, of subjectivity or infinite form which is equivalent to substance. We may give the name of knowledge, of pure intelligence, to this subjectivity, this infinite form, this infinite elasticity of substance whereby it breaks itself up within itself, and makes itself an object for itself. Its content is therefore a content which is identical with itself, because it is the infinitely substantial subjectivity which makes itself both object and content. Then in this content itself the finite subject is further distinguished from the infinite object. God regarded as Spirit, when He remains above, when He is not present in His Church as a living Spirit, is Himself characterized in a merely one-sided way as object.

This is the Notion, it is the Notion of the Idea, of the absolute Idea, and the reality is now Spirit which exists for Spirit, which has made itself its object, and this religion is the revealed religion, the religion in which God reveals Himself. Revelation means this differentiation of the infinite form, the act of self-determination, the being for an Other, and this self-manifestation is of the very essence of Spirit. Spirit which is not revealed is not Spirit. We say that God has created the world, and we state this as a fact which has happened once and which will not happen again, and we thus ascribe to the event the character of something which may be or may not be. God, we say, might have revealed Himself or He might not. The character we ascribe to God's revelation of Himself is that of something arbitrary, accidental as it were, and not that of something belonging to the Notion of God. But God as Spirit is essentially this very self-revelation; He does not create the world once for all, but He is the eternal Creator, this eternal self-revelation, this *actus*. This is His Notion, His essential characteristic.

70

Religion, the revealed religion, Spirit as for Spirit, is as such the Religion of Spirit. It is not something which does not open itself out for an Other, which is an Other merely momentarily. God posits or lays down the Other, and takes it up again into His eternal movement. Spirit just is what appears to itself or manifests itself; this constitutes its act, or form of action, and its life; this is its only act, and it is itself only its act. What does God reveal, in fact, but just that He is this revelation of Himself? What He reveals is the infinite form. Absolute subjectivity is determination, and this is the positing or bringing into actual existence of distinctions or difference. The positing of the content, what He thus reveals, is that He is the one Power who can make these distinctions in Himself. It is His Being to make these distinctions eternally, to take them back and at the same time to remain with Himself, not to go out of Himself. What is revealed, is, that He is for an Other. This is the essential character, the definition, of revelation.

2. This religion, which is manifest or revealed to itself, is not only the revealed religion, but the religion which is actually known as a religion which has been revealed; and by this is understood, on the one hand, that it has been revealed by God, that God has actually communicated the knowledge of Himself to men; and, on the other hand, that being a revealed religion, it is a positive religion in the sense that it has come to men, and has been given to them from the outside.

In view of this peculiarity which attaches to the idea of what is positive, it becomes interesting to see what the Positive is.

The absolute religion is undoubtedly a positive religion in the sense that everything which exists for consciousness is for it something objective. Everything must come to us in an outward way. What belongs to sense is thus something positive, and, to begin with, there is nothing so positive as what we have before us in immediate perception.

Everything spiritual, as a matter of fact, comes to us in this way also, as the spiritual in a finite form, the spiritual in the form of history, and the mode in which the spiritual is thus external and externalizes itself is likewise positive.

A higher and purer form of the spiritual is found in what is moral, in the laws of freedom. This, however, is not in its real nature any such outward form of the spiritual as has just been referred to, it is not something external or accidental, but expresses the nature of pure Spirit itself. It too, however, comes to us in an outward way, at first in education, training, definite teaching; there its truth or validity is simply given to us, pointed out to us.

And so, too, laws, civil laws, the laws of the State, are something positive; they come to us, they exist for us, they have authority or validity, they *are*, not in the sense that we can leave them alone or pass by them, but as implying that in this external form of theirs they ought also to exist *for us* as something subjectively essential, subjectively binding.

When we get a grasp of the law that crime should be punished, when we recognize its validity and find it to be rational, it is not something essential for us in the sense that it has authority for us only *because* it is positive, because it is what it is; but it has authority for us inwardly as well, for our reason, as being something essential, because it is also inward and rational.

The fact of its being positive in no way deprives it of its character as something rational, as something which is our own. The laws of freedom, when they actually appear, have always a positive side, a side marked by reality, externality, and contingency. Laws must get a specific character, and into the specification, into the quality of the punishment, there already enters the element of externality, and still more into the quantity of the punishment.

In the case of punishment the positive element cannot at all be absent—it is absolutely necessary. This final determination or specification of the immediate is something positive which is in no sense rational. In the case of punishment, round numbers, for instance, decide the amount; you cannot find out by reason what is the absolutely just penalty. It is the irrational which is naturally positive. It must get a definite character, and it is characterized in a way which has nothing rational about it, or which contains nothing rational in it.

It is necessary to regard revealed religion in the following aspect also. Since in it there is present something historical, something which appears in an outward form, there is also present in it something positive, something contingent, which may take either one form or another. Thus it occurs in the case of religion as well, that owing to the externality, the appearance in an outward form which accompanies it, there is always something positive present.

But we must distinguish between the Positive as such, the abstract Positive, and the Positive in the form of and as the law of freedom. The law of freedom should not possess validity or authority because it is actually there, but rather because it is the essential characteristic of our rational nature itself. It is not, therefore, anything positive, not any-thing which simply has validity, if it is known to be a characteristic of this kind. Religion, too, appears in a positive form in all that constitutes its doctrines; but it is not meant to remain in this condition, or to be a matter of mere popular ideas or of pure memory.

The positive element connected with the verification of religion consists in the idea that what is external should establish the truth of a religion, and should be regarded as the foundation of its truth. Here in this instance the verification takes the form of something positive as such. There are miracles and evidences which it is held prove the divinity of the person who reveals and prove that this person has communicated to men certain definite doctrines.

Miracles are changes connected with the world of sense, changes in the material world which are actually perceived, and this perception is itself connected with the senses because it has to do with changes in the world of sense. It has been already remarked in reference to this positive element of miracle, that it undoubtedly can produce a kind of verification for the man who is guided by his senses; but this is merely the beginning of verification, an unspiritual kind of verification by which what is spiritual cannot be verified.

The Spiritual, as such, cannot be directly verified or authenticated by what is unspiritual and connected with sense. The chief thing to be noticed in connexion with this view of miracles is that in this way they are put on one side.

The understanding may attempt to explain miracles naturally, and may bring many plausible arguments against them—i.e. it may confine its attention simply to the outward fact, to what has happened, and direct its criticism against this. The essential standpoint of reason in the matter of miracles is that the truth of the Spiritual cannot be attested in an outward way; for what is spiritual is higher than what is outward, its truth can be attested only by itself and in itself, and demonstrated only through itself and in itself. This is what has been called the witness of the Spirit.

This very truth has found expression in the history of religion. Moses performs miracles before Pharaoh, and the Egyptian sorcerers imitate them, and this very fact implies that no great value is to be put on them. The main thing, however, is that Christ Himself says, 'Many will come who will do miracles in My name, but I know them not'. Here He Himself rejects miracles as a true criterion of truth. This is the essential point of view in regard to this question, and we must hold fast to the principle that the verification of religion by means of miracles, as well as the attacking of miracles, belong to a sphere which has no interest for us. The Witness of the Spirit is the true witness.

This witness may take various forms; it may be indefinite, general, something which is, broadly speaking, in harmony with Spirit, and which awakens a deeper response within it. In history all that is noble, lofty, moral, and divine, appeals to us; our spirit bears witness to it. The witness may not be more than this general response, this assent of the inner life, this sympathy. But it may also be united to intellectual grasp, to thought; and this intellectual grasp, inasmuch as it has no element of sense in it, belongs directly to the sphere of thought. It appears in the form of reasons, distinctions, and such like; in the form of mental activity, exercised along with and according to the specific forms of thought, the categories. It may appear in a more matured form or in a less matured form. It may have the character of something which constitutes the necessary basis of a man's inner heart-life, of his spiritual life in general, the presupposition of general fundamental principles which have authoritative value for him and accompany him through life. These maxims don't require to be consciously followed; rather, they represent the mode and manner in which his character is formed, the universal element which has got a firm footing in his spirit, and which accordingly is something permanent within his mind and governs him.

Starting from a firm foundation or presupposition of this sort, he can begin to reason logically, to define or arrange under categories. Here the stages of intellectual advance and the methods of life are of very many kinds, and the needs felt are very various. The highest need of the human spirit, however, is thought—the witness of the Spirit, which is not present only in the merely responsive form of a kind of primary sympathy, nor in that other form according to which such firm foundations and fundamental principles do exist in the spirit, and have reflective thought built upon them, firmly based presuppositions from which conclusions can be drawn and deductions made.

The witness of the Spirit in its highest form takes the form of philosophy, according to which the Notion, purely as such, and without the presence of any presupposition, develops the truth out of itself, and we recognize it as developing, and perceive the necessity of the development in and through the development itself.

Belief has often been opposed to Thought in such a way as to imply that we can have no true conviction regarding God and the truths of religion by any other method than that of Thought, and thus the proofs of the existence of God have been pointed to as supplying the only method by which we can know and be convinced of the truth.

The witness of the Spirit may, however, be present in manifold and various ways; we have no right to demand that the truth should in the case of all men be got at in a philosophical way. The spiritual necessities of men vary according to their culture and free development; and so, too, the demand, the conviction that we should believe on authority, varies according to the different stages of development reached.

Even miracles have their place here, and it is interesting to observe that they have been reduced down to this minimum. There is thus still something positive present in this form of the witness of the Spirit as well. Sympathy, which is immediate certainty, is itself something positive in virtue of its immediacy, and the process of inference which starts from something laid down or given has a similar basis. It is man only who has a religion, and religion has its seat and its soil in thought. Heart or feeling is not the heart or feeling of an animal, but the heart of *thinking* man, a thinking heart, or feeling; and what shows itself in the heart as the feeling for religion, exists in the thinking element of the heart, or feeling. In so far as we begin to draw conclusions, to draw inferences, to suggest reasons, to advance to thought-determinations or categories of thought, we do this always by the exercise of thought.

Inasmuch as the doctrines of the Christian religion are found in the Bible, they are given in a positive way; and if they become subjective, if the Spirit bears witness to their truth, this can happen only in a purely immediate way, by a man's inner nature, his spirit, his thought, his reason being impressed with their truth and assenting to it. Thus, for the Christian it is the Bible which is this basis, the fundamental basis, and which has upon him the effect referred to, which touches a chord in his heart, and gives firmness to his convictions.

We get a stage further, however, when it is seen that just because he is a thinking being he cannot rest in this state of immediate consent or witnessing to truth, but turns it over by thinking, meditating, and reflecting upon it. This accordingly leads to a further development in religion; and in its highest and most developed form it is theology, scientific religion; it is this content of religion known in a scientific way as the witness of Spirit.

75

But here a principle which is the opposite of this comes in, and which is expressed by saying that we should simply keep to the Bible. Looked at in one aspect, that is a perfectly correct principle. There are people who are very religious, who do nothing but read the Bible and repeat sayings out of it, and whose piety and religious feeling are of a lofty kind, but they are not theologians; religion does not, so far, take with them a scientific form, the form of theology. Götze, the Lutheran zealot, had a celebrated collection of Bibles; the devil, too, quotes the Bible, but that by no means makes the theologian.

As soon, however, as this ceases to be simply the reading and repetition of passages, as soon as what is called explanation begins, as soon as an attempt is made by reasoning and exegesis to find out the meaning of what is in the Bible, then we pass into the region of inference, reflexion, and thought, and then the question comes to be as to whether our thinking is correct or not, and as to *how* we exercise this power of thought.

It is of no use to say that these particular thoughts or these principles are based on the Bible. As soon as they cease to be anything more than the mere words of the Bible, a definite form is given to what constitutes them, to their content; this content gets a logical form, or, to put it otherwise, certain presuppositions are formed in connexion with this content, and we approach the explanation of the passages with these presuppositions which represent the permanent element so far as the explanation is concerned. We bring with us certain ideas which guide us in the explanation given. The explanation of the Bible exhibits the substance or content of the Bible in the form or style of thought belonging to each particular age. The explanation which was first given was wholly different from that given now.

These presuppositions consist, for instance, of such an idea as this, that man is naturally good, or that we cannot know God. Consider how any one with such preconceived ideas in his mind must distort the Bible. Yet people bring such ideas to the interpretation of the Bible, although the Christian religion just means that we know God, and is just the religion in which God has revealed Himself and has shown what He is.

Thus here again the positive element may enter in in another form, and in this connexion it is a matter of great importance to determine whether this content, these ideas and principles, are true or not.

It is no longer the Bible which we have here, but the words as these have been conceived of within the mind or spirit. If the spirit gives expression to them, then they have already a form got from the spirit, the form of thought. It is necessary to examine this form which is thus given to the content of these words. Here again the positive element comes in. In this connexion it means, for instance, that the existence of the formal logic of syllogistic reasoning, of the relations of thought belonging to what is finite, has been presupposed.

According to the ordinary view of the nature of reasoning, it is only what is finite, only what may be grasped by the understanding, that can be conceived of and known. Reason, as ordinarily understood, is not adequate to deal with a divine element or content. Thus this content is rendered totally useless.

As soon as theology ceases to be a rehearsal of what is in the Bible, and goes beyond the words of the Bible, and concerns itself with the character of the feelings within the heart, it employs forms of thought and passes into thought. If, however, it uses these forms in a haphazard way so that it has presuppositions and preconceived ideas, then its use of them is of an accidental and arbitrary kind, and it is the examination of these forms of thought which alone makes philosophy.

When theology turns against philosophy, it is either not conscious that it uses such forms, that it thinks itself, and that its main concern is to advance in accordance with thought, or else its opposition is not seriously meant, but is simply deception; it wishes to reserve for itself the right to think as it chooses, to indulge in thinking which does not follow laws and which is here the positive element.

The recognition of the true nature of thought lessens the value of this arbitrary kind of thought. This sort of thought, which is a matter of choice and does not follow strict laws, is the positive element which comes in here. It is only the Notion in its true nature, the Notion for itself, which truly frees itself absolutely from this positive element, for both in philosophy and religion freedom in its highest form is thought itself as such.

The doctrine or content also takes on the form of something positive; it is something having a valid existence, and it passes as such in society. All law, all that is rational, and in general all that has true value or validity, takes the form of something which exists or is possessed of being, and as such it is for each one something essential, something having true value or validity. This, however, is merely the form in which what is positive appears; the content or substance must be constituted by the true Spirit.

The Bible represents the Positive in this form; but it is one of its own sayings, that the letter killeth, while the spirit giveth life; and here the important point is the kind of spirit which is brought into connexion with the letter, what kind of spirit gives life to the word. We must know that we bring with us a concrete spirit, a thinking, reflecting, or feeling spirit, and we must have a consciousness of the presence of this spirit which is active and forms a conception of the content before it.

This act of apprehending or forming a conception is not a passive reception of something into the mind, but, on the contrary, just because the spirit forms a conception, this conceiving of something is at the same time a manifestation of its activity. It is only in the mechanical sphere that one of the sides remains passive in connexion with the process of reception. Thus Spirit plays a part here, and this spirit has its ideas and conceptions, it is a logical Essence, a form of thinking activity, and the spirit must know this activity. Thought in this form, however, can also pass into the various categories of finitude.

It is Spirit which after this fashion starts from what is positive but is essentially in it; it must be the true, right spirit, the Holy Spirit which apprehends and knows the Divine, and which apprehends and knows this content as divine. This is the witness of the Spirit, and it may have a more or less developed form.

The main thing, therefore, so far as the Positive is concerned, is that Spirit occupies a thinking relation to things, that it appears in an active form in the categories or specific forms of thought, that Spirit is active here and may take the shape of feeling, reasoning, etc. Some don't know this, and are not conscious when they have impressions that they are active in receiving them.

Many theologians, while treating their subject exegetically, and as they imagine taking up a purely receptive attitude to what is in the Bible, are not aware that they are at the same time thinking actively and reflecting. Since this kind of thinking is accidental, governed by no necessary laws, it yields itself up to the guidance of the categories of finitude, and is consequently incapable of grasping the divine element in the content; it is not the divine but the human spirit which is actively present in such categories.

It is owing to this finite way of conceiving of the Divine, of what has full and complete Being, what is in and for itself, and to this finite way of thinking of the absolute content, that the fundamental doctrines of

Christianity have for the most part disappeared from Dogmatics. At the present time it is philosophy which is not only orthodox, but orthodox *par excellence*; and it is it which maintains and preserves the principles which have always held good, the fundamental truths of Christianity.

In treating of this religion we do not go to work historically after the fashion of that form of mental action which starts from what is outward, but, on the contrary, we start from the Notion. That form of activity which starts from what is outward takes the shape of something which apprehends or receives impressions only when we look at it in *one* of its two aspects, while looked at in the other it is activity.

Our attitude here is essentially an attitude of activity of this kind; we are, in fact, conscious that we are thinking on thought itself, on the course taken by the categories of thought, a kind of thinking which has tested itself and knows itself, which knows how it thinks, and knows which are the finite and which the true categories of thought. That, regarding the matter from the other point of view, we start from what is positive, is true in reference to education, and is even necessary; but here we must abandon this mode of procedure in so far as we employ the scientific method.

3. The absolute religion is thus the religion of Truth and Freedom. For truth means that the mind does not take up such an attitude to the objective as would imply that this is something foreign to it. Freedom brings out the real meaning of truth, and gives it a specific character by means of negation. Spirit is for Spirit; that expresses its nature, and it is thus its own presupposition. We start with Spirit as subject, it is identical with itself, it is the eternal perception of itself, and it is at the same time conceived of only as a result, as the end of a process. It is the presupposition of itself, and it is at the same time the result, and it exists only as the end of a process. This is truth, this condition of being adequate, of being object and subject. The fact that it is itself the object makes it the reality, the Notion, the Idea, and it is this which makes the Truth. So, too, it is the religion of freedom. Freedom considered abstractly means that the mind is related to something objective which is not regarded as foreign to its nature, its essential character is the same as that of truth, only that in the case of freedom the negation of the difference of Otherness has been done away with and absorbed in something higher, and thus it appears in the form of Reconciliation. Reconciliation starts from the fact that there are different forms of

existence which stand to each other in a relation of opposition, namely, God, who has opposed to Him an estranged world, and a world which is estranged from its own essential Being. Reconciliation is the negation of this separation, of this division; it means that each recognizes itself, finds itself and its essential nature, in the other. Reconciliation is thus freedom; but it is not something in a state of repose, something which simply is; on the contrary, it is activity. All that we mean by reconciliation, truth, freedom, represents a universal process, and cannot therefore be expressed in a single proposition without becoming one-sided. The main idea which in a popular form expresses the truth, is that of the unity of the divine and human natures; God has become Man. This unity is at first *potential* only, but being such it has to be eternally produced or brought into actual existence; and this act of production is the freeing process, the reconciliation which in fact is possible only by means of the potentiality. The Substance which is identical with itself is this unity, which as such is the basis, but which as subjectivity is what eternally produces itself.

The final result of the whole of philosophy is that this Idea only is the absolute truth. In its pure form it is the logical result, but it is likewise the result of a study of the concrete world. What constitutes the truth is that Nature, life, Spirit, are thoroughly organic, that each separate thing is merely the mirror of this Idea, in such a way that the Idea exhibits itself in it as in something isolated, as a process in it, and thus it manifests this unity in itself.

The Religion of Nature is the religion which occupies the standpoint of consciousness only. This standpoint is to be found in the Absolute Religion as well, but it exists within it only as a transitory moment. In the Religion of Nature God is represented as an 'Other', as present in a natural shape; or, to put it otherwise, religion appears in the form merely of consciousness. The second form was that of the spiritual religion, of Spirit which does not get beyond finite characterization. So far it is the religion of self-consciousness, that is, of absolute power, of necessity in the sense which we have given to these terms. The One, the Power, is something defective, because it is abstract Power only, and is not in virtue of its content absolute subjectivity, but is only abstract necessity, abstract, simple, undifferentiated Being.

The condition of abstraction in which the Power and the necessity are conceived of as still existing at this stage, constitutes their finitude, and it is the particular powers, namely, the gods who when characterized in accordance with their spiritual content first make totality, since they add a real content to that abstraction. Lastly, we have the third form of religion, the religion of freedom, of self-consciousness, which, however, is at the same time a consciousness of the all-embracing reality which constitutes the determinateness of the eternal Idea of God Himself, and a consciousness which does not go outside of itself, which remains beside itself in this objectivity. Freedom is the essential characteristic of self-consciousness.

The Philosophy of Religion (1832) (trans. E. B. Speirs and J. B. Sanderson)

— something important for the church to learn from Hegel: that the action of God in human existence, in all of existence, is necessarily synthetic; that is, God is creating in the midst of the existence we perceive, and therefore if we are to really know God in existence we must realize his creative, synthetic activity, and not simply "reduce" all claims about knowledge of God to the existential relationship with him. This is to say that Kierk.'s critique is not enough, it is also necessary for the Christian to see the creative activity of God in current existence, and not stop at the existential analysis of judgement/grace, despair/hope

Hegel to Marx: ideal to empirical
Hegel to Kierkegaard: ideal to existential

alienation in Hegel: the cross, the center, the sign and means of synthesis of A.S. with finite consciousness

" in Marx: the social/existential situation from which social analysis proceeds to action, the beginning of realization and order

" in Kierkegaard: the essence of the Christian life and existence

CHAPTER 3

FEUERBACH

Ludwig Feuerbach, author of *Das Wesen des Christenthums*, was born, the son of a lawyer, at Landshut in Bavaria in 1804, receiving his university education first at Heidelberg and then, after 1824, at Berlin, where he became a pupil of Hegel's. In 1828 he was appointed *Privatdozent* in philosophy at Erlangen, but later gave up academic teaching altogether for the retired life of a private scholar. From 1860 until his death in 1872 he made his home on the Rechenberg, near Nuremberg; an uneventful existence, dedicated only to the traffic of ideas, although of *mere* ideas he was always contemptuous: *Der Mensch*, he said, in a famous phrase, *ist was er isst*— 'Man is what he eats'. Indeed in Feuerbach's writings there is more of the prophet and reformer than of the pure thinker or scholar. His *œuvre* includes, besides *Das Wesen des Christenthums* (1841)—translated into English by George Eliot in 1854—a critique of the philosophy of Hegel (1839), *Grundsätze der Philosophie der Zukunft* (1843), and *Das Wesen der Religion* (1851), a series of lectures delivered by him at Heidelberg in 1848. Whatever Feuerbach's place may be in the general course of modern philosophy, his contribution to the philosophy of religion and in particular to the philosophical interpretation of Christianity, emerges, in the light both of Marxism and of recent existentialism, as worthy of serious study. This 'philosophically grounded negation to all theology' was, as Karl Barth states, 'essentially a summons, an appeal, a proclamation', and its message, more than a century since, has lost nothing of its interest. For his influence on Marx alone Feuerbach would of course be a key-figure; but Kierkegaard, Nietzsche, Freud, Heidegger and Sartre all to some extent bear the impress of his mind.

Atheist though Feuerbach may be, Engels was correct in saying that his aim was not to abolish religion but to 'perfect' it and that he believed that even philosophy itself would have to be absorbed in religion. He quotes Feuerbach's own statements that 'the periods of humanity are distinguished only by religious changes' and that 'the heart is the essence of religion'. Yet the truth of Marx's comment, that Feuerbach's achievement consists in 'the dissolution of the religious world into its secular basis', is obvious. Religion, as Feuerbach understood it, is essentially the relation, founded deep in the emotions, between man and man. As he himself puts it: 'The question as to the existence or non-existence of God, the opposition between theism and atheism, belongs to the sixteenth and seventeenth centuries, but not to the nineteenth. I deny God. But that means for me that I deny *the negation of man*' (italics ours). What he claimed to be doing was to substitute for the 'illusory, fantastic, heavenly' position of man—which in fact tends to his degradation—the 'tangible, actual' position, including, necessarily, his political and social position. Thus he holds that the question of God is no more or other than the question of man. The error of religion in every age has been to project an all-important human relationship upon the screen of eternity, so that man mistakes his own terrestrial being for the Brocken-spectre of a celestial deity. The truth to which religion must in future witness is the love between the *I* and the *Thou* of a purely earthly and temporal encounter. To fix our eyes on the heavens is to misconceive our humanity. In other words, the 'friends of God' must be turned into the 'friends of man', believers into thinkers, worshippers into workers. Man's chief task is to reach an authentic self-understanding. In clinging to the creed of a 'supernatural' faith, he has hitherto been self-alienated. In place of 'sterile baptismal water' let him now look to the 'beneficent effects of real water'.

Feuerbach's materialism is fundamental. 'I differ *toto coelo*', he wrote, 'from philosophers who pluck out their eyes that they may see better.' Objects are not generated from thought, but thought from objects. The doctrines of Christianity, if we are to comprehend what they really mean, must be concretized. We must interpret them not in the mythico-meta-physical language of traditional theology, which has now ceased to be intelligible, but in that of actual human experience. Hence theology is to be reduced to *anthropology*, 'very much', so Feuerbach argues, 'as Christianity, while lowering God into man, made man into God'. Our interest should be to make God 'real and human', since the problem of Christianity is not metaphysical but historical and psychological. The metaphysical question can never be answered because it can never be meaningfully stated; it belongs only to a realm of abstract notions which prove their falsity in their latent contradictions. Feuerbach's inquiry is made to fall, therefore, into two parts, a positive and a negative, or a destructive and a constructive, although in Marxism, as in popular rationalism, it is the negative and destructive side that receives most attention. The polemic, as the author of *The Essence of Christianity* himself insists, is necessary: the need for radical criticism entails demolition, and dogmatic Christianity, as the obsolete inheritance of a bygone era in human culture, cannot escape it. But Feuerbach is no vulgar 'debunker' of religion, as Engels was quick to point out. The religious aspect of life, so far from being an absurdity, was in his view a basic component of man's self-consciousness, its subject being nothing other than man himself. This is shown by an analysis of religious experience which goes beyond the confused images of theology. God is simply man's self-reflexion, 'the commonplace book where he registers his highest feelings and thoughts, the genealogical album in which he enters the names of the things most dear and sacred to him'. As a conceptual ideal—the epitome of all realities and perfections—deity is only a 'compendious summary devised for the benefit of the limited individual'. What it denotes is certain generic human qualities necessary to the self-realization of the species in the course of world-history. Even orthodox theism, when pressed, drops back on the method of definition by negation, the *via negativa*, so that if the idea of God is to have negotiable content we are bound to resort to human categories. But it is more than a matter of *analogy*, since man can know nothing beyond his own strictly conditioned experience: 'The divine essence is the glorified human essence transfigured from the death of abstraction.' In religion he frees himself from life's frustrations, for here alone, 'where he celebrates his Sunday', does he live in his true character.

The first half of Feuerbach's book is a close examination of Christian doctrine along purely experiential lines. What he believed himself able to offer was a faith for an age of *un*faith. With Hegel the era of metaphysics ended and whatever we may happen to prefer or desire the thought-forms of an age as remote as that in which Christian dogma took shape are no longer serviceable. Supernatural doctrines have no need to be disproved; they merely cease to be credible, and apologetic argument, however ingenious, will not restore their intellectual purchasing power. So much Feuerbach takes for granted; but in the second half of the book he applies his principle of negation to the whole range of dogmatic theology, the root error of which is to ascribe to an 'other-worldly' plane a set of images which in the nature of things can relate only to the world we know. When, however, we take the more modest and realistic course of transferring these same images to their proper sphere we discover that religion becomes solidly intelligible as a form of *human* knowledge, and one moreover which cannot be satisfactorily replaced by the abstract schematisms of the sciences.

According to a theology thus transposed into anthropology there can be no distinction between the predicates of the divine and human nature, and consequently between the divine and human subjects. For example, the Son of God is in religion—not theology—a real son, the son of God in the same sense in which man is the son of man, a profoundly human relation being conceived—or misconceived—as divine, and all that we need to do to find the true basis of faith is to recognize the fact. The theological proposition, on the other hand, in its conception of the 'Son of God', involves a being who is not a son in the natural sense but 'in an entirely different manner, contradictory to Nature and reason', i.e. mythologically. But mythology, Feuerbach urges, is for us today the negation of religion, the vital elements of which 'are those only which make man an object to man'. This humanistic criterion, when applied to the Christian creed, is seen to resolve it into a figure or symbol of man's own subjectivity. But the result is a liberation—the discharge of a needless and oppressive burden, demanded not by scepticism or atheism or moral libertinism but by the exigences of the religious consciousness itself.

Bibliographical note

Feuerbach's *Gesammelte Werke*, edited by W. Bolin and Fr. Jodl, were published at Stuttgart, 1903–11. There is a separate edition of *Das Wesen des Christenthums*, with an introduction by K. Quenzel. George Eliot's translation of *The Essence of Christianity* was reissued in 1957 with a preface by H. Richard Niebuhr and an introductory essay by Karl Barth. See Henri Arvon, *Ludwig Feuerbach ou la transformation du Sacré* (1957); as also Fr. Engels, 'Ludwig Feuerbach and the Outcome of Classical German Philosophy', in *Karl Marx: Selected Works* (ed. V. Adoratsky), vol. I.

MAN AND RELIGION

1. *The essential nature of man*

Religion has its basis in the essential difference between man and the brute—the brutes have no religion. It is true that the old uncritical writers on natural history attributed to the elephant, among other laudable qualities, the virtue of religiousness; but the religion of elephants belongs to the realm of fable. Cuvier, one of the greatest authorities on the animal kingdom, assigns, on the strength of his personal observations, no higher grade of intelligence to the elephant than to the dog.

But what is this essential difference between man and the brute? The most simple, general, and also the most popular answer to this question is—consciousness; but consciousness in the strict sense; for the consciousness implied in the feeling of self as an individual, in discrimination by the senses, in the perception and even judgement of outward things according to definite sensible signs, cannot be denied to the brutes. Consciousness in the strictest sense is present only in a being to whom his species, his essential nature, is an object of thought. The brute is indeed conscious of himself as an individual—and he has accordingly the feeling of self as the common centre of successive sensations—but not as a species: hence, he is without that consciousness which in its nature, as in its name, is akin to science. Where there is this higher consciousness there is a capability of science. Science is the cognizance of species. In practical life we have to do with individuals; in science, with species. But only a being to whom his own species, his own nature, is an object of thought, can make the essential nature of other things or beings an object of thought.

Hence the brute has only a simple, man a twofold life: in the brute, the inner life is one with the outer; man has both an inner and an outer life. The inner life of man is the life which has relation to his species, to his general, as distinguished from his individual, nature. Man thinks—that is, he converses with himself. The brute can exercise no function which has relation to its species without another individual external to itself; but man can perform the functions of thought and speech, which strictly imply such a relation, apart from another individual. Man is himself at once I and thou; he can put himself in the place of another, for this reason, that to him his species, his essential nature, and not merely his individuality, is an object of thought.

Religion being identical with the distinctive characteristic of man, is then identical with self-consciousness—with the consciousness which man has of his nature. But religion, expressed generally, is consciousness of the infinite; thus it is and can be nothing else than the consciousness which man has of his own—not finite and limited, but infinite nature. A really finite being has not even the faintest adumbration, still less consciousness, of an infinite being, for the limit of the nature is also the limit of the consciousness. The consciousness of the caterpillar, whose life is confined to a particular species of plant, does not extend itself beyond this narrow domain. It does, indeed, discriminate between this plant and other plants, but more it knows not. A consciousness so limited, but on account of that very limitation so infallible, we do not call consciousness, but instinct. Consciousness, in the strict or proper sense, is identical with consciousness of the infinite; a limited consciousness is no consciousness; consciousness is essentially infinite in its nature.[1] The consciousness of the infinite is nothing else than the consciousness of the infinity of the consciousness; or, in the consciousness of the infinite, the conscious subject has for his object the infinity of his own nature.

What, then, *is* the nature of man, of which he is conscious, or what

[1] 'Objectum intellectus esse illimitatum sive omne verum ac, ut loquuntur, omne ens ut ens, ex eo constat, quod ad nullum non genus rerum extenditur, nullumque est, cujus cognoscendi capax non sit, licet ob varia obstacula multa sint, quæ re ipsa non norit' (Gassendi, *Opp. Omn. Phys.*).

constitutes the specific distinction, the proper humanity of man?[1] Reason, Will, Affection. To a complete man belong the power of thought, the power of will, the power of affection. The power of thought is the light of the intellect, the power of will is energy of character, the power of affection is love. Reason, love, force of will, are perfections—the perfections of the human being—nay, more, they are absolute perfections of being. To will, to love, to think, are the highest powers, are the absolute nature of man as man, and the basis of his existence. Man exists to think, to love, to will. Now that which is the end, the ultimate aim, is also the true basis and principle of a being. But what is the end of reason? Reason. Of love? Love. Of will? Freedom of the will. We think for the sake of thinking; love for the sake of loving; will for the sake of willing—i.e. that we may be free. True existence is thinking, loving, willing existence. That alone is true, perfect, divine, which exists for its own sake. But such is love, such is reason, such is will. The divine trinity in man, above the individual man, is the unity of reason, love, will. Reason, Will, Love, are not powers which man possesses, for he is nothing without them, he is what he is only by them; they are the constituent elements of his nature, which he neither has nor makes, the animating, determining, governing powers—divine, absolute powers—to which he can oppose no resistance.[2]

How can the feeling man resist feeling, the loving one love, the rational one reason? Who has not experienced the overwhelming power of melody? And what else is the power of melody but the power of feeling? Music is the language of feeling; melody is audible feeling—feeling communicating itself. Who has not experienced the power of love, or at least heard of it? Which is the stronger—love or the individual man? Is it man that possesses love, or is it not much rather love that possesses man? When love impels a man to suffer death even joyfully for the beloved one, is this death-conquering power his own individual power, or is it not rather the power of love? And who that ever truly thought has not experienced that quiet, subtle power—the power of thought? When thou sinkest into deep reflexion, forgetting

[1] The obtuse materialist says: 'Man is distinguished from the brute *only* by consciousness—he is an animal with consciousness superadded'; not reflecting, that in a being which awakes to consciousness, there takes place a qualitative change, a differentiation of the entire nature. For the rest, our words are by no means intended to depreciate the nature of the lower animals. This is not the place to enter further into that question.

[2] 'Toute opinion est assez forte pour se faire exposer au prix de la vie' (Montaigne).

thyself and what is around thee, dost thou govern reason, or is it not reason which governs and absorbs thee? Scientific enthusiasm—is it not the most glorious triumph of intellect over thee? The desire of knowledge—is it not a simply irresistible, and all-conquering power? And when thou suppressest a passion, renouncest a habit, in short, achievest a victory over thyself, is this victorious power thy own personal power, or is it not rather the energy of will, the force of morality, which seizes the mastery of thee, and fills thee with indignation against thyself and thy individual weaknesses?

Man is nothing without an object. The great models of humanity, such men as reveal to us what man is capable of, have attested the truth of this proposition by their lives. They had only one dominant passion —the realization of the aim which was the essential object of their activity. But the object to which a subject essentially, necessarily relates, is nothing else than this subject's own, but objective, nature. If it be an object common to several individuals of the same species, but under various conditions, it is still, at least as to the form under which it presents itself to each of them according to their respective modifications, their own, but objective, nature.

Thus the Sun is the common object of the planets, but it is an object to Mercury, to Venus, to Saturn, to Uranus, under other conditions than to the Earth. Each planet has its own sun. The Sun which lights and warms Uranus has no physical (only an astronomical, scientific) existence for the earth; and not only does the Sun appear different, but it really is *another* sun on Uranus than on the Earth. The relation of the Sun to the Earth is therefore at the same time a relation of the Earth to itself, or to its own nature, for the measure of the size and of the intensity of light which the Sun possesses as the object of the Earth is the measure of the distance which determines the peculiar nature of the Earth. Hence each planet has in its sun the mirror of its own nature.

In the object which he contemplates, therefore, man becomes acquainted with himself; consciousness of the objective is the self-consciousness of man. We know the man by the object, by his conception of what is external to himself; in it his nature becomes evident; this object is his manifested nature, his true objective *ego*. And this is true not merely of spiritual, but also of sensuous objects. Even the objects which are the most remote from man, *because* they are objects to him, and to the extent to which they are so, are revelations of human nature. Even the moon, the sun, the stars, call to man Γνῶθι σεαυτόν.

That he sees them, and so sees them, is an evidence of his own nature. The animal is sensible only of the beam which immediately affects life; while man perceives the ray, to him physically indifferent, of the remotest star. Man alone has purely intellectual, disinterested joys and passions; the eye of man alone keeps theoretic festivals. The eye which looks into the starry heavens, which gazes at that light, alike useless and harmless, having nothing in common with the earth and its necessities— this eye sees in that light its own nature, its own origin. The eye is heavenly in its nature. Hence man elevates himself above the earth only with the eye; hence theory begins with the contemplation of the heavens. The first philosophers were astronomers. It is the heavens that admonish man of his destination, and remind him that he is destined not merely to action, but also to contemplation.

The *absolute* to man is his own nature. The power of the object over him is therefore the power of his own nature. Thus the power of the object of feeling is the power of feeling itself; the power of the object of the intellect is the power of the intellect itself; the power of the object of the will is the power of the will itself. The man who is affected by musical sounds is governed by feeling; by the feeling, that is, which finds its corresponding element in musical sounds. But it is not melody as such, it is only melody pregnant with meaning and emotion, which has power over feeling. Feeling is only acted on by that which conveys feeling, i.e. by itself, its own nature. Thus also the will; thus, and infinitely more, the intellect. Whatever kind of object, therefore, we are at any time conscious of, we are always at the same time conscious of our own nature; we can affirm nothing without affirming ourselves. And since to will, to feel, to think, are perfections, essences, realities, it is impossible that intellect, feeling, and will should feel or perceive themselves as limited, finite powers, i.e. as worthless, as nothing. For finiteness and nothingness are identical; finiteness is only a euphemism for nothingness. Finiteness is the metaphysical, the theoretical— nothingness the pathological, practical expression. What is finite to the understanding is nothing to the heart. But it is impossible that we should be conscious of will, feeling, and intellect, as finite powers, because every perfect existence, every original power and essence, is the immediate verification and affirmation of itself. It is impossible to love, will, or think, without perceiving these activities to be perfections— impossible to feel that one is a loving, willing, thinking being, without experiencing an infinite joy therein. Consciousness consists in a being becoming objective to itself; hence it is nothing apart, nothing distinct from the being which is conscious of itself. How could it otherwise become conscious of itself? It is therefore impossible to be conscious of a perfection as an imperfection, impossible to feel feeling limited, to think thought limited.

Consciousness is self-verification, self-affirmation, self-love, joy in one's own perfection. Consciousness is the characteristic mark of a perfect nature; it exists only in a self-sufficing, complete being. Even human vanity attests this truth. A man looks in the glass; he has complacency in his appearance. This complacency is a necessary, involuntary consequence of the completeness, the beauty of his form. A beautiful form is satisfied in itself; it has necessarily joy in itself—in self-contemplation. This complacency becomes vanity only when a man piques himself on his form as being his individual form, not when he admires it as a specimen of human beauty in general. It is fitting that he should admire it thus; he can conceive no form more beautiful, more sublime than the human.[1] Assuredly every being loves itself, its existence—and fitly so. To exist is a good. *Quidquid essentia dignum est, scientia dignum est.* Everything that exists has value, is a being of distinction—at least this is true of the species: hence it asserts, maintains itself. But the highest form of self-assertion, the form which is itself a superiority, a perfection, a bliss, a good, is consciousness.

Every limitation of the reason, or in general of the nature of man, rests on a delusion, an error. It is true that the human being, as an individual, can and must—herein consists his distinction from the brute —feel and recognize himself to be limited; but he can become conscious of his limits, his finiteness, only because the perfection, the infinitude of his species is perceived by him, whether as an object of feeling, of conscience, or of the thinking consciousness. If he makes his own limitations the limitations of the species, this arises from the mistake that he identifies himself immediately with the species—a mistake which is intimately connected with the individual's love of ease, sloth, vanity, and egoism. For a limitation which I know to be merely mine humiliates, shames, and perturbs me. Hence to free myself from this feeling of shame, from this state of dissatisfaction, I convert the limits of my individuality into the limits of human nature in general. What

[1] 'Homini homine nihil pulchrius' (Cic. *de Nat.* D. I. i). And this is no sign of limitation, for he regards other beings as beautiful besides himself; he delights in the beautiful forms of animals, in the beautiful forms of plants, in the beauty of nature in general. But only the absolute, the perfect form, can delight without envy in the forms of other beings.

is incomprehensible to me is incomprehensible to others; why should I trouble myself further? it is no fault of mine; my understanding is not to blame, but the understanding of the race. But it is a ludicrous and even culpable error to define as finite and limited what constitutes the essence of man, the nature of the species, which is the absolute nature of the individual. Every being is sufficient to itself. No being can deny itself, i.e. its own nature; no being is a limited one to itself. Rather, every being is in and by itself infinite—has its God, its highest conceivable being, in itself. Every limit of a being is cognizable only by another being out of and above him. The life of the ephemera is extraordinarily short in comparison with that of longer lived creatures; but nevertheless, for the ephemera this short life is as long as a life of years to others. The leaf on which the caterpillar lives is for it a world, an infinite space.

That which makes a being what it is—is its talent, its power, its wealth, its adornment. How can it possibly hold its existence non-existence, its wealth poverty, its talent incapacity? If the plants had eyes, taste and judgement, each plant would declare its own flower the most beautiful; for its comprehension, its taste, would reach no farther than its natural power of production. What the productive power of its nature has brought forth as the highest, that must also its taste, its judgement, recognize and affirm as the highest. What the nature affirms, the understanding, the taste, the judgement, cannot deny; otherwise the understanding, the judgement, would no longer be the understanding and judgement of this particular being, but of some other. The measure of the nature is also the measure of the understanding. If the nature is limited, so also is the feeling, so also is the understanding. But to a limited being its limited understanding is not felt to be a limitation; on the contrary, it is perfectly happy and contented with this understanding; it regards it, praises and values it, as a glorious, divine power; and the limited understanding, on its part, values the limited nature whose understanding it is. Each is exactly adapted to the other; how should they be at issue with each other? A being's understanding is its sphere of vision. As far as thou seest, so far extends thy nature; and conversely. The eye of the brute reaches no farther than its needs, and its nature no farther than its needs. And so far as thy nature reaches, so far reaches thy unlimited self-consciousness, so far art thou God. The discrepancy between the understanding and the nature, between the power of conception and the power of production in the human consciousness, on the one hand is merely of individual significance and has not a universal application; and, on the other hand, it is only apparent. He who having written a bad poem knows it to be bad, is in his intelligence, and therefore in his nature, not so limited as he who, having written a bad poem, admires it and thinks it good.

It follows, that if thou thinkest the infinite, thou perceivest and affirmest the infinitude of the power of thought; if thou feelest the infinite, thou feelest and affirmest the infinitude of the power of feeling. The object of the intellect is intellect objective to itself; the object of feeling is feeling objective to itself. If thou hast no sensibility, no feeling for music, thou perceivest in the finest music nothing more than in the wind that whistles by thy ear, or than in the brook which rushes past thy feet. What then is it which acts on thee when thou art affected by melody? What dost thou perceive in it? What else than the voice of thy own heart? Feeling speaks only to feeling; feeling is comprehensible only by feeling, that is, by itself—for this reason, that the object of feeling is nothing else than feeling. Music is a monologue of emotion. But the dialogue of philosophy also is in truth only a monologue of the intellect; thought speaks only to thought. The splendours of the crystal charm the sense; but the intellect is interested only in the laws of crystallization. The intellectual only is the object of the intellect.[1]

All therefore which, in the point of view of metaphysical, transcendental speculation and religion, has the significance only of the secondary, the subjective, the medium, the organ—has in truth the significance of the primary, of the essence, of the object itself. If, for example, feeling is the essential organ of religion, the nature of God is nothing else than an expression of the nature of feeling. The true but latent sense of the phrase, 'Feeling is the organ of the divine', is, feeling is the noblest, the most excellent, i.e. the divine, in man. How couldst thou perceive the divine by feeling, if feeling were not itself divine in its nature? The divine assuredly is known only by means of the divine—God is known only by himself. The divine nature which is discerned by feeling, is in truth nothing else than feeling enraptured, in ecstasy with itself— feeling intoxicated with joy, blissful in its own plenitude.

It is already clear from this that where feeling is held to be the organ of the infinite, the subjective essence of religion, the external data of religion lose their objective value. And thus, since feeling has been

[1] 'The understanding is percipient only of understanding, and what proceeds thence' (Reimarus, *Wahrh. der Natürl. Religion*, IV, Abth. §8).

held the cardinal principle in religion, the doctrines of Christianity, formerly so sacred, have lost their importance. If from this point of view some value is still conceded to Christian ideas, it is a value springing entirely from the relation they bear to feeling; if another object would excite the same emotions, it would be just as welcome. But the object of religious feeling is become a matter of indifference, only because when once feeling has been pronounced to be the subjective essence of religion, it in fact is also the objective essence of religion, though it may not be declared, at least directly, to be such. I say directly; for indirectly this is certainly admitted, when it is declared that feeling, as such, is religious, and thus the distinction between specifically religious and irreligious, or at least non-religious, feelings, is abolished—a necessary consequence of the point of view in which feeling only is regarded as the organ of the divine. For on what other ground than that of its essence, its nature, dost thou hold feeling to be the organ of the infinite, the divine being? And is not the nature of feeling in general, also the nature of every special feeling, be its object what it may? What, then, makes this feeling religious? A given object? Not at all; for this object is itself a religious one only when it is not an object of the cold understanding or memory, but of feeling. What then? The nature of feeling—a nature of which every special feeling, without distinction of objects, partakes. Thus, feeling is pronounced to be religious, simply because it is feeling; the ground of its religiousness is its own nature—lies in itself. But is not feeling thereby declared to be itself the absolute, the divine? If feeling in itself is good, religious, i.e. holy, divine, has not feeling its God in itself?

But if, notwithstanding, thou wilt posit an object of feeling, but at the same time seekest to express thy feeling truly, without introducing by thy reflexion any foreign element, what remains to thee but to distinguish between thy individual feeling and the general nature of feeling;—to separate the universal in feeling from the disturbing, adulterating influences with which feeling is bound up in thee, under thy individual conditions? Hence what thou canst alone contemplate, declare to be the infinite, and define as its essence, is merely the nature of feeling. Thou hast thus no other definition of God than this; God is pure, unlimited, free Feeling. Every other God, whom thou supposest, is a God thrust upon thy feeling from without. Feeling is atheistic in the sense of the orthodox belief, which attaches religion to an external object; it denies an objective God—it is itself God. In this point of

93

view, only the negation of feeling is the negation of God. Thou art simply too cowardly or too narrow to confess in words what thy feeling tacitly affirms. Fettered by outward considerations, still in bondage to vulgar empiricism, incapable of comprehending the spiritual grandeur of feeling, thou art terrified before the religious atheism of thy heart. By this fear thou destroyest the unity of thy feeling with itself, in imagining to thyself an objective being distinct from thy feeling, and thus necessarily sinking back into the old questions and doubts—is there a God or not?—questions and doubts which vanish, nay, are impossible, where feeling is defined as the essence of religion. Feeling is thy own inward power, but at the same time a power distinct from thee, and independent of thee; it is in thee, above thee: it is itself that which constitutes the objective in thee—thy own being which impresses thee as another being; in short, thy God. How wilt thou then distinguish from this objective being within thee another objective being? how wilt thou get beyond thy feeling?

But feeling has here been adduced only as an example. It is the same with every other power, faculty, potentiality, reality, activity—the name is indifferent—which is defined as the essential organ of any object. Whatever is a subjective expression of a nature is simultaneously also its objective expression. Man cannot get beyond his true nature. He may indeed by means of the imagination conceive individuals of another so-called higher kind, but he can never get loose from his species, his nature; the conditions of being, the positive final predicates which he gives to these other individuals, are always determinations or qualities drawn from his own nature—qualities in which he in truth only images and projects himself. There may certainly be thinking beings besides men on the other planets of our solar system. But by the supposition of such beings we do not change our standing point—we extend our conceptions *quantitatively*, not *qualitatively*. For as surely as on the other planets there are the same laws of motion, so surely are there the same laws of perception and thought as here. In fact, we people the other planets, not that we may place there different beings from ourselves, but *more* beings of our own or of a similar nature.[1]

[1] 'Verisimile est, non minus quam geometriæ, etiam musicæ oblectationem ad plures quam ad nos pertinere. Positis enim aliis terris atque animalibus ratione et auditu pollentibus, eur tantum his nostris contigisset ea voluptas, quæ sola ex sono percipi potest?' (Christ. Hugenius, *Cosmotheor*, I, i).

2. *The essence of religion considered generally*

What we have hitherto been maintaining generally, even with regard to sensational impressions, of the relation between subject and object, applies especially to the relation between the subject and the religious object.

In the perceptions of the senses consciousness of the object is distinguishable from consciousness of self; but in religion, consciousness of the object and self-consciousness coincide. The object of the senses is out of man, the religious object is within him, and therefore as little forsakes him as his self-consciousness or his conscience; it is the intimate, the closest object. 'God', says Augustine, for example, 'is nearer, more related to us, and therefore more easily known by us, than sensible, corporeal things.'[1] The object of the senses is in itself indifferent—independent of the disposition or of the judgement; but the object of religion is a selected object; the most excellent, the first, the supreme being; it essentially presupposes a critical judgement, a discrimination between the divine and the non-divine, between that which is worthy of adoration and that which is not worthy.[2] And here may be applied, without any limitation, the proposition: the object of any subject is nothing else than the subject's own nature taken objectively. Such as are a man's thoughts and dispositions, such is his God; so much worth as a man has, so much and no more has his God. Consciousness of God is self-consciousness, knowledge of God is self-knowledge. By his God thou knowest the man, and by the man his God; the two are identical. Whatever is God to a man, that is his heart and soul; and conversely, God is the manifested inward nature, the expressed self of a man—religion the solemn unveiling of a man's hidden treasures, the revelation of his intimate thoughts, the open confession of his love-secrets.

But when religion—consciousness of God—is designated as the self-consciousness of man, this is not to be understood as affirming that the religious man is directly aware of this identity; for, on the contrary, ignorance of it is fundamental to the peculiar nature of religion. To preclude this misconception, it is better to say, religion is man's earliest and also indirect form of self-knowledge. Hence, religion everywhere precedes philosophy, as in the history of the race, so also in that of the individual. Man first of all sees his nature as if *out of* himself, before

---

[1] *De Genesi ad litteram*, I. v. c. 16.
[2] 'Unusquisque vestrum non cogitat, *prius* se debere Deum *nosse*, quam *colere*' (M. Minucii Felicis Octavianus, c. 24).

he finds it in himself. His own nature is in the first instance contemplated by him as that of another being. Religion is the childlike condition of humanity; but the child sees his nature—man—out of himself; in childhood a man is an object to himself, under the form of another man. Hence the historical progress of religion consists in this: that what by an earlier religion was regarded as objective, is now recognized as subjective; that is, what was formerly contemplated and worshipped as God is now perceived to be something *human*. What was at first religion becomes at a later period idolatry; man is seen to have adored his own nature. Man has given objectivity to himself, but has not recognized the object as his own nature: a later religion takes this forward step; every advance in religion is therefore a deeper self-knowledge. But every particular religion, while it pronounces its predecessors idolatrous, excepts itself—and necessarily so, otherwise it would no longer be religion—from the fate, the common nature of all religions: it imputes only to other religions what is the fault, if fault it be, of religion in general. Because it has a different object, a different tenour, because it has transcended the ideas of preceding religions, it erroneously supposes itself exalted above the necessary eternal laws which constitute the essence of religion—it fancies its object, its ideas, to be superhuman. But the essence of religion, thus hidden from the religious, is evident to the thinker, by whom religion is viewed objectively, which it cannot be by its votaries. And it is our task to show that the antithesis of divine and human is altogether illusory, that it is nothing else than the antithesis between the human nature in general, and the human individual: that, consequently, the object and contents of the Christian religion are altogether human.

Religion, at least the Christian, is the relation of man to himself, or more correctly to his own nature (i.e. his subjective nature); but a relation to it, viewed as a nature apart from his own. The divine being is nothing else than the human being, or rather, the human nature purified, freed from the limits of the individual man, made objective—i.e. contemplated and revered as another, a distinct being. All the attributes of the divine nature are, therefore, attributes of the human nature.[1]

[1] 'Les perfections de Dieu sont celles de nos âmes, mais il les possède sans bornes—il y a en nous quelque puissance, quelque connaissance, quelque bonté, mais elles sont toutes entières en Dieu' (Leibniz, *Théod. Preface*). 'Nihil in anima esse putemus eximium, quod non etiam divinae naturae proprium sit—Quidquid a Deo alienum extra definitionem animae' (S. Gregorius Nyss). 'Est ergo, ut videtur, disciplinarum omnium pulcherrima et maxima se ipsum nosse; si quis enim se ipsum norit, Deum cognoscet' (Clemens Alex. *Paed.* I. iii. c. I).

In relation to the attributes, the predicates, of the Divine Being, this is admitted without hesitation, but by no means in relation to the subject of these predicates. The negation of the subject is held to be irreligion, nay, atheism; though not so the negation of the predicates. But that which has no predicates or qualities, has no effect upon me; that which has no effect upon me, has no existence for me. To deny all the qualities of a being is equivalent to denying the being himself. A being without qualities is one which cannot become an object to the mind; and such a being is virtually non-existent. Where man deprives God of all qualities, God is no longer anything more to him than a negative being. To the truly religious man, God is not a being without qualities, because to him he is a positive, real being. The theory that God cannot be defined, and consequently cannot be known by man, is therefore the offspring of recent times, a product of modern unbelief.

As reason is and can be pronounced finite only where man regards sensual enjoyment, or religious emotion, or aesthetic contemplation, or moral sentiment, as the absolute, the true; so the proposition that God is unknowable or undefinable can only be enunciated and become fixed as a dogma, where this object has no longer any interest for the intellect; where the real, the positive, alone has any hold on man, where the real alone has for him the significance of the essential, of the absolute, divine object, but where at the same time, in contradiction with this purely worldly tendency, there yet exist some old remains of religiousness. On the ground that God is unknowable, man excuses himself to what is yet remaining of his religious conscience for his forgetfulness of God, his absorption in the world: he denies God practically by his conduct—the world has possession of all his thoughts and inclinations—but he does not deny him theoretically, he does not attack his existence; he lets that rest. But this existence does not affect or incommode him; it is a merely negative existence, an existence without existence, a self-contradictory existence—a state of being, which, as to its effects, is not distinguishable from non-being. The denial of determinate, positive predicates concerning the divine nature, is nothing else than a denial of religion, with, however, an appearance of religion in its favour, so that it is not recognized as a denial; it is simply a subtle, disguised atheism. The alleged religious horror of limiting God by positive predicates, is only the irreligious wish to know nothing more of God, to banish God from the mind. Dread of limitation is dread of existence. All real existence, i.e. all existence which is truly such, is

97

qualitative, determinate existence. He who earnestly believes in the Divine existence is not shocked at the attributing even of gross sensuous qualities to God. He who dreads an existence that may give offence, who shrinks from the grossness of a positive predicate, may as well renounce existence altogether. A God who is injured by determinate qualities has not the courage and the strength to exist. Qualities are the fire, the vital breath, the oxygen, the salt of existence. An existence in general, an existence without qualities, is an insipidity, an absurdity. But there can be no more in God than is supplied by religion. Only where man loses his taste for religion, and thus religion itself becomes insipid, does the existence of God become an insipid existence—an existence without qualities.

There is, however, a still milder way of denying the Divine predicates than the direct one just described. It is admitted that the predicates of the divine nature are finite, and, more particularly, human qualities, but their rejection is rejected; they are even taken under protection, because it is necessary to man to have a definite conception of God, and since he is man, he can form no other than a human conception of him. In relation to God, it is said, these predicates are certainly without any objective validity; but to me, if he is to exist for me, he cannot appear otherwise than as he does appear to me, namely, as a being with attributes analogous to the human. But this distinction between what God is in himself, and what he is for me, destroys the peace of religion, and is besides in itself an unfounded and untenable distinction. I cannot know whether God is something else in himself or for himself, than he is for me; what he is to me, is to me all that he is. For me, there lies in these predicates under which he exists for me, what he is in himself, his very nature; he is for me what he can alone ever be for me. The religious man finds perfect satisfaction in that which God is in relation to himself; of any other relation he knows nothing, for God is to him what he can alone be to man. In the distinction above stated, man takes a point of view above himself, i.e. above his nature, the absolute measure of his being; but this transcendentalism is only an illusion; for I can make the distinction between the object as it is in itself, and the object as it is for me, only where an object can really appear otherwise to me, not where it appears to me such as the absolute measure of my nature determines it to appear—such as it must appear to me. It is true that I may have a merely subjective conception, i.e. one which does not arise out of the general constitution of my species; but if my conception is determined by the constitution of my species, the distinction between what an object is in itself, and what it is for me ceases; for this conception is itself an absolute one. The measure of the species is the absolute measure, law, and criterion of man. And, indeed, religion has the conviction that its conceptions, its predicates of God, are such as every man ought to have, and must have, if he would have the true ones—that they are the conceptions necessary to human nature; nay, further, that they are objectively true, representing God as he is. To every religion the gods of *other* religions are only notions concerning God, but its own conception of God is to it God himself, the true God—God such as he is in himself. Religion is satisfied only with a complete Deity, a God without reservation; it will not have a mere phantasm of God; it demands God himself. Religion gives up its own existence when it gives up the nature of God; it is no longer a truth, when it renounces the possession of the true God. Scepticism is the arch-enemy of religion; but the distinction between object and conception—between God as he is in himself, and God as he is for me, is a sceptical distinction, and therefore an irreligious one.

That which is to man the self-existent, the highest being, to which he can conceive nothing higher—that is to him the Divine being. How then should he inquire concerning this being, what He is in himself? If God were an object to the bird, he would be a winged being: the bird knows nothing higher, nothing more blissful, than the winged condition. How ludicrous would it be if this bird pronounced: to me God appears as a bird, but what he is in himself I know not. To the bird the highest nature is the bird-nature; take from him the conception of this, and you take from him the conception of the highest being. How, then, could he ask whether God in himself were winged? To ask whether God is in himself what he is for me, is to ask whether God is God, is to lift oneself above one's God, to rise up against him.

Wherever, therefore, this idea, that the religious predicates are only anthropomorphisms, has taken possession of a man, there has doubt, has unbelief obtained the mastery of faith. And it is only the inconsequence of faint-heartedness and intellectual imbecility which does not proceed from this idea to the formal negation of the predicates, and from thence to the negation of the subject to which they relate. If thou doubtest the objective truth of the predicates, thou must also doubt the objective truth of the subject whose predicates they are. If thy predicates are anthropomorphisms, the subject of them is an anthropomorphism too. If love, goodness, personality, etc., are human attributes, so also is the subject which thou pre-supposest, the existence of God, the belief that there is a God, an anthropomorphism—a pre-supposition purely human. Whence knowest thou that the belief in a God at all is not a limitation of man's mode of conception? Higher beings—and thou supposest such—are perhaps so blest in themselves, so at unity with themselves, that they are not hung in suspense between themselves and a yet higher being. To know God and not oneself to be God, to know blessedness, and not oneself to enjoy it, is a state of disunity, of unhappiness. Higher beings know nothing of this unhappiness; they have no conception of that which they are not.

Thou believest in love as a divine attribute because thou thyself lovest; thou believest that God is a wise, benevolent being, because thou knowest nothing better in thyself than benevolence and wisdom; and thou believest that God exists, that therefore he is a subject—whatever exists is a subject, whether it be defined as substance, person, essence, or otherwise—because thou thyself existest, art thyself a subject. Thou knowest no higher human good, than to love, than to be good and wise; and even so thou knowest no higher happiness than to exist, to be a subject; for the consciousness of all reality, of all bliss, is for thee bound up in the consciousness of being a subject, of existing. God is an existence, a subject to thee, for the same reason that he is to thee a wise, a blessed, a personal being. The distinction between the divine predicates and the divine subject is only this, that to thee the subject, the existence, does not appear an anthropomorphism, because the conception of it is necessarily involved in thy own existence as a subject, whereas the predicates do appear anthropomorphisms, because their necessity—the necessity that God should be conscious, wise, good, etc.—is not an immediate necessity, identical with the being of man, but is evolved by his self-consciousness, by the activity of his thought. I am a subject, I exist, whether I be wise or unwise, good or bad. To exist is to man the first datum; it constitutes the very idea of the subject; it is presupposed by the predicates. Hence, man relinquishes the predicates, but the existence of God is to him a settled, irrefragable, absolutely certain, objective truth. But, nevertheless, this distinction is merely an apparent one. The necessity of the subject lies only in the necessity of the predicate. Thou art a subject only in so far as thou art a human subject; the certainty and reality of thy existence lie only in the certainty and reality of thy human attributes. What the subject is, lies only in the predicate; the predicate is the *truth* of the subject—the subject only the personified, existing predicate, the predicate conceived as existing. Subject and predicate are distinguished only as existence and essence. The negation of the predicates is therefore the negation of the subject. What remains of the human subject when abstracted from the human attributes? Even in the language of common life the divine predicates—Providence, Omniscience, Omnipotence—are put for the divine subject.

The certainty of the existence of God, of which it has been said that it is as certain, nay, more certain to man than his own existence, depends only on the certainty of the qualities of God—it is in itself no immediate certainty. To the Christian the existence of the Christian God only is a certainty; to the heathen that of the heathen God only. The heathen did not doubt the existence of Jupiter, because he took no offence at the nature of Jupiter, because he could conceive of God under no other qualities, because to him these qualities were a certainty, a divine reality. The reality of the predicate is the sole guarantee of existence.

Whatever man conceives to be true, he immediately conceives to be real (that is, to have an objective existence), because, originally, only the real is true to him—true in opposition to what is merely conceived, dreamed, imagined. The idea of being, of existence, is the original idea of truth; or, originally, man makes truth dependent on existence, subsequently, existence dependent on truth. Now God is the nature of man regarded as absolute truth—the truth of man; but God, or, what is the same thing, religion, is as various as are the conditions under which man conceives this his nature, regards it as the highest being. These conditions, then, under which man conceives God, are to him the truth, and for that reason they are also the highest existence, or rather they are existence itself; for only the emphatic, the highest existence, is existence, and deserves this name. Therefore, God is an existent, real being, on the very same ground that he is a particular, definite being; for the qualities of God are nothing else than the essential qualities of man himself, and a particular man is what he is, has his existence, his reality, only in his particular conditions. Take away from the Greek the quality of being Greek, and you take away his existence. On this ground, it is true that for a definite positive religion—that is, relatively—the certainty of the existence of God is *immediate*; for just as involuntarily, as necessarily, as the Greek was a Greek, so necessarily were his gods Greek beings, so necessarily were they real, existent beings. Religion is that conception of the nature of the world and of man which is essential to, i.e. identical with, a man's nature. But man does not stand above this his necessary conception; on the contrary, it stands above him; it animates, determines, governs him. The necessity of a proof, of a middle term to unite qualities with existence, the possibility of a doubt, is abolished. Only that which is apart from my own being is capable of being doubted by me. How then can I doubt of God, who is my being? To doubt of God is to doubt of myself. Only when God is thought of abstractly, when his predicates are the result of philosophic abstraction, arises the distinction or separation between subject and predicate, existence and nature—arises the fiction that the existence or the subject is something else than the predicate, something immediate, indubitable, in distinction from the predicate, which is held to be doubtful. But this is only a fiction. A God who has abstract predicates has also an abstract existence. Existence, being, varies with varying qualities.

The identity of the subject and predicate is clearly evidenced by the progressive development of religion, which is identical with the progressive development of human culture. So long as man is in a mere state of nature, so long is his god a mere nature-god—a personification of some natural force. Where man inhabits houses, he also encloses his gods in temples. The temple is only a manifestation of the value which man attaches to beautiful buildings. Temples in honour of religion are in truth temples in honour of architecture. With the emerging of man from a state of savagery and wildness to one of culture, with the distinction between what is fitting for man and what is not fitting, arises simultaneously the distinction between that which is fitting and that which is not fitting for God. God is the idea of majesty, of the highest dignity: the religious sentiment is the sentiment of supreme fitness. The later more cultured artists of Greece were the first to embody in the statues of the gods the ideas of dignity, of spiritual grandeur, of imperturbable repose and serenity. But why were these qualities in their view attributes, predicates of God? Because they were in themselves regarded by the Greeks as divinities. Why did those artists exclude all disgusting and low passions? Because they perceived them to be unbecoming, unworthy, unhuman, and consequently ungodlike. The Homeric gods eat and drink—that implies: eating and drinking is a divine pleasure. Physical strength is an attribute of the Homeric gods: Zeus is the strongest of the gods. Why? Because physical strength, in and by itself, was regarded as something glorious, divine. To the ancient

Germans the highest virtues were those of the warrior; therefore, their supreme god was the god of war, Odin—war, 'the original or oldest law'. Not the attribute of the divinity, but the divineness or deity of the attribute, is the first true Divine Being. Thus what theology and philosophy have held to be God, the Absolute, the Infinite, is not God; but that which they have held not to be God, is God: namely, the attribute, the quality, whatever has reality. Hence, he alone is the true atheist to whom the predicates of the Divine Being—for example, love, wisdom, justice, are nothing; not he to whom merely the subject of these predicates is nothing. And in no wise is the negation of the subject necessarily also a negation of the predicates considered in themselves. These have an intrinsic, independent reality; they force their recognition upon man by their very nature; they are self-evident truths to him; they prove, they attest themselves. It does not follow that goodness, justice, wisdom, are chimaeras, because the existence of God is a chimaera, nor truths because this is a truth. The idea of God is dependent on the idea of justice, of benevolence; a God who is not benevolent, not just, not wise, is no God; but the converse does not hold. The fact is not that a quality is divine because God has it, but that God has it because it is in itself divine: because without it God would be a defective being. Justice, wisdom, in general every quality which constitutes the divinity of God, is determined and known by itself, independently, but the idea of God is determined by the qualities which have thus been previously judged to be worthy of the divine nature; only in the case in which I identify God and justice, in which I think of God immediately as the reality of the idea of justice, is the idea of God self-determined. But if God as a subject is the determined, while the quality, the predicate is the determining, then in truth the rank of the godhead is due not to the subject, but to the predicate.

Not until several, and those contradictory, attributes are united in one being, and this being is conceived as personal—the personality being thus brought into especial prominence—not until then is the origin of religion lost sight of, is it forgotten that what the activity of the reflective power has converted into a predicate distinguishable or separable from the subject, was originally the true subject. Thus the Greeks and Romans deified accidents as substances: virtues, states of mind, passions, as independent beings. Man, especially the religious man, is to himself the measure of all things, of all reality. Whatever strongly impresses a man, whatever produces an unusual effect on his mind, if it be only a peculiar, inexplicable sound or note, he personifies as a divine being. Religion embraces all the objects of the world; everything existing has been an object of religious reverence; in the nature and consciousness of religion there is nothing else than what lies in the nature of man and in his consciousness of himself and of the world. Religion has no material exclusively its own. In Rome even the passions of fear and terror had their temples. The Christians also made mental phenomena into independent beings, their own feelings into qualities of things, the passions which governed them into powers which governed the world, in short, predicates of their own nature, whether recognized as such or not, into independent subjective existences. Devils, cobolds, witches, ghosts, angels, were sacred truths as long as the religious spirit held undivided sway over mankind.

In order to banish from the mind the identity of the divine and human predicates, and the consequent identity of the divine and human nature, recourse is had to the idea that God, as the absolute, real Being, has an infinite fulness of various predicates, of which we here know only a part, and those such as are analogous to our own; while the rest, by virtue of which God must thus have quite a different nature from the human or that which is analogous to the human, we shall only know in the future—that is, after death. But an infinite plenitude or multitude of predicates which are really different, so different that the one does not immediately involve the other, is realized only in an infinite plenitude or multitude of different beings or individuals. Thus the human nature presents an infinite abundance of different predicates, and for that very reason it presents an infinite abundance of different individuals. Each new man is a new predicate, a new phasis of humanity. As many as are the men, so many are the powers, the properties of humanity. It is true that there are the same elements in every individual, but under such various conditions and modifications that they appear new and peculiar. The mystery of the inexhaustible fulness of the divine predicates is therefore nothing else than the mystery of human nature considered as an infinitely varied, infinitely modifiable, but, consequently, phenomenal being. Only in the realm of the senses, only in space and time, does there exist a being of really infinite qualities or predicates. Where there are really different predicates, there are different times. One man is a distinguished musician, a distinguished author, a distinguished physician; but he cannot compose music, write books, and perform cures in the same moment of time. Time, and not the

Hegelian dialectic, is the medium of uniting opposites, contradictories, in one and the same subject. But distinguished and detached from the nature of man, and combined with the idea of God, the infinite fulness of various predicates is a conception without reality, a mere phantasy, a conception derived from the sensible world, but without the essential conditions, without the truth of sensible existence, a conception which stands in direct contradiction with the Divine Being considered as a spiritual, i.e. an abstract, simple, single being; for the predicates of God are precisely of this character, that one involves all the others, because there is no real difference between them. If, therefore, in the present predicates I have not the future, in the present God not the future God, then the future God is not the present, but they are two distinct beings.[1] But this distinction is in contradiction with the unity and simplicity of the theological God. Why is a given predicate a predicate of God? Because it is divine in its nature; i.e. because it expresses no limitation, no defect. Why are other predicates applied to Him? Because, however various in themselves, they agree in this, that they all alike express perfection, unlimitedness. Hence I can conceive innumerable predicates of God, because they must all agree with the abstract idea of the Godhead, and must have in common that which constitutes every single predicate a divine attribute. Thus it is in the system of Spinoza. He speaks of an infinite number of attributes of the divine substance, but he specifies none except Thought and Extension. Why? because it is a matter of indifference to know them; nay, because they are in themselves indifferent, superfluous: for with all these innumerable predicates, I yet always mean to say the same thing as when I speak of thought and extension. Why is Thought an attribute of substance? Because, according to Spinoza, it is capable of being conceived by itself, because it expresses something indivisible, perfect, infinite. Why Extension or Matter? For the same reason. Thus, substance can have an indefinite number of predicates, because it is not their specific definition, their difference, but their identity, their equivalence, which makes them attributes of substance. Or rather, substance has innumerable predicates only because (how strange!) it has properly no predicate; that is, no definite, real predicate. The indefinite unity, which is the product of thought, completes itself by the indefinite multiplicity which is the

[1] For religious faith there is no other distinction between the present and future God than that the former is an object of faith, of conception, of imagination, while the latter is to be an object of immediate, that is, personal, sensible perception. In this life, and in the next, he is the same God; but in the one he is incomprehensible, in the other, comprehensible.

product of the imagination. Because the predicate is not *multum*, it is *multa*. In truth, the positive predicates are Thought and Extension. In these two, infinitely more is said than in the nameless innumerable predicates; for they express something definite, in them I have something. But substance is too indifferent, too apathetic, to be *something*; that is, to have qualities and passions; that it may not be something, it is rather nothing.

Now, when it is shown that what the subject is lies entirely in the attributes of the subject; that is, that the predicate is the true subject; it is also proved that if the divine predicates are attributes of the human nature, the subject of those predicates is also of the human nature. But the divine predicates are partly general, partly personal. The general predicates are the metaphysical, but these serve only as external points of support to religion; they are not the characteristic definitions of religion. It is the personal predicates alone which constitute the essence of religion—in which the Divine Being is the object of religion. Such are, for example, that God is a Person, that he is the moral Law-giver, the Father of mankind, the Holy One, the Just, the Good, the Merciful. It is however at once clear, or it will at least be clear in the sequel, with regard to these and other definitions, that, especially as applied to a personality, they are purely human definitions, and that consequently man in religion—in his relation to God—is in relation to his own nature; for to the religious sentiment these predicates are not mere conceptions, mere images, which man forms of God, to be distinguished from that which God is in himself, but truths, facts, realities. Religion knows nothing of anthropomorphisms; to it they are not anthropomorphisms. It is the very essence of religion, that to it these definitions express the nature of God. They are pronounced to be images only by the understanding, which reflects on religion, and which while defending them yet before its own tribunal denies them. But to the religious sentiment God is a real Father, real Love and Mercy; for to it he is a real, living, personal being, and therefore his attributes are also living and personal. Nay, the definitions which are the most sufficing to the religious sentiment, are precisely those which give the most offence to the understanding, and which in the process of reflexion on religion it denies. Religion is essentially emotion; hence, objectively also, emotion is to it necessarily of a divine nature. Even anger appears to it an emotion not unworthy of God, provided only there be a religious motive at the foundation of this anger.

But here it is also essential to observe, and this phenomenon is an extremely remarkable one, characterizing the very core of religion, that in proportion as the divine subject is in reality human, the greater is the apparent difference between God and man; that is, the more, by reflexion on religion, by theology, is the identity of the divine and human denied, and the human, considered as such, is depreciated.[1] The reason of this is, that as what is positive in the conception of the divine being can only be human, the conception of man, as an object of consciousness can only be negative. To enrich God, man must become poor; that God may be all, man must be nothing. But he desires to be nothing in himself, because what he takes from himself is not lost to him, since it is preserved in God. Man has his being in God; why then should he have it in himself? Where is the necessity of positing the same thing twice, of having it twice? What man withdraws from himself, what he renounces in himself, he only enjoys in an incomparably higher and fuller measure in God.

The monks made a vow of chastity to God; they mortified the sexual passion in themselves, but therefore they had in Heaven, in the Virgin Mary, the image of woman—an image of love. They could the more easily dispense with real woman, in proportion as an ideal woman was an object of love to them. The greater the importance they attached to the denial of sensuality, the greater the importance of the Heavenly Virgin for them: she was to them in the place of Christ, in the stead of God. The more the sensual tendencies are renounced, the more sensual is the God to whom they are sacrificed. For whatever is made an offering to God has an especial value attached to it; in it God is supposed to have especial pleasure. That which is the highest in the estimation of man, is naturally the highest in the estimation of his God—what pleases man, pleases God also. The Hebrews did not offer to Jehovah unclean, ill-conditioned animals; on the contrary, those which they most highly prized, which they themselves ate, were also the food of God (*cibus Dei*, Lev. iii. 2). Wherever, therefore, the denial of the sensual delights is made a special offering, a sacrifice well-pleasing to God, there the highest value is attached to the senses, and the sensuality which has been renounced is unconsciously restored, in the fact that God takes

[1] 'Inter creatorem et creaturam non potest tanta similitudo notari, quin inter eos major sit dissimilitudo notanda' (Later. Conc. can. 2, *Summa Omn. Conc. Carranza*, Antwerp 1559, p. 326). The last distinction between man and God, between the finite and infinite nature, to which the religious speculative imagination soars, is the distinction between Something and Nothing, Ens and Non-Ens; for only in Nothing is all community with other beings abolished.

the place of the material delights which have been renounced. The nun weds herself to God; she has a heavenly bridegroom, the monk a heavenly bride. But the heavenly virgin is only a sensible presentation of a general truth, having relation to the essence of religion. Man denies as to himself only what he attributes to God. Religion abstracts from man, from the world; but it can only abstract from the limitations, from the phenomena, in short, from the negative, not from the essence, the positive, of the world and humanity: hence, in the very abstraction and negation it must recover that from which it abstracts, or believes itself to abstract. And thus, in reality, whatever religion consciously denies—always supposing that what is denied by it is something essential, true, and consequently incapable of being ultimately denied—it unconsciously restores in God. Thus, in religion man denies his reason; of himself he knows nothing of God, his thoughts are only worldly, earthly; he can only believe what God reveals to him. But on this account the thoughts of God are human, earthly thoughts: like man, he has plans in his mind, he accommodates himself to circumstances and grades of intelligence, like a tutor with his pupils; he calculates closely the effect of his gifts and revelations; he observes man in all his doings; he knows all things, even the most earthly, the commonest, the most trivial. In brief, man in relation to God denies his own knowledge, his own thoughts, that he may place them in God. Man gives up his personality; but in return, God, the Almighty, infinite, unlimited being, is a person; he denies human dignity, the human *ego*; but in return God is to him a selfish, egoistical being, who in all things seeks only himself, his own honour, his own ends; he represents God as simply seeking the satisfaction of his own selfishness, while yet he frowns on that of every other being; his God is the very luxury of egoism.[1] Religion further denies goodness as a quality of human nature; man is wicked, corrupt, incapable of good; but on the other hand, God is only good—the Good Being. Man's nature demands as an object goodness, personified as God; but is it not hereby declared that goodness is an essential tendency of man? If my heart is wicked, my understanding perverted, how can I perceive and feel the holy to be holy, the good to be good? Could I perceive the beauty of a fine picture, if my mind were aesthetically an absolute piece of perversion?

[1] Gloriam suam plus amat Deus quam omnes creaturas. 'God can only love himself, can only think of himself, can only work for himself. In creating man, God seeks his own ends, his own glory,' etc. (see P. Bayle, *Ein Beitrag zur Geschichte der Philos. u. Menschh.* pp. 104–7).

Though I may not be a painter, though I may not have the power of producing what is beautiful myself, I must yet have aesthetic feeling, aesthetic comprehension, since I perceive the beauty that is presented to me externally. Either goodness does not exist at all for man, or, if it does exist, therein is revealed to the individual man the holiness and goodness of human nature. That which is absolutely opposed to my nature, to which I am united by no bond of sympathy, is not even conceivable or perceptible by me. The Holy is in opposition to me only as regards the modifications of my personality, but as regards my fundamental nature it is in unity with me. The Holy is a reproach to my sinfulness; in it I recognize myself as a sinner; but in so doing, while I blame myself, I acknowledge what I am not, but ought to be, and what, for that very reason, I, according to my destination, can be; for an 'ought' which has no corresponding capability, does not affect me, is a ludicrous chimaera without any true relation to my mental constitution. But when I acknowledge goodness as my destination, as my law, I acknowledge it, whether consciously or unconsciously, as my own nature. Another nature than my own, one different in quality, cannot touch me. I can perceive sin as sin, only when I perceive it to be a contradiction of myself with myself—that is, of my personality with my fundamental nature. As a contradiction of the absolute, considered as another being, the feeling of sin is inexplicable, unmeaning.

The distinction between Augustinianism and Pelagianism consists only in this, that the former expresses after the manner of religion what the latter expresses after the manner of rationalism. Both say the same thing, both vindicate the goodness of man; but Pelagianism does it directly, in a rationalistic and moral form, Augustinianism indirectly, in a mystical, that is, a religious form.[1] For that which is given to man's God, is in truth given to man himself; what a man declares concerning God, he in truth declares concerning himself. Augustinianism would be a truth, and a truth opposed to Pelagianism, only if man had the devil

[1] 'Pelagianism denies God, religion—isti tantam tribuunt potestatem voluntati, ut pietati auferant orationem' (Augustin, de Nat. et Grat. cont. Pelagium, c. 58). It has only the Creator, i.e. Nature, as a basis, not the Saviour, the true God of the religious sentiment—in a word, it denies God; but, as a consequence of this, it elevates man into a God, since it makes him a being not needing God, self-sufficing, independent. (See on this subject Luther against Erasmus and Augustine, 1. c. c. 33.) Augustinianism denies man; but, as a consequence of this, it reduces God to the level of man, even to the ignominy of the cross, for the sake of man. The former puts man in the place of God, the latter puts God in the place of man; both lead to the same result—the distinction is only apparent, a pious illusion. Augustinianism is only an inverted Pelagianism; what to the latter is a subject, is to the former an object.

for his God, and with the consciousness that he was the devil, honoured, reverenced, and worshipped him as the highest being. But so long as man adores a good being as his God, so long does he contemplate in God the goodness of his own nature.

As with the doctrine of the radical corruption of human nature, so is it with the identical doctrine, that man can do nothing good, i.e. in truth, nothing of himself—by his own strength. For the denial of human strength and spontaneous moral activity to be true, the moral activity of God must also be denied; and we must say, with the oriental nihilist or pantheist: the Divine being is absolutely without will or action, indifferent, knowing nothing of the discrimination between evil and good. But he who defines God as an active being, and not only so, but as morally active and morally critical—as a being who loves, works, and rewards good, punishes, rejects, and condemns evil— he who thus defines God, only in appearance denies human activity, in fact making it the highest, the most real activity. He who makes God act humanly, declares human activity to be divine; he says: a god who is not active, and not morally or humanly active, is no god; and thus he makes the idea of the Godhead dependent on the idea of activity, that is, of human activity, for a higher he knows not.

Man—this is the mystery of religion—projects his being into objectivity,[1] and then again makes himself an object to this projected image of himself thus converted into a subject; he thinks of himself, is an object to himself, but as the object of an object, of another being than himself. Thus here. Man is an object to God. That man is good or evil is not indifferent to God; no! He has a lively, profound interest in man's being good; he wills that man should be good, happy—for without goodness there is no happiness. Thus the religious man virtually retracts the nothingness of human activity, by making his dispositions and actions an object to God, by making man the end of God—for that which is an object to the mind is an end in action; by making the divine activity a means of human salvation. God acts, that man may be good and happy. Thus man, while he is apparently humiliated to the lowest degree, is in truth exalted to the highest. Thus, in and through God, man has in view himself alone. It is true that man places the aim of his action in God, but God has no other aim of action than

[1] The religious, the original mode in which man becomes objective to himself, is (as is clearly enough explained in this work) to be distinguished from the mode in which this occurs in reflexion and speculation; the latter is voluntary, the former involuntary, necessary—as necessary as art, as speech. With the progress of time, it is true, theology coincides with religion.

the moral and eternal salvation of man: thus man has in fact no other aim than himself. The divine activity is not distinct from the human.

How could the divine activity work on me as its object, nay, work in me, if it were essentially different from me; how could it have a human aim, the aim of ameliorating and blessing man, if it were not itself human? Does not the purpose determine the nature of the act? When man makes his moral improvement an aim to himself, he has divine resolutions, divine projects; but also, when God seeks the salvation of man, He has human ends and a human mode of activity, corresponding to these ends. Thus in God man has only his own activity as an object. But, for the very reason that he regards his own activity as objective, goodness only as an object, he necessarily receives the impulse, the motive, not from himself, but from this object. He contemplates his nature as external to himself, and this nature as goodness, thus it is self-evident, it is mere tautology to say, that the impulse to good comes only from thence where he places the good.

God is the highest subjectivity of man abstracted from himself; hence man can do nothing of himself, all goodness comes from God. The more subjective God is, the more completely does man divest himself of his subjectivity, because God is, *per se*, his relinquished self, the possession of which he however again vindicates to himself. As the action of the arteries drives the blood into the extremities, and the action of the veins brings it back again, as life in general consists in a perpetual systole and diastole; so is it in religion. In the religious systole man propels his own nature from himself, he throws himself outward; in the religious diastole he receives the rejected nature into his heart again. God alone is the being who acts of himself—this is the force of repulsion in religion; God is the being who acts in me, with me, through me, upon me, for me, is the principle of my salvation, of my good dispositions and actions, consequently my own good principle and nature—this is the force of attraction in religion.

The course of religious development which has been generally indicated, consists specifically in this, that man abstracts more and more from God, and attributes more and more to himself. This is especially apparent in the belief in revelation. That which to a later age or a cultured people is given by nature or reason, is to an earlier age, or to a yet uncultured people, given by God. Every tendency of man, however natural—even the impulse to cleanliness, was conceived by the Israelites as a positive divine ordinance. From this example we again see that God is lowered, is conceived more entirely on the type of ordinary humanity, in proportion as man detracts from himself. How can the self-humiliation of man go further than when he disclaims the capability of fulfilling spontaneously the requirements of common decency?[1] The Christian religion, on the other hand, distinguished the impulses and passions of man according to their quality, their character; it represented only good emotions, good dispositions, good thoughts, as revelations, operations—that is, as dispositions, feelings, thoughts— of God; for what God reveals is a quality of God himself: that of which the heart is full overflows the lips, as is the effect such is the cause, as the revelation such the being who reveals himself. A God who reveals himself in good dispositions is a God whose essential attribute is only moral perfection. The Christian religion distinguishes inward moral purity from external physical purity; the Israelites identified the two.[2] In relation to the Israelitish religion, the Christian religion is one of criticism and freedom. The Israelite trusted himself to do nothing except what was commanded by God; he was without will even in external things; the authority of religion extended itself even to his food. The Christian religion, on the other hand, in all these external things, made man dependent on himself, i.e. placed in man what the Israelite placed out of himself, in God. Israel is the most complete presentation of positivism in religion. In relation to the Israelite, the Christian is an *esprit fort*, a free-thinker. Thus do things change. What yesterday was still religion, is no longer such today; and what today is atheism, tomorrow will be religion.

The Essence of Christianity (1841) (trans. George Eliot)

[1] Deut. xxiii. 12, 13.
[2] See, for example, Gen. xxxv. 2; Lev. xi. 44, xx. 26; and the Commentary of Le Clerc on these passages.

CHAPTER 4

D. F. STRAUSS

The fundamental weakness of Hegel's interpretation of Christianity lay in its failure to appreciate the significance of the historical personality of Jesus Christ himself. Hegelian theology is an abstract system for which history provides much less the indispensable ground than a series of apposite illustrations. Hegel's disciple, David Friedrich Strauss, realized this and whilst hardly more than a youth set himself the task of rendering a strictly historical account of Jesus in which—the author's presuppositions being what they were—no miraculous element would be allowed to remain. Hitherto a 'life' of Christ had always required a dogmatic framework and had been presented with an apologetic interest. The historicity of the gospel narratives, even in their details, had been assumed instead of investigated. Further, although orthodox writers, as was to be expected, took the supernatural for granted, the professed rationalists themselves, in rejecting the supernatural, did no more than offer alternative and naturalistic explanations of the same alleged phenomena. This procedure had often been carried (as, for example, by Paulus) to absurd lengths, making the rationalized story not only no more credible than the original but misrepresenting the truth underlying it. What, in Strauss' view, must be understood is that the gospel records sometimes testify, 'not to outward facts, but to ideas, often most poetical and beautiful ideas...reflexions and imaginings such as were natural to the time and at the author's level of culture'. The issue therefore is not a simple distinction between fact and fiction, actual divine interposition and deliberate fraud. What we see before us is 'a plastic, naïve, and, at the same time, often most profound apprehension of truth, within the area of religious feeling and poetic insight'. The gospel tradition represents the growth of a narrative legendary or even mythical in character, though it may embody spiritual truth 'in a manner more perfect than any hard prosaic statement could achieve'. In this conviction Strauss undertook what he believed would be an inquiry into the facts about the founder of Christianity as sympathetic as it was both clear-sighted and novel. The result was the publication in 1835–6 of his *Leben Jesu*, a work which, although today mainly of historical interest, still repays the effort of reading it. Despite its obvious defects, and notably its excessive dependence on the Hegelian philosophy, it stands as a landmark in the development both of the study of the New Testament and of modern religious thought.

Strauss was born at Ludwigsburg, in Württemberg, in 1808, and attended the university of Tübingen. After a brief period as assistant to a country pastor, with a temporary teaching post at Marlbronn, he went in 1831 to Berlin to study under Schleiermacher and Hegel, though the latter died shortly after his arrival. His first full-time academic appointment was as lecturer in philosophy at Tübingen. There it was that he wrote his *Life of Jesus*, the appearance of which, to his astonishment, provoked a storm of criticism. In 1839 he accepted the chair of dogmatic theology at Zürich, but the intense opposition which his nomination had aroused prevented him from taking up his duties. Election in 1848 to the Württemberg Diet, gave him a position which he found little to his liking and which he subsequently resigned. His true *métier* was that of a writer. The years 1839–41 saw the publication in two volumes of his *Christliche Glaubenslehre*. His popular *Leben Jesu für das Deutsche Volk* came out in 1860 (an English translation in 1865). But he also published a number of biographies before the appearance of his final contribution to the theological debate of his time with *Der alte und der neue Glaube* in 1872, a book in which he expresses his maturest reflexions—now undisguisedly hostile—upon the whole problem of Christianity. He died two years later.

Strauss' *Life of Jesus*, translated into English by George Eliot in 1843, attempts to explain the origins of Christianity in purely historical terms, the dogmatic and rationalistic approaches being alike rejected. The first requirement was to eliminate miracle as outside the sphere of history; the second, to appreciate the role of myth and legend in the expression and development of the religious consciousness. Nature is now recognized to be a nexus of cause and effect, suffering no interruption. 'The conviction is so much a habit of thought with the modern world, that in actual life, the belief in a supernatural manifestation, an immediate divine agency, is at once attributed to ignorance or imposture.' As for myth and legend, the process, unconscious at a certain cultural level, of objectifying ideas and beliefs in historical form, is but testimony to the force in all genuine religion of the poetic spirit. For the world in which the gospels came to be written knew no clear-cut distinction between poetry and prose, fact and fiction. An emotion could distil itself into a myth, which in turn would be presented in the guise of an event. The Messianic idea is an illustration. Messianism was a myth which faith and hope attached to the historical person of Jesus of Nazareth.

Strauss' examination of the gospels is painstaking, given the limitations of his viewpoint. What he lacked was a searching critique of the gospels as documents, which at the time he wrote had not yet been effectively undertaken, scientific New Testament study being still in its infancy. The result was that Strauss, having no criteria by which to sift the gospel material for its historical reliability, tended to explain the whole tradition in terms of the mythopoeic imagination. His estimate of Jesus' historical personality is inadequate. As one of his earliest critics objected, if Christ was the creation of the Church by whom was the Church itself created? And to this, on Strauss' showing, no ready answer can be given. Moreover, as Pfleiderer points out, Strauss' error lay not in his regarding certain gospel incidents as legends or the miracle-stories as symbols of ideal truths, for that no serious criticism can deny. His real fault, into which the influence of Hegel misled him, was in locating the religious truths thus symbolized not in religious experience—in the facts of 'the devout heart and moral will'—but in metaphysical speculation. This failure to appreciate the place of both history and ethics in the primitive Christian tradition deprives his work of much of the value it might otherwise have had. For although his declared aim was positive—at the time of writing the *Life of Jesus* he was a sincere Christian believer—its immediate effect was negative. Yet he had sought to be constructive, even apologetic—'to re-establish dogmatically what had been destroyed critically'. Christ, he was confident, would emerge from history no longer as a myth in metaphysical attire but as the symbol of humanity itself. Was not the unity of the divine and human natures true in a far higher sense when the whole race of mankind was seen as its realization than when restricted to a single life? 'Is not an incarnation of God from eternity a truer one than incarnation limited to a particular point in time?' Strauss hoped that his interpretation would bring to many thinking Christians, Christian ministers included, such an intellectual liberation as the continuing life of the spirit demanded. The effect of mental adjustment might, in individual instances, prove difficult, and the author, who was in no sense an ecclesiastical reformer, had no specific counsel to offer. But although the old doctrines were in his opinion dead he had little doubt that Christianity itself would survive. What in fact could be achieved by his methods time would show. In his own case, however, his optimism proved unfounded and his final conviction was that, although Christian institutions may continue, Christian belief belongs only to the world of things past.

Bibliographical note

There is no modern reprint of Strauss' *Life of Jesus*. For an authoritative discussion of Strauss' views see A. Schweitzer, *Von Reimarus zu Wrede* (1906), pp. 67–119 (English trans., *The Quest of the Historical Jesus*, 1910, pp. 68–120).

I. MYTH IN THE NEW TESTAMENT

Seeing from what has already been said that the external testimony respecting the composition of our Gospels, far from forcing upon us the conclusion that they proceeded from eyewitnesses or well-informed contemporaries, leaves the decision to be determined wholly by internal grounds of evidence, that is, by the nature of the Gospel narratives themselves: we might immediately proceed from this introduction to the peculiar object of the present work, which is an examination of those narratives in detail. It may however appear useful, before entering upon this special inquiry, to consider the general question, how far it is consistent with the character of the Christian religion that mythi should be found in it, and how far the general construction of the Gospel narratives authorizes us to treat them as mythi. Although, indeed, if the following critical examination of the details be successful in proving the actual existence of mythi in the New Testament, this preliminary demonstration of their possibility becomes superfluous.

If with this view we compare the acknowledged mythical religions of antiquity with the Hebrew and Christian, it is true that we are struck by many differences between the sacred histories existing in these religious forms and those in the former. Above all, it is commonly alleged that the sacred histories of the Bible are distinguished from the legends of the Indians, Greeks, Romans, etc., by their moral character and excellence. 'In the latter, the stories of the battles of the gods, the loves of Krishna, Jupiter, etc., contain much which was offensive to the moral feeling even of enlightened heathens, and which is revolting to ours: whilst in the former, the whole course of the narration offers only what is worthy of God, instructive, and ennobling.' To this it may be answered with regard to the heathens, that the appearance of immorality in many of their narratives is merely the consequence of a subsequent misconception of their original meaning: and with regard to the Old Testament, that the perfect moral purity of its history has been contested. Often indeed, it has been contested without good grounds, because a due distinction is not made between that which is ascribed to individual men (who, as they are represented, are by no means spotless examples of purity) and that which is ascribed to God:[1]

[1] This same want of distinction has led the Alexandrians to allegorize, the Deists to scoff, and the Supernaturalists to strain the meaning of words.

nevertheless it is true that we have commands called divine, which, like that to the Israelites on their departure out of Egypt to purloin vessels of gold, are scarcely less revolting to an enlightened moral feeling, than the thefts of the Grecian Hermes. But even admitting this difference in the morality of the religions to its full extent (and it must be admitted at least with regard to the New Testament) still it furnishes no proof of the historical character of the Bible; for though every story relating to God which is immoral is necessarily fictitious, even the most moral is not necessarily true.

'But that which is incredible and inconceivable forms the staple of the heathen fables; whilst in the biblical history, if we only presuppose the immediate intervention of the Deity, there is nothing of the kind.' Exactly, if this be presupposed. Otherwise, we might very likely find the miracles in the life of Moses, Elias, or Jesus, the Theophany and Angelophany of the Old and New Testament, just as incredible as the fables of Jupiter, Hercules, or Bacchus: presuppose the divinity or divine descent of these individuals, and their actions and fate become as credible as those of the biblical personages with the like presupposition. Yet not quite so, it may be returned. Vishnu appearing in his three first avatars as a fish, a tortoise, and a boar; Saturn devouring his children; Jupiter turning himself into a bull, a swan, etc.—these are incredibilities of quite another kind from Jehovah appearing to Abraham in a human form under the terebinth tree, or to Moses in the burning bush. This extravagant love of the marvellous is the character of the heathen mythology. A similar accusation might indeed be brought against many parts of the Bible, such as the tales of Balaam, Joshua, and Samson; but still it is here less glaring, and does not form as in the Indian religion and in certain parts of the Grecian, the prevailing character. What however does this prove? Only that the biblical history *might* be true, sooner than the Indian or Grecian fables; not in the least that on this account it *must* be true, and can contain nothing fictitious.

'But the subjects of the heathen mythology are for the most part such, as to convince us beforehand that they are mere inventions: those of the Bible such as at once to establish their own reality. A Brahma, an Ormusd, a Jupiter, without doubt never existed; but there still is a God, a Christ, and there have been an Adam, a Noah, an Abraham, a Moses.' Whether an Adam or a Noah, however, were such as they are represented, has already been doubted, and may still be doubted. Just

so, on the other side, there may have been something historical about
Hercules, Theseus, Achilles, and other heroes of Grecian story. Here,
again, we come to the decision that the biblical history *might* be true
sooner than the heathen mythology, but is not necessarily so. This
decision, however, together with the two distinctions already made,
brings us to an important observation. How do the Grecian divinities
approve themselves immediately to us as non-existing beings, if not
because things are ascribed to them which we cannot reconcile with our
idea of the divine? whilst the God of the Bible is a reality to us just
in so far as he corresponds with the idea we have formed of him in our
own minds. Besides the contradiction to our notion of the divine
involved in the plurality of heathen gods, and the intimate description
of their motives and actions, we are at once revolted to find that the
gods themselves have a history; that they are born, grow up, marry,
have children, work out their purposes, suffer difficulties and weariness,
conquer and are conquered. It is irreconcilable with our idea of the
Absolute to suppose it subjected to time and change, to opposition and
suffering; and therefore where we meet with a narrative in which these
are attributed to a divine being, by this test we recognize it as unhistorical or mythical.

It is in this sense that the Bible, and even the Old Testament, is said
to contain no mythi. The story of the creation with its succession of
each day's labour ending in a rest after the completion of the task;
the expression often recurring in the farther course of the narrative,
God repented of having done so and so—these and similar representations cannot indeed be entirely vindicated from the charge of making
finite the nature of the Deity, and this is the ground which has been
taken by mythical interpreters of the history of the creation. And in
every other instance where God is said to reveal himself exclusively at
any definite place or time, by celestial apparition, or by miracle wrought
immediately by himself, it is to be presumed that the Deity has become
finite and descended to human modes of operation. It may, however,
be said in general, that in the Old Testament the divine nature does not
appear to be essentially affected by the temporal character of its operation, but that the temporal shows itself rather as a mere form, an
unavoidable appearance, arising out of the necessary limitation of
human, and especially of uncultivated powers of representation. It is
obvious to every one, that there is something quite different in the Old
Testament declarations, that God made an alliance with Noah, and

Abraham, led his people out of Egypt, gave them laws, brought them
into the promised land, raised up for them judges, kings and prophets,
and punished them at last for their disobedience by exile—from the
tales concerning Jupiter, that he was born of Rhea in Crete, and hidden
from his father Saturn in a cave; that afterwards he made war upon his
father, freed the Uranides, and with their help and that of the lightning
with which they furnished him, overcame the rebellious Titans, and
at last divided the world amongst his brothers and children. The
essential difference between the two representations is, that in the latter,
the Deity himself is the subject of progression, becomes another being
at the end of the process from what he was at the beginning, something
being effected in himself and for his own sake: whilst in the former,
change takes place only on the side of the world; God remains fixed in
his own identity as the I AM, and the temporal is only a superficial
reflexion cast back upon his acting energy by that course of mundane
events which he both originated and guides. In the heathen mythology
the gods have a history: in the Old Testament, God himself has none,
but only his people: and if the proper meaning of mythology be the
history of gods, then the Hebrew religion has no mythology.

From the Hebrew religion, this recognition of the divine unity and
immutability was transmitted to the Christian. The birth, growth,
miracles, sufferings, death and resurrection of Christ are circumstances
belonging to the destiny of the Messiah, above which God remains
unaffected in his own changeless identity. The New Testament therefore knows nothing of mythology in the above sense. The state of the
question is, however, somewhat changed from that which it assumed
in the Old Testament: for Jesus is called the Son of God, not merely
in the same sense as kings under the theocracy were so called, but as
actually begotten by the divine spirit, or from the incarnation in his
person of the divine λόγος. Inasmuch as he is one with the Father,
and in him the whole fullness of the godhead dwells bodily, he is more
than Moses. The actions and sufferings of such a being are not external
to the Deity: though we are not allowed to suppose a *theopaschitic* union
with the divine nature, yet still, even in the New Testament, and more
in the later doctrine of the Church, it is a divine being that here lives
and suffers, and what befalls him has an absolute worth and significance.
Thus according to the above accepted notion of the mythus, the New
Testament has more of a mythical character than the Old. But to call
the history of Jesus mythical in this sense, is as unimportant with regard

to the historical question as it is unexceptionable; for the idea of God is in no way opposed to such an intervention in human affairs as does not affect his own immutability; so that as far as regards this point, the gospel history, notwithstanding its mythical designation, might be at the same time throughout historically true.

Admitting that the biblical history does not equally with the heathen mythology offend our idea of Deity, and that consequently it is not in like manner characterized by this mark of the unhistorical, however far it be from bearing any guarantee of being historical—we are met by the further question whether it be not less accordant with our idea of the world, and whether such discordancy may not furnish a test of its unhistorical nature.

In the ancient world, that is, in the east, the religious tendency was so preponderating, and the knowledge of nature so limited, that the law of connexion between earthly finite beings was very loosely regarded. At every link there was a disposition to spring into the Infinite, and to see God as the immediate cause of every change in nature or the human mind. In this mental condition the biblical history was written. Not that God is here represented as doing all and everything himself—a notion which, from the manifold direct evidence of the fundamental connexion between finite things, would be impossible to any reasonable mind—but there prevails in the biblical writers a ready disposition to derive all things down to the minutest details, as soon as they appear particularly important, immediately from God. He it is who gives the rain and sunshine; he sends the east wind and the storm; he dispenses war, famine, pestilence; he hardens hearts and softens them, suggests thoughts and resolutions. And this is particularly the case with regard to his chosen instruments and beloved people. In the history of the Israelites we find traces of his immediate agency at every step: through Moses, Elias, Jesus, he performs things which never would have happened in the ordinary course of nature.

Our modern world, on the contrary, after many centuries of tedious research, has attained a conviction, that all things are linked together by a chain of causes and effects, which suffers no interruption. It is true that single facts and groups of facts, with their conditions and processes of change, are not so circumscribed as to be unsusceptible of external influence; for the action of one existence or kingdom in nature intrenches on that of another: human freedom controls natural development, and material laws react on human freedom. Nevertheless, the totality of finite things forms a vast circle, which, except that it owes its existence and laws to a superior power, suffers no intrusion from without. This conviction is so much a habit of thought with the modern world, that in actual life, the belief in a supernatural manifestation, an immediate divine agency, is at once attributed to ignorance or imposture. It has been carried to the extreme in that modern explanation, which, in a spirit exactly opposed to that of the Bible, has either totally removed the divine causation, or has so far restricted it that it is immediate in the act of creation alone, but mediate from that point onwards—i.e. God operates on the world only in so far as he gave to it this fixed direction at the creation. From this point of view, at which nature and history appear as a compact tissue of finite causes and effects, it was impossible to regard the narratives of the Bible, in which this tissue is broken by innumerable instances of divine interference, as historical.

It must be confessed on nearer investigation, that this modern explanation, although it does not exactly deny the existence of God, yet puts aside the idea of him, as the ancient view did the idea of the world. For this is, as it has been often and well remarked, no longer a God and Creator, but a mere finite Artist, who acts immediately upon his work only during its first production, and then leaves it to itself; who becomes excluded with his full energy from one particular sphere of existence. It has therefore been attempted to unite the two views so as to maintain for the world its law of sequence, and for God his unlimited action, and by this means to preserve the truth of the biblical history. According to this view, the world is supposed to move in obedience to the law of consecutive causes and effects bound up with its constitution, and God to act upon it only mediately: but in single instances, where he finds it necessary for particular objects, he is not held to be restricted from entering into the course of human changes immediately. This is the view of modern Supranaturalism; evidently a vain attempt to reconcile two opposite views, since it contains the faults of both, and adds a new one in the contradiction between the two ill-assorted principles. For here the consecutiveness of nature and history is broken through as in the ancient biblical view; and the action of God limited as in the contrary system. The proposition that God works sometimes mediately, sometimes immediately, upon the world, introduces a changeableness, and therefore a temporal element, into the nature of his action, which brings it under the same condemnation as both the other systems; that, namely, of distinguishing the maintaining power, in the one case from individual instances of the divine agency, and in the other from the act of creation.[1]

Since then our idea of God requires an immediate, and our idea of the world a mediate divine operation; and since the idea of combination of the two species of action is inadmissible—nothing remains for us but to regard them both as so permanently and immovably united, the operation of God on the world continues for ever and everywhere twofold, both immediate and mediate; which comes just to this, that it is neither of the two, or this distinction loses its value. To explain more closely: if we proceed from the idea of God, from which arose the demand for his immediate operation, then the world is to be regarded in relation to him as a Whole: on the contrary, if we proceed from the idea of the finite, the world is a congeries of separate parts, and hence has arisen the demand for a merely mediate agency of God— so that we must say—God acts upon the world as a Whole immediately, but on each part only by means of his action on every other part, that is to say, by the laws of nature.

This view brings us to the same conclusion with regard to the historical value of the Bible as the one above considered. The miracles which God wrought for and by Moses and Jesus, do not proceed from his immediate operation on the Whole, but presuppose an immediate action in particular cases, which is a contradiction to the type of the divine agency we have just given. The supranaturalists indeed claim an exception from this type on behalf of the biblical history; a pre-supposition which is inadmissible from our point of view, according to which the same laws, although varied by various circumstances, are supreme in every sphere of being and action, and therefore every narrative which offends against these laws, is to be recognized as so far unhistorical.

The result, then, however surprising, of a general examination of the biblical history, is that the Hebrew and Christian religions, like all others, have their mythi. And this result is confirmed, if we consider

---

[1] If the supranatural view contains a theological contradiction, so the new evangelical theology, which esteems itself raised so far above the old supranatural view, contains a logical contradiction. To say that God acts only mediately upon the world as the general rule, but sometimes, by way of exception, immediately, has some meaning, though perhaps not a wise one. But to say that God acts always immediately on the world, but in some cases more particularly immediately, is a flat contradiction in itself. On the principle of the immanence or immediate agency of God in the world, to which the new evangelical theology lays claim, the idea of the miraculous is impossible.

the inherent nature of religion, what essentially belongs to it and there-fore must be common to all religions, and what on the other hand is peculiar and may differ in each. If religion be defined as the perception of truth, not in the form of an idea, which is the philosophic perception, but invested with imagery; it is easy to see that the mythical element can be wanting only when religion either falls short of, or goes beyond, its peculiar province, and that in the proper religious sphere it must necessarily exist. *The Life of Jesus* (1835) (trans. George Eliot)

II. DEFINITION AND CHARACTERISTICS OF THE GOSPEL MYTH

The precise sense in which we use the expression *mythus*, applied to certain parts of the gospel history, is evident from all that has already been said; at the same time the different kinds and gradations of the mythi which we shall meet with in this history may here by way of anticipation be pointed out.

We distinguish by the name *evangelical mythus* a narrative relating directly or indirectly to Jesus, which may be considered not as the expression of a fact, but as the product of an idea of his earliest followers: such a narrative being mythical in proportion as it exhibits this char-acter. The mythus in this sense of the term meets us, in the Gospel as elsewhere, sometimes in its pure form, constituting the substance of the narrative, and sometimes as an accidental adjunct to the actual history.

The pure mythus in the Gospel will be found to have two sources, which in most cases contributed simultaneously, though in different proportions, to form the mythus. The one source is, as already stated, the Messianic ideas and expectations existing according to their several forms in the Jewish mind before Jesus, and independently of him; the other is that particular impression which was left by the personal character, actions, and fate of Jesus, and which served to modify the Messianic idea in the minds of his people. The account of the Trans-figuration, for example, is derived almost exclusively from the former source; the only amplification taken from the latter source being— that they who appeared with Jesus on the Mount spake of his decease. On the other hand, the narrative of the rending of the veil of the temple at the death of Jesus seems to have had its origin in the hostile position which Jesus, and his church after him, sustained in relation to the Jewish temple worship. Here already we have something historical, though consisting merely of certain general features of character, position etc.; we are thus at once brought upon the ground of the historical mythus.

The historical mythus has for its groundwork a definite individual fact which has been seized upon by religious enthusiasm, and twined around with mythical conceptions culled from the idea of the Christ. This fact is perhaps a saying of Jesus such as that concerning 'fishers of men' or the barren fig-tree, which now appear in the Gospels transmuted into marvellous histories: or, it is perhaps a real transaction or event taken from his life; for instance, the mythical traits in the account of the baptism were built upon such a reality. Certain of the miraculous histories may likewise have had some foundation in natural occurrences, which the narrative has either exhibited in a supernatural light, or enriched with miraculous incidents.

All the species of imagery here enumerated may justly be designated as mythi, even according to the modern and precise definition of George, inasmuch as the unhistorical which they embody—whether formed gradually by tradition, or created by an individual author—is in each case the product of an *idea*. But for those parts of the history which are characterized by indefiniteness and want of connexion, by misconstruction and transformation, by strange combinations and confusion—the natural results of a long course of oral transmission; or which, on the contrary, are distinguished by highly coloured and pictorial representations, which also seem to point to a traditionary origin—for those parts the term *legendary* is certainly the more appropriate.

Lastly. It is requisite to distinguish equally from the mythus and the legend, that which, as it serves not to clothe an idea on the one hand, and admits not of being referred to tradition on the other, must be regarded as *the addition of the author*, as purely individual, and designed merely to give clearness, connexion, and climax, to the representation.

It is to the various forms of the unhistorical in the gospels that this enumeration exclusively refers; it does not involve the renunciation of the *historical* which they may likewise contain.

The Life of Jesus (1835) (trans. George Eliot)

∴ can't possibly know the historical Jesus

CHAPTER 5

LOTZE

The desire to establish the fundamental rights of religious belief whilst fully admitting the claims of natural science found an undaunted champion in Hermann Lotze, even though today his once solid-seeming achievement is largely forgotten. Born at Bautzen in Saxony in 1817, he studied both medicine and philosophy at Leipzig, where in 1839 he was appointed professor *extraordinarius* in the latter subject. In 1842 he was given the chair of philosophy at Göttingen which he held until his nomination, only a short while before his death in 1881, to the corresponding post at Berlin. As a thinker he may be classified as a teleological idealist, but his views represent a considerable modification of Hegelianism. His influence on subsequent German philosophy was not marked, but liberal theologians, especially Albrecht Ritschl, owed him much. His attempt to give ultimacy to personal values in an age of science had its repercussions in this country in the form of the 'personal idealist' movement at the turn of the century. The works by which he is best known are his *Metaphysik*, first published in 1841 but substantially revised and enlarged in 1879—an English translation by Bernard Bosanquet appeared in 1884; a *Logik* (1843; revised 1874), and the *Mikrokosmus* (1854–6), a comprehensive and in intention popularizing exposition of his ideas and in particular of his conception of the development of human culture (Eng. trans. by Hamilton and Jones, 1885). These were to be brought together in a general *System der Philosophie*, along with a detailed treatment of ethical, aesthetic and religious questions, but the ambitious scheme was never completed. His lecture-notes were edited by E. Rheinisch in a series of volumes published in 1881 and later.

Lotze's discussion of a subject is always copious and clear, though perhaps his most original work was done in the field of psychology, in which, so far as its modern study is concerned, he was something of a pioneer. He realized, as against the uncritical vitalism then widely current, that the mechanism of nature cannot be confined to the inorganic sphere alone and implies the assumption of a universal law of causal connexion. What indeed is properly to be understood by causal connexion was a problem which gave him a good deal of concern. How, for example, was a change occurring in one object to be connected, under a general principle, with the change occurring also in an object separately existing? His conclusion was that the difficulty of 'transitive action', as he called it, indicates that separate entities do not and cannot have an independent existence and that the seemingly disparate elements which constitute reality are necessarily correlated in the unity of universal being, the Infinite. Transitive action between separate objects should accordingly be interpreted as an immanent movement or operation within a subsisting whole or 'world-ground'. But this infinite reality, if the facts of experience are to be adequately explained, can, Lotze thinks, be conceived only on the analogy of spiritual or personal being. To the objection that personality is inconceivable apart from distinction and limitation he replies that true personality, an 'inner core' of selfhood 'previous to and out of' every relationship, is of its nature infinite and that our finite humanity informs us not of the necessary conditions of personal existence but only of the restraints which space and time impose on it. Ultimately therefore the equation of the ground of existence with personal being *per se* requires for its due expression the language of theism. God is he in whom the entire process of the universe must be thought of as immanent—in whom, that is, it is correlated, sustained and orientated.

The predominant feature of Lotze's doctrine is its refusal to accord metaphysics, as the science of being, a right of existence independent of ethics. Man is a creature not of reason alone but of feeling, and the emotional demands of his nature have to be met. Because of this *values* arise—moral, aesthetic, religious. Indeed we cannot properly speak of ultimate 'reality' except in terms of ultimate 'value'. The mechanistic principle applies fully in the realms of nature, but it is wholly subordinate, Lotze argues, to ends which mechanism itself cannot determine, so that nature, philosophically viewed, is essentially an instrument of purpose. Knowledge itself, as the purposive activity of reason, must be said to originate in value-judgements, for science exists only in the convictions of those who are wholly persuaded of its truth. 'And it will never produce such convictions if it forgets that every region which it investigates, all the departments of the mental and the physical world, had been explored and taken possession of by our hopes and wishes and anticipations long before any systematic investigation was thought of.' Mechanism, then, cannot be held to negate the freedom of the will which we are obliged to postulate on moral grounds; it is simply the condition without which volition could not issue in effective action. Hence the fear, in an age of positivistic science, that materialism is the only appropriate philosophy is really baseless. Mechanism provides a means, no more; the ends by which man interprets his own life and historical development lie beyond it and alone determine its function and limits. Being and value are not disjoined but have their common source in the personal Infinite, that ground of all existence which at the same time is value-creating and value-conserving. The elements of which reality is composed are, Lotze thinks, but modifications or 'actions' of the Infinite: we may categorize them into material particles or atoms—'the elementary actions of the world-ground'—

and souls. Apart from the Infinite there is no universal truth, no antecedently valid 'law of occurrence' (*Recht des Geschehens*). The very notions of law and truth, that is to say, are themselves indicative of the modes or conditions under which the Infinite achieves the realization of its, or his, purposes. They have no meaning except in relation to the ultimate ends wherein the Infinite establishes its self-identity—ends that are not determined by metaphysical necessity but arise only from the intrinsically ethical nature of the Person in whose consciousness the world-ground achieves selfhood.

Such, in outline, is the attempt which Lotze makes to meet the difficulty of the growing antithesis between cognition and faith. 'Taking truth as a whole', he claims, 'we are not justified in regarding it as a mere self-centred splendour, having no necessary connexion with those stirrings of the soul from which, indeed, the impulse to seek it first proceeded.' The solution, however, of absolute idealism he cannot accept, since knowledge and reality are set over against one another: human thinking can only *represent* it. But it is doubtful whether he succeeded in resolving the antitheses of naturalism and idealism. He was at pains to stress the idealistic character of his doctrine and sought to include the whole of reality in a teleological and ethical perspective, but it is very questionable whether he is able to dispose of a residuum of naturalism, and his confidence that the ultimate is 'a living Love that wills the blessedness of others' is the expression of a personal faith which his system cannot underpin with consistently rational argument. His follower Ritschl, a theologian without philosophical interest, chose to retain the value-judgement whilst dispensing with the metaphysic.

Bibliographical note

The English translations of the *Microcosmus* and *Metaphysics* mentioned above should be supplemented by *Outlines of the Philosophy of Religion*, translated by F. C. Conybeare (1892). See also Henry Jones, *A Critical Account of the Philosophy of Lotze* (1895) and J. R. Illingworth, *Personality, Human and Divine* (1894).

THE DIVINE PERSONALITY

Two distinct series of attributes through which man tries to comprehend the being of God recall to us the two impulses from which arose the notion of God and belief in Him. Metaphysical attributes of Unity, Eternity, Omnipresence, and Omnipotence determine Him as the ground of all finite reality; ethical attributes of Wisdom, Justice, and Holiness satisfy our longing to find in that which has supreme reality, supreme worth also. We have no need to give a complete account of these attributes or to touch doubtful questions as to their reciprocal limits; the only really important point for us is to reach a conviction as to the mode of existence that is to give a definite form to this essence of all perfection, determining also at the same time the special significance of several of the attributes referred to. If these reflexions, which are now struggling to a conclusion, were allowed once more to run into the prolixity of systematic completeness, it would be easy to develop from the preceding investigations as to the nature of existence the answer which we should have to give to this last question as to the nature of that Infinite which we have there discovered. But just because it is easy for the reader to supply this transition we will regard the goal to which it would lead, the notion of a Personal God, as being already reached, and endeavour to defend this against doubts as to its possibility, as being the only logical conclusion to which our considerations could come.

The longing of the soul to apprehend as reality the Highest Good which it is able to feel, cannot be satisfied by or even consider any form of the existence of that Good except Personality. So strong is its conviction that some living Ego, possessing and enjoying Self, is the inevitable presupposition and the only possible source and abode of all goodness and all good things, so filled is it with unspoken contempt for all existence that is apparently lifeless, that we always find the myth-constructing beginnings of religion busied in transforming natural to spiritual reality; but never find them actuated by any desire to trace back living spiritual activity to unintelligent Realness as to a firmer foundation. From this right path the progressive development of reflexion turned off for a time. With increasing cosmic knowledge, it grew more clear what must be required in the notion of God, if He were not only to contain in Himself all that is greatest and most worthy, but also to contain it after such a fashion as to appear at the same time as the creative and formative ground of all reality; and on the other hand, in more refined observation of spiritual life, the conditions became clear to which in us finite beings the development of personality is attached; both trains of thought seemed to combine in showing that the form of spiritual life is incompatible with the notion of the Supreme Being, or that the form of personal existence is incompatible with the notion of the Infinite Spirit. And there arose attempts to find more satisfying forms of existence for the Highest Good in ideas of an Eternal

World-Order, of an Infinite Substance, of a Self-developing Idea, and to deprecate the form of personal existence which had previously seemed to the unsophisticated mind to be the only one that was worthy....

*   *   *

An Ego (or Self, *Ich*) is not thinkable without the contrast of a Non-Ego or Not-Self; hence personal existence cannot be asserted of God without bringing even Him down to that state of limitation, of being conditioned by something not Himself, which is repugnant to Him—The objections that speculative knowledge makes to the personality of God fall back upon this thought: in order to estimate their importance, we shall have to test the apparently clear content of the proposition which they take as their point of departure. For unambiguous it is not; it may be intended to assert that what the term Ego denotes can be comprehended in reflective analysis only by reference to the Non-Ego; it may also mean that it is not conceivable that this content of the Ego should be experienced without that contrasted Non-Ego being experienced at the same time; finally, it may point to the existence and active influence of a Non-Ego as the condition without which the being upon which this influence works could not be an Ego.

The relations which we need in ideation for making clear the object ideated, are not in a general way decisive as to its nature; they are not conditions of the possibility of the thing as they are for us conditions of the possibility of its presentation in idea. But the special nature of the case before us seems to involve something which is not generally included—for it is just in the act of ideation that Selfhood (*Ichheit*) consists, and hence what is necessary for carrying out such an act is at the same time a condition of the thing. Hence the first two interpretations which we gave of the proposition referred to seem to run together into the assertion that the Ego has significance only as contrasted with the Non-Ego, and can be experienced only in such contrast. Whether we agree with this assertion will depend in part upon the significance attached to the words used. We see in the first place that at any rate Ego and Non-Ego cannot be two notions of which each owes its whole content only to its contrast with the other; if this were so they would both remain without content, and if neither of them apart from the contrast had a fixed meaning of its own, not only would there be no ground for giving an answer one way or the other to the question which of the two members of the contrast should take the place of the Ego and which that of the Non-Ego, but the very question would cease to have any meaning. Language has given to the Ego alone its own independent name, to the Non-Ego only the negative determination which excludes the Ego without indicating any positive content of its own. Hence every being which is destined to take the part of the Ego when the contrast has arisen, must have the ground of its determination in that nature which it had *previous to* the contrast, although before the existence of the contrast it is not yet entitled to the predicate which in that contrast comes to belong to it. Now if this is to remain the meaning of the term, if the being is to be Ego only at the moment when it is distinguished from the Non-Ego, then we have no objection to make to this mode of expression, but we shall alter our own. For it is our opponents' opinion and not ours that personality is to be found exclusively where, in ideation (or presentation), Self-consciousness sets itself as Ego in opposition to the Non-Ego; in order to establish the self hood (*Selbstheit*) which we primarily seek, that nature is sufficient in virtue of which, when the contrast does arise, the being becomes an Ego, and it is sufficient even before the appearance of the contrast. Every feeling of pleasure or of dislike, every kind of self-enjoyment (*Selbstgenuss*), does in our view contain the primary basis of personality, that immediate self-existence which all later developments of self-consciousness may indeed make plainer to thought by contrasts and comparisons, thus also intensifying its value, but which is not in the first place produced by them. It may be that only the being who in thought contrasts with himself a Non-Ego from which he also distinguishes himself, can say *I* (*Ich*) to himself, but yet in order that in thus distinguishing he should not mistake and confound himself with the Non-Ego, this discriminating thought of his must be guided by a certainty of self which is immediately experienced, by a self-existence which is earlier than the discriminative relation by which it becomes Ego as opposed to the Non-Ego. A different consideration has already led us by an easier path to the same result, and we may refer the reader to this passage for explanation and completion of what is said here. The discussion referred to showed us that all self-consciousness rests upon the foundation of direct sense of self which can by no means arise from becoming aware of a contrast with the external world, but is itself the reason that this contrast can be felt as unique, as not comparable to any other distinction between two objects. Self-consciousness is only the subsequent endeavour to analyse with the resources of cognition this experienced fact—to frame in thought a picture of the Ego that in cognition apprehends itself with the most vivid feeling, and in this manner to place it artificially among the objects of our consideration, to which it does not really belong. So we take up our position with regard to the first two interpretations of the proposition of which we are speaking, thus: We admit that the Ego *is thinkable* only in relation to the Non-Ego, but we add that it *may be experienced* previous to and out of every such relation, and that to this is due the possibility of its subsequently becoming thinkable in that relation.

But it is not these two interpretations but the third that is most obstructive to that faith in the Personality of God which we are seeking to establish. In one form indeed in which it sometimes occurs we need not make it an object of renewed investigation; for we may now consider it as, in our view, established that no being in the nature of which self-existence was not given as primary and underived, could be endowed with selfhood by any mechanism of favouring circumstances however wonderful. Hence we may pass over in complete silence all those attempts which think to show by ill-chosen analogies from the world of sense how in a being as yet selfless an activity originally directed entirely outwards is, by the resistance opposed to it by the Non-Ego (comparable to that which a ray of light encounters in a plane surface), thrown back upon itself and thereby transformed into the self-comprehending light of self-consciousness. In such ideas everything is arbitrary, and not a single feature of the image employed is applicable to the actual case which it is intended to make clear; that outgoing activity is an unmeaning imagination, the resistance which it is to meet with is something that cannot be proved, the inference that that activity is by that resistance turned back along the path by which it came is unfounded, and it is wholly incomprehensible how this reflexion could transform its nature, so that from blind activity it should turn into the selfhood of *self-existence*.

Setting aside these follies which have influenced philosophic thought to an unreasonable extent, we find a more respectable form of the view which we are combating occupied in proving that though that self-existence cannot be produced by any external condition in a being to which it does not belong by nature, yet it could never be developed even in one whose nature is capable of it, without the co-operation and educative influences of an external world. For that from the impressions which we must receive from the external world, there comes to us not only all the content of our ideas, but also the occasion of all those feelings in which the Ego, existing for self, can enjoy self without as yet being conscious of a relation of contrast to the Non-Ego. That all feeling must be conceived as (in some definite form of pleasure or displeasure) interested in some definite situation of the being to which it belongs, some particular phase of its action and its passion; but that neither is passion possible without some foreign impression which calls it forth, nor activity possible without an external point of attraction which guides it and at which it aims. That in any single feeling the being which is self-existent is only partially self-possessing; that whether it has self-existence truly and completely depends upon the variety of the external impulses which stimulate by degrees the whole wealth of its nature, making this wealth matter of self-enjoyment— that thus the development of all personality is bound up with the existence and influence of an external world and the variety and succession of those influences; and that such development would be possible even for God only under similar conditions.

It is not sufficient to lessen the weight of this objection by the assertion that this educative stimulation is necessary only for finite and changing beings, and not for the nature of God, which, as a self-cognizant Idea, eternally unchangeable, always possesses its whole content simultaneously. Though this assertion grazes the truth, yet in this form it would be injurious in another respect to our idea of God, for it would make the being of God similar to that of an eternal truth—a truth indeed not merely valid but also conscious of itself. But we have a direct feeling of the wide difference there is between this personification of a thought and living personality; not only do we find art tedious when it expects us to admire allegorical statues of Justice or of Love, but even speculation rouses our opposition forthwith, when it offers to us some self-cognizant Principle of Identity, or some self-conscious Idea of Good, as completely expressing personality. Either of these is obviously lacking in an essential condition of all true reality in the capacity of *suffering*. Every Idea by which in reproductive cognition we seek to exhaust the nature of some being, is and remains nothing more than the statement of a thought-formula by which we fix, as an aid to reflexion, the inner connexion between the living activities of the Real; the real thing itself is that which applies this Idea to itself, which feels contradiction to it as disturbance of itself, and wills and attempts as its own endeavour the realization of the Idea. The only living subject of personality is this inner core, which cannot be resolved into thoughts, the meaning and significance of which we know in the immediate experience of our mental life, and which we always misunderstand when we seek to construe it—hence personality can never belong to any unchangeably valid truth, but only to something which changes, suffers, and reacts. We will only briefly point out in passing the insurmountable difficulties which the attempt to personify Ideas thus would encounter if there were any question of determining the relation between the Ideas so personified and the changing course of the world; it would immediately appear that these could as little do without the additions necessary to transform them into suffering and acting beings as the World-Order to which we have before referred.

Yet the transference of the conditions of finite personality to the personality of the Infinite is not justified. For we must guard ourselves against seeking in the alien nature of the external world, in the fact that it is *Non*-Ego, the source of the strength with which it calls out the development of the Ego; it operates only by bringing to the finite mind stimuli which occasion the activity, which that mind cannot produce from its own nature. It is involved in the notion of a finite being that it has its definite place in the whole, and thus that it is not what any other is, and yet that at the same time it must as a member of the whole in its whole development be related to and must harmonize with that other. Even for the finite being the forms of its activity flow from its own inner nature, and neither the content of its sensations nor its feelings, nor the peculiarity of any other of its manifestations, is given to it from without; but the incitements of its action certainly all come to it from that external world, to which, in consequence of the finiteness of its nature, it is related as a part, having the place, time, and character of its development marked out by the determining whole. The same consideration does not hold of the Infinite Being that comprehends in itself all that is finite, and is the cause of its nature and reality; this Infinite Being does not need—as we sometimes, with a strange perversion of the right point of view, think—that its life should be called forth by external stimuli, but from the beginning its concept is without that deficiency which seems to us to make such stimuli necessary for the finite being, and its active efficacy thinkable. The Infinite Being, not bound by any obligation to agree in any way with something not itself, will, with perfect self-sufficingness, possess in its own nature the causes of every step forward in the development of its life. An analogy which though weak yet holds in some important points and is to some extent an example of the thing itself, is furnished to us by the course of memory in the finite mind. The world of our ideas, though certainly called into existence at first by external impressions, spreads out into a stream which, without any fresh stimulation from the external world, produces plenty that is new by the continuous action and reaction of its own movements, and carries out in works of imagination, in the results reached by reflexion, and in the conflicts of passion, a great amount of living development—as much, that is, as can be reached by the nature of a finite being without incessantly renewed orientation, by action and reaction with the whole in which it is comprehended; hence the removal of these limits of finiteness does not involve the removal of any producing condition of personality which is not compensated for by the self-sufficingness of the Infinite, but that which is only approximately possible for the finite mind, the conditioning of its life by itself, takes place without limit in God, and no contrast of an external world is necessary for Him.

Of course there remains the question what it is that in God corresponds to the primary impulse which the train of ideas in a finite mind receives from the external world. But the very question involves the answer. For when through the impulse received from without there is imparted to the inner life of the mind an initiatory movement which it subsequently carries on by its own strength, whence comes the movement in the external world which makes it capable of giving that impulse? A brief consideration will suffice to convince us that our theory of the cosmos, whatever it may be, must somehow and somewhere recognize the actual movement itself as an originally given reality, and can never succeed in extracting it from rest. And this indication may suffice for the present, since we wish here to avoid increasing our present difficulties by entering upon the question as to the nature of time. When we characterize the inner life of the Personal God, the current of His thoughts, His feelings, and His will, as everlasting and without beginning, as having never known rest, and having never been roused to movement from some state of quiescence, we call upon imagination to perform a task no other and no greater than that which is required from it by every materialistic or pantheistic view. Without an eternal uncaused movement of the World-Substance, or the assumption of definite initial movements of the countless world-atoms, movements which have to be simply recognized and accepted, neither materialistic nor pantheistic views could attain to any explanation of the existing cosmic course, and all parties will be at last driven to the conviction that the splitting up of reality into a quiescent being and a movement which subsequently takes hold of it, is one of those fictions which, while they are of some use in the ordinary business of reflexion, betray their total inadmissibility as soon as we attempt to rise above the reciprocal connexion of cosmic particulars to our first notions of the cosmos as a whole.

The ordinary doubts as to the possibility of the personal existence of the Infinite have not made us waver in our conviction. But in seeking to refute them, we have had the feeling that we were occupying a standpoint which could only be regarded as resulting from the strangest perversion of all natural relations. The course of development of philosophic thought has put us who live in this age in the position of being obliged to show that the conditions of personality which we meet with in finite things, are not lacking to the Infinite; whereas the natural concatenation of the matter under discussion would lead us to show that of the full personality which is possible only for the Infinite a feeble reflexion is given also to the finite; for the characteristics peculiar to the finite are not producing conditions of self-existence, but obstacles to its unconditioned development, although we are accustomed, unjustifiably, to deduce from these characteristics its capacity of personal existence. The finite being always works with powers with which it did not endow itself, and according to laws which it did not establish—that is, it works by means of a mental organization which is realized not only in it but also in innumerable similar beings. Hence in reflecting on self, it may easily seem to it as though there were in itself some obscure and unknown substance—something which is in the Ego though it is not the Ego itself, and to which, as to its subject, the whole personal development is attached. And hence there arise the questions —never to be quite silenced—What are we ourselves? What is our soul? What is our self—that obscure being, incomprehensible to ourselves, that stirs in our feelings and our passions, and never rises into complete self-consciousness? The fact that these questions can arise shows how far personality is from being developed in us to the extent which its notion admits and requires. It can be perfect only in the Infinite Being which, in surveying all its conditions or actions, never finds any content of that which it suffers or any law of its working, the meaning and origin of which are not transparently plain to it, and capable of being explained by reference to its own nature. Further, the position of the finite mind, which attaches it as a constituent of the whole to some definite place in the cosmic order, requires that its inner life should be awakened by successive stimuli from without, and that its course should proceed according to the laws of a psychical mechanism, in obedience to which individual ideas, feelings, and efforts press upon and supplant one another. Hence the whole self can never be brought together at one moment, our self-consciousness never presents to us a complete and perfect picture of our Ego—not even of its whole nature at any moment, and much less of the unity of its development in time. We always appear to ourselves from a one-sided point of view, due to those mental events which happen to be taking place within us at the time—a point of view which only admits of our surveying a small part of our being; we always react upon the stimuli which reach us, in accordance with the one-sided impulses of this accidental and partial self-consciousness; it is only to a limited extent that we can say with truth that *we* act; for the most part action is carried on in us by the individual feelings or groups of ideas to which at any moment the psychical mechanism gives the upper hand. Still less do we exist wholly *for ourselves* in a temporal point of view. There is much that disappears from memory, but most of all individual moods, that escape it by degrees. There are many regions of thought in which while young we were quite at home, which in age we can only bring before our mind as alien phenomena; feelings in which we once revelled with enthusiasm we can now hardly recover at all, we can now hardly realize even a pale reflexion of the power which they once exercised over us; endeavours which once seemed to constitute the most inalienable essence of our Ego seem, when we reach the path along which later life conducts us, to be unintelligible aberrations, the incentives to which we can no longer understand. In point of fact we have little ground for speaking of the personality of finite beings; it is an ideal, which, like all that is ideal, belongs unconditionally only to the Infinite, but like all that is good appertains to us only conditionally and hence imperfectly.

The more simple content of this section hardly needs the brief synoptical repetition in which we now proceed to gather up its results and to add them to those already reached.

Selfhood, the essence of all personality, does not depend upon any opposition that either has happened or is happening of the Ego to a

Non-Ego, but it consists in an immediate self-existence which constitutes the basis of the possibility of that contrast wherever it appears.
Self-consciousness is the elucidation of this self-existence which is
brought about by means of knowledge, and even this is by no means
necessarily bound up with the distinction of the Ego from a Non-Ego
which is substantially opposed to it.

In the nature of the finite mind as such is to be found the reason why
the development of its personal consciousness can take place only
through the influences of that cosmic whole which the finite being
itself is not, that is through stimulation coming from the Non-Ego, not
because it needs the contrast with something *alien* in order to have self-
existence, but because in this respect, as in every other, it does not
contain in itself the conditions of its existence. We do not find this
limitation in the being of the Infinite; hence for it alone is there possible
a self-existence, which needs neither to be initiated nor to be continuously developed by something not itself, but which maintains itself
within itself with spontaneous action that is eternal and had no
beginning.

Perfect Personality is in God only, to all finite minds there is allotted
but a pale copy thereof; the finiteness of the finite is not a producing
condition of this Personality but a limit and a hindrance of its development.

Mikrokosmus (1854–6) (trans. Elizabeth Hamilton and Constance Jones)

CHAPTER 6

RITSCHL

Born in Berlin in 1822, Albrecht Ritschl, the most influential of nineteenth-century German theologians, studied at the universities of Bonn, Halle, Heidelberg and Tübingen, at the first of which he was appointed professor in 1852. In 1864 he moved to Göttingen. Like most of his contemporaries he came under Hegelian influence, particularly from the radical Tübingen school of New Testament critics led by F. C. Baur. A work on the gospels of Mark and Luke published in 1846 revealed him as among Baur's closest followers, but in the ensuing years his enthusiasm for Hegelian principles waned, as is clear from the considerably revised second edition (1857) of his *Entstehung der altkatholische Kirche*. Ritschl's thinking now bore the marks of Kant and Schleiermacher, but the culminating influence was to be that of Rudolf Lotze, apparent in all his major publications. Most important of these is *Die christliche Lehre von der Rechtfertigung und der Versöhnung* (1870–4; 2nd ed., 1882; 4th ed., 1895–1902), the work on which his reputation as a theologian largely rests, although *Die Geschichte des Pietismus* (1880–6), *Über die christliche Vollkommenheit* (1874)—a study of 'Christian perfection'—and *Theologie und Metaphysik* (1881) are also noteworthy. His *Unterricht in die christliche Religion* (1875) is a summary, none too lucid, of his general theological position. Ritschl found Göttingen much to his liking and subsequent calls to Strasbourg and Berlin were refused. He died in 1889, after a lifetime as little remarkable for external event—apart from theological controversy, which he relished—as that of Kant himself.

The character of Ritschl's theology is determined by its apologetic aim: namely, to justify religious belief in an age of positive science. This was to be achieved by the total severance of religion from theoretical knowledge; but unlike Kant, Ritschl will accept no subordination of religion to morality: on the contrary, it is as independent of ethics as it is of speculative philosophy. And to the latter certainly he allows no place. The test of faith is pragmatic; the solution of the intellectual problem which religion poses—that of resolving 'the contradiction in which man finds himself as both a part of the natural world and a spiritual personality claiming to rule nature'—cannot be a matter of abstract necessity. What man seeks in religion is the attainment of a *personal* good. All religions show that 'the knowledge of the world made use of in them is not constituted theoretically, without interest, but according to practical objects'. This practical incentive finds its highest expression in Christianity, 'the monotheistic, completely spiritual and ethical religion' based on the life of its founder, Jesus of Nazareth, by whom was established that Kingdom of God whose end is the pardon of sinners, the motivation of conduct by love and the deepening of men's sense of filial relation to God.

Plainly then all merely speculative concern is irrelevant. Spiritual reality must be apprehended empirically; it cannot be comprehended rationally. Contrary to Hegel's view, it is the *Vorstellung*, the 'representation', which is possible; the *Begriff*, the 'abstract idea', is beyond our grasp. Ritschl goes on to invoke a theory of knowledge which he derives, somewhat uncritically, from Kant and Lotze and which has more the appearance of an apologetic device than of an independent and consistent doctrine. But although we cannot pass from the 'phenomenal' to the 'noumenal' the reality or objectivity of the noumenal is not, he thinks, open to doubt. If we do not understand God's intrinsic nature we may yet discern him in his actions. Similarly we can recognize the work of Christ without resort to metaphysical explanations of his person. What matters is the impact of his moral personality, historically testified, upon our own.

Ritschl's theology has little in common with the pantheistic immanentism favoured by many nineteenth-century thinkers. He taught a personal theism grounded in man's experience as a moral being, and although he denies the competence of speculative philosophy in the theological realm he is ready to defend the theistic position—as against the objections of D. F. Strauss, for example—by the familiar rational arguments. It is never quite clear, in fact, whether Ritschl's idea of God is purely 'practical', in the Kantian sense, or in the last resort a matter of theoretically valid knowledge. He describes it, in a term with which the Ritschlian theology is especially associated, as a 'value-judgement' (*Werthurtheile*), by which he means the affirmation of 'an essential belief in the good and the possibility of attaining it'. The word 'God' signifies the good and the influence which moves us to pursue it. It is right to say that God is love, love being both the foundation and the consummation of the good. But what he is 'in himself' we do not know and metaphysics cannot tell us. The one justification for speaking of God is the vital experience we have of him.

Surprisingly, however, Ritschl had no interest in mysticism and suspected its claims. Mystical revelations he thought were too various, too uncertain and possibly too bizarre in content either for the grounding of belief or for moral guidance. Himself of a practical and rather prosaic nature, Ritschl had very little sympathy with pietism or religious emotionalism of any sort. The one sure basis of faith was the example of the historic Jesus, whose unique consciousness of God is our only standard and model. The Christian revelation is essentially a historical one, and Ritschl relies heavily on the testimony of history as embodied in the New Testament. He was well aware of the extent to which the credibility of the gospel tradition had been impugned by Strauss and the Tübingen critics, yet he assumes that its authenticity is sufficient to give us the needed insight into Jesus' own mind. Neither Church nor dogma nor even a verbally guaranteed Bible, but Christ alone is the believer's authority, as he meets him, not in some 'illuministic' inner sanctuary of personal devotion, but in a positive historical record. The position is one that many would judge precarious, yet upon it the whole Ritschlian doctrine is made to rest. For the facts, Ritschl held, are objective and unassailable. They are the data which theology interprets in its value-judgements.

Ritschl's *Christian Doctrine of Justification and Reconciliation*, or rather its third volume, the first two being historical and exegetical in scope, is one of the outstanding theological treatises of the nineteenth century. By giving centrality to the doctrine of Christ's work the author presents a theological scheme differing markedly from the traditional expositions. He breaks with what he considered the arbitrary and fruitless method of propounding theological ideas in logical sequence and falls back on the facts of experience. What is needed is a *scientific* theology based on man's conviction of sin and desire for redemption, things which constitute the substance of the religious life. The evidence of psychology and history cannot be denied, and although value-judgements are not scientific in form they none the less are truth-conveying.

Ritschl's project, however, fell short of its aim. Apart from the difficulties involved in its historical positivism, the delimiting of revelation to the Judaeo-Christian tradition and the author's lack of interest in non-Christian religions meant that no adequate account could be offered of religious experience as an evidently universal phenomenon in the life of mankind. Ritschl's inability to appreciate the nature and incidence of mysticism is a further weakness. Yet his refusal to allow religious experience to be equated with its intellectual forms can hardly fail to evoke sympathy. In arguing that religious truth is pragmatic and not theoretical and that the dynamic of faith declines under pressure of logical inferences he has helped to set theological thought upon a course from which it is unlikely again to deviate far.

Bibliographical note

There is no collected edition of Ritschl's works. *The Christian Doctrine of Justification and Reconciliation*, translated by J. S. Black (1872) and edited by H. R. Mackintosh and A. B. Macaulay (1900; 2nd ed., 1902) has been long out of print. On the Ritschlian theology see A. E. Garvie, *The Ritschlian Theology* (1899), J. K. Mozley *Ritschlianism* (1909), E. A. Edghill, *Faith and Fact: a Study of Ritschlianism* (1910), H. R. Mackintosh, *Types of Modern Theology* (1937) and Karl Barth, *From Rousseau to Ritschl* (1959).

I. GOD AND METAPHYSICS

There are no sufficient grounds for combining a theory of things in general with the conception of God. That is done, however, when Aristotle gives the name God to the idea of the highest end which he postulates as winding up the cosmic series of means and ends, and so as an expression of the unity of the world. This conjunction of the two forms the content of the teleological argument for God's existence constructed by Scholastic theology. We have a similar case in the cosmological argument. It exhibits a metamorphosis of the Neo-platonic view of the world, which rests merely upon the idea of things and their causal connexion. Now in religion the thought of God is given. But the religious view of the world, in all its species, rests on the fact that man in some degree distinguishes himself in worth from the phenomena which surround him and from the influences of nature which press in upon him. All religion is equivalent to an explanation of the course of the world—to whatever extent it may be known—in the sense that the sublime spiritual powers (or the spiritual power) which rule in or over it, conserve and confirm to the personal spirit its claims and its independence over-against the restrictions of nature and the natural effects of human society. Thus the thought of God, when by the word is understood conscious personality, lies beyond the horizon of metaphysic, as metaphysic is defined above. And both these proofs for God's existence, whose construction is purely metaphysical, lead not to the Being the idea of which Scholastic theology receives as a datum from Christianity, but merely to conceptions of the world-unity which have nothing to do with any religion. This use of meta-physic, consequently, must be forbidden in theology, if the latter's positive and proper character is to be maintained.

The Christian Doctrine of Justification and Reconciliation (1870–4)
(trans. J. S. Black, ed. H. R. Mackintosh and A. B. Macaulay)

II. THE SPECIAL CHARACTER OF RELIGIOUS KNOWLEDGE

In every religion what is sought, with the help of the superhuman spiritual power reverenced by man, is a solution of the contradiction in which man finds himself, as both a part of the world of nature and a spiritual personality claiming to dominate nature. For in the former *rôle* he is a part of nature, dependent upon her, subject to and confined by other things; but as spirit he is moved by the impulse to maintain his independence against them. In this juncture, religion springs up as faith in superhuman spiritual powers, by whose help the power which man possesses of himself is in some way supplemented, and elevated into a unity of its own kind which is a match for the pressure of the natural world. The idea of gods, or Divine powers, everywhere includes belief in their spiritual personality, for the support to be received from above can only be reckoned on in virtue of an affinity between God and men. Even where merely invisible natural powers are regarded as Divine, they are conceived in a way analogous to that in which man distinguishes himself from nature. For the rest, the ease with which definite stupendous natural phenomena, whether beneficent or destructive, are personified, proves that it is in the spiritual personality of the gods that man finds the foothold which he seeks for in every religion. The assertion that the religious view of the world is founded upon the idea of a whole[1] certainly holds true of Christianity: as regards the other religions it must be modified thus far, that in them what is sought is a supplementary addition to human self-feeling or to human independence over against and above the restrictions of the world. For in order to know the world as a totality, and in order himself to become a totality in or over it by the help of God, man needs the idea of the oneness of God, and of the consummation of the world in an end which is for man both knowable and realizable. But this condition is fulfilled in Christianity alone....

★   ★   ★

How, then, is *religious knowledge* related to theoretical or philosophical knowledge? This question, indeed, has already been raised by the very fact of Greek Philosophy; still, much more tangible and comprehensive reasons for raising it are to be found in the mutual relations of Christianity and philosophy. Accordingly, it is best that we should limit the question to Christianity in so far as it is a religion, intelligible as such from the characteristics noted above. The possibility of both kinds of knowledge mingling, or, again, colliding, lies in this, that they deal with the same object, namely, the world. Now we cannot rest content with the amiable conclusion that Christian knowledge comprehends the world as a whole, while philosophy fixes the special and universal

---

[1] Lotze, *Mikrokosmus*, III, 331.

laws of nature and spirit. For with this task every philosophy likewise combines the ambition to comprehend the universe under one supreme law. And for Christian knowledge also one supreme law is the form under which the world is comprehensible as a whole under God. Even the thought of God, which belongs to religion, is employed in some shape or other by every non-materialistic philosophy. Thus no principle of discrimination between the two kinds of knowledge is, at least provisionally, to be found in the object with which they deal.

Now, in order to elicit the distinction between the two from the realm of the subject, I recall the twofold manner in which the mind (*Geist*) further appropriates the sensations aroused in it. They are determined, according to their value for the Ego, by the feeling of pleasure or pain. Feeling is the basal function of mind, inasmuch as in it the Ego is originally present to itself. In the feeling of pleasure or pain, the Ego decides whether a sensation, which touches the feeling of self, serves to heighten or depress it. On the other hand, through an idea the sensation is judged in respect of its cause, the nature of the latter, and its connexion with other causes: and by means of observation, etc., the knowledge of things thus gained is extended until it becomes scientific. The two functions of spirit mentioned are always in operation simultaneously, and always also in some degree mutually related, even though it be in the inverse ratio of prominence. In particular, it must not be forgotten that all continuous cognition of the things which excite sensation is not only accompanied, but likewise guided, by feeling. For in so far as attention is necessary to attain the end of knowledge, will, as representing the desire for accurate cognition, comes in between; the proximate cause of will, however, is feeling as expressing the consciousness that a thing or an activity is worth desiring, or that something ought to be put away. Value-judgements therefore are determinative in the case of all connected knowledge of the world, even when carried out in the most objective fashion. Attention during scientific observation, and the impartial examination of the matter observed, always denote that such knowledge has a value for him who employs it. This fact makes its presence all the more distinctly felt when knowledge is guided through a richly diversified field by attention of a technical or practical kind.

But even if we have made up our mind that religious knowledge in general, and therefore Christian knowledge too, consists of value-judgements, such a definition is as lacking in precision as it would be to describe philosophical knowledge contrariwise as disinterested. For without interest we do not trouble ourselves about anything. We have therefore to distinguish between *concomitant* and *independent* value-judgements. The former are operative and necessary in all theoretical cognition, as in all technical observation and combination. But *independent* value-judgements are all perceptions of moral ends or moral hindrances, in so far as they excite moral pleasure or pain, or, it may be, set in motion the will to appropriate what is good or repel the opposite. If the other kinds of knowledge are called 'disinterested', this only means that they are without these moral effects. But even in them pleasure or pain must be present, according as they succeed or fail. Religious knowledge forms another class of independent value-judgements. That is, it cannot be traced back to the conditions which mark the knowledge belonging to moral will, for there exists religion which goes on without any relation whatever to the moral conduct of life. Besides, in many religions religious pleasure is of a purely natural kind, and is independent of those conditions which lift religious above natural pleasure. For only at the higher stages do we find religion combined with the ethical conduct of life. Religious knowledge moves in independent value-judgements, which relate to man's attitude to the world, and call forth feelings of pleasure or pain, in which man either enjoys the dominion over the world vouchsafed him by God, or feels grievously the lack of God's help to that end. This theory is almost more easily intelligible if it be tested by religions which possess no moral character. Orgiastic worships represent contending natural feelings with extraordinary intensity and with abrupt changes, in virtue of their recognition of the value which the identity of the Godhead with the vegetation as it decays and again revives, has for the man who modifies his attitude towards the world of nature in sympathy with the Godhead which he adores. The peculiar nature of religious value-judgements is less clear in the case of religions of an explicitly ethical character. Nevertheless, in Christianity we can distinguish between the religious functions which relate to our attitude towards God and the world, and the moral functions which point directly to men, and only indirectly to God, Whose end in the world we fulfil by moral service in the Kingdom of God. In Christianity, the religious motive of ethical action lies here, that the Kingdom of God, which it is our task to realize, represents also the highest good which God destines for us as our supramundane goal. For here there emerges the value-judgement that our blessedness consists in that elevation above the world in the Kingdom of God which accords with our true destiny. This is a religious judgement, inasmuch as it indicates the value of this attitude taken up by believers towards the world, just as those judgements are religious in which we set our trust in God, even when He condemns us to suffering.

In its day the Hegelian philosophy represented theoretical knowledge as not merely the most valuable function of spirit, but likewise the function which has to take up the problem of religion and solve it. To this Feuerbach opposed the observation that in religion the chief stress falls upon the wishes and needs of the human heart. But as the latter philosopher also continued to regard professedly pure and disinterested knowledge as the highest achievement of man, religion, and especially the Christian religion—which he held to be the expression of a purely individual and therefore egoistic interest, and a self-delusion in respect of its object, God—was by him declared to be worthless, as compared not merely with the knowledge of philosophic truth, but also with purely moral conduct. But an interest in salvation in the Christian sense, when rightly understood, is incompatible with egoism. Egoism is a revolt against the common tasks of action. Now, people might say that faith in God for our salvation, and a dutiful public spirit towards our fellows, have nothing to do with one another, and that therefore there is no conceivable reason why religion, as a rule, should not be egoistic. But in Christianity precisely faith in God and moral duty within the Kingdom of God *are* related to one another. As a rule, therefore, it is impossible that Christian faith in God should be egoistic. On the other hand, theoretical knowledge in itself, as has been shown, is not disinterested; but moral conduct is still less so. For in the latter domain the vital point is that one realizes as one's own interest the interest of others to whom the service is rendered. The moral disposition can nowhere strike root save in such motives. It is true that, contrary to the rule, faith in God may be combined with egoistic arrogance towards others. But the same danger attaches to both of the other kinds of activity which have been compared. It is possible for one occupied with theoretical knowledge to be vain and haughty, and for one devoted to the moral service of others to be tyrannical or sycophantic.

Scientific knowledge is accompanied or guided by a judgement affirming the worth of impartial knowledge gained by observation. In

Christianity, religious knowledge consists in independent value-judgements, inasmuch as it deals with the relation between the blessedness which is assured by God and sought by man, and the whole of the world which God has created and rules in harmony with His final end. Scientific knowledge seeks to discover the laws of nature and spirit through observation, and is based on the presupposition that both the observations and their arrangement are carried out in accordance with the ascertained laws of human cognition. Now the desire for scientific knowledge carries with it no guarantee that, through the medium of observation and the combination of observations according to known laws, it will discover the supreme universal law of the world, from which, as a starting-point, the differentiated orders of nature and spiritual life, each in its kind, might be explained, and understood as forming one whole. On the contrary, the intermingling and collision of religion and philosophy always arises from the fact that the latter claims to produce in its own fashion a unified view of the world. This, however, betrays rather an impulse religious in its nature, which philosophers ought to have distinguished from the cognitive methods they follow. For in all philosophical systems the affirmation of a supreme law of existence, from which they undertake to deduce the world as a whole, is a departure from the strict application of the philosophic method, and betrays itself as being quite as much an object of the intuitive imagination, as God and the world are for religious thought. This is the case at all stages and in all forms of Greek philosophy, especially in those forms in which the ultimate universal grounds of existence, through which the universe is interpreted, are identified with the idea of God. In these cases the combination of heterogeneous kinds of knowledge—the religious and the scientific—is beyond all doubt; and it is to be explained by the fact that philosophers who, through their scientific observation of nature, had destroyed the foundations of the popular faith, sought to obtain satisfaction for their religious instincts by another path. In a certain respect, too, they were able to follow this tendency with especial confidence, so far as they succeeded in making out the unity of the Divine Being to be the ground of the universe. But in another respect they failed to satisfy the essential conditions of the religious view of the world, partly in so far as they surrendered the personality of the Godhead thus identified with the ground of the world, partly because they had to give up the active influence of a personal God upon the world. Nor, under these circumstances, could any worship be deduced from the idea of God. Thus the collision of Greek philosophy with the popular faith was twofold, and in both respects inevitable. For one thing, the actual observation of nature and her laws is incompatible with the religious combination of popular views of nature and the idea of God. Further, the rigidly unified view of the world held by philosophers is incompatible with the religious view of the world which is only loosely developed in polytheism. But the real force of the latter incompatibility is to be found in the fact that, under the guise of philosophic knowledge, what was really only the religious imagination has been operative in designing the general philosophic view of the world, the supreme principle of which is never proved as such, but always merely anticipatively assumed.

The Christian Doctrine of Justification and Reconciliation (1870–4)
(trans. J. S. Black, ed. H. R. Mackintosh and A. B. Macaulay)

III. VALUE-JUDGEMENTS

When we mark the attitude taken up by the human spirit towards the world of nature, two analogous facts present themselves. In theoretical knowledge, spirit treats nature as something which exists for it; while in the practical sphere of the will, too, it treats nature as something which is directly a means to the realization of the common ethical end which forms the final end of the world. The cognitive impulse and the will both take this course without regard to the fact that nature is subject to quite other laws than those which spirit obeys, that it is independent of spirit, and that it forms a restraint on spirit, and so far keeps it in a certain way in dependence on itself. Hence we must conclude either that the estimate which spirit, as a power superior to nature, forms of its own worth—in particular, the estimate which it forms of moral fellowship, which transcends nature—is a baseless fancy, or that the view taken by spirit is in accordance with truth and with the supreme law which is valid for nature as well. If that be so, then its ground must lie in a Divine Will, which creates the world with spiritual life as its final end. To accept the idea of God in this way is, as Kant observes, practical faith, and not an act of theoretical cognition. While, therefore, the Christian religion is thereby proved to be in harmony with reason, it is always with the reservation that knowledge of God embodies itself in judgements which differ in kind from those of theoretical science.

The meaning, therefore, of this moral argument for the necessity of the thought of God differs altogether from the aim of the other arguments; and for that reason the success it attains surpasses that of the others. The cosmological and teleological arguments are intended to show that the conception of God—necessary to complete the circle of knowledge—is similar in kind to the results of science. A truth which for religious faith is certain is thus proved, it is held, to be at the same time the result of scientific cognition as it advances from observation to observation and crystallizes into conclusions, and should be set up as the criterion of theological science. But this method ends in failure, partly because neither argument takes us beyond the limits of the world, partly because their pretended results, even if they were correct, differ from the Christian conception of God in this, that they fail to express His worth for men, and in particular His worth for men as sinners. On the other hand, while Kant regards practical faith in God, conceived as endowed with the attributes which Christianity ascribes to Him, as necessary to complete our knowledge of the world, yet he does not posit this idea—which is an object merely of practical faith, and cannot be proved apart from such faith—as a conception which is theoretical or rational in the sense of general science. On the contrary, he maintains it in its original and specific character. Now it is the duty of theology to conserve the special characteristic of the conception of God, namely, that it can only be represented in value-judgements. Consequently it ought to base its claim to be a science, when looked at in itself, on the use of the method described above, and, when looked at in its relation to other sciences, by urging that, as Kant was the first to show, the Christian view of God and the world enables us comprehensively to unify our knowledge of nature and the spiritual life of man in a way which otherwise is impossible. When we have once got a true conception of this point, a review of the moral constitution of man, based upon the principles of Kant, will serve as the *ratio cognoscendi* of the validity of the Christian idea of God when employed as the solution of the enigma of the world.

The Christian Doctrine of Justification and Reconciliation (1870-4)
(trans. J. S. Black, ed. H. R. Mackintosh and A. B. Macaulay)

CHAPTER 7

HARNACK

Harnack's lectures on the 'essence' of Christianity were delivered at the University of Berlin during the winter of 1899–1900 and published shortly afterwards. Their success was immediate and *Das Wesen des Christenthums* was repeatedly reprinted and translated. The widespread controversy it aroused was but further testimony to its importance as an expression of current liberal Protestantism. The deep sincerity of its author, one of the most eminent scholars of his generation, combined with the simplicity and directness of its approach, marked it out from the first as a work of historic significance. This reputation it has maintained, even if it is seldom read today. (The English translation, *What is Christianity?*, by T. B. Saunders has, however, been reprinted in recent years in two different editions.) As a document of late nineteenth-century religious thought it is of the highest interest.

Adolf von Harnack—he was ennobled in 1914 by the Kaiser Wilhelm II—was born at Dorpat in Estonia in 1851, the son of a professor of pastoral theology. He studied at the university of Leipzig, later joining its teaching staff. He himself occupied professorial chairs, first at Giessen (1879) and Marburg (1886) and then, with international fame, at Berlin (1889–1924). From 1905 until 1921 he was Director of the Prussian National Library and for ten years (1902–12) President of the Evangelical Church Congress. He died in 1930.

His *opus magnum* is his monumental *Lehrbuch der Dogmengeschichte* (1886–90; 6th ed., 1922; reprinted 1963), an English translation of which was completed in 1899. This elaborately detailed historical survey, covering the development of Christian doctrine from its beginnings to the Reformation of the sixteenth century, contains the thesis that primitive Christian belief became increasingly distorted under Hellenistic influences and that it is precisely the effect of this process which renders Christianity unacceptable to the modern mind, a view of which *What is Christianity?* was but a popular exposition. Among Harnack's many other works of historical scholarship are his *Geschichte der altchristlichen Literatur bis Eusebius* (1893–1904; 2nd ed., K. Aland, 1958), *Die Mission und Ausbreitung des Christenthums in der drei ersten Jahrhunderten* (1902; Eng. trans. 1904–5), and *Beiträge zur Einleitung in der Neue Testament* (1906–11), some of which, such as the well-known *Luke the Physician* (1907), also appeared in English.

In *What is Christianity?* Harnack sets himself the task, not as a theologian, for that he did not profess to be, but as a historian, employing the objective methods of historical science 'and the experience of life gained by studying the actual course of history'. The answer he gives to his question is short and simple: the essence of Christianity is the gospel, as found in the historic life and teaching of Jesus of Nazareth. Here we have a kernel of precious spiritual truth from which the husk of dogma and ecclesiastical polity must be removed. The written gospels themselves contain a good deal of extraneous matter in the way of 'Jewish limitations' and this too must be set aside. That Jesus himself taught the coming of the 'Kingdom of God' is indubitable, but his own personal conception of it and that of his contemporaries were by no means identical. Apocalyptic ideas he would have imbibed from his early religious environment and he used them in presenting his own message; but at the heart of the latter lay the conviction that the Kingdom 'cometh not with observation', but as an experience for the individual, 'by entering his soul and laying hold of it'. The burden of Jesus' preaching can be stated in a few words: God is our Father and the human soul may be 'so ennobled that it can and does unite with him'. Hence the relevance of the gospel for individualistic modern man. What Jesus sought to kindle was *personal* faith. He never 'had anyone but the individual in mind, and the abiding disposition of the heart in love'.

But what of Jesus' own position in regard to his gospel? Here again no real difficulty presents itself. The metaphysical Christology devised by the Fathers of the early Church must be discounted. Jesus, Harnack allows, was assuredly 'Son of God' in that no man has ever attained to a like consciousness of God within himself. 'Rightly understood, the name of Son means nothing but the knowledge of God.' It is thus that his Messiahship is to be explained: the sense of divine Sonship naturally led him to a conviction of his own Messianic role. But the theology subsequently read into this historically conditioned belief is an excrescence. 'The Gospel is no theoretical system of doctrine or philosophy of the universe; it is a doctrine only in so far as it proclaims the reality of God the Father.' The gradual metamorphosis of this uncomplicated teaching into the Catholicism of later ages is clearly traceable. The religion of 'strong feeling', of the 'heart', became the religion of 'custom' and so of 'forms' and of 'law'. Its eventual embodiment in the outward and visible institution of a church claiming divine dignity has in the gospel no foundation whatever. 'It is a case, not of distortion, but of total perversion.' Reformation Protestantism had halted this inordinate growth and reduced Christianity to its 'essential factors', the Word of God and faith. But the Protestant movement had itself been arrested; catholicizing elements remained which would have to be swept away if the religion of the spirit were finally to be delivered from the bonds of dogma, ordinance and ceremony.

The appeal of liberal Protestantism to an age rendered sceptical of traditional supernaturalist religion but still feeling the need of a religious faith and an ethical ideal is obvious. It extolled Christian morality whilst thrusting creeds and ecclesiasticism aside. The challenge it presented to Catholicism—as no less to orthodox Protestantism—was therefore formidable. A refutation of Harnack's argument was undertaken by a French Catholic priest and biblical scholar, Alfred Loisy (1857–1940), of the Paris Institut Catholique, whose brilliant reply, *L'Évangile et l'Église*, appeared in 1902. Harnack had invoked the judgement of history in his attempt to determine Christianity's essence and Loisy, confident of a different verdict, took him at his word. What, then, did history prove? That Jesus of Nazareth did not teach only a simple humanitarian ethic tinged with religious emotion but, as Johannes Weiss and Schweitzer had lately demonstrated, the coming of a supernatural 'Kingdom of God'—an other-worldly, eschatological hope, disappointed no doubt as to the form in which it was expected to be realized but certainly achieved in the historic existence of the Catholic Church. Of Harnack's individualist piety the gospel knows nothing, and the Christ which it presents does not divide his teaching into two categories, 'the one comprising all that had an absolute value, the other all that had only a relative value, fitted to the present time'. Rather must we see the absolute under the shape of the relative. The gospel entered the world not as 'a unique and steadfast truth' but as a living faith, a dynamic idea. The vital seed, planted in the soil of historical conditions, became by a natural evolution the complex structure of belief and organization which the world now sees. 'To reprove the Catholic Church for the development of her constitution is to reproach her for having chosen to live.'

Loisy's account of the eventual outcome of New Testament Christianity may be deemed a more realistic answer to Harnack's question than that of the Lutheran scholar himself. The Christian religion, as a human phenomenon, certainly reveals a pragmatic development. Harnack's book, however, is an estimate less of fact than of value, and although the evaluation is open to challenge it cannot, without frivolity, be dismissed.

Bibliographical note

Recent editions of the English translation of *What is Christianity?* are those respectively of R. Bultmann (1957) and W. R. Matthews (1958). There is an account of Harnack's life and work by Agnes von Zahn-Harnack (1936). See also J. de Ghellinck, *Patristique et Moyen-âge*, vol. III (1948), Étude iii, pp. 1–102. An English translation of Loisy's *L'Évangile et l'Église*, by C. Home, appeared in 1903.

I. JESUS' ESSENTIAL TEACHING

God the Father and the infinite value of the human soul

To our modern way of thinking and feeling, Christ's message appears in the clearest and most direct light when grasped in connexion with the idea of God the Father and the infinite value of the human soul. Here the elements which I would describe as the restful and rest-giving in Jesus' message, and which are comprehended in the idea of our being children of God, find expression. I call them *restful* in contrast with the impulsive and stirring elements; although it is just they that are informed with a special strength. But the fact that the whole of Jesus' message may be reduced to these two heads—God as the Father, and the human soul so ennobled that it can and does unite with him—shows us that the Gospel is in no-wise a positive religion like the rest; that it contains no statutory or particularistic elements; *that it is, there-fore, religion itself.* It is superior to all antithesis and tension between this world and a world to come, between reason and ecstasy, between work and isolation from the world, between Judaism and Hellenism. It can dominate them all, and there is no factor of earthly life to which it is confined or necessarily tied down. Let us, however, get a clearer idea of what being children of God, in Jesus' sense, means, by briefly considering four groups containing sayings of his, or, as the case may be, a single saying, viz.: (1) The Lord's Prayer; (2) that utterance, 'Rejoice not that the spirits are subject unto you; but rather rejoice because your names are written in heaven'; (3) the saying, 'Are not two sparrows sold for a farthing? and one of them shall not fall to the ground without your Father. But the very hairs of your head are all numbered'; (4) the utterance, 'What shall it profit a man if he shall gain the whole world and lose his own soul?'

Let us take the Lord's Prayer first. It was communicated by Jesus to his disciples at a particularly solemn moment. They had asked him to teach them how to pray, as John the Baptist had taught his disciples. Thereupon he uttered the Lord's Prayer. It is by their prayers that the character of the higher religions is determined. But this prayer was spoken—as every one must feel who has ever given it a thought in his soul—by one who has overcome all inner unrest, or overcomes it the moment that he goes before God. The very apostrophe of the prayer, 'Our Father', exhibits the steady faith of the man who knows that he is safe in God, and it tells us that he is certain of being heard. Not to hurl violent desires at heaven or to obtain this or that earthly blessing does he pray, but to preserve the power which he already possesses and strengthen the union with God in which he lives. No one, then, can utter this prayer unless his heart is in profound peace and his mind wholly concentrated on the inner relation of the soul with God. All other prayers are of a lower order, for they contain particularistic elements, or are so framed that in some way or other they stir the imagination in regard to the things of sense as well; whilst this prayer leads us away from everything to the height where the soul is alone with its God. And yet the earthly element is not absent. The whole of the second half of the prayer deals with earthly relations, but they are placed in the light of the Eternal. In vain will you look for any request for particular gifts of grace, or special blessings, even of a spiritual kind. 'All else shall be added unto you.' The name of God, His will, and His kingdom—these elements of rest and permanence are poured out over the earthly relations as well. Everything that is small and selfish melts away, and only four things are left with regard to which it is worth while to pray—the daily bread, the daily trespass, the daily temptations, and the evil in life. There is nothing in the Gospels that tells us more certainly what the Gospel is, and what sort of disposition and temper it produces, than the Lord's Prayer. With this prayer we ought also to confront all those who disparage the Gospel by representing it as an ascetic or ecstatic or sociological pronouncement. It shows the Gospel to be the Fatherhood of God applied to the whole of life; to be an inner union with God's will and God's kingdom, and a joyous certainty of the possession of eternal blessings and protection from evil.

As to the second utterance: when Jesus says 'Rejoice not that the spirits are subject unto you; but rejoice rather that your names are written in heaven', it is another way of laying special emphasis on the idea that the all-important element in this religion is the consciousness of being safe in God. The greatest achievements, nay the very works which are done in the strength of this religion, fall below the assurance, at once humble and proud, of resting for time and eternity under the fatherly care of God. Moreover, the genuineness, nay the actual existence, of religious experience is to be measured, not by any transcendency of feeling nor by great deeds that all men can see, but by the joy and the peace which are diffused through the soul that can say 'My Father'.

6-2

How far did Christ carry this idea of the fatherly providence of God? Here we come to the third saying: 'Are not two sparrows sold for a farthing? and one of them shall not fall to the ground without your Father. But the very hairs of your head are all numbered.' The assurance that God rules is to go as far as our fears go, nay, as far as life itself —life down even to its smallest manifestations in the order of nature. It was to disabuse his disciples of the fear of evil and the terrors of death that he gave them the sayings about the sparrows and the flowers of the field; they are to learn how to see the hand of the living God everywhere in life, and in death too.

Finally, in asking—and after what has gone before the question will not sound surprising—'What shall it profit a man if he shall gain the whole world and lose his own soul?' he put a man's value as high as it can be put. The man who can say 'My Father' to the Being who rules heaven and earth, is thereby raised above heaven and earth, and himself has a value which is higher than all the fabric of this world. But this great saying took the stern tone of a warning. He offered them a gift and with it set them a task. How different was the Greek doctrine! Plato, it is true, had already sung the great hymn of the mind; he had distinguished it from the whole world of appearance and maintained its eternal origin. But the mind which he meant was the knowing mind; he contrasted it with blind, insensible matter; his message made its appeal to the wise. Jesus Christ calls to every poor soul; he calls to every one who bears a human face: You are children of the living God, and not only better than many sparrows but of more value than the whole world. The value of a truly great man, as I saw it put lately, consists in his increasing the value of all mankind. It is here, truly, that the highest significance of great men lies: to have enhanced, that is, to have progressively given effect to human value, to the value of that race of men which has risen up out of the dull ground of Nature. But Jesus Christ was the first to bring the value of every human soul to light, and what he did no one can any more undo. We may take up what relation to him we will: in the history of the past no one can refuse to recognize that it was he who raised humanity to this level.

This highest estimate of a man's value is based on a transvaluation of all values. To the man who boasts of his possessions he says: 'Thou fool.' He confronts everyone with the thought: 'Whosoever will lose his life shall save it.' He can even say: 'He that hateth his life in this world shall keep it unto life eternal.' This is the transvaluation of values of which many before him had a dim idea; of which they perceived the truth as through a veil; the redeeming power of which—that blessed mystery—they felt in advance. He was the first to give it calm, simple, and fearless expression, as though it were a truth which grew on every tree. It was just this that stamped his peculiar genius, that he gave perfectly simple expression to profound and all-important truths, as though they could not be otherwise; as though he were uttering something that was self-evident; as though he were only reminding men of what they all know already, because it lives in the innermost part of their souls.

In the combination of these ideas—God the Father, Providence, the position of men as God's children, the infinite value of the human soul —the whole Gospel is expressed. But we must recognize what a paradox it all is; nay, that the paradox of religion here for the first time finds its full expression. Measured by the experience of the senses and by exact knowledge, not only are the different religions a paradox, but so are all religious phenomena. They introduce an element, and pronounce it to be the most important of all, which is not cognizable by the senses and flies in the face of things as they are actually constituted. But all religions other than Christianity are in some way or other so bound up with the things of the world that they involve an element of earthly advantage, or, as the case may be, are akin in their substance to the intellectual and spiritual condition of a definite epoch. But what can be less obvious than the statement: the hairs of your head are all numbered; you have a supernatural value; you can put yourselves into the hands of a power which no one has seen? Either that is nonsense, or else it is the utmost development of which religion is capable; no longer a mere phenomenon accompanying the life of the senses, a coefficient, a transfiguration of certain parts of that life, but something which sets up a paramount title to be the first and the only fact that reveals the fundamental basis and meaning of life. Religion subordinates to itself the whole motley world of phenomena, and defies that world if it claims to be the only real one. Religion gives us only a single experience, but one which presents the world in a new light: the Eternal appears; time becomes means to an end; man is seen to be on the side of the Eternal. This was certainly Jesus' meaning, and to take anything from it is to destroy it. In applying the idea of Providence to the whole of humanity and the world without any exception; in showing that humanity is rooted in the Eternal; in proclaiming the fact that we are God's children as at once a gift and a task, he took a firm grip of all fumbling and stammering attempts at religion and brought them to their issue. Once more let it be said: we may assume what position we will in regard to him and his message, certain it is that thence onward the value of our race is enhanced; human lives, nay, we ourselves, have become dearer to one another. A man may know it or not, but a real reverence for humanity follows from the practical recognition of God as the Father of us all.

The higher righteousness and the commandment of love

This is the third head, and the whole of the Gospel is embraced under it. To represent the Gospel as an ethical message is no depreciation of its value. The ethical system which Jesus found prevailing in his nation was both ample and profound. To judge the moral ideas of the Pharisees solely by their childish and casuistical aspects is not fair. By being bound up with religious worship and petrified in ritual observance, the morality of holiness had, indeed, been transformed into something that was the clean opposite of it. But all was not yet hard and dead; there was some life still left in the deeper parts of the system. To those who questioned him Jesus could still answer: 'You have the law, keep it; you know best yourselves what you have to do; the sum of the law is, as you yourselves say, to love God and your neighbour.' Nevertheless, there is a sphere of ethical thought which is peculiarly expressive of Jesus' Gospel. Let us make this clear by citing four points.

First: Jesus severed the connexion existing in his day between ethics and the external forms of religious worship and technical observance. He would have absolutely nothing to do with the purposeful and self-seeking pursuit of 'good works' in combination with the ritual of worship. He exhibited an indignant contempt for those who allow their neighbours, nay, even their parents, to starve, and on the other hand send gifts to the temple. He will have no compromise in the matter. Love and mercy are ends in themselves; they lose all value and are put to shame by having to be anything else than the service of one's neighbour.

Secondly: in all questions of morality he goes straight to the root, that is, to the disposition and the intention. It is only thus that what he calls the 'higher righteousness' can be understood. The 'higher righteousness' is the righteousness that will stand when the depths of the heart are probed. Here, again, we have something that is seemingly very simple and self-evident. Yet the truth, as he uttered it, took the severe form: 'It was said of old...but I say unto you.' After all, then, the truth was something new; he was aware that it had never yet been expressed in such a consistent form and with such claims to supremacy. A large portion of the so-called Sermon on the Mount is occupied with what he says when he goes in detail through the several departments of human relationships and human failings so as to bring the disposition and intention to light in each case, to judge a man's works by them, and on them to hang heaven and hell.

Thirdly: what he freed from its connexion with self-seeking and ritual elements, and recognized as the moral principle, he reduces to *one* root and to *one* motive—love. He knows of no other, and love itself, whether it takes the form of love of one's neighbour or of one's enemy, or the love of the Samaritan, is of one kind only. It must completely fill the soul; it is what remains when the soul dies to itself. In this sense love is the new life already begun. But it is always the love which *serves*, and only in this function does it exist and live.

Fourthly: we saw that Jesus freed the moral element from all alien connexions, even from its alliance with the public religion. Therefore to say that the Gospel is a matter of ordinary morality is not to mis-understand him. And yet there is one all-important point where he combines religion and morality. It is a point which must be felt; it is not easy to define. In view of the Beatitudes it may, perhaps, best be described as *humility*. Jesus made love and humility one. Humility is not a virtue by itself; but it is pure receptivity, the expression of inner need, the prayer for God's grace and forgiveness, in a word, the opening up of the heart to God. In Jesus' view, this humility, which is the love of God of which we are capable—take, for instance, the parable of the Pharisee and the publican—is an abiding disposition towards the good, and that out of which everything that is good springs and grows. 'Forgive us our trespasses even as we forgive them that trespass against us' is the prayer at once of humility and of love. This, then, is the source and origin of the love of one's neighbour; the poor in spirit and those who hunger and thirst after righteousness are also the peacemakers and the merciful.

It was in this sense that Jesus combined religion and morality, and in this sense religion may be called the soul of morality, and morality the body of religion. We can thus understand how it was that Jesus could place the love of God and the love of one's neighbour side by side; the love of one's neighbour is the only practical proof on earth of that love of God which is strong in humility.

In thus expressing his message of the higher righteousness and the new commandment of love in these four leading thoughts, Jesus defined the sphere of the ethical in a way in which no one before him had ever defined it. But should we be threatened with doubts as to what he meant, we must steep ourselves again and again in the Beatitudes of the Sermon on the Mount. They contain his ethics and his religion, united at the root, and freed from all external and particularistic elements.

What is Christianity? (1900) (trans. E. B. Saunders)

II. PROTESTANTISM

Anyone who looks at the external condition of Protestantism, especially in Germany, may, at first sight, well exclaim: 'What a miserable spectacle!' But no one can survey the history of Europe from the second century to the present time without being forced to the conclusion that in the whole course of this history the greatest movement and the one most pregnant with good was the Reformation in the sixteenth century; even the great change which took place at the transition to the nineteenth is inferior to it in importance. What do all our discoveries and inventions and our advances in outward civilization signify in comparison with the fact that today there are thirty millions of Germans, and many more millions of Christians outside Germany, who possess a religion without priests, without sacrifices, without 'fragments' of grace, without ceremonies—a spiritual religion!

Protestantism must be understood, first and foremost, by the contrast which it offers to Catholicism, and here there is a double direction which any estimate of it must take, first as *Reformation* and secondly as *Revolution*. It was a reformation in regard to the doctrine of salvation; a revolution in regard to the Church, its authority, and its apparatus. Hence Protestantism is no spontaneous phenomenon, created as it were by a *generatio equivoca*; but, as its very name implies, it was called into being by the misdeeds of the Roman Church having become intolerable. It was the close of a long series of cognate but ineffectual attempts at reform in the Middle Ages. If the position which it thus holds in history proves its continuity with the past, the fact is still more strongly

in evidence in its own and not inappropriate contention that it wa
an innovation in regard to religion, but a restoration and renewal
But from the point of view of the Church and its authority Protesta
ism was undoubtedly a revolutionary phenomenon. We must, th ,
take account of it in both these relations.

Protestantism was a *Reformation*, that is to say, a renewal, as regards the
core of the matter, as regards religion, and consequently as regards the
doctrine of salvation. That may be shown in the main in three points.

In the first place, religion was here brought back again to itself, in
so far as the Gospel and the corresponding religious experience were
put into the foreground and freed of all alien accretions. Religion was
taken out of the vast and monstrous fabric which had been previously
called by its name—a fabric embracing the Gospel and holy water,
the priesthood of all believers and the Pope on his throne, Christ the
Redeemer and St Anne—and was *reduced* to its essential factors, to the
Word of God and to faith. This truth was imposed as a *criterion* on
everything that also claimed to be 'religion' and to unite on terms of
equality with those great factors. In the history of religions every really
important reformation is always, first and foremost, *a critical reduction
to principles*; for in the course of its historical development, religion,
by adapting itself to circumstances, attracts to itself much alien matter,
and produces, in conjunction with this, a number of hybrid and apocryphal elements, which it is necessarily compelled to place under the
protection of what is sacred. If it is not to run wild from exuberance,
or be choked by its own dry leaves, the reformer must come who
purifies it and brings it back to itself. This critical reduction to principles
Luther accomplished in the sixteenth century, by victoriously declaring
that the Christian religion was given only in the Word of God and in
the inward experience which accords with this Word.

In the *second* place, there was the definite way in which the 'Word
of God' and the 'experience' of it were grasped. For Luther the
'Word' did not mean Church doctrine; it did not even mean the Bible;
it meant the message of the free grace of God in Christ which makes
guilty and despairing men happy and blessed; and the 'experience' was
just the certainty of this grace. In the sense in which Luther took them,
both can be embraced in one phrase: *the confident belief in a God of grace*.
They put an end—such was his own experience, and such was what he
taught—to all inner discord in a man; they overcome the burden of
every ill; they destroy the sense of guilt; and, despite the imperfection

of a man's own acts, they give him the certainty of being inseparably united with the holy God:

> Now I know and believe
> And give praise without end
> That God the Almighty
> Is Father and Friend,
> And that in all troubles,
> Whatever betide,
> He hushes the tempest
> And stands at my side.

Nothing, he taught, is to be preached but the God of Grace, with whom we are reconciled through Christ. Conversely, it is not a question of ecstasies and visions; no transports of feeling are necessary; it is *faith* that is to be aroused. Faith is to be the beginning, middle, and end of all religious fervour. In the correspondence of Word and faith 'justification' is experienced, and hence justification holds the chief place in the Reformers' message; it means nothing less than the attainment of peace and freedom in God through Christ, dominion over the world, and an eternity within.

Lastly, the third feature of this renewal was the great transformation which *God's worship* now inevitably underwent, God's worship by the individual and by the community. Such worship—this was obvious—can and ought to be nothing but putting *faith* to practical proof. As Luther declared over and over again, 'all that God asks of us is faith, and it is through faith alone that He is willing to treat with us'. To let God be God, and to pay Him honour by acknowledging and invoking Him as Father—it is thus alone that a man can serve Him. Every other path on which a man tries to approach Him and honour Him leads astray, and vain is the attempt to establish any other relation with Him. What an enormous mass of anxious, hopeful, and hopeless effort was now done away with, and what a revolution in worship was effected! But all that is true of God's worship by the individual is true in exactly the same way of public worship. Here, too, it is only the Word of God and prayer which have any place. All else is to be banished; the community assembled for God's worship is to proclaim the message of God with praise and thanksgiving, and call upon His name. Anything that goes beyond this is not worship at all.

These three points embrace the chief elements in the Reformation. What they involved was a *renewal* of religion; for not only do they denote, albeit in a fashion of their own, a return to Christianity as it originally was, but they also existed themselves in Western Catholicism, although buried in a heap of rubbish.

But, before we go further, permit me two brief digressions. We were just saying that the community assembled for God's worship must not solemnize its worship in any other way than by proclaiming the Word and by prayer. To this, however, we must add, according to the Reformers' injunctions, that all that is to stamp this community as a Church is its existence as a community of the faith in which God's Word is preached aright. Here we may leave the sacraments out of account, as, according to Luther, they, too, derive their entire importance from the Word. But if Word and faith are the only characteristics of worship, it looks as if those who contend that the Reformation did away with the visible Church and put an invisible one in its place were right. But the contention does not tally with the facts. The distinction between a visible and an invisible Church dates back as far as the Middle Ages, or even, from one point of view, as far as Augustine. Those who defined the true Church as 'the number of the predestined' were obliged to maintain that it was wholly invisible. But the German Reformers did not so define it. In declaring the Church to be a community of the faith in which God's Word is preached aright, they rejected all the coarser characteristics of a Church, and certainly excluded the visibility that appeals to the senses; but—to take an illustration—who would say that an intellectual community, for example, a band of young men all alike eagerly devoted to knowledge or the interests of their country, was 'invisible', because it possesses no external characteristics, and cannot be counted on one's fingers? Just as little is the evangelical Church an 'invisible' community. It is a community of the spirit, and therefore its 'visibility' takes different phases and different degrees of strength. There are phases of it where it is absolutely unrecognizable, and others, again, where it stands forth with the energy of a power that appeals to the senses. It can never, indeed, take the sharp contours of a State like the Venetian republic or the kingdom of France—such was the comparison which a great exponent of Catholic dogmatics declared to be applicable to his Church —but as Protestants we ought to know that we belong, not to an 'invisible' Church, but to a spiritual community which disposes of the forces pertaining to spiritual communities; a spiritual community resting on earth, but reaching to the Eternal.

And now as to the other point: Protestantism maintains that, objectively, the Christian community is based upon the Gospel alone, but that the Gospel is contained in Holy Scripture. From the very beginning it has encountered the objection that, if that be so, and at the same time there be no recognized authority to decide what the purport and meaning of the Gospel is and how it is to be ascertained from the Scriptures, general confusion will be the result; that of this confusion the history of Protestantism affords ample testimony; that if every man has a warrant to decide what the 'true understanding' of the Gospel is, and in this respect is bound to no tradition, no council, and no pope, but exercises the free right of research, any unity, community, or Church is absolutely impossible; that the State, therefore, must interfere, or some arbitrary limit be fixed. That no Church possessing the Sacred Office of the Inquisition can arise in this way is certainly true; further, that to impose any *external* limits on a community *from the inside* is a simple impossibility. What has been done by the State or under pressure of historical necessities does not affect the question at all; the structures which have arisen in the way are, in the evangelical sense, only figuratively called 'Churches'. *Protestantism reckons*—this is the solution—*upon the Gospel being something so simple, so divine, and therefore so truly human, as to be most certain of being understood when it is left entirely free, and also as to produce essentially the same experiences and convictions in individual souls.* In this it may often enough make mistakes; differences of individuality and education may issue in very heterogeneous results; but still, in this its attitude, it has not up to now been put to shame. A real, spiritual community of evangelical Christians; a common conviction as to what is most important and as to its application to life in all its forms, has arisen and is in full force and vigour. This community embraces Protestants in and outside Germany, Lutherans, Calvinists, and adherents of other denominations. In all of them, so far as they are earnest Christians, there lives a common element, and this element is of infinitely greater importance and value than all their differences. It keeps us to the Gospel and it protects us from modern heathenism and from relapse into Catholicism. More than this we do not need; nay, any other fetter we reject. This, however, is no fetter, but the condition of our freedom. And when we are reproached with our divisions and told that Protestantism has as many doctrines as heads, we reply, 'So it has, but we do not wish it otherwise; on the contrary, we want still more freedom, still greater individuality in utterance and in doctrine; the historical circumstances necessitating the formation of national and free churches have imposed only too many rules and limitations upon us, even though they be not proclaimed as divine ordinances; we want still more confidence in the inner strength and unifying power of the Gospel, which is more certain to prevail in free conflict than under guardianship; we want to be a spiritual realm and we have no desire to return to the fleshpots of Egypt; we are well aware that in the interests of order and instruction outward and visible communities must arise; we are ready to foster their growth, so far as they fulfil these aims and deserve to be fostered; but we do not hang our hearts upon them, for they may exist today and tomorrow give place, under other political or social conditions, to new organizations; let anyone who has such a Church have it as though he had it not; our Church is not the particular Church in which we are placed, but the *societas fidei* which has its members everywhere, even among Greeks and Romans.' That is the evangelical answer to the reproach that we are 'divided', and that is the language which the liberty that has been given to us employs. Let us now return from these digressions to the exposition of the essential features of Protestantism.

Protestantism was not only a Reformation but also a *Revolution*. From the legal point of view the whole Church system against which Luther revolted could lay claim to full obedience. It had just as much legal validity in Western Europe as the laws of the State themselves. When Luther burnt the papal bull he undoubtedly performed a revolutionary act—revolutionary, not in the bad sense of a revolt against legal ordinance which is also moral ordinance as well, but certainly in the sense of a violent breach with a given legal condition. It was against this state of things that the new movement was directed, and it was to the following chief points that its protest in word and deed extended. First: it protested against the entire hierarchical and priestly system in the Church, demanded that it should be abolished, and abolished it in favour of a common priesthood and an established order formed on the basis of the congregation. What a range this demand had, and to what an extent it interfered with the previously existing state of things, cannot be told in a few sentences. To explain it all would take hours. Nor can we here show how the various arrangements actually took shape in the evangelical churches. That is not a matter of fundamental importance, but what is of fundamental importance is that the 'divine' rights of the Church were abolished.

Secondly: it protested against all formal, external authority in religion; against the authority, therefore, of councils, priests, and the whole tradition of the Church. That alone is to be authority which shows itself to be such within and effects a deliverance; the thing itself, therefore, the Gospel. Thus Luther also protested against the authority of the letter of the Bible; but we shall see that this was a point on which neither he nor the rest of the Reformers were quite clear, and where they failed to draw the conclusions which their insight into fundamentals demanded.

Thirdly: it protested against all the traditional arrangements for public worship, all ritualism, and every sort of 'holy work'. As it neither knows nor tolerates, as we have seen, any specific form of worship, any material sacrifice and service to God, any mass and any works done for God and with a view to salvation, the whole traditional system of public worship, with its pomp, its holy and semi-holy articles, its gestures and processions, came to the ground. How much could be retained in the way of form for *aesthetic* or *educational* reasons was, in comparison with this, a question of entirely secondary importance.

Fourthly: it protested against Sacramentalism. Baptism and the Lord's Supper it left standing, as institutions of the primitive Church, or, as it might be, of the Lord himself; but it desired that they should be regarded either as symbols and marks by which the Christian is known, or as acts deriving their value exclusively from that message of the forgiveness of sins which is bound up with them. All other sacraments it abolished, and with them the whole notion of God's grace and help being accessible in bits, and fused in some mysterious way with definite corporeal things. To sacramentalism it opposed the *Word*, and to the notion that grace was given by bits, the conviction that there is only one grace, namely, to possess *God himself* as the source of grace. It was not because Luther was so very enlightened that in his tract 'On the Babylonian Captivity' he rejected the whole system of Sacramentalism—he had enough superstition left in him to enable him to advance some very shocking contentions—but because he had had inner experience of the fact that where 'grace' does not endow the soul with the living God Himself it is an illusion. Hence for him the whole doctrine of sacramentalism was an infringement of God's majesty and an enslavement of the soul.

Fifthly: it protested against the double form of morality, and accordingly against the higher form; against the contention that it is particularly well-pleasing to God to make no use of the powers and gifts which are part of creation. The Reformers had a strong sense of the fact that the world passes away with the lusts thereof; we must certainly not represent Luther as the modern man cheerfully standing with his feet firmly planted on the earth; on the contrary, like the men of the Middle Ages he had a strong yearning to be rid of this world and to depart from the 'vale of tears'. But because he was convinced that we neither can nor ought to offer God anything but trust in Him, he arrived, in regard to the Christian's position in the world, at quite different theses from those which were advanced by the grave monks of previous centuries. As fastings and ascetic practices had no value before God, and were of no advantage to one's fellow-men, and as God is the Creator of all things, the most useful thing that a man can do is to remain in the position in which God has placed him. This conviction gave Luther a cheerful and confident view of earthly ordinances, which contrasts with and actually got the upperhand of his inclination to turn his back upon the world.

He advanced the definite thesis that all positions in life—constituted authority, the married state, and so on, down to domestic service—existed by the will of God, and were therefore genuinely spiritual positions in which we are to serve God; a faithful maidservant stands higher, with him, than a contemplative monk. Christians are not to be always devising how they may find some new paths of their own, but to show patience and love of neighbour within the sphere of their given vocation. Out of this there grew up in his mind the notion that all worldly laws and spheres of activity have an independent title. It is not that they are to be merely tolerated, and have no right to exist until they receive it from the Church. No! they have rights of their own, and they form the vast domain in which the Christian is to give proof of his faith and love; nay, they are even to be respected in places which are as yet ignorant of God's revelation in the Gospel.

It was thus that the same man who asked nothing of the world, so far as his own personal feelings were concerned, and whose soul was troubled only by thought for the Eternal, delivered mankind from the ban of asceticism. He was thereby really and truly the life and origin of a new epoch, and he gave it back a simple and unconstrained attitude towards the world, and a good conscience in all earthly labour. This fruitful work fell to his share, not because he secularized religion, but because he took it so seriously and so profoundly that, while in his view it was to pervade all things, it was itself to be freed from everything external to it. *What is Christianity?* (1900) (trans. E. B. Saunders)

CHAPTER 8

KIERKEGAARD

Although most of Kierkegaard's life was covered by the first half of the nineteenth century—he died in 1855—his influence belongs to the twentieth. Not that he was ignored, by his fellow-countrymen at least, in his own day; on the contrary, he was a conspicuous and controversial figure. But beyond Denmark his voluminous writings made no impact until after the First World War. Since then they have been translated into many languages and the man and his work—for the two are inseparable—have been the subject of endless comment and discussion. Kierkegaard is regarded as the originator— as he remains the most forceful exponent—of the type of modern philosophy known as existentialism, and thinkers as diverse as Karl Jaspers, Karl Barth and Jean-Paul Sartre are alike in being his recognizable heirs.

Born at Copenhagen in 1813, the son of a well-to-do wool merchant, Søren Kierkegaard spent practically the whole of his life in his native city, leaving it only for two or three brief periods—in all but a few months—in Berlin, which he first visited in order to hear Schelling lecture on Hegel, an experience which he found disappointing. The great personal influence in his life was that of his dourly religious father, Michael Pedersen Kierke-gaard, who had been brought up in poverty amid the desolate heaths of Jutland but whose success in business permitted him to retire at the age of 40, soon after the death of his first wife. Søren was the last of seven children by a second marriage to a distant relative whose status in the Kierkegaard household was virtually that of a servant. At the time of the wedding she was already pregnant, and her husband's burdening sense of personal guilt— he could never forget that as a child he had cursed God—may have been deepened by brooding upon his own conduct towards her. The gloomy seriousness of Michael Pedersen's disposition was reflected in his son's temperament. 'I was already', he wrote, 'an old man when I was born', and Søren himself knew little happiness as a child. In 1828 he attended the university of Copenhagen as a theological student—it was his father's wish that he should become a pastor—but the study of theology was deferred in favour of philosophy and general literature. Ten years later he did sit for his theological examination but was never ordained, an event for which, in any case, his frivolous and spendthrift manner of life ill-fitted him. He was already noted, moreover, for his mordant wit, a gift of which he was himself eminently conscious. Yet despite his extravagant tastes and eccentricity he was a born *studiosus* and desired no other career. In 1841 he became engaged to a seventeen-year-old girl, Regine Olsen, to whom he had long been attached. His sudden breaking off of the engagement created a scandal. His reasons for doing so are not clear. It may be that his ingrained sense of guilt caused him to doubt his suitability for matrimony at all; or possibly he suspected that she herself could not join her life to his at his own spiritual level. But his love for her is beyond question. Had he not had, he tells us, a conscientious scruple to sustain him she must have won. 'I had to fight the case before a much higher tribunal, and hence my firmness, which was taken for heartlessness.'

His father's death in 1838 left Kierkegaard in affluence, so that he could devote himself to writing without thought of economic necessities. In 1843 *Either/Or* appeared pseudonymously, but the fact that he was its author was generally known. Thereafter more than twenty books came from his pen. His reputation as a writer was quickly established, but he was angered by the continual misrepresentation, often malicious, to which he was subjected, particularly in a scurrilous periodical called *The Corsair*, which for a twelve-month exposed him to vulgar ridicule. In his last years he launched a bitter attack upon the Danish State Church as, by New Testament standards, a dishonest travesty of what Christianity really is. He prophesied a new and 'frightful' Reformation, compared with which that of Luther would be hardly more than 'a jest'. For the fact was that Christianity 'really does not exist, and it is horrible when a generation coddled by a childish Christianity, deluded into the vain notion that they are Christians, have to receive again the death-blow of learning what it is to become a Christian, to be a Christian'. His satirical genius here reached its apex, but in the midst of his onslaught he died. He was still only 42.

Kierkegaard's thought does not constitute a system. Indeed he abhorred the very idea of any such thing, for life cannot be enclosed in systems. He was not even interested in 'intellectual problems'. It was, rather, his conviction of the utter inadequacy of the merely intellectual standpoint which set him against Hegelianism. 'A philosophy of pure thought is for an existing individual a chimera, if the truth that is sought is something to exist in.' An *existing*, not simply a reflecting, individual is what a philosopher must be, as was the case, Kierkegaard believed, in ancient Greece. One should exist in and with the whole of one's being, and one should be an individual, not just a unit in an impersonal crowd—'the crowd is untruth'. ('None', he shrewdly adds, 'has more contempt for what it is to be a man than they who make it their profession to lead the crowd.') Kierkegaard's own thinking sprang from his life and is the indispensable commentary thereon. His writings as a whole provide full documentation for both, but none is more revealing than *Stages on Life's Way*, published in 1845 and probably its author's most mature literary achievement. It resumes and repeats the theme of *Either/Or*. The stages in question are three: the aesthetic, concerned with the immediate and sensible; the ethical; and the religious. The first of these represents the romantic attitude and is supremely exemplified in Don Juan—especially the Don Juan of Mozart—who is the very embodiment of restless desire. But for one who realizes the emptiness of the merely aesthetic life and yet continues to cling to it the only outcome is despair. Man has within him an awareness of the eternal, which cannot be satisfied by the pleasures of the senses. He is a synthesis of body and spirit, necessity and freedom, finite and infinite, time and eternity. The aesthetic standpoint stresses only one element in this synthesis, but the other is there, making itself felt by a strange anxiety—'a sympathetic antipathy and an antipathetic sympathy'—in which fear and fascination combine. *Angst*, dread, is the term Kierkegaard uses to denote it: it is the presence of Angst which reminds us that we belong to eternity. The dual concepts of dread and despair provide the subject of two of Kierkegaard's most striking essays: *The Concept of Dread* (1844) and *Sickness unto Death* (1849). To pass from the aesthetic stage to the ethical is to prove oneself mature enough to make a real and significant choice. The aesthetic is not indeed repudiated—Kierkegaard never doubts its lasting value; but it is transcended. The ethical man, that is, has submitted to the claim upon him of the eternal and proceeds to realize the eternal in the temporal, sensible world. Aesthetic and ethical are thus united; and of this union marriage—as it might and should be—is the expression and symbol. Yet there also is the third stage, the religious, for the ethical offers no final goal. On the contrary, it manifests in an acute form the conflict between universal demands and individual inwardness. In the long run morality itself is impotent, since it inevitably subordinates the individual and personal to the social and legal, the subjective to the objective. The more a man believes in his power to fulfil himself in ethics the more likely is he to become aware of his failure to do so.

The respective demands of ethics and faith are vividly illustrated in the story of Abraham and Isaac, recalled by Kierkegaard in *Fear and Trembling* (1843). Abraham showed faith, even in defiance of ethics, because he understood the profound meaning of absolute obedience to the absolute. He was confident that for God all things are possible. But the paradox is that the man who has faith need *not* renounce—Abraham did not lose his son—whereas the man who renounces proves that in doing so he lacks faith. 'Faith, therefore,' Kierkegaard notes in his journal (May 1843), 'has hope of this life as well, but only by virtue of the absurd, not because of human reason.' Here precisely is the challenge of Christianity. Religion is not, and without self-betrayal cannot be, a wisdom of this world, a scheme of rational belief anticipating and answering all questions. Faith and philosophy are essentially opposed. Faith does not aim at certainty—without risk it cannot exist: it is like 'lying out over 70,000 fathoms of water'. In the *Concluding Unscientific Postscript* (1846), in some respects Kierkegaard's most important work, he ventures to define truth itself as 'objective uncertainty held fast by the personal appropriation of the most passionate inwardness'. Truth, in fact, is in subjectivity. For religious belief certain corollaries are obvious. The very 'absurdity' of the Christian doctrines, the affront they give to level-headed logic, is the real proof of their truth. The effort to rationalize belief and 'to bring God to light objectively' is 'in all eternity impossible because God is a subject, and therefore exists only for subjectivity in inwardness'. He is never a 'third party'. Above all the incarnation, the advent of the 'God-man' in history, is beyond rational explanation. It is the sheer heart of paradox, and neither philosophical nor historical inquiry can authenticate it. Belief in the incarnation is an act at once of absolute defiance and of trust. Thus the question to be faced is not the customary one of the 'truth of Christianity' but, rather, of 'how to become a Christian'. Faced by it Kierkegaard increasingly felt that to describe himself as a Christian was something he dare not do.

Kierkegaard was a master of his native tongue and one of the foremost writers of his time, but his thickly woven prose often presents difficulties to the reader. His style is elliptical, allusive, ironic and frequently aggressive. His individualism, moreover, is apt to be obsessive, his pessimism morbid. One of the last entries in his journal records that 'the purpose of this life is— to be carried to the highest degree of weariness of life'. But his implacable opposition to all attempts to evade the real issues under cover of objective 'reason' has left a mark on modern thought which is not likely now to be erased.

Bibliographical note

A second edition of the *Samlede Voeker* appeared during the years 1920–31. The several volumes of the standard English translation, by W. Lowrie and others, have been published at intervals since 1938. See also J. Hohlenberg, *Søren Kierkegaard* (Eng. trans. by T. H. Croxall, 1954), W. Lowrie, *Kierkegaard* (1938) and *A Short Life of Kierkegaard* (1942), R. Thomte, *Kierkegaard's Philosophy of Religion* (1948), R. Jolivet, *An Introduction to Kierkegaard* (Eng. trans. by W. H. Barber, 1950), D. Roberts, *Existentialism and Religious Belief* (1957) and H. Diem, *Kierkegaard's Dialectic of Existence* (1959).

FAITH AND REASON

In spite of the fact that Socrates studied with all diligence to acquire a knowledge of human nature and to understand himself, and in spite of the fame accorded him through the centuries as one who beyond all other men had an insight into the human heart, he has himself admitted that the reason for his shrinking from reflexion upon the nature of such beings as Pegasus and the Gorgons was that he, the life-long student of human nature, had not yet been able to make up his mind whether he was a stranger monster than Typhon, or a creature of a gentler and simpler sort, partaking of something divine (*Phaedrus*, 229 E). This seems to be a paradox. However, one should not think slightingly of the paradoxical; for the paradox is the source of the thinker's passion, and the thinker without a paradox is like a lover without feeling: a paltry mediocrity. But the highest pitch of every passion is always to will its own downfall; and so it is also the supreme passion of the Reason to seek a collision, though this collision must in one way or another prove its undoing. The supreme paradox of all thought is the attempt to discover something that thought cannot think. This passion is at bottom present in all thinking, even in the thinking of the individual, in so far as in thinking he participates in something transcending himself. But habit dulls our sensibilities, and prevents us from perceiving it. So for example the scientists tell us that our walking is a constant falling. But a sedate and proper gentleman who walks to his office in the morning and back again at noon, probably thinks this to be an exaggeration, for his progress is clearly a case of mediation; how should it occur to him that he is constantly falling when he religiously follows his nose!

But in order to make a beginning, let us now assume a daring proposition; let us assume that we know what man is.[1] Here we have that criterion of the Truth, which in the whole course of Greek philo-

---

[1] It may seem ridiculous to give this proposition a doubtful form by 'assuming' it, for in this theocentric age such matters are of course known to all. Aye, if it were only so well with us! Democritus also knew what man is, for he defines man as follows: 'Man is what we all know', and then goes on to say: 'for we all know what a dog, a horse, a plant is, and so forth; but none of these is a man'. We do not aspire to the malice of Sextus Empiricus, nor have we his wit; for he concludes as we know, from the above definition, and quite correctly, that man is a dog; for man is what we all know, and we all know what a dog is, *ergo*—but let us not be so malicious. Nevertheless, has this question been so thoroughly cleared up in our own time that no one need feel a little uneasy about himself when he is reminded of poor Socrates and his predicament?

sophy was either *sought*, or *doubted*, or *postulated*, or *made fruitful*. Is it not remarkable that the Greeks should have borne us this testimony? And is it not an epitome, as it were, of the significance of Greek culture, an epigram of its own writing, with which it is also better served than with the frequently voluminous disquisitions sometimes devoted to it? Thus the proposition is well worth positing, and also for another reason, since we have already explained it in the two preceding chapters; while anyone who attempts to explain Socrates differently may well beware lest he fall into the snare of the earlier or later Greek scepticism. For unless we hold fast to the Socratic doctrine of Recollection, and to his principle that every individual man is Man, Sextus Empiricus stands ready to make the transition involved in 'learning' not only difficult but impossible; and Protagoras will begin where Sextus Empiricus leaves off, teaching that man is the measure of all things, in the sense that the individual man is the measure for others, but by no means in the Socratic sense that each man is his own measure, neither more nor less.

So then we know what man is, and this wisdom, which I shall be the last to hold in light esteem, may progressively become richer and more significant, and with it also the Truth. But now the Reason hesitates, just as Socrates did; for the paradoxical passion of the Reason is aroused and seeks a collision; without rightly understanding itself, it is bent upon its own downfall. This is like what happens in connexion with the paradox of love. Man lives undisturbed a self-centered life, until there awakens within him the paradox of self-love, in the form of love for another, the object of his longing. (Self-love is the underlying principle, or the principle that is made to lie under, in all love; whence if we conceive a religion of love, this religion need make but one assumption, as epigrammatic as true, and take its realization for granted: namely the condition that man loves himself, in order to command him to love his neighbor as himself.) The lover is so completely transformed by the paradox of love that he scarcely recognizes himself; so say the poets, who are the spokesmen of love, and so say also the lovers themselves, since they permit the poets merely to take the words from their lips, but not the passion from their hearts. In like manner the paradoxical passion of the Reason, while as yet a mere presentiment, retroactively affects man and his self-knowledge, so that he who thought to know himself is no longer certain whether he is a more strangely composite animal than Typhon, or if perchance his

nature contains a gentler and diviner part (σκοπῶ οὐ ταῦτα, ἀλλὰ
ἐμαυτόν, εἴτε τι θηρίον ὢν τυγχάνω πολυπλοκώτερον καὶ μᾶλλον
ἐπιτεθυμμένον εἴτε ἡμερώτερόν τε καὶ ἁπλούστερον ζῷον, θείας τινὸς
καὶ ἀτύφου μοίρας φύσει μετέχον. *Phaedrus*, 230A).

But what is this unknown something with which the Reason collides
when inspired by its paradoxical passion, with the result of unsettling
even man's knowledge of himself? It is the Unknown. It is not a
human being, in so far as we know what man is; nor is it any other
known thing. So let us call this unknown something: *God*. It is
nothing more than a name we assign to it. The idea of demonstrating
that this unknown something (God) exists, could scarcely suggest
itself to the Reason. For if God does not exist it would of course be
impossible to prove it; and if he does exist it would be folly to attempt
it. For at the very outset, in beginning my proof, I will have presupposed
it, not as doubtful but as certain (a presupposition is never doubtful,
for the very reason that it is a presupposition), since otherwise I would
not begin, readily understanding that the whole would be impossible
if he did not exist. But if when I speak of proving God's existence I
mean that I propose to prove that the Unknown, which exists, is God,
then I express myself unfortunately. For in that case I do not prove
anything, least of all an existence, but merely develop the content of a
conception. Generally speaking, it is a difficult matter to prove that
anything exists; and what is still worse for the intrepid souls who undertake the venture, the difficulty is such that fame scarcely awaits those
who concern themselves with it. The entire demonstration always
turns into something very different from what it assumes to be, and
becomes an additional development of the consequences that flow
from my having assumed that the object in question exists. Thus I
always reason from existence, not toward existence, whether I move
in the sphere of palpable sensible fact or in the realm of thought. I do
not for example prove that a stone exists, but that some existing thing
is a stone. The procedure in a court of justice does not prove that a
criminal exists, but that the accused, whose existence is given, is a
criminal. Whether we call existence an *accessorium* or the eternal *prius*,
it is never subject to demonstration. Let us take ample time for consideration. We have no such reason for haste as have those who from
concern for themselves or for God or for some other thing, must make
haste to get its existence demonstrated. Under such circumstances there
may indeed be need for haste, especially if the prover sincerely seeks

to appreciate the danger that he himself, or the thing in question, may be non-existent unless the proof is finished; and does not surreptitiously entertain the thought that it exists whether he succeeds in proving it or not.

If it were proposed to prove Napoleon's existence from Napoleon's deeds, would it not be a most curious proceeding? His existence does indeed explain his deeds, but the deeds do not prove *his* existence, unless I have already understood the word 'his' so as thereby to have assumed his existence. But Napoleon is only an individual, and in so far there exists no absolute relationship between him and his deeds; some other person might have performed the same deeds. Perhaps this is the reason why I cannot pass from the deeds to existence. If I call these deeds the deeds of Napoleon the proof becomes superfluous, since I have already named him; if I ignore this, I can never prove from the deeds that they are Napoleon's, but only in a purely ideal manner that such deeds are the deeds of a great general, and so forth. But between God and his works there exists an absolute relationship; God is not a name but a concept. Is this perhaps the reason that his *essentia involvit existentiam*?[1] The works of God are such that only God can perform

---

[1] So Spinoza, who probes the depths of the God-idea in order to bring existence out of it by way of thought, but not it should be noted as if existence were an accidental circumstance, but rather as if it constituted an essential determination of content. Here lies Spinoza's profundity, but let us examine his reasoning. In *principia philosophiae Cartesianae, pars I, propositio VII, lemma I*, he says: '*quo res sua natura perfectior est, eo majorem existentiam et magis necessariam involvit; et contra, quo magis necessariam existentiam res sua natura involvit, eo perfectior.*' The more perfect therefore a thing is, the more being it has; the more being it has, the more perfect it is. This is, however, a tautology, which becomes still more evident in a note, *nota II*: '*quod hic non loquimur de pulchritudine et aliis perfectionibus, quas homines ex superstitione et ignorantia perfectiones vocare voluerunt. Sed per perfectionem intelligo tantum realitatem sive esse.*' He explains *perfectio* by *realitas, esse*; so that the more perfect a thing is, the more it is; but its perfection consists in having more *esse* in itself; that is to say, the more a thing is, the more it is. So much for the tautology, but now further. What is lacking here is a distinction between factual being and ideal being. The terminology which permits us to speak of more or less of being, and consequently of degrees of reality or being, is in itself lacking in clearness, and becomes still more confusing when the above distinction is neglected; when, in other words, Spinoza does indeed speak profoundly, but fails first to consider the difficulty. In the case of factual existence it is meaningless to speak of more or less of being. A fly, when it exists, has as much being as God; the stupid remark I here set down has as much factual existence as Spinoza's profundity; for factual existence is subject to the dialectic of Hamlet: to be or not to be. Factual existence is wholly indifferent to any and all variations in essence, and everything that exists participates without petty jealousy in being, and participates in the same degree. Ideally to be sure, the case is quite different. *But the moment I speak of being in the ideal sense I no longer speak of being, but of essence.* The highest ideality is necessary, and therefore it is. But this its being is identical with its essence; such being does not involve it dialectically in the determinations of factual existence, since it is; nor can it be said to have more or less of being in relation to other things. In the old days this used to be expressed, if somewhat imperfectly, by saying that if God is possible, he is *eo ipso* necessary (Leibniz). Spinoza's principle is thus quite correct and his tautology in order; but it is also certain that he altogether evades the difficulty. For the difficulty is to lay hold of God's factual existence, and to introduce God's ideal essence dialectically into the sphere of factual existence.

them. Just so, but where then are the works of God? The works from which I would deduce his existence are not immediately given. The wisdom of God in nature, his goodness, his wisdom in the governance of the world—are all these manifest, perhaps, upon the very face of things? Are we not here confronted with the most terrible temptations to doubt, and is it not impossible finally to dispose of all these doubts? But from such an order of things I will surely not attempt to prove God's existence; and even if I began I would never finish, and would in addition have to live constantly in suspense, lest something so terrible should suddenly happen that my bit of proof would be demolished. From what works then do I propose to derive the proof? From the works as apprehended through an ideal interpretation, i.e. such as they do not immediately reveal themselves. But in that case it is not from the works that I prove God's existence. I merely develop the ideality I have presupposed, and because of my confidence in *this* I make so bold as to defy all objections, even those that have not yet been made. In beginning my proof I presuppose the ideal interpretation, and also that I will be successful in carrying it through; but what else is this but to presuppose that God exists, so that I really begin by virtue of confidence in him?

And how does God's existence emerge from the proof? Does it follow straightway, without any breach of continuity? Or have we not here an analogy to the behaviour of these toys, the little Cartesian dolls? As soon as I let go of the doll it stands on its head. As soon as I let it go—I must therefore let it go. So also with the proof for God's existence. As long as I keep my hold on the proof, i.e. continue to demonstrate, the existence does not come out, if for no other reason than that I am engaged in proving it; but when I let the proof go, the existence is there. But this act of letting go is surely also something; it is indeed a contribution of mine. Must not this also be taken into the account, this little moment, brief as it may be—it need not be long, for it is a *leap*. However brief this moment, if only an instantaneous now, this 'now' must be included in the reckoning. If anyone wishes to have it ignored, I will use it to tell a little anecdote, in order to show that it really does exist. Chrysippus was experimenting with a sorites to see if he could not bring about a break in its quality, either progressively or retrogressively. But Carneades could not get it in his head when the new quality actually emerged. Then Chrysippus told him to try making a little pause in the reckoning, and so—so it would be easier to understand. Carneades replied: With the greatest pleasure, please do not hesitate on my account; you may not only pause, but even lie down to sleep, and it will help you just as little; for when you awake we will begin again where you left off. Just so; it boots as little to try to get rid of something by sleeping as to try to come into the possession of something in the same manner.

Whoever therefore attempts to demonstrate the existence of God (except in the sense of clarifying the concept, and without the *reservatio finalis* noted above, that the existence emerges from the demonstration by a leap) proves in lieu thereof something else, something which at times perhaps does not need a proof, and in any case needs none better; for the fool says in his heart that there is no God, but whoever says in his heart or to men: Wait just a little and I will prove it—what a rare man of wisdom is he![1] If in the moment of beginning his proof it is not absolutely undetermined whether God exists or not, he does not prove it; and if it is thus undetermined in the beginning he will never come to begin, partly from fear of failure, since God perhaps does not exist, and partly because he has nothing with which to begin. A project of this kind would scarcely have been undertaken by the ancients. Socrates at least, who is credited with having put forth the physico-teleological proof for God's existence, did not go about it in any such manner. He always presupposes God's existence, and under this presupposition seeks to interpenetrate nature with the idea of purpose. Had he been asked why he pursued this method, he would doubtless have explained that he lacked the courage to venture out upon so perilous a voyage of discovery without having made sure of God's existence behind him. At the word of God he casts his net as if to catch the idea of purpose; for nature herself finds many means of frightening the inquirer, and distracts him by many a digression.

The paradoxical passion of the Reason thus comes repeatedly into collision with the Unknown, which does indeed exist, but is unknown, and in so far does not exist. The Reason cannot advance beyond this point, and yet it cannot refrain in its paradoxicalness from arriving at this limit and occupying itself therewith. It will not serve to dismiss its relation to it simply by asserting that the Unknown does not exist, since this itself involves a relationship. But what then is the Unknown, since the designation of it as God merely signifies for us that it is unknown? To say that it is the Unknown because it cannot be known,

---

[1] What an excellent subject for a comedy of the higher lunacy!

and even if it were capable of being known, it could not be expressed, does not satisfy the demands of passion, though it correctly interprets the Unknown as a limit; but a limit is precisely a torment for passion, though it also serves as an incitement. And yet the Reason can come no further, whether it risks an issue *via negationis* or *via eminentia*.

What then is the Unknown? It is the limit to which the Reason repeatedly comes, and in so far, substituting a static form of conception for the dynamic, it is the different, the absolutely different. But because it is absolutely different, there is no mark by which it could be distinguished. When qualified as absolutely different it seems on the verge of disclosure, but this is not the case; for the Reason cannot even conceive an absolute unlikeness. The Reason cannot negate itself absolutely, but uses itself for the purpose, and thus conceives only such an unlikeness within itself as it can conceive by means of itself; it cannot absolutely transcend itself, and hence conceives only such a superiority over itself as it can conceive by means of itself. Unless the Unknown (God) remains a mere limiting conception, the single idea of difference will be thrown into a state of confusion, and become many ideas of many differences. The Unknown is then in a condition of dispersion (διασπορά), and the Reason may choose at pleasure from what is at hand and the imagination may suggest (the monstrous, the ludicrous, etc.).

But it is impossible to hold fast to a difference of this nature. Every time this is done it is essentially an arbitrary act, and deepest down in the heart of piety lurks the mad caprice which knows that it has itself produced its God. If no specific determination of difference can be held fast, because there is no distinguishing mark, like and unlike finally become identified with one another, thus sharing the fate of all such dialectical opposites. The unlikeness clings to the Reason and confounds it, so that the Reason no longer knows itself and quite consistently confuses itself with the unlikeness. On this point paganism has been sufficiently prolific in fantastic inventions. As for the last-named supposition, the self-irony of the Reason, I shall attempt to delineate it merely by a stroke or two, without raising any question of its being historical. There lives an individual whose appearance is precisely like that of other men; he grows up to manhood like others, he marries, he has an occupation by which he earns his livelihood, and he makes provision for the future as befits a man. For though it may be beautiful to live like the birds of the air, it is not lawful, and may

lead to the sorriest of consequences: either starvation if one has enough
persistence, or dependence on the bounty of others. This man is also
God. How do I know? I cannot know it, for in order to know it I
would have to know God, and the nature of the difference between
God and man; and this I cannot know, because the Reason has reduced
it to likeness with that from which it was unlike. Thus God becomes
the most terrible of deceivers, because the Reason has deceived itself.
The Reason has brought God as near as possible, and yet he is as far
away as ever.

Now perhaps someone will say: 'You are certainly a crotcheteer, as I
know very well. But you surely do not believe that I would pay any
attention to such a crotchet, so strange or so ridiculous that it has
doubtless never occurred to anyone, and above all so absurd that I
must exclude from my consciousness everything that I have in it in order
to hit upon it.'—And so indeed you must. But do you think yourself
warranted in retaining all the presuppositions you have in your consciousness, while pretending to think about your consciousness without
presuppositions? Will you deny the consistency of our exposition: that
the Reason, in attempting to determine the Unknown as the unlike,
at last goes astray, and confounds the unlike with the like? From this
there would seem to follow the further consequence, that if man is to
receive any true knowledge about the Unknown (God) he must be
made to know that it is unlike him, absolutely unlike him. This knowledge the Reason cannot possibly obtain of itself; we have already seen
that this would be a self-contradiction. It will therefore have to obtain
this knowledge from God. But even if it obtains such knowledge it
cannot understand it, and thus is quite unable to possess such knowledge. For how should the Reason be able to understand what is
absolutely different from itself? If this is not immediately evident, it
will become clearer in the light of the consequences; for if God is
absolutely unlike man, then man is absolutely unlike God; but how
could the Reason be expected to understand this? Here we seem to
be confronted with a paradox. Merely to obtain the knowledge that
God is unlike him, man needs the help of God; and now he learns that
God is absolutely different from himself. But if God and man are
absolutely different, this cannot be accounted for on the basis of what
man derives from God, for in so far they are akin. Their unlikeness
must therefore be explained by what man derives from himself, or by

177

what he has brought upon his own head. But what can this unlikeness be? Aye, what can it be but sin; since the unlikeness, the absolute unlikeness, is something that man has brought upon himself. We have expressed this in the preceding by saying that man was in Error, and had brought this upon his head by his own guilt; and we came to the conclusion, partly in jest and yet also in earnest, that it was too much to expect of man that he should find this out for himself. Now we have again arrived at the same conclusion. The connoisseur in self-knowledge was perplexed over himself to the point of bewilderment when he came to grapple in thought with the unlike; he scarcely knew any longer whether he was a stranger monster than Typhon, or if his nature partook of something divine. What then did he lack? The consciousness of sin, which he indeed could no more teach to another than another could teach it to him, but only God—if God consents to become a Teacher. But this was his purpose, as we have imagined it. In order to be man's Teacher, God proposed to make himself like the individual man, so that he might understand him fully. Thus our paradox is rendered still more appalling, or the same paradox has the double aspect which proclaims it as the Absolute Paradox; negatively by revealing the absolute unlikeness of sin, positively by proposing to do away with the absolute unlikeness in absolute likeness.

But can such a paradox be conceived? Let us not be over-hasty in replying; and since we strive merely to find the answer to a question, and not as those who run a race, it may be well to remember that success is to the accurate rather than to the swift. The Reason will doubtless find it impossible to conceive it, could not of itself have discovered it, and when it hears it announced will not be able to understand it, sensing merely that its downfall is threatened. In so far the Reason will have much to urge against it; and yet we have on the other hand seen that the Reason, in its paradoxical passion, precisely desires its own downfall. But this is what the Paradox also desires, and thus they are at bottom linked in understanding; but this understanding is present only in the moment of passion. Consider the analogy presented by love, though it is not a perfect one. Self-love underlies love; but the paradoxical passion of self-love when at its highest pitch wills precisely its own downfall. This is also what love desires, so that these two are linked in mutual understanding in the passion of the moment, and this passion is love. Why should not the lover find this conceivable? But he who in self-love shrinks from the touch of love can neither

understand it nor summon the courage to venture it, since it mean
his downfall. Such is then the passion of love; self-love is indeed submerged but not annihilated; it is taken captive and become love's
spolia opima, but may again come to life, and this is love's temptation.
So also with the Paradox in its relation to the Reason, only that the
passion in this case has another name; or rather, we must seek to find
a name for it.

Appendix: The Paradox and the offended consciousness
(An acoustic illusion)

If the Paradox and the Reason come together in a mutual understanding
of their unlikeness their encounter will be happy, like love's understanding, happy in the passion to which we have not yet assigned a
name, and will postpone naming until later. If the encounter is not in
understanding the relationship becomes unhappy, and this unhappy
love of the Reason if I may so call it (which it should be noted is
analogous only to that particular form of unhappy love which has its
root in misunderstood self-love; no further stretching of the analogy
is possible, since accident can play no role in this realm), may be
characterized more specifically as *Offense*.

All offense is in its deepest root passive.[1] In this respect it is like that
form of unhappy love to which we have just alluded. Even when such
a self-love (and does it not already seem contradictory that love of self
should be passive?) announces itself in deeds of audacious daring, in
astounding achievements, it is passive and wounded. It is the pain of
its wound which gives it this illusory strength, expressing itself in what
looks like self-activity and may easily deceive, since self-love is especially
bent on concealing its passivity. Even when it tramples on the object
of affection, even when it painfully schools itself to a hardened indifference and tortures itself to show this indifference, even then, even when
it abandons itself to a frivolous triumph over its success (this form is
the most deceptive of all), even then it is passive. Such is also the case
with the offended consciousness. Whatever be its mode of expression,
even when it exultantly celebrates the triumph of its unspirituality, it
is always passive. Whether the offended individual sits broken-hearted,

---

[1] The Danish language correctly calls emotion (Dan. '*Affekten*') 'Sinds*lidelse*' (compare Ger.
'*Leiden*schaft'). When we use the word '*Affekt*' we are likely to think more immediately of the
convulsive daring which astounds us, and makes us forget that it is a form of passivity. So for
example: pride, defiance, etc.

staring almost like a beggar at the Paradox, paralysed by his suffering, or he sheathes himself in the armor of derision, pointing the arrows of wit as if from a distance—he is still passive and near at hand. Whether offense came and robbed the offended individual of his last bit of comfort and joy, or made him strong—the offended consciousness is nevertheless passive. It has wrestled with the stronger, and its show of strength is like the peculiar agility induced in the bodily sphere by a broken back.

However, it is quite possible to distinguish between an active and a passive form of the offended consciousness, if we take care to remember that the passive form is so far active as not to permit itself wholly to be annihilated (for offense is always an act, never an event); and that the active form is always so weak that it cannot free itself from the cross to which it is nailed, or tear the arrow from out its wound.[1]

But precisely because offense is thus passive, the discovery, if it be allowable to speak thus, does not derive from the Reason, but from the Paradox. The offended consciousness does not understand itself[2] but is understood by the Paradox. While therefore the expressions in which offense proclaims itself, of whatever kind they may be, sound as if they came from elsewhere, even from the opposite direction, they are nevertheless echoings of the Paradox. This is what is called an acoustic illusion. But if the Paradox is *index* and *judex sui et falsi*, the offended consciousness can be taken as an indirect proof of the validity of the Paradox; offense is the mistaken reckoning, the invalid consequence, with which the Paradox repels and thrusts aside. The offended individual does not speak from his own resources, but borrows those of the Paradox; just as one who mimics or parodies another does not invent, but merely copies perversely. The more profound the passion with which the offended consciousness (active or passive) expresses itself, the more apparent it is how much it owes to the Paradox. Offense was not discovered by the Reason, far from it, for then the

---

[1] The idiom of the language also supports the view that all offense is passive. We say: 'to be offended', which primarily expresses only the state or condition; but we also say, as identical in meaning with the foregoing: 'to take offense', which expresses a synthesis of active and passive. The Greek word is σκανδαλίζεσθαι. This word comes from σκάνδαλον (offense or stumbling-block), and hence means to take offense, or to collide with something. Here the movement of thought is clearly indicated; it is not that offense provokes the collision, but that it meets with a collision, and hence passively, although so far actively as itself to take offense. Hence the Reason is not the discoverer of offense; for the paradoxical collision which the Reason develops in isolation discovers neither the Paradox nor the reaction of offense.

[2] In this sense the Socratic principle that sin is ignorance finds justification. Sin does not understand itself in the Truth, but it does not follow that it may not will itself in Error.

Reason must also have been able to discover the Paradox. No, offense comes into being with the Paradox; it *comes into being*. Here again we have the Moment, on which everything depends. Let us recapitulate. If we do not posit the Moment we return to Socrates; but it was precisely from him that we departed, in order to discover something. If we posit the Moment the Paradox is there; for the Moment is the Paradox in its most abbreviated form. Because of the Moment the learner is in Error; and man, who had before possessed self-knowledge, now becomes bewildered with respect to himself; instead of self-knowledge he receives the consciousness of sin, and so forth; for as soon as we posit the Moment everything follows of itself.

From the psychological point of view the offended consciousness will display a great variety of nuances within the more active and the more passive forms. To enter into a detailed description of these would not further our present purpose; but it is important to bear fixedly in mind that all offense is in its essence a misunderstanding of the *Moment*, since it is directed against the Paradox, which again is the Moment.

The dialectic of the *Moment* is not difficult. From the Socratic point of view the Moment is invisible and indistinguishable; it is not, it has not been, it will not come. Hence the learner is himself the Truth, and the moment of occasion is but a jest, like a bastard title that does not essentially belong to the book. From this point of view the Moment of decision becomes *folly*; for if a decision in time is postulated, then (by the preceding) the learner is in Error, which is precisely what makes a beginning in the Moment necessary. The reaction of the offended consciousness is to assert that the Moment is folly, and that the Paradox is folly; which is the contention of the Paradox that the Reason is absurd, now reflected back as in an echo from the offended consciousness. Or the Moment is regarded as constantly about to come; it is so regarded, and the Reason holds it as *worthy of regard*; but since the Paradox has made the Reason absurd, the regard of the Reason is no reliable criterion.

The offended consciousness holds aloof from the Paradox, and the reason is: *quia absurdum*. But it was not the Reason that made this discovery; on the contrary it was the Paradox that made the discovery, and now receives this testimony from the offended consciousness. The Reason says that the Paradox is absurd, but this is mere mimicry, since the Paradox is the Paradox, *quia absurdum*. The offended consciousness holds aloof from the Paradox and keeps to the probable, the Paradox being the most improbable of things. Again it is not the Reason that made this discovery; it merely snatches the words from the mouth of the Paradox, strange as this may seem; for the Paradox itself says: Comedies and romances and lies must needs be probable, but why should I be probable? The offended consciousness holds aloof from the Paradox, and what wonder, since the Paradox is the Miracle! This discovery was not made by the Reason; it was the Paradox that placed the Reason on the stool of wonderment and now replies: But why are you so astonished? It is precisely as you say, and the only wonder is that you regard it as an objection; but the truth in the mouth of a hypocrite is dearer to me than if it came from the lips of an angel or an apostle. When the Reason boasts of its splendors in comparison with the Paradox, which is most wretched and despised, the discovery was not made by the Reason but by the Paradox itself; it is content to leave to the Reason all its splendors, even the splendid sins (*vitia splendida*). When the Reason takes pity on the Paradox, and wishes to help it to an explanation, the Paradox does not indeed acquiesce, but nevertheless finds it quite natural that the Reason should do this; for why do we have our philosophers, if not to make supernatural things trivial and commonplace? When the Reason says that it cannot get the Paradox into its head, it was not the Reason that made the discovery but the Paradox, which is so paradoxical as to declare the Reason a blockhead and a dunce, capable at the most of saying yes and no to the same thing, which is not good divinity. And so always. All that the offended consciousness has to say about the Paradox it has learned from the Paradox, though it would like to pose as the discoverer, making use of an acoustic illusion.

But I think I hear someone say: 'It is really becoming tiresome the way you go on, for now we have the same story over again; not one of the expressions you have put into the mouth of the Paradox belongs to you.'—'Why should they belong to me, when they belong to the Paradox?'—'You can spare us your sophistry, you know very well what I mean. These expressions are not yours, nor by you put into the mouth of the Paradox, but are familiar quotations, and everybody knows who the authors are.'—'My friend, your accusation does not grieve me, as you perhaps believe; what you say rather makes me exceedingly glad. For I must admit that I could not repress a shudder when I wrote them down; I scarcely recognized myself, that I who am usually so timid and apprehensive dared say such things. But if the expressions are not by me, perhaps you will explain to whom they belong?'—'Nothing is easier. The first is by Tertullian, the second by Hamann, the third by Hamann, the fourth is by Lactantius and is frequently quoted; the fifth is by Shakespeare, in a comedy called *All's Well that Ends Well*, Act II, scene iii; the sixth is by Luther, and the seventh is a remark by King Lear. You see that I am well informed, and that I have caught you with the goods.'—'Indeed I do perceive it; but will you now tell me whether all these men have not spoken of the relation between some paradox and an offended consciousness, and will you now note that the individuals who spoke thus were not themselves offended, but precisely persons who held to the paradox; and yet they speak as if they were offended, and offense cannot find a more characteristic expression for itself. Is it not strange that the Paradox should thus as it were take the bread from the mouth of the offended consciousness, reducing it to the practice of an idle and unprofitable art? It seems as curious as if an opponent at a disputation, instead of attacking the author's thesis, defended him in his distraction. Does it not seem so to you? However, one merit unquestionably belongs to the offended consciousness, in that it brings out the unlikeness more clearly; for in that happy passion which we have not yet given a name, the Unlike is on good terms with the Reason. There must be a difference if there is to be a synthesis in some third entity. But here the difference consisted in the fact that the Reason yielded itself while the Paradox bestowed itself (*halb zog sie ihn, halb sank er hin*), and the understanding is consummated in that happy passion which will doubtless soon find a name; and this is the smallest part of the matter, for even if my happiness does not have a name—when I am but happy, I ask for no more.'

Philosophical Fragments (1844) (trans. D. F. Swenson)

CHAPTER 9

LAMENNAIS

'The life of an Ultramontane who became a Deist inevitably presents the sharpest contrasts. Honoured by one pope, condemned by another; master of distinguished disciples, and abandoned by them all; winning by his genius, and repelling by his austerities; craving for sympathy, yet flinging it away; intolerant of social life, yet crushed by solitude; meteoric alike in brilliancy and eclipse; alternating between noble conceptions and small-minded perversities; singularly capable in intellect, yet practically as helpless as a child; merciless in criticism, yet acutely sensitive; affected with constant ill-health and the morbid depression of a Breton temperament; logical and imaginative; martyr to noble aims, unworldly, superior to all personal ambitions while serenely conscious of his power'[1]—such, with little exaggeration, was Félicité Robert de Lamennais, priest, philosopher and political theorist, and among the Catholic clergy of the nineteenth century the only rival in personal magnetism as in literary gift of J. H. Newman himself. In both the ultramontane and liberal Catholic movements he is the key-figure, yet he remains, like Newman, an individualist. At one time the fervent advocate of a Catholic renaissance, the course he took only carried him in the end to a disillusioned rejection of all orthodox religious belief.

Born at St Malo in 1782, the son of an ennobled shipbuilder, his health was never robust, whilst temperamentally he was sensitive to an almost morbid degree. Inclined in youth to rationalism, his philosophical and historical studies convinced him of the necessity of faith and in particular of the importance of the social function of religion. In 1808 he published, in co-operation with his brother, a volume of *Réfléxions sur l'état de l'Église en France pendant le XVIIIe siècle, et sa situation actuelle*, in which he urged the need of a religious revival and a more active role in society for the clergy. Napoleon's police considered the work too controversial and suppressed it, thus delaying its appearance for some six years. Testimony of Lamennais' literary powers was afforded by his translation, under the title *Le Guide spirituel* (1809), of the *Speculum Monachorum* of Ludovicus Blosius (Louis of Blois).

In 1811 he took up work as a teacher of mathematics at an ecclesiastical college in his native town, but during the Hundred Days fled to England, where he obtained a post at a school for the children of *émigrés*. Returning to Paris in 1815, he was ordained priest the following year at Rennes. Shortly

---

[1] W. J. Sparrow-Simpson, *French Catholics in the Nineteenth Century*, p. 9.

afterwards he began publication of his *Essai sur l'indifférence en matière de religion* (4 vols., 1817–23; Eng. trans. of part, by Lord Stanley of Alderley, 1895), an elaborate apology for Roman Catholicism in which he argues the need of a fresh approach to the apologetic problem. The traditional appeal to miracle and prophecy was, he felt, no longer serviceable. The apologist's first task was to enlist his readers' sympathies. Faith must be shown to be something that is *natural* to man. Yet in the process the insufficiency of mere reasoning would become manifest, since rationalism only ends in scepticism and universal doubt, whereas man is constrained by his own nature to believe. But what general principle determines belief? The only possible answer is Authority, resting ultimately upon the common consent of mankind. The individual judgement in isolation is weak, but certainty can be built upon common experience. The truth, then, is most likely to be found where authority is clearest and most assured.

From the testimony of the general reason to that of the Catholic Church and the papacy is thus for Lamennais but a step. Yet it is always the *use* of religion in society rather than any abstract consideration of its validity with which his argument is concerned. Toleration is a mistake: Europe needs a restoration of its traditional faith; Luther, Descartes and Rousseau have taught it the exercise of private judgement, and the result has been atheism and political subversion. What Lamennais envisages is the submission of the temporal to ecclesiastical authority, and even a form of democracy if inspired by the theocratic ideal. The *Essai* had a mixed reception, however, from the Gallican bishops and the monarchists, although many of the younger clergy were warm in its praise. It also won the approval of Pope Leo XII, who invited the author to Rome and even offered him a cardinal's hat, but Lamennais chose to return to France where he felt he had a mission and might possibly gain a wide influence. At La Chênaie he gathered around him a brilliant following, including such men as the Comte de Montalembert, Henri Dominique Lacordaire and Maurice de Guérin, and in his two independent journals, the *Drapeau blanc* and the *Mémorial catholique*, strongly advocated the ultramontane cause. He also published a treatise *De la religion considerée dans ses rapports avec l'ordre politique et civil* (1826), in which the philosophy of the *Essai* was given a practical goal. What Lamennais and his friends now sought was to organize public opinion against the continued connexion of Church and State. The so-called liberties of the Gallican Church they denounced. But the continued strain of work proved too much for Lamennais' energy and his health broke. Retiring to the Pyrenees to recuperate, his speedy recovery seemed to him providential, and by 1828 the project of a theocratic republic had again become the absorbing interest of his life. A new periodical, *L'Avenir*, was founded, with 'God and Liberty' for its motto, its first number appearing on 16 October 1830. In civil matters it championed a radical democracy and demanded complete freedom for the Church from state control.

Conservative opposition, not unnaturally, became more stubborn, and for a while Lamennais found it politic to suspend his journal. In November 1831 he set out for Rome in company with Montalembert and Lacordaire, but Gregory XVI's reception of these 'pilgrims of liberty', as they described themselves, was cool and the Vatican declined to endorse their views. Lamennais' own hopes for eventual papal support were dashed by the publication of the encyclical *Mirari vos* (August 1832), in which his liberal ultramontanism was unequivocally condemned. At first he was half prepared to submit, but his passionate outburst two years later in *Paroles d'un croyant* brought his ecclesiastical career to an end, and with it also his profession of faith as a Catholic. Henceforth he could be regarded only as a deist and a Voltairean, fervently committed to the struggle for popular rights. In 1837 he published *Le livre du peuple*, followed, in 1840, by *Le pays et le gouvernement*, for which he was indicted and sentenced to twelve months' imprisonment. These books, like the revolutionary *Paroles*, are an expression of Lamennais' deepest convictions. His religious beliefs had been but scaffolding for his real faith—the destiny of man in society; and the scaffolding had now collapsed with an ease he himself had not perhaps expected. The metaphysical grounds of Catholic teaching did not interest him fundamentally, a fact which links him with both Saint-Simon and Auguste Comte, who also based their socio-political systems on a reading of history rather than on any abstract philosophy.

Yet the years 1840–6 saw the publication of what is in some ways Lamennais' principal literary achievement: the four-volume *Esquisse d'une philosophie*. His aim here is system and comprehensiveness—a grandiose scheme of doctrine for which the impassioned rhetoric that characterizes so much of his work was felt to be unsuitable. The method is ontological, not psychological: God is Being—one, infinite and eternal, and the presupposition and basis of all human thinking. He also is personal, since there is no perfection without mind. The significance of the Christian dogma of the Trinity is in its symbolization of the Absolute's intrinsic life. The Father signifies power, through which all things possess their being; the Son, the divine self-knowledge; the Spirit, the unity of Father and Son each with the other. Lamennais goes on to discuss creation and the universe, the problem of evil, and the nature of man, and ends by reviewing the works of man in art, science, industry and the institutions of society. The whole enterprise shows its author's capacity for reflective thinking, but did little to extend his influence. It was as the creator first of ultramontanism and then of liberal Catholicism that he became a force in the intellectual and religious life of nineteenth-century France. In 1848, the year of revolutions, he was elected to the National Constituent Assembly, sitting on the extreme Left until the *coup d'état* of 1851. His last days, marred by sickness and poverty, were spent in translating Dante. He died in Paris, unreconciled to the Church, in 1854.

Bibliographical note

Extracts from the *Essai sur l'indifférence en matière de religion* and *Paroles d'un croyant* are published in a single volume by La Renaissance du Livre (n.d.). An edition, by Y. le Hir, of a hitherto unpublished *Essai d'un système de philosophie catholique*, appeared in 1954. See F. Duine, *Lamennais: sa vie, ses idées, ses ouvrages* (1922), A. R. Vidler, *Prophecy and Papacy* (1954), R. Bovard, *Drame de conscience* (1961), and L. Foucher, *La philosophie catholique en France au XIXe siècle* (1955), chapters II and III.

AUTHORITY IN RELIGION

In attempting to discover the basis of certainty, we have recognized two important truths: the first is that all philosophical systems result in absolute doubt; the second, that absolute doubt is impossible for man. Hence when he consults reason alone, he is placed in an unnatural state; for while reason constrains him to doubt, nature compels him to believe.

Now, to believe is simply to defer to a testimony or to obey an authority; and in fact every mind begins by obeying. We receive language on the authority of those who speak to us, and with it our first ideas, or the truths necessary for our self-preservation. No race is without these truths; at the moment when he drew man from nothingness, God revealed them by manifesting himself through the power of his word; and the life of the intellect, whose law is to obey, is merely a participation in the supreme reason, a full consent to the testimony which the Infinite Being has himself given to his creature. Every created intelligence springs to life in the rays of the eternal intelligence. Divine reason, communicating by means of language, is the cause of their existence, and faith is its essential mode.

Thence it follows that the principle of certainty and the principle of life are one and the same thing; nor should this surprise us, since certainty must obviously be a property of the infinite reason which embraces all truth, and since that which is true is simply that which exists. Thus he who receives existence or life, receives truth; he receives it through language or testimony; so testimony or language is the principle of our reason, of our intellectual being. It is through language that we exist, it is through testimony that we are sure of existing or of possessing truth; the more general the authority or the reason which testifies, the greater the certainty; and since the testimony on which rest the primordial truths constituting our reason, our life, is of necessity the testimony of the author of that life himself—in other words, of the highest authority or of infinite reason—it carries absolute certainty.

Furthermore, one sees that the initial ideas of which language in its essential nature is the expression could not be lost without language itself being lost, and without intelligence being destroyed. If man were deprived of these traditional ideas, he would lapse into a complete powerlessness to act or think, since he would no longer possess an instrument for action, nor anything upon which to act. So when particular circumstances separate some men from others, and the primal truths are obscured, or, as Scripture so admirably puts it, 'diminish'[1] in their rationality, these men, partially deprived of those elements of all thought which tradition alone preserves, are left with an extremely poor language, and a small number of secondary concepts. To this category belong all savages.

The workings of the human mind are restricted to combining the concepts which it received initially and to drawing consequences from them. And since human reason is made for truth, since it is through truth alone that it exists, the general reason cannot err or destroy itself; otherwise there would be in God a contradiction of wills, or lack of power.

It is quite another matter with individual reason. In isolating itself, it loses the support of tradition. Incapable henceforth of returning to the principle of its being, it sees itself as a mere effect without a cause. Doubt invades it on all sides. It finds no ground of certainty in itself, since it finds no necessity there. Equally able to be, or not to be, existence poses for it an eternally insoluble problem; evidence is the sole means by which this problem can be solved, but individual reason cannot furnish itself with infallible or certain evidence. And this helps us to understand the profound saying of the supreme reason, of the eternal Word clothed in our flesh: 'If I bear witness of myself, my witness is not true. There is another that beareth witness of me.'[2] Thus simply in separating itself from society, reason dies; it violates

---

[1] Ps. xi. 1: 'Diminutae sunt veritates' (Vulgate). [2] John v. 31–2.

188

the law of evidence or authority which is for intelligent beings a law of life.

No law is more general; it admits of no exception; it embraces the entire duration of our existence. If man, blind and corrupt, did not try to escape it, his magnificent destiny could be accomplished without effort. As far as the present life is concerned, he resigns himself easily to obeying authority, because above all else he wants to live, and sees that disobedience results in death. But eternal life, and the life of the soul, affect him very much less. Since he has no conception of the nature of that life, and has no consciousness of it, he is not equally horrified at being deprived of it—that is, at eternal death. Naturally disinclined to recognize any master, he seeks within himself the laws of truth and of order, whose conception he has drawn from society. First he asks his reason to furnish them, and it replies, 'How do I know?' Then he asks his emotions, but they do not reply, for they have no language; or, if we take as a reply the inclination which draws us towards certain objects, or the aversion which they give us, truth and order become as uncertain and as variable as our loves and our hates. Thus man, who can only think and feel, turns now to reason in scorn of emotion, now to emotion in scorn of reason. Panting with desire, he pursues truth, which flees from him; and when he thinks that he is about to reach it, his eyes become dim, he stumbles and in the darkness doubt is the only support he finds.

Pride, eternal principle of disobedience; pride, in constant revolt against power, is the first cause of the great disorder by which man, fixed within himself, remains as if suspended between darkness and light, between life and death. He convinces himself that the sacrifice of his reason is demanded when he is urged to obey authority; but on the contrary, as authority is simply 'the general reason manifested by testimony', it is supremely reasonable to submit to it, since even leaving on one side the evidences of its infallibility, it has the strongest presumptions to support its validity. If to submit to authority's decisions were to renounce reason, man's every act would be unreasonable, for all his actions, as a physical being and as a member of society, presuppose complete faith in testimony and complete obedience to authority; it is enough to remark that man does not owe language to his reason; he has received it, and he uses it as it was given him; to speak is to obey.

Thus everywhere authority is revealed to our eyes; it animates and preserves the universe which it has created. Without it there would be no existence, no truth, no order. Principle and ruler of our thoughts, our attachments and our duties, it reigns over the whole soul, which itself lives solely by faith, and dies the instant that it ceases to obey. And this should not astonish us, since the sway of authority is simply that of reason manifested through speech. He who has not heard it knows nothing, recognizes nothing. Intelligence has no other foundation; certainty neither has nor can have any other basis but this great testimony originally given by God himself, immutable, infinite reason.

Thus one cannot find the certainty of religion elsewhere; and Bossuet insists on this truth in the strongest terms: 'I say that earth never lacked a visible, audible authority to which it should submit...I say that there must be an external means of resolving these doubts, and that this means must be certain.'[1]

In other words, religion must be certain. But, incapable of acquiring by reason alone, by his individual judgement, the certainty of any knowledge, even the simplest, how could man find in this same reason the certainty of the most lofty dogmas and of the most incomprehensible mysteries; mysteries of which he has no idea before they are revealed to him, and which he knows only by the teaching of the authority which commands him to believe them?

But Religion is not only a corpus of knowledge; it is more, a law first and foremost, since it includes every truth and all order, or everything which must hold sway over the reason, heart and actions of men, all that he must believe and practise. But there can be no law without authority: the two ideas are correlative. Thus Religion necessarily rests on authority, and true Religion on the greatest authority, without which men could not recognize it, or know what God commands them to obey.

We have proved that everyone should arrive at the knowledge of true Religion. Hence there must exist a general means of discerning it. Now Religion is truth, and the only means we have to discern truth from error is authority; thus authority is both the only and the universal means of discerning true Religion; and consequently that Religion which rests upon the highest authority is certainly or necessarily the true one.

Religion is the corpus of the laws which result from the nature of

---

[1] 'Conférence avec M. Claude', *Œuvres de Bossuet*, XXIII, 294, 295 (Edition de Versailles).—*Ed.*

intelligent beings. Now human nature would perish if each man had to discover or even clearly to understand natural laws, which, however, he cannot transgress without dying: thus we must be instructed by testimony, and so authority is the only, the universal, means of knowing the laws of the intelligence or of discerning the true Religion; and consequently that Religion which rests upon the highest authority is certainly or necessarily the true one.

In a word, Religion is the expression of God's will, since he wants man to live, and since man cannot live the life of the soul without conforming to the laws of Religion. It is therefore a duty to submit to them; and as all duty presupposes an authority which commands, authority is the only, the universal, means of assuring us of our duties as intelligent beings, or of discerning the true Religion; and consequently that religion which rests upon the highest authority is certainly or necessarily the true one.

See how everything is linked in the order established by the Creator:

Intelligence develops only through speech or through testimony; testimony exists only in society:

Thus man can live only in a social context; thus there necessarily existed a social relationship between God and the first man; thus God spoke to him and gave him testimony of his existence.

The necessity of testimony implies that of faith, without which evidence would remain ineffectual:

Thus faith is in man's nature, and is the first condition of life.

The certainty of faith depends on its conformity with reason, on the weight of the authority which testifies to it:

Thus the testimony of God is infinitely certain, since it is simply the manifestation of infinite reason, or of the greatest authority.

Testimony is possible only in society:

Thus authority and certainty exist in society alone.

No human society can exist except by virtue of the social relationship originally established between God and man, or by the truths or laws which his word made known in the beginning.

Thus these truths cannot be lost in any society without its being destroyed; thus they must be found in all societies.

These truths necessary to society can be preserved only by testimony, and it is authority which gives testimony its force and effect; since the reason for believing in testimony depends on its certainty, which itself depends on the weight of the authority which testifies:

So just as authority exists only in society, society exists only through authority; thus wherever there is no authority, there is no society.

Man's relationships with his fellows are set in a temporal context; but those with God and the other intelligences are eternal:

Thus there are two societies, political or civil society which is on the level of time, and spiritual society which is on the level of eternity; so there are two authorities, each one infallible in its sphere.

Political society testifies to contingent truths, namely the facts on which it rests, its institutions, laws, etc.; and its testimony is certain, being the expression of the general reason.

Spiritual society testifies to the immutable truths on which it rests, namely its dogmas, precepts, etc.; and its testimony is certain, being the expression of the general reason.

As this society embraces all men and all epochs, and the truths which constitute it—in other words, those necessary for man to maintain himself as an intelligent and moral being—must be testified to by the human race, or rest on the greatest visible authority.

But since man, like every being, must attain his perfection, and since he cannot do this without the aid of truth, it is in the order of things, that is to say, it is natural or necessary, that the primal truths develop; and they cannot do so if spiritual society does not itself develop or perfect itself.

If the primal truths really have developed, they must all be found in the perfected spiritual society, which must make itself known by the mark of the greatest authority, since it would impose new duties on man's spirit, heart and senses, and since it is to a greater authority alone that man owes a greater obedience. Thus no visible authority would equal that of this society; and, in fact, as a corollary of what has just been said, it would be composed of the authority of humanity testifying to the primal truths, and of a subsequent authority testifying both to the primal truths and to those which have developed from them. And just as from this development known with certainty one could logically infer the existence of the perfected spiritual society, and even its certain existence, so one must infer the development of truth, the only possible cause of perfection.

So in choosing a Religion the only question to consider is whether there exists somewhere an authority as we have defined it; or, in other words, if there exists a spiritual and visible society which declares that it possesses this authority. We say first of all a visible society because all evidence is external; secondly, we say that such evidence would prove with certainty the authority in question, as it would be the expression of the most general reason.[1]

If there were no society with these characteristics, the only true Religion would be the traditional Religion of humanity, in other words the corpus of dogmas and precepts hallowed by the traditions of every race, and originally revealed by God.

If such a society exists, true Religion is the corpus of the dogmas and precepts preserved by tradition within this society, and perpetually manifested through its testimony. These precepts and dogmas are no more than a development of the dogmas and precepts which form the general beliefs of the human race.

Any man rendered incapable by circumstances of knowing the developed or perfected spiritual society would be required to obey only the authority known to him, namely that of the human race.

Any man capable of knowing the developed or perfected spiritual society would be required to obey its authority, since it would be the greatest visible authority.

In a word, man is always obliged to obey the greatest authority that it is possible for him to know, since his rule is reason, and since a higher authority is and can be nothing less than a higher reason.

Thus there exists for all men a means of perceiving the true Religion: although some men are incapable of knowing it in all its perfection, or of being acquainted with all its developments.

This means is universal, since it has its source in the nature of man, who everywhere believes in reason or obeys authority.

This means is easy, since at every instant man employs it; for it is through it that he forms his judgements and controls his actions in everything connected with his present existence.

Finally, as we have shown, this means is sure, since it is the very law of certainty and of life.

Here we may have recourse once more to universal testimony. Was there ever a Religion which did not rest upon authority? Have not all races believed because they have been told to believe; because they have been addressed in the name of a higher reason? Of all these races

---

[1] Particular testimony or individual denial on the part of one or a few men neither adds nor removes any degree of force to the testimony of society. Thus when Bossuet and Newton affirmed that God exists, or when Spinoza and Diderot denied it, God's existence, attested throughout the centuries by the human race, was neither more nor less certain. The witness of authority cannot be either weakened or confirmed, in the strict sense of the word, except by an authority still greater.

there is not one in which one does not find the primitive traditions; thus they have obeyed the authority of humanity. It is true that a great many races, in preserving these traditions, have altered them to a greater or less extent by the errors they have added to them; but these errors themselves were established only through authority, they subsist through it alone, namely through a false application of the rule which, if better used, would cause them to be recognized as human inventions, and would lead souls back to the truth.

So some, confusing political with religious society, have taken their beliefs from the hand of the civil power, obeying an authority which has no rights over them. Others, impatient with the duties which the general authority of the spiritual society imposed on their reason and hearts, have revolted against it, obeying the particular authority of one or of several men; but always they have obeyed; and he who obeys no authority has no Religion, not even a false one.

Since all men have the same means for discerning the true Religion, it is their will alone that is responsible when they stray. Distracted by passions, ruled by pride, either they do not seek the highest authority or they refuse to obey it. Indifference or rebellion; these are their crimes; these are for intelligent beings the two great causes of death. Woe betide him who shuts his ears to testimony! Woe betide him who separates himself from society! 'Vae soli!' As we emerged from nothingness, society repeats to each of us the word which the first man heard from the lips of the Creator. Time opens to receive the newborn understanding which, in one single act, takes possession of the past and the future. It believes, and faith unites it to the supreme reason; it is born, and it adores; for to believe is to adore. Entering (if I may dare so put it) the infinite Being, it feeds there on truth, always listening, always obeying, and eternal life consists simply in eternal obedience.

Assured of the means by which we can discern the true Religion, we shall now easily be able to discover it; there is no need to discuss dogma; it is solely a question of knowing which is the visible spiritual society that possesses the greatest authority. Once this society is recognized, all uncertainty vanishes. To dispute its testimony, to deny that to which it testifies, is to abjure reason; to disobey its laws is a crime. Developing the consequences of the principle established in this chapter, we shall thus conclude:

1. That before Jesus Christ there existed a spiritual and visible society, universal yet purely domestic, which preserved the stock

of necessary truths; so that true Religion consisted of the dogmas and precepts originally revealed by God and attested by the tradition of every family and every race; that this Religion, which we have ever since been able to distinguish from particular errors and local superstitions, evidently rested on the highest authority, or on the testimony of the human race, which is the permanent manifestation of the general reason.

2. That as the primitive Religion developed according to universal expectation based on divine promises, so the spiritual society developed simultaneously; that perfected in its constitution and its laws it became a public society; that since this moment, namely since Jesus Christ, the Christian society always held the highest authority; whence it follows that every man who is in a position to be acquainted with it should obey its commandments and believe its testimony, which, as far as ancient traditions are concerned, mingles with the testimony of the human race, being no less than the testimony of God himself.

3. That among the different Christian communions the essential characteristic of the greatest authority belongs visibly to the Catholic Church; so that in her alone dwell all the truths necessary to man, the full consciousness of the duties or of the laws of intelligence, certainty, salvation and life.

The particular proofs of Christianity will be seen to arise from the principle of authority as its logical consequences. We shall see that it alone shows all the marks of the true Religion, just as one finds only in the Catholic Church the distinctive marks of the society which is the trustee of this true Religion. These marks, necessary conditions of the highest authority, belong both to Christian doctrine considered in itself, and to the Church which preserves it and perpetuates it by its unchanging teaching; a natural enough thing, since these marks are basically no more than the characteristics inherent in the very being of God who, in his all-embracing unity and in the relationship which he wished to establish between himself and his intelligent creatures, is the totality of Religion.

Essay on Indifference in Matters of Religion (1817–24) (trans. Stephen Abbott)

CHAPTER 10

AUGUSTE COMTE

Auguste Comte, originator of the positivist philosophy, is a writer today more often referred to than read. But while his more idiosyncratic notions are usually dismissed with an amused contempt the general tendency of his thought has exercised considerable if unacknowledged influence. By many of his contemporaries he was hailed as a prophet, a revealer of ultimate truths. In the eyes of his English disciple, G. H. Lewes, for example, 'a new era' had dawned with the appearance of the *Philosophie positive*. 'For the first time in history,' Lewes proclaimed, 'an explanation of the World, Society and Man is presented which is thoroughly in accordance with accurate knowledge.'

The author of this all-comprehending system was born at Montpellier in 1798, entering the Paris École Polytechnique in 1814. Although the school was disbanded for political reasons only two years later the young Comte remained in the capital, where he soon became a close friend of the political philosopher, Saint-Simon, whose ideas deeply impressed him. He was especially moved by the latter's demand for a new principle of spiritual cohesion in a society whose inherited political and religious traditions were in dissolution. But a breach occurred between the two men when Comte published a scheme for the reorganization of society on the basic assumption that the Revolution of 1789 had been a calamitous mistake. In 1825 he married Caroline Masson, but the union was ill-starred and brought the pair no happiness. The following year he began public lecturing on philosophy, but this congenial occupation was interrupted by a mental breakdown, although on his recovery he took it up again with unabated vigour. There after his principal literary labour was the composition of his *Cours de philosophie positive*, the sixth and final volume of which came out in 1842. Meantime he had been appointed examiner—he earlier had been tutor—at the revived École Polytechnique, but his unpopularity with his colleagues led to his dismissal. Luckily, much-needed financial support was forthcoming from his devoted English followers, George Grote and J. S. Mill, and later a public subscription was raised for his benefit in France. By now separated from his wife, he formed in 1845 an attachment with one Clotilde de Vaux, his admiration for whom quickly turned to adulation. He declared her to be above all women he had 'read of in the past, had seen in the present, or could conceive in the future'. But signs of renewed mental instability were to be observed. He applied himself, with a zeal unblemished by the slightest touch of humour, to the invention of a new Religion of Humanity, of which he was to be high priest. Nor did his project lack enthusiasts who, like himself, were stirred by the thought of enlisting religious sentiment in the task of the intellectual and moral betterment of mankind. Indeed the Comtists, as an organized sect, long survived their founder, who died in Paris in 1857.

Comte's other writings include a *Discours sur l'esprit positif* (1844; Eng. trans. 1905), a *Système de politique positive* (4 vols., 1851–4; Eng. trans. 1875–9), a *Catéchisme positive* (1852; Eng. trans. 1858) and a *Système de logique positive* (1856). The author's aim was an encyclopædic unification of all knowledge on a strictly scientific basis, a scheme designed to comprise history, morals and politics under the novel title of *sociology*. The arrangement of the various disciplines is hierarchical: mathematics at the summit is followed in a dependent series by astronomy, physics, chemistry and biology, sociology, also 'positivized', completing it. In the latter the presiding idea is that of the 'Loi des trois états', according to which human thought passes through three stages of development. Of these the earliest is the theological, in which natural phenomena are attributed to or associated with the agency of spirits or divinities identified at the more primitive level with the natural objects themselves, but later, in a mythological phase, depicted as discarnate spiritual beings. The second stage is metaphysical: spiritual entities are replaced as causal forces by abstract ideas. Phenomena are now explained in terms of ultra-phenomenal principles, free-ranging imagination having given way to logical reasoning and argument, often abstruse. But this stage, which is transitional only, must finally succumb to the positive or scientific. Here observation is the sole test of truth and teleology an irrelevance: the only question man may ask is How? Inquiry is directed to general theories concerning the constant relations subsisting between classes of phenomena, and the function of philosophy, of which Comte's own doctrine is the exemplar, is purely that of systematizing scientific knowledge. Hence positive philosophy, by condensing—again in the words of G. H. Lewes—'all knowledge into a homogeneous body of doctrine', is 'capable of supplying a Faith and consequently a Polity'. At the same time, although the sciences are to be classified according to their respective degrees of generality, any attempt to reduce them to a single *corpus* of laws deriving from some ultimate and unitary principle is excluded.

For what Comte envisaged was not merely the satisfaction of intellectual curiosity, important though this is when achieved by means of a proper methodology, but, like Karl Marx, the reformation of society. Here too the use of scientific reason could yield definite and permanent results. The social situation in his day was, as he saw it, one of intellectual and moral chaos; the theological and metaphysical stages had passed or were passing, but the implications of the positive were not fully recognized. The process of critical erosion had begun with the Protestant Reformation, and the French Revolution had carried it much further, but the principles of the Revolution had themselves hardened into a new dogmatism inimical to progress. The idealist notions which it had left strewn in its wake must be cleared away if a scientific account of man and society is to find practical expression. What was needed was a new social *order* in which revolutionary 'freedom' must be subordinated to an authority based on positive knowledge. 'The requisite convergence of the best minds', Comte's readers were informed, 'cannot be obtained without the voluntary renunciation, on the part of most of them, of the sovereign rights of free inquiry'; though doubtless they would be 'willing to abdicate, as soon as they have found organs worthy to exercise appropriately their vain provisional supremacy'.

Apart from the formulation of his by no means implausible Law of the Three Stages, Comte is most often remembered for his doctrinaire and somewhat bizarre Religion of Humanity. The emotional impulse behind this singular project may have sprung from his infatuation for Madame de Vaux. He at all events was convinced not only that a 'sound Philosophy' must become the foundation of 'true Religion' but that the latter's creation was to be his own destined responsibility. The revolt of reason against feeling had left nineteenth-century civilization without the moral inspiration which traditional religion once supplied but could do so no longer. The claims of the modern intellect had first to be met, 'but this being done, moral requirements at once reassume the place that belongs to them'. In realizing a complete synthesis Love was to be 'the one universal principle', along with Order and Progress. But Comte was not satisfied only with a moral ideal. No less necessary was its expression in a concrete religious system. The result, in Carlyle's words, was 'Catholicism without Christianity'. No detail was omitted: philosophers would be its priests, with Comte himself as supreme pontiff. Even the new hierarchy's pay-scale was not left to chance. That there would have to be an appropriate hagiology was obvious—'the best types we can find to personify Humanity', and on them would public worship be based. Women would enjoy a place of special honour, and a succession of rites and ceremonies would consecrate life's successive phases. Widowhood, as in the primitive Church, was to be looked on as a virtuous condition not to be sullied by a second marriage. Divorce would be permitted only in exceptional circumstances.

It is easy to scoff at Comte's religiosity and to deride a system which at once aped and travestied the ancestral faith of his fellow-countrymen. But for all the bemused ardour with which he pursued a vision that to the Christian believer was a scandal and to the non-believer—unless himself a Comtean—mere folly, Comte's perception of the need of a positive morality as well as of positive knowledge, reveals an understanding of man's actual situation in the modern world as relevant now as then. His historical generalizations are indeed no less striking than Karl Marx's; and like Marx Comte sought not only to describe the world but to change it. Yet the respective fates of their two systems could not, in the event, have been more diverse.

Bibliographical note

Comte's *Cours de philosophie positive, discours sur l'esprit positif,* is obtainable in a new edition by C. Le Verrier (1949–50). A translation, with explanatory notes, by E. S. Beesly, was published in 1903. It is from this that the following extract is taken. On Comte's system G. H. Lewes' *Comte's Philosophy of the Sciences* (1853) is still worth reading. See also E. Caird, *The Social Philosophy and Religion of Auguste Comte* (1893). L. Levy-Bruhl, *La philosophie d'Auguste Comte* (1900; Eng. trans. New York, 1903) remains a standard work. There is a life of Comte by H. Gouhier (1931).

THE LAW OF THE THREE STATES

According to the fundamental doctrine [of Positivism], all our speculations on every subject of human inquiry are bound to pass successively, both in the individual and the race, through three different theoretical states, usually known as Theological, Metaphysical, and Positive. To those who quite understand the true general sense of these words, their meaning, as used here, will be sufficiently clear. The first of these states, though in every respect indispensable at the outset, must henceforth be regarded as purely provisional and preparatory. The second is but a modified and destructive form of the first, and thus has only the transitional office of leading gradually to the third. This last is the only normal and final state of human reason in all departments of knowledge.

At their first rise all human speculations necessarily take a theological shape. They are marked by an instinctive predilection for the most insoluble questions relating to subjects that no investigation can ever decide. In our day it must at first sight seem unaccountable, though in reality it was perfectly in accordance with the primitive situation of the human mind, that when it was still unequal to dealing with the simplest scientific problems it should have busied itself eagerly and almost exclusively with such questions as the origin of all things, the essential causes, whether first or final, of the sundry phenomena which struck its attention, the ultimate mode of their production—in a word, with absolute knowledge. This primitive propensity was satisfied in a natural way, as far as the then situation required (and indeed as far as it can ever be satisfied), by the tendency of man in the infancy of the race to attribute human qualities to every object in nature. All phenomena whatsoever were supposed to resemble those which we ourselves produce, and which for that reason seem to us at first sufficiently known through the direct intuition accompanying them. This rudimentary condition of the intellect is developed more and more systematically until it becomes the theological state properly so called. If we would rightly understand that state we must not confine ourselves to observing it in its last phase which is drawing to its close under our eyes among the most advanced populations; for this is far from being its most marked type. We must take a really philosophic survey of its whole course in order to detect its essential identity under the three principal forms which it successively assumes.

The most direct and thorough of these forms is Fetichism properly so called. In this all external objects are supposed to possess a life essentially analogous to our own, but almost always more energetic, because their action is seen to be usually more powerful than ours. Again, this first phase of theologism has gradations of its own. Its earliest form differs little from the mental state at which the superior animals have stopped short; its highest is marked by star-worship. Fetichism can be traced in the early intellectual history of all peoples; but in its naked simplicity it now prevails only among the least numerous of the three great branches of the human race.

The second phase is that of true Polytheism—too often confounded by modern observers with Fetichism. Here uncontrolled Imagination plays the chief part in speculation, whereas in Fetichism human theories had sprung chiefly from Instinct and Feeling. In assuming this phase theological philosophy undergoes the most profound change that is compatible with its real purpose as a whole. It consists in this: life is no longer attributed to material objects themselves, but is mysteriously transferred to sundry fictitious beings, usually invisible, whose active interposition is thenceforth considered to be the direct cause of all external and even, as the theory gains ground, human phenomena. It is during this well-marked phase, now so ill understood, that we shall best study the Theological Spirit; for here we find it developed with a completeness and consistency which became impossible under Monotheism. Look at it how you will this is the period when Theologism had its greatest influence on both thought and society. The majority of the human species have not yet emerged from this phase. It still prevails among the most numerous of the three great races, and also among the most advanced Blacks and the most backward Whites.

The third phase is Monotheism, properly so called. With this begins the decay, bound to come sooner or later, of the theological philosophy. A great social influence it long retains; though even in the monotheistic phase this is more apparent than real. But its intellectual influence begins thenceforward to decrease rapidly. This decline is the natural consequence of the simplification which is its distinguishing mark. Reason begins to restrict more and more the former predominance of imagination; and a universal feeling, till then hardly noticeable, that all the phenomena of nature are necessarily subject to invariable laws, gradually gains ground. Under many different and even irreconcilable forms this final phase of the theological régime still prevails, though with very unequal degrees of energy, among the vast majority of the white race. It is thus more easily observable. On the other hand personal bias is more apt to come in and to prevent this phase from being fairly judged, for want of a sufficiently rational and impartial comparison of it with its two predecessors.

Imperfect as the theological manner of philosophizing must seem now, it is very important to recognize that it was for a long time not only inevitable but indispensable to progress. We thus realize that there has not been and could not be any breach of continuity between the present state of the human mind and the whole of its preceding states. Estimating the theological hypothesis here merely from the intellectual point of view, I need hardly dwell on the involuntary propensity which even at the present day evidently impels us all to fly to theological explanations the moment we want to get direct to the inaccessible mystery of the ultimate mode of production of any phenomena, especially those whose real laws are still unknown to us. In such cases the most eminent thinkers may notice that they are themselves apt to fall instinctively into the naïvest fetichism if their ignorance happens to be for the moment combined with some vehement feeling. If therefore among the Western peoples in modern times all theological explanations have been more and more going out of use, it is only because researches into the mystery of causation have been laid aside as being radically inaccessible to the human mind, which has slowly but surely exchanged them for studies more fruitful and more suitable to our real needs. The speculations of Malebranche on so easy a subject as the elementary theory of impact, and at a time when the true philosophical spirit already prevailed with respect to the simplest phenomena, will always be memorable as showing that whenever man tries to penetrate to the First Cause of any event he is obliged to recur to the hypothesis of a direct and continual intervention of supernatural power. But further; childish as such attempts to explain causes by divine volition are now justly considered to be, they were certainly the only means by which human speculation could first be set in motion. It was a spontaneous way of escape from the vicious circle in which the intellect was at first confined by two incompatible and yet equally imperative conditions. For while on the one hand it is quite true, as we Moderns proclaim, that no solid theory can be built except on a sufficient combination of suitable observations, it is on the other hand equally incontestable that the human mind could never combine or even collect such observations unless it were directed by some previously adopted theory. There was, therefore, only one source from which these earliest conceptions could emanate; namely from a philosophy which by its very nature needed no long preparation, but could arise, to put it in one word, spontaneously, that is by sheer instinct; though of course speculations so destitute of any real foundation could not be otherwise than chimerical. Observe, then, this happy property of theological beliefs: without them the human mind would assuredly never have been able to emerge from its primitive torpor; they alone could give the first direction to its speculative activity, and so make gradual preparation for a more rational philosophy. Another instinctive tendency which powerfully helped to stimulate the human intellect was its taste, in its infancy, for precisely those problems which are insoluble. Until Man had sufficiently exercised his mental powers he could not gauge them, and consequently could not know to what tasks it is wise to limit them. But how was he to be induced to make this indispensable exertion, especially as these are the feeblest of his faculties? No stimulus would have been strong enough but that administered by the theological philosophy to which so many ill-cultivated minds still look for the readiest and completest solutions of the questions that usually confront them. To overcome the native sluggishness of the human intellect there was need, even for a long time, of the attractive illusions naturally inspired by a philosophy which encouraged man to think that he could modify the world almost as he pleased. For the world was then supposed to be essentially ordained for man's use, and no great law withdrawing it from the arbitrary government of supernatural power had yet been discovered. As late as three centuries ago, and among the most advanced peoples, the hope excited by astrology and alchemy, those last traces of theology in science, was still of real service in stimulating a daily accumulation of astronomical and chemical observations, as Kepler has remarked in the first case and Berthollet in the second.

So much for the various intellectual impulses which contributed to create the theological mode of thought. It was also irresistibly imposed by high social motives. They have been fully set forth in my *System of Positive Philosophy*; but in the present treatise they must only have brief mention. In the first place it can be convincingly shown how indispensable the theological mode of thought must long have been for a durable building up of ideas in the field of Morals and Politics, even more peculiarly so than in the lower departments of knowledge, both because Morals and Politics are more complex, and because their phenomena were, in primitive times, too indistinct and could not acquire a well-marked development until after a very prolonged growth of human civilization. It is a strange inconsistency, for which the blindly critical spirit of our time is hardly a sufficient excuse, to admit that the ancients could not possibly speculate in the simpler departments of knowledge otherwise than theologically, and yet not to see that theologism was equally inevitable in social speculations, especially among the polytheists. But further we must feel, though this is not the place for demonstrating it, that Theologism was also indispensable to the first stage of social growth, quite as much as to that of intellectual growth. Its service was twofold. It furnished in those early times certain common doctrines, without which the social union could not have acquired sufficient extension or cohesion, and it spontaneously called into existence the only spiritual authority that could then arise.

Theologism, then, was the only philosophy suited to the infancy of Humanity. The general explanations I have here given as to its provisional nature and preparatory service have been necessarily brief. But they suffice to make clear how profoundly this first stage of thought differs in all respects from that Positive spirit which I shall presently show to be appropriate to our intellectual manhood. So wide is the gap that the passage from the one state to the other could not originally have been accomplished, either in the individual or the species, without the increasing help of a sort of intermediate philosophy, useful only for this transitory purpose. This is the special share of the Metaphysical State, properly so called, in the fundamental intellectual evolution. In this way the human mind, which is averse to any brusque change, is enabled to rise almost insensibly from the purely Theological to the frankly Positive state, although the ambiguous intermediate state has much more affinity with Theologism than with Positivism. The questions with which it chiefly busies itself involve the same habitual pursuit of absolute knowledge. Only, in the metaphysical philosophy the solutions offered undergo a notable change in form, and one which smooths the way towards Positive conceptions. Metaphysic, in fact, like Theology strives to explain the inner nature of beings, the origin and purpose of all things, the essential mode of the production of all phenomena. But instead of employing for that purpose supernatural agents properly so called, it step by step substitutes for them, entities or personified abstractions. The usage of these is so thoroughly characteristic of Metaphysic that it has often been called Ontology. It is only too easy to find instances of this manner of philosophizing at the present day. In reasoning about the most complicated phenomena most people still employ it. And even in speculations relating to the simplest and most highly perfected sciences distinct traces of its long sway may every day be noticed.[1] It was precisely their equivocal character which made these entities so useful in the past. For each of these metaphysical existences was supposed to be inherent in the body to which it related, and yet at the same time to be something distinct from that body. If therefore the metaphysical thinker was but little removed from the theological state, 'entity' meant for him a real emanation of supernatural power. If on the other hand he was nearer the positive stage he could use the word merely as an abstract denomination of the phenomenon observed. In the Metaphysical stage pure imagination no longer reigns supreme; neither as yet does

---

[1] Almost all the current explanations of social phenomena, most of those relating to man's intellectual and moral nature, many of our physiological and medical theories, and even several chemical theories, etc., still forcibly remind one of the strange manner of philosophizing depicted so amusingly by Molière, for instance as to the 'dormitive virtue' of opium. Molière was following up the decisive blow just dealt by Descartes at the whole system of entities.

genuine observation; but reason comes far more into play than it did in Theologism, and gets prepared, in a confused way, for true scientific work. Indeed, we must remark that when the mind first enters this transitional stage, ratiocination plays an even excessive part in speculation. For an obstinate proneness to argue rather than observe, whatever be the subject of inquiry, is characteristic of the metaphysical spirit even in its most eminent representatives. Again, the system of entities being so flexible it could not enjoy the stability which was so long the privilege of the theological system. It was bound to arrive much more rapidly at its own form of unity. The process consisted in a gradual merging of the sundry particular entities in a single general entity called NATURE. Just as Monotheism had furnished a vague universal bond of connexion for all phenomena, so Nature, though in a much feebler way, served the same purpose in the Metaphysical state.

The use of the Metaphysical philosophy in the past cannot be properly understood, especially in our day, unless we recognize that its spontaneous effect on beliefs, and, *a fortiori*, on social institutions, must always be to criticize and dissolve them. This is its very nature. It can never organize any belief or institution of its own. There is a radical inconsistency in this equivocal mode of philosophizing; it retains all the fundamental principles of the theological system, while more and more depriving them of the vigour and stability without which they can exercise no useful authority. But in this weakening of Theologism lies the chief temporary utility of the metaphysical philosophy. It began to be of service when the theological régime, which through long ages had played a progressive part in the human evolution, looked at as a whole, reached—as sooner or later it was bound to do— a stage of mischievous prolongation, and threatened to keep man for ever in the infancy which it at first so advantageously directed. At bottom, therefore, Metaphysics are nothing but a sort of enervated theology losing something of its vigour at each successive simplification. By this simplifying process it spontaneously loses its direct power of impeding the isolated use of positive conceptions in special branches of knowledge, while still retaining its provisional aptitude for keeping up a certain indispensable exercise of the spirit of generalization until the time comes when that spirit can find better aliment. As a consequence of its self-contradictory character the metaphysical or ontological régime is always oscillating between two inevitable alternatives. It can only satisfy the requirements of order by attempting an unmeaning restoration of Theology. It can only escape from the oppressive domination of Theology by moving towards a state of pure negation. This unavoidable oscillation is now only observable in the case of the most difficult theories. But it was formerly quite as marked with regard to the simplest, as long as they remained in the Metaphysical state, because that manner of philosophizing is always impotent for organic purposes. If popular good sense had not long ago pushed aside the absurd metaphysical doubts raised twenty centuries ago as to so fundamental a notion as the existence of external bodies we may be sure that they would still survive in one shape or another; for they have certainly never been decisively dissipated by any argumentation. The Metaphysical state then may be regarded as a sort of chronic distemper naturally supervening in the mental evolution, whether of the individual or the race, between the periods of infancy and adult manhood.

To the modern philosopher who hardly ever carries his consideration of history further back than polytheistic times, the metaphysical spirit must seem to be almost as ancient as the theological spirit itself. And he is not altogether wrong. For the metaphysical spirit did necessarily play an important though not very obvious part in the primitive change from fetichism to polytheism. When purely supernatural activity was withdrawn from separate concrete objects, and lodged in gods representing abstract classes of phenomena, its place was supplied by a corresponding entity supposed to be inherent in the concrete object. But this first and greatest change in theology could not at that early time be accompanied by anything deserving the name of discussion. It was, therefore, not until the next revolution (when Polytheism was to be condensed into Monotheism) that the intervention of the ontological spirit began to be plainly marked. Ontological reasoning was indeed the natural instrument by which that revolution was effected. Its influence went on increasing, and as long as it remained subordinate to the theological instinct it even seemed to be capable of building up belief. But the appearance was deceptive. The essential nature of the metaphysical spirit is dissolvent. And this became plain enough later on when it tried by degrees to push the simplification of theology even beyond the monotheistic type suitable to ordinary minds, which was, for every reason, the last really possible phase of the theological régime. Thus the help given by the metaphysical spirit to the fundamental development of our modern

civilization has been of a negative kind. The value of Catholic monotheism had lain in its *social* usefulness. By the end of the Middle Age
this was exhausted. Thenceforward, therefore, the theological system
became finally retrograde, and in decomposing it bit by bit the metaphysical spirit was rendering a service—if only of a negative kind—to
progress. Unfortunately, after having fulfilled this indispensable but
transitory office in each department of knowledge, it always lingered
on and tended to obstruct any new and real organization of opinions;
so that the most dangerous hindrance to the final installation of a true
philosophy comes in our day from the very spirit which still often
claims to have almost a monopoly of philosophic thought.

A Discourse on the Positive Spirit (1844) (trans. E. S. Beesly)

AUGUSTE SABATIER

Louis Auguste Sabatier was born at Vallon in 1839 and educated at Montpellier and Montauban. Later he studied at Basle, Tübingen and Heidelberg. His first appointment was as agent of the Société centrale protestante d'évangelisation at Aubenas, Ardèche, but in 1870 he became professor of dogmatics in the Protestant faculty at Strasbourg. On the outbreak in the same year of the Franco-Prussian War he helped to organize a Protestant ambulance service and after France's defeat refused to continue academic work under a German government. Indeed he so antagonized the German authorities in the city that he was obliged to leave. Settling in Paris as secretary of the École libre des sciences religieuses—he had declined the offer of a university post at Lausanne—he devoted much of his time for economic reasons to journalism. When, however, in 1877 the Protestant faculty was transferred from Strasbourg to Paris—and the establishment of such a faculty in the capital he had himself repeatedly urged—he at last was able to resume his former career. He was subsequently appointed associate director of the section for the history of religion at the École des hautes études and finally, in 1895, dean of the faculty. His numerous publications include, besides the well-known *Esquisse d'une philosophie de la religion* (1897), a history of the canon of the New Testament (1877), an address, *De l'esprit théologique*, to the Paris Société de Théologie (1878), a study of the Apocalypse of St John (1888), a notable volume on St Paul—*L'Apôtre Paul. Esquisse d'une histoire de sa pensée* (1870; Eng. trans. 1891)—lectures delivered at Stockholm on *La religion et la culture moderne* (1897) and a treatise on the atonement, *La doctrine de l'expiation et son évolution historique* (Eng. trans., *The Doctrine of the Atonement and its Historical Evolution*, 1904). The last-named, together with what is perhaps the best-known of all his works, *Les religions d'autorité et la religion de l'esprit* (Eng. trans., *The Religions of Authority and the Religion of the Spirit*, 1904), was published posthumously in 1903.

Sabatier was brought up an orthodox Huguenot and all his life remained deeply religious. Religion, he writes in the opening paragraph of his *Outlines*, is 'a moral necessity of my being', adding: 'The necessity which I experience in my individual life I find to be still more invincible in the collective life of humanity. Humanity is not less incurably religious than I am. The cults it has espoused and abandoned have deceived it in vain; in vain has the criticism of savants and philosophers shattered its dogmas and mythologies; in vain has religion left such tracks of blood and fire throughout the annals of humanity; it has survived all change, all revolution, all stages of culture and progress. Cut down a thousand times, the ancient stem has always sent new branches forth.' But this inextinguishable vitality left no reason for ignoring the difficulty of religious belief in an increasingly non-religious environment. His own century was an age of science, not of faith; somehow the two had to be reconciled as aspects alike necessary of the life of modern man. But the attempt, in his personal thinking, to bring this about led him further and further from orthodoxy. After Renan, he was among the earliest of his fellow-countrymen to steep himself in the methods of modern biblical criticism; and the result again proved what a solvent of traditional belief this could be. For Sabatier realized that a critical approach to the Scriptures and the history of primitive Christianity is bound to point to certain negative conclusions in the field of dogma. The origin of all religion he discovered in the struggle to overcome man's sense of contra-diction between his empirical and his ideal ego. 'Man cannot know himself without knowing himself to be limited. But he cannot feel these fatal limitations without going beyond them in thought and by desire, so that he is never satisfied with what he possesses, and cannot be happy except with that he cannot attain.' The protraction of this struggle marks the growth of the spiritual life. Religion is 'the rent in the rock through which the living and life-giving waters flow'. Not that it proposes any theoretical solution to man's problems: the issue it puts before us is essentially practical. 'It does not save us by adding to our knowledge, but by a return to the very principle on which our being depends, and by a moral act of confidence in the origin and aim of life.' One may describe it as the spiritual aspect of the instinct of conservation in the physical world. In the actual religious evolution of the race Sabatier observes three stages: the mythological, represented by ancient paganism; the dogmatic, represented by Catholicism and orthodox Protes-tantism; and the psychological, in which the divine revelation is seen to be interior, evident—'the veil is withdrawn'—and progressive—dependent, that is, on 'the progress of the moral and religious life which God begets and nourishes in the bosom of humanity'. Psychological religion alone will satisfy the needs of both piety and reason.

The history of man's religion may fairly be claimed to have culminated in Christianity. For the Christian it is unquestionably the perfect religion. This perfection, however, is not that of a complete system of supernatural knowledge but the perfect realization, rather, of the believer's relation to God and of God's relation to him. The assurance is, again, not speculative, but the immediate and practical result of an inward experience, an experience first and most fully reached in the consciousness of Jesus Christ. For Christ was not only the 'author' of Christianity; the 'first germ' of it was formed in his own inner life, in which, to begin with, 'that divine revelation was made which, repeating and multiplying itself, has enlightened and quickened all mankind'. Christianity is not merely an ideal, therefore; it is a historical phenomenon inseparably connected not only with the recorded teaching of Jesus but with his person itself and with 'the permanent action of the new spirit which animated him', and which lives from generation to generation in his followers. Thus the real truth of the Christian religion (as something inward and personal), is beyond scientific criticism. Nevertheless Christian theology is not so immune. Here criticism has the task of purifying the doctrine by purging it of the merely temporary or adventitious, though no doubt it 'will always be a just cause of alarm' to those who would elevate some historical or contingent form of it into an absolute. But the fact is that nothing historically conditioned can be absolute. The function of dogmatics is to effect a constant revision and restatement of dogma, inasmuch as a religious society cannot dispense with some degree of formal and authoritative teaching; indeed, 'the more moral it is in its character, the more it needs a dogmatic symbol which defines and explains its *raison d'être*'. Yet the creeds, with which dogmatics is primarily concerned, have inevitably with the lapse of time become obsolete. The manner in which a modern dogmatics can best serve the Church is to avoid, on the one hand, such 'a tyrannical usurpation of tradition' as Sabatier sees in Roman Catholicism, and, on the other, that 'intransigence of individual convictions and of Illuminism' which is 'the plague of Protestant communities'. The truth, he holds, will lie in a *tertium quid* 'and in the organization of a traditional Church stable enough to receive and help the heritage of the past, large and flexible enough to permit in it the legitimate expansion of the Christian consciousness and the acquisition of new treasure'. For all his emphasis on the need for a modern outlook in theology and a style of doctrine adapted to the times, Sabatier had a deep respect for tradition and a keen sense of the value of continuity.

Although, as he acknowledged, he owed much to Schleiermacher, and akin as his opinions were to Harnack's, Sabatier's work made no great impression in Germany. But in his native France its interest was at once recognized; and not only in Protestant circles, since it had no small influence upon Catholic Modernism. His books were also widely read in England, where they readily appealed to Anglican liberals.

Bibliographical note

Of the works translated into English only the *Outlines of a Philosophy of Religion* has been recently reprinted (1957). The English edition of *Religions of Authority and the Religion of the Spirit* has a memoir by Jean Réville. See also H. Mounier, *Auguste Sabatier, sa vie, sa pensée et ses travaux* (1903),

E. Ménégoz, 'The Theology of Auguste Sabatier of Paris', *The Expository Times*, xv (1903-4) and G. B. Stevens, 'Auguste Sabatier and the Paris School of Theology', *The Hibbert Journal*, I (1903).

WHAT IS A DOGMA?

1. *Definition*

Dogma, in the strictest sense, is one or more doctrinal propositions which, in a religious society, and as the result of the decisions of the competent authority, have become the object of faith, and the rule of belief and practice.

It would not be enough to say that a religious society has dogmas as a political society has laws. For the first, it is a much greater necessity. Moral societies not only need to be governed; they need to define themselves and to explain their *raison d'être*. Now, they can only do this in their dogma.

Dogma therefore is a phenomenon of social life. One cannot conceive either dogma without a Church, or a Church without dogma. The two notions are correlative and inseparable.

There are three elements in dogma: a religious element, which springs from piety; an intellectual or philosophic element, which supposes reflexion and discussion; and an element of authority, which comes from the Church. Dogma is a doctrine of which the Church has made a law.

All the peoples of antiquity believed that their legislation came from heaven. In like manner all the Churches have believed, and many of them still believe, that their dogmas, in their official form, have been directly given to them by God Himself. The history of evolution, political and religious, has dissipated these illusions. Every law of righteousness and truth should, doubtless, be referred to the mysterious action of the Divine Spirit which works incessantly in the spirits of men; but, in its historical form, it bears, nevertheless, the stamp of the contingent conditions in which it is born. The genius of a people is nowhere more manifest than in its constitution and its laws, nor the soul and the original inspiration of a Church than in its dogmatic creations. The work always bears the moral impress of the workman.

It follows that a Church cannot claim for its dogma more authority than it possesses itself. Only a Church which is infallible can issue immutable dogmas. When Protestantism sets up such a pretension, it falls into a radical contradiction with its own principle, and that contradiction ruins all attempts of this kind.

In Catholicism the theory of the immutability of dogmas is opposed to history; in Protestantism it is opposed to logic. In both cases the affirmation is shown to be illusory. It is with dogmas, so long as they are alive, as it is with all living things; they are in a perpetual state of transformation. They only become immutable when they are dead, and they begin to die when they cease to be studied for their own sakes —that is, to be discussed.

Dogma, therefore, which serves as a law and visible bond to the Church, is neither the principle nor the foundation of religion. It is not primitive; it never appears until late in the history of religious evolution. 'There were poets and orators,' says Voltaire, 'before there was a grammar and a rhetoric.' Man chanted before he reasoned. Everywhere the prophet preceded the rabbi, and religion theology. It may be said, no doubt, that dogma is in religion, since it comes out of it; but it is in it as the fruits of Autumn are in the blossoms of Spring. Dogmas and fruits, in order to form and ripen, need long summers and much sunshine. The best way to describe their nature will be to trace their genesis.

2. *The genesis of dogma*

Dogma has its tap-root in religion. In every positive religion there is an internal and an external element, a soul and a body. The soul is inward piety, the movement of adoration and of prayer, the divine sensibility of the heart; the body consists of external forms, of rites and dogmas, institutions and codes. Life consists in the organic union of these two elements. Without the soul, religion is but an empty form, a mere corpse. Without the body, which is the expression and the instrument of the soul, religion is indiscernible, unconscious, and unrealized.

Which of these two elements is primitive and generative? The answer is not doubtful. Modern psychology has learnt it in a manner never to be forgotten from Schleiermacher, Benjamin Constant, and Alexander Vinet. The principle of all religion is in piety, just as the principle of language is in thought, although it is not possible now to conceive of them as being separate. Consider a moment. That religion which time and custom have transformed, perhaps, into a mechanical round of ceremonies, or into a system of abstractions and metaphysical theories, what was it at first? Trace it to its source, and you will find that these cold blocks of lava once came burning hot from an interior fire.

But this is the parting of the ways. This is the point at which religious minds separate into widely different groups.

Regarding religion as a saving institution in the form of a visible organized Church maintained by God and provided with all the means of grace, Catholicism was bound to end in a sort of mechanical psychology, and to explain the sentiment of piety as the inward effect of the outward and supernatural institution. This is done by Bellarmine and de Bonald, the most consistent of the Catholic theologians. Protestantism, on the contrary, which makes of the faith of the heart, of the immediate and personal relation of the soul to God, the very principle of justification, and of all religious life, was bound none the less logically to end, by analysis, in a more profound psychology, and to refer to an inward principle all the forms and manifestations of religion. Religious history thus becomes homogeneous, and runs parallel with that of all the other activities of the human mind.

None the less, this subjectivity of the religious principle frightens many good men. Persons devoted to practice, and unconsciously dominated by the habits and necessities of ecclesiastical government and religious teaching, hesitate to enter upon a road so naturally opened. As, from generation to generation, religion has been taught and propagated externally by the Church, the family, or special agents, it is impossible for them to imagine that it was not always so, and not to trace back to God Himself that chain or tradition of external instruction. In which they are certainly right. Their only error, but it is a grave one, is to represent God as an ordinary teacher, the first of a series, who once acted, like the rest of them, upon His pupils from without; whereas God works in all souls, acts and teaches without ceasing through all human masters, and is present throughout the whole religious education of humanity.

Who does not see that to represent things otherwise is to remain in the crudest and least religious of anthropomorphisms? At bottom, these men are afraid of losing revelation, which they rightly judge to be inseparable from the very idea of religion. They object that piety and the awakening of the religious sentiment must have an objective cause, and that that cause can only be a revelation of God Himself. Nothing is more true; but this revelation which is effected without, in the events of Nature or of History, is only known within, in and by the human consciousness. This inward inspiration alone enables religious men to interpret Nature and History religiously. Now, this interpretation is made by their intellect and according to the laws and conditions which regulate it. The religious phenomenon therefore has not two moments only, the objective revelation as a cause and the subjective piety as an effect; it has three, which always follow each other in the same order: the inner revelation of God, which produces the subjective piety of man, which, in its turn, engenders the historical religious forms, rites, formularies of faith, sacred books, social creations, which we can know and describe as external facts. It will be seen what an error they commit, what a mistake they make, who identify the third term with the first, suppressing the second, which is the necessary link and forms the transition between the other two. Whoever will fathom this little problem in psychology, and reflect upon it with a little attention, will see that all religious revelation of God must necessarily pass through human subjectivity before arriving at historical objectivity.

Passing now from the intellectual interpretation to the intellectual expression of religion, and noting the successive stages through which it must necessarily advance towards dogma, I remark once more that man's first language is that of the imagination. The imagination of the child or of the savage animates, dramatizes, and transfigures everything. It spontaneously engenders vivid and poetic images. At the beginning, religion, consisting chiefly of emotions, presentiments, movements of the heart, clothed itself in mythologic forms...But the age of individual reflexion comes. The image tends to change into the idea. Men interpret, define, translate it. The religious myth is replaced by the religious doctrine. These are at first entirely personal interpretations. Nevertheless, these opinions desire to propagate themselves, to become general, and, as they are imperfect and diverse, they engender conflicts which threaten to become schisms. Myths, appealing to the imagination merely, and only professing to translate the common emotion, draw souls together and fuse them into a real unity; individual reason, private exegesis, inevitably separates them. But the consciousness of the community, thus menaced, naturally reacts by the instincts of conservation. There is therefore a struggle between the two, and out of this conflict dogma is born.

A new element must intervene. There must be a Church. Now, all religions do not form churches. The phenomenon is only produced in the universalist and moral religions. Strictly speaking, there is no

Church except in Christianity; and no dogmas save Christian dogmas. In ancient societies, where religion was confounded either with the State, or with the nationality, the religious unity was maintained and guaranteed by the same means as the political unity. There were no dogmas, because dogmas were of no use. As much may be said of Hebraism and of Islam: in them there were rites, external signs and seals, which sufficed to weld and to maintain the religious bond.

Dogma only arises when the religious society, distinguishing itself from the civil, becomes a moral society, recruiting itself by voluntary adherents. This society, like every other, gives to itself what it needs in order to live, to defend itself, and propagate itself. Doctrine necessarily becomes for it an essential thing; for in its doctrine it expresses its soul, its mission, its faith. It is necessary also that it should carry its doctrine to a degree at once of generality and precision high enough to embrace and to translate all the moments of its religious experience and to eliminate all alien and hostile elements. Controversy springs up and threatens to rend it. The Church then chooses and formulates a definition of the point contested: it enacts it as the adequate expression of its faith, and sanctions it with all its objective authority: dogma is born. From that moment also the two correlative notions of *orthodoxy* and *heresy* are formed. Orthodoxy is official and collective doctrine; heresy is individual doctrine or interpretation...By and by symbols or confessions of faith are formed, and these become the standards of faith and practice in the various churches that adopt them.

This long evolution is fully justified in the eyes of reason. It is a movement of the mind as legitimate as it is necessary. The germ must become a tree, the child grow to manhood, the image be transformed into the idea, and poetry give place to prose. It is possible to be mistaken as to the nature, origin, and value of dogma, but not as to its necessity. The Church may make a different use of it in the future, but it will not be able to dispense with it, for the doctrinal form of religion answers to an imperative need of the epoch of intellectual growth at which we have arrived. No one can either reverse or arrest its development....

The word dogma is anterior to Catholicism. It had two senses in Greek antiquity: a political and authoritarian sense, designating the decrees of popular assemblies and of kings; this is the meaning which dominates and characterizes the Catholic notion of dogma. But the word had also in the schools of Greece an essentially philosophical and doctrinal meaning; it designated the characteristic doctrine of each school. The Protestant Churches have inherited this latter sense of the word: it is in perfect harmony with the spirit and the principle of Protestantism. Dogma, in the Protestant sense, means the doctrinal type generally received in a Church, and publicly expressed in its liturgy, its catechisms, its official teaching, and especially in its Confession of Faith.[1]

3. *The religious value of dogma*

The intolerance of Catholic dogmatism has had consequences so revolting, and, in Protestantism, wherever this dogmatism has revived, it has given rise to conflicts so sterile and so lamentable, that certain minds have gone so far as to deny the utility of dogma in the largest sense of the word, and have wished to suppress all doctrinal definition of the Christian Faith. To call dogma either divine in itself or evil in itself is to go to an unwarrantable extreme. In religious development, whether individual or social, it has an organic place that cannot be taken away from it, and a practical importance that cannot be contested.

Religious faith is a phenomenon of consciousness. God Himself is its author and its cause; but it has for psychological factors all the elements of consciousness—feeling, volition, idea. It must never be forgotten that these verbal distinctions are pure abstractions; that these elements co-exist, and are enveloped and implicated with each other in the unity of the ego. In the living reality there has never existed feeling which did not carry within it some embryo of an idea and translate itself into some voluntary movement... As it is impossible for thought not to manifest itself organically by gesture or language, so it is impossible for religion not to express itself in rites and doctrines.

No doubt, in the first period of physical life, sensation dominates, and at the *début* of religious life, feeling and imagination. But as science springs from sensation, so religious doctrine springs from piety. To say that 'Christianity is a life, therefore it is not a doctrine' is to reason very badly. We should rather say, 'Christianity is a life and therefore it engenders doctrine'; for man cannot live his life without thinking it. The two things are not hostile; they go together. In apostolic times the greatest of missionaries was the greatest of theologians. St Augustine

---

[1] Originally the word dogma signified a command, a precept, and not a truth (Luke ii. 1, and the Septuagint of Dan. ii. 13; vi. 8; Esth. iii. 9; 2 Macc. x. 8, etc.). Ignatius of Antioch still uses the word in this sense. It is not until towards the time of Athanasius or of Augustine that it begins to be used of the doctrinal decisions of the Fathers, the Councils, and the pope. (Cf. also Acts xv. 28, 29. This is afterwards called a dogma, the only time it is used in the N.T. with reference to a decision of the Church.)

at the end of the old world, Calvin, Luther, Zwingli, at the beginning
of the modern world, followed the example of St Paul. When the sap
of piety fails, theology withers. Protestant scholasticism corresponds
to a decline of religious life. Spener, by reopening the springs of piety,
renewed the streams of theology. Without Pietism Germany would
have had no Schleiermacher; without the religious revival at the
beginning of this century we should have had neither Samuel Vincent
nor Alexander Vinet.

If the life of a Church be compared to that of a plant, doctrine holds
in it the place of the seed. Like the seed, doctrine is the last to be
formed; it crowns and closes the annual cycle of vegetation; but it is
necessary that it should form and ripen; for it carries within it the power
of life and the germ of a new development. A Church without dogmas
would be a sterile plant. But let not the partisans of dogmatic immutability triumph: let them pursue the comparison to the end: 'Except a
grain of wheat fall into the ground and *die*,' said Jesus, 'it bears no fruit.'
To be fruitful, dogma must be decomposed—that is to say, it must mix
itself unceasingly with the evolution of human thought and die in it;
it is the condition of perpetual resurrection.

Without being either absolute, or perfect in itself, then, dogma is
absolutely necessary to the propagation and edification of the religious
life. The Church has a pedagogic mission that could not be fulfilled
without it. It bears souls, nourishes them and brings them up. Its role
is that of a mother. In that educative mission, we may add, the mother
finds the principle and aim of her authority, the reason and the limit
of her tutelage. In this sense, dogma is never without authority. But
this same pedagogic authority is neither absolute nor eternal; it has a
double limit, in the nature of the pupil's soul, which it ought to respect,
and in the end it would attain, the making of free men, adult Christians,
sons of God in the image of Christ and in immediate relationship to
the Father. If dogma is the heritage of the past transmitted by the
Church, it is the children's duty first to receive it, and then to add to its
value by continually reforming it, since that is the only way to keep it
alive and to render it truly useful and fruitful in the moral development
of humanity. It is therefore to this idea of necessary dogma, but of
dogma necessarily historical and changing, that we must henceforth
accustom ourselves; and we shall most easily habituate ourselves to it
by tracing its evolution in the past.

Outlines of a Philosophy of Religion based on Psychology and History (1897) (trans. T. A. Seed)

CHAPTER 12

SOLOVYOV

Vladimir Sergeyevich Solovyov, philosopher, critic and poet, was born at Moscow in 1853, the son of a well-known historian and rector of the city's university. He himself studied there and in 1874 gained his doctorate with a thesis on *The Crisis of Western Civilization*, on the strength of which he was awarded a fellowship in the faculty of philosophy. He subsequently travelled abroad, visiting England, France, Italy and Egypt. On his return to Russia he was given a post in the Ministry of Public Education at St Petersburg, where he also lectured at the university. His lectures on 'Godmanhood', delivered at this time, drew a large audience that included both Dostoyevsky and Tolstoy. But a speech of his (March 1881) on capital punishment—shortly after the assassination of the Tsar Alexander II—aroused so much excitement that he resigned his position, though no pressure was brought upon him to do so. From then on he devoted himself entirely to literary work and to the task—at the time a good deal misunderstood—of promoting relations between the Orthodox and Roman Catholic Churches. He died, very prematurely, in 1900. Of his numerous publications *The Philosophical Foundations of Integral Knowledge* (1877), the *Lectures on Godmanhood* (1878) and *A Criticism of Abstract Principles* (1880) are the most important. His *Russia and the Universal Church*, published in Paris in 1889, was bitterly attacked by the Holy Synod of the Russian Orthodox Church. Several of his works have appeared in English translation.

Solovyov, who claimed to have experienced certain visions of the divine Wisdom—the first at the age of 9, two more whilst travelling in Egypt—was deeply influenced by his studies in mysticism, both western and eastern, and by German idealist philosophy. His great aim, which admitted even certain Gnostic elements, was to create an organic synthesis of all aspects of the human understanding upon the directing and energizing principle of this same personified divine Wisdom (*Sophia*). He may be described therefore as a Christian philosopher in the sense of one who constructs a general philosophy of life on the basis of the Christian creed; but the spirit which informs his work is predominantly mystical and theosophical. The question he sought to answer was What is the purpose of life?, and no philosophy, he held, which failed to consider it seriously was worth the name. Inquiry would have to start with the individual consciousness, but would necessarily comprise all mankind and ultimately the universe itself, since reality is a consistent and co-ordinated whole, the lesser being explicable only by reference to the greater. The key to life's meaning must be a spiritual experience that affords a unique knowledge of ends, and philosophy cannot as a rational pursuit be isolated from it.

Solovyov sees in the incarnation, death and resurrection of Jesus Christ the central event of history, with implications that are cosmic. The Christian dogma proclaims that man has himself been deified through the perfect union in Christ of humanity and deity. Formally stated this is a paradox which cannot be accommodated to reason except by the suppression of one or other of its terms. Accordingly Christianity is not to be reduced to a common pattern of religious belief. It has a content *sui generis*, which is 'solely and exclusively Christ'—a truth 'very often asserted but little assimilated'. For the singularity of Christ lies not in his moral teaching but in his claim that he and he only is 'the way, the truth and the life'. Here, then, is mystery; reason cannot explain it and a rationalizing theology which simply attempts to eliminate it would but cut the core from the gospel message. On the other hand the meaning of the incarnation for human life can be rationally inferred. Hence the uses of a Christian philosophy. The reason why the incarnation took place at a point in history and not—for so some would think proper—as a grand climax at its end is that God purposed a Kingdom on earth, a new human order the principle of which had to be a signal revelation of its essential nature in the person of an actual individual. The historical disclosure of 'Godmanhood' provided this.

The starting-point in Solovyov's system is the idea of the cosmos or whole, the ground of which is ultimate Unity. To achieve complete integration within the whole, and so to realize unity, is the aim of all finite existence. Yet human experience is experience of multiplicity. To overcome the disharmony between experience and what we intuitively apprehend to be the truth—that all things do in fact inhere in an ultimate unity—is possible only through belief in God. 'For if we do not recognize in Divinity the entire fulness of reality—which is plurality—then inevitably the positive significance is transferred to the diverse reality of this world. The Divinity retains only a negative significance and little by little is denied.' Plurality therefore must be understood as contained within the unity of God. He is that by which diversity is unified and unity diversified. With this the Christian dogma of the Trinity is plainly congruent. The Father, whose unified will holds the possibility of all things in itself, begets the Son who is the principle of multiplicity. The final unity to which realized multiplicity is necessarily restored is represented by the Holy Spirit. The doctrine is thus the expression not only of men's experience of the divine in its concrete and historical manifestations but of an ultimate and eternal truth.

The Kingdom of God, Solovyov believed, is to be thought of not only as *another* world hereafter, nor only as a terrestrial order attainable by goodwill, humanitarian idealism and political action. The incarnation of God in the person of Jesus Christ as the God-Man implies, rather, that the Kingdom is both human and divine. But the union must be freely willed and sought on man's part. Indeed the possibility of the Kingdom is already latent within him, although he needs the aid of divine grace to realize it. It is a task to be achieved and constitutes man's overall vocation in this world. Moreover, its achievement involves the entire race, which in practice means the application of Christian beliefs and values to the collective life of mankind with, as its goal or ideal, a perfect social order, national and international. The existence of the divinely instituted Christian Church is proof that redemption is corporate. Yet the pity and scandal has been that this divine Society is itself only too visibly divided. Eastern Orthodoxy, in Solovyov's view, failed to understand the *human* aspect of the Church, whilst Roman Catholicism conceived it too much as a *magisterium* resting upon compulsion. The result was the predominance in the East of the secular power—Caesaropapism—and the revolt, in the West, of the individual conscience—the Reformation. But Protestantism, having found the criterion of truth in personal opinion, has in consequence destroyed objective standards of right and wrong. The result is the engrossment of secularized Western society in the material world and its disposition to limit truth to scientific description and classification. Modern democracy is but a projection on the political and social plane of this same process of disintegration. Individuality degenerates into a crude egoism, equality into the pursuit of material prosperity. 'This path', Solovyov observes, 'has not yet been followed to the end.' The final product will be Anti-Christ, not a prodigy of wickedness but simply man, rational, self-sufficient and dedicated to technical progress. He is Anti-Christ because in the midst of utopia he remains unregenerate, the slave of his own will.

Solovyov's sympathy with Western Catholicism, in spite of the faults he saw in it, was strong enough to impel him towards the Roman Church. Whether or not he actually became a Roman Catholic, as is claimed, is disputed. The fact would seem to be that for him ecclesiastical boundaries were indistinct. What he really beheld, away beyond them, was the universal Church of Christ. 'All men who acknowledge the paternal authority of the apostolic hierarchy, who confess the Son of God and the Son of Man, and who participate in the gracious gifts of the Holy Spirit, belong to Christ's Church on earth. They are in the Church and the Church is in them.' The underlying truth of the Church's essential oneness imposes, however, the concrete task of visibly demonstrating it. A herald of twentieth-century ecumenism, he urges that the fragments of Christendom must be reunited and insists that the outcome of such union will be neither 'Orthodoxy' nor 'Catholicism', but in the fullest sense Universality. Further, 'when Orthodox

and Catholics, who abide in the unity of the Body of Christ, become aware
of that mystical unity and are moved to confirm it by the moral bond of love
and communion, the Protestant principle of freedom will find its true
application and occupy a high position in the completion of the Church,
for that completion is free theocracy'. Yet the one Church will also need,
in its present state of militancy, a visible centre of authority; and this Solovyov
has no hesitation in identifying with the papacy, provided the papal authority
be that only of 'the sovereign guidance of the Church's earthly affairs' and
so, in the long run, a matter of expediency, not of principle. The Church
itself is a means, not an end. The end is the Kingdom of God, where human
egoism will be expunged by the divine love.

Bibliographical note

A German edition of Solovyov's complete works is in course of publication. English translations of *War and Christianity* (with an introduction by
Stephen Graham) and *War, Progress and the End of History* (by A. Bakshy,
with a biographical notice by H. Wright) were published in 1915 and 1918
respectively; of *God, Man and the Church* (by D. Attwater) in 1938, of
Lectures on Godmanhood (by P. Zouboff) in 1944, of *The Meaning of Love* (by
Jane Marshall) in 1945, and of *Russia and the Universal Church* (by H. Rees)
in 1948. See also *A Solovyov Anthology*, arranged by S. C. Frank and translated by N. Duddington (1950), N. Zernov, *Three Russian Prophets* (1944)
and I. Müller, *Das Religionsphilosophische System Solovjevs* (1956).

GODMANHOOD

In general, man is a certain union of Divinity with material nature;
and that presupposes in man three constituent elements: the divine, the
material, and that which binds both together, the properly human. The
conjunction of these three elements is what really forms the actual man,
and the properly-human element is the mind (*ratio*), i.e. the relationship
of the two others. When this relation consisted of a direct and immediate subjection of the natural element to the divine [beginning] we
had the primordial man, the prototype of humanity, not yet detached
from but enclosed within, the eternal unity of the divine life; here the
natural human element was contained in the actuality of the divine
being as an embryo, *potentia*. When, on the contrary, the actuality
of man belongs to his material element, when he knows himself [only]
as a fact or as a phenomenon of nature, and [regards] the divine begin-

ning in himself only as a possibility of a different being, then we have the natural man. The third possible relationship takes place when Divinity and nature are of equal actuality in man, and his human life, properly so called, consists in an active co-ordination of the natural element with the divine, or in a free subjection of the former to the latter. Such relationship forms the *spiritual man*. From this general conception of the spiritual man certain conclusions follow. First: in order that concordance of the natural element with the divine beginning in man be an actuality, it is necessary that it take place in a single person —otherwise there would be only a real or ideal interaction between God and the natural man, but there would be no new spiritual man— in order to have an actual union of Divinity with nature, a person is necessary in whom this union might take place. Secondly, in order that this union be an actual union of the *two* beginnings, the actual presence of both of these beginnings is necessary; it is necessary that this personality be God as well as the actual, natural man—both natures are necessary. Third, in order that the concordance of the two natures in the personality of the God-man be a free spiritual act, it is necessary that the human will take part in it, [a will] distinct from the divine will; it is necessary that, rejecting any possible contradiction with the divine will, the human will would freely submit to it and bring human nature into complete inner harmony with Divinity. Thus, the conception of the spiritual man presupposes a *single God-man personality, uniting in itself two natures and possessing two wills*.[1]

The original immediate union of the two beginnings in man—the unity represented by the first Adam in his state of innocence in the Garden of Eden, which was destroyed in his fall, could not be simply restored. A new unity could not be immediate, [could not be] innocence; it had to be *attained*. It can only be the result of a free act, of an exploit, and a double exploit—[that] of the divine and human self-denial; because for the true union or concordance of the two principles, free participation and action of both are necessary. We have seen previously how the interaction of the divine and natural beginnings defines the whole life of the world and humanity, and (how) the whole course of this life consists in the gradual coming together and inter-

---

[1] This definition, which follows from our conception of the 'spiritual man', or the second Adam, is unconditionally identical with the dogmatic definitions of the Oecumenical Councils of the fifth to the seventh centuries, which were developed in refutation of the Nestorian, Monophysite, and Monothelite heresies, each of which represented a direct contradiction to one of the three essential logical conditions of the true idea of Christ.

penetration of these two beginnings, which were at first far apart and external to each other, then came more and more closely together, permeating each other deeper and deeper until nature appeared in Christ as the human soul ready for total self-denial, and God [appears] as the spirit of love and mercy communicating to this soul the whole fullness of divine life—not suppressing it [the soul] by force, not illuminating its understanding, but in His graciousness quickening it. Here we have an actual divine-human personality, able to accomplish the double exploit of the divine and human self-abnegation. To a certain extent such a self-abnegation had already taken place in the whole cosmic as well as historical process. For here, on one hand, the divine Logos, by a free act of His divine will or love, abnegated His divine dignity (the glory of God) refraining from any manifestation of it; [in the cosmic process] He left the peace of eternity, entered upon the struggle with the evil beginning, and subjected Himself to the anxieties of the world process, appearing in the chains of external being, in the limits of space and time; and then [in history] He appeared to the natural humanity, acting upon it in different finite forms of the world life, which concealed rather than revealed the true being of God. On the other hand, the nature of the world and humanity, in its constant yearning and striving for the ever fuller reception of the divine image, continuously negates itself in its given, actual forms. But here (i.e. in the cosmic and historic process) this self-denial is not perfect on either side because the boundaries of the cosmic and historic theophanies are external limits for Divinity, determining Its manifestation for the 'other' (for nature and humanity) but in no manner affecting its inner being or awareness of Itself.[1] Nature and natural humanity, on the other hand, in their perpetual progress abnegate themselves not by a free act, but only by an instinctive tendency. In the personality of the God-man, however, the divine beginning, precisely as a consequence of the fact that it is related to its antipode not through an external act, which would limit the antipode (without changing itself [i.e. the divine beginning]) but through an inner self-limitation [by] which [it] gives room in itself to the 'other one'—such an inner union with the antipode is the real self-denial on the part of the divine beginning, here it actually

---

[1] This may be explained [by a] comparison [taken] from the natural world: man, as a comparatively higher being, acting upon some lower animal, cannot appear to it in all the fullness of his human life; but those limited forms in which, for example, a dog perceives the appearance of its master, belong only to the mind of the animal, by no means limiting or changing the proper being of the man himself.

descends, annihilates itself, takes on itself the likeness of a slave. The divine beginning here is not hidden from man by the limits of human consciousness, as was the case in the previous, incomplete theophanies: here it itself adopts these limitations. Not that it wholly enters into the limits of natural consciousness (that is impossible) but it actually *feels* these limits as *its own at the given moment*; and this self-limitation of Divinity in Christ liberates His humanity, allowing its natural will to abnegate itself freely in favour of the divine beginning—[to abnegate it] not as an external force (in that case His denial would not be free) but as an inner good—and thereby to acquire that good actually. Christ, as God, freely renounces the glory of God and thereby as man acquires the possibility of *attaining* that glory. On the way to this attainment the human nature and [the human] will of the Saviour unavoidably encounter the *temptation* of evil. The divine-human personality represents a dual consciousness: the consciousness of the limits of natural existence, and the consciousness of its divine essence and power. And so, experiencing the limitations of a natural being, the God-man may be subjected to the temptation to make His divine power a means for the aims which develop as the result of those limitations.

First, to a being subjected to the conditions of material existence is presented the temptation to make material welfare the goal, and his divine power, the means for attaining it: 'if thou be the Son of God, command that these stones be made bread'. Here the divine nature—'if thou be the Son of God'—and the manifestation of that nature, the word 'command', are to serve as means for the satisfaction of a material need. Christ in answer to this temptation asserts that the Word of God is not an instrument of material life, but itself is the source of the true life for man: 'Man shall not live by bread alone but by every word that proceedeth out of the mouth of God.' Having overcome this temptation of the flesh, the Son of Man receives authority over all flesh.

Secondly, to the God-man, free from the material motives, is presented a new temptation—to make His divine power an instrument for the self-assertion of His human personality, to fall into the sin of the intellect—that of pride: 'if thou be the Son of God, cast thyself down: for it is written, He shall give his angels charge over thee: and in their hands they shall bear thee up, lest at any time thou dash thy foot against a stone'. This act ('cast thyself down') would be a proud call of man to God, a temptation of God by man, and Christ answers: 'it is written again, Thou shalt not tempt the Lord thy God'.[1] Having conquered the sin of the mind, the Son of Man receives authority over the minds.

The third temptation was the last and the strongest one. The enslavement to the flesh and the pride of the mind have been removed: the human will finds itself now on a high moral level, is conscious of being higher than the rest of creation; in the name of this moral height, man can wish for the mastery over the world in order to lead the latter to perfection; but the world lieth in sin and will not voluntarily submit to moral superiority: [it may seem] therefore that the world should be forced into subjection, that it is necessary [for Christ] to use His divine power to force the world into subjection. But such a use of coercion, i.e. of evil, for the attainment of a good would be [equivalent to] a confession that evil is stronger than the good, that the good by itself has no force. It would be [equivalent to] *falling down* before that *element of evil* which dominates the world: 'and [he] sheweth Him all the kingdoms of the world, and the glory of them; and saith unto Him, All these things will I give Thee, if Thou wilt fall down and worship me'. Here the human will is directly challenged with the fateful question: what does it believe, and what does it wish to serve—the invisible might of God or the force of evil that openly reigns in the world? And the human will of Christ, having overcome the temptation of a plausible desire for power, freely subjected itself to the true good, denying any agreement with the evil which reigns in the world: 'Then saith Jesus unto him: Get thee hence, Satan: for it is written, Thou shalt worship the Lord thy God and Him *only* shalt thou serve.' Having conquered the sin of the spirit, the Son of Man received supreme authority in the realm of the spirit; refusing to submit to the earthly power for the sake of dominion over the earth, He acquired for Himself the service of the powers of heaven: 'and, behold, angels came and ministered unto Him'.

Thus, having overcome the temptations of the evil beginning which were trying to incline His human will to self-assertion, Christ subjected and co-ordinated this human will with the divine will, [thereby]

---

[1] Sometimes these words are understood as if Christ says to the tempter: Do not tempt Me, for I am the Lord thy God. But this would have no sense, because Christ was subjected to temptations not as God but as man. In fact, the second reply of Christ, as well as the first one, represents a direct answer to what is presented by the tempter: it is offered to tempt God by a daring deed, and against this as against the first proposition, Christ refers to the Scriptures, which forbid tempting God.

deifying His manhood after the inhumanization[1] of His Divinity. But the high deed of Christ was not exhausted by the inner self-denial of His human will. Fully man, Christ had in Himself not only the purely human element (the rational will), but also the natural material element: He not only was inhumanized, but also incarnated (in Greek, Sarx egeneto). The spiritual exploit—the overcoming of the internal temptation—had to be completed with the exploit of the flesh, i.e. of the sensual soul, in the experience of His passion and death: therefore it is that in the Gospel, after the narrative about the temptations in the wilderness, it is stated that the devil departed from Christ *for a season*. The evil beginning, inwardly conquered by the self-denial of the will, [and] not being admitted into the centre of the human being, yet retained power over its periphery—over the sensual nature; and this latter could be delivered from it also by the process of self-denial— [which in the case of the human body meant] suffering and death. After the human will of Christ freely subjected itself to His Divinity, and thereby subjected to itself the sensual nature of man in Him; and, regardless of the infirmity of the latter (the prayer for the passing of the cup), [the human will of Christ] forced it [the human body] to realize in itself the divine will to the end—in the physical process of suffering and death. Thus in the second Adam has been restored the normal relationship of all the three principles which had been violated by the first Adam. The human beginning, having placed itself in the proper relationship of voluntary subjection to, or accord with, the divine beginning, as its inner good, thereby once more received the significance of the intermediary [or] uniting element between God and nature; and the latter, purified by the death on the cross, lost its material separateness and weight, became a direct expression and instrument of the divine spirit, a true *spiritual body*. It was with that body that Christ arose [from the dead] and appeared to His Church.

The due relationship between Divinity and nature in humanity, which was reached by the person of Jesus Christ as the spiritual centre or head of mankind, must be assimilated by all of mankind as His body.

The humanity which has been reunited with its divine beginning through the mediation of Jesus Christ, is the *Church*; and if in the eternal primordial world the ideal humanity had been the body of the

---

[1] The term 'inhumanization' is used in the Orthodox Church even more frequently than the term 'incarnation', and signifies a much fuller meaning of the incarnation than the mere 'taking on of human flesh'—'And the Word was made man', it would mean, rather than 'And the Word was made flesh'. Translator.

divine Logos, so in the natural world, that has come into existence, the Church appears as the body of the same Logos, only [One who has become] incarnate, i.e. historically individualized in the divine-human personality of Jesus Christ.

This body of Christ, which first appeared as a small embryo in the form of the not very numerous community of the early Christians, gradually grows and develops so as to embrace, at the end of time, all humanity and the whole of nature in one universal organism of God-manhood; because the rest of nature, in the words of the Apostle, is awaiting, with hope, the manifestation of the sons of God; for the creature became subjected to vanity not voluntarily, but by the will of Him who had so subjected it, in the hope that the creature itself was to be liberated from the enslavement to corruption into the freedom of the glory of the sons of God; for we know that the whole creation groaneth travailing together until now.

This manifestation and glory of the sons of God, hopefully awaited by all creation, is the full realization of the free God-man union in the whole of mankind in all the spheres of its life and activity; all these spheres must be brought into concordant divine-human unity, must become parts of the free theocracy in which the Universal Church will reach the full measure of the stature of Christ.

Thus, starting from the conception of the Church as the body of Christ (not in the sense of a metaphor, but [in that of] a metaphysical formula), we must remember that this body necessarily grows and develops, consequently changes and becomes perfected. Being the body of Christ, the Church until now is not yet His glorified, fully deified body. The present terrestrial existence of the Church corresponds to the [life of the] body of Jesus on earth (before the resurrection)—of the body which, manifesting in some particular cases miraculous properties (which even at present are manifested in the Church also), yet generally speaking [was] material and subject to death, not free from the infirmities and sufferings of the flesh—for all the infirmities and sufferings of human nature were taken on by Christ. But, as in Christ, all that is weak and earthly was 'swallowed up' in the resurrection of the spiritual body, thus must it be also in the Church, His universal body, when it will have reached its fullness.

The attainment of that state in mankind is conditioned, as in the personality of the God-man, by the self-negation of the human will and a free subjection of it to Divinity.

But if in Christ, as in a single person, the moral exploit of victory over the temptations of evil and of the voluntary subjection to the divine beginning, was pre-eminently an internal action, as a subjective psychological process, then in the aggregate of mankind it has been an objective, historical process—and the objects of temptation, which in the psychological process [were primarily subjective] receive an objective reality, so that a part of mankind actually becomes subject to the temptations of evil and only through their personal experience becomes convinced of the falsity of the ways which were previously rejected by the conscience of the God-man.

Since the whole of mankind represents the same three substantial elements as a single man—the spirit, the mind, and the sensual soul—the temptations of evil appear for all humanity also to be threefold, but in a sequence different from that [in which they appeared] to the personality of Christ. Humanity has already received the revelation of the divine truth in Christ, it possesses this truth as an actual *fact*—the first temptation, therefore, is that of a misuse of this truth as such in the name of this same truth, an evil in the name of the good, [which is] the sin of the spirit: a pre-eminently moral evil, i.e. that which was with Christ the last temptation (according to the Gospel of St Matthew).

Historically, the Christian Church has been composed of all people who have accepted Christ, but Christ can be accepted either inwardly or outwardly.

The inner acceptance of Christ, i.e. of the new spiritual man, consists in the spiritual regeneration, in that birth from above or of the spirit which was spoken of in the discourse with Nicodemus; [it starts] when man, having become aware of the untruth of the fleshly, material life, feels in himself the positive source of the other true life (independent of the flesh as well as of the mind of man), [accepts] the law which was given in the revelation of Christ, and, having acknowledged this new life opened [to man] by Christ as that which unconditionally ought to be [the true life of man], as the good and the truth, voluntarily subjects to it his fleshly and human life, inwardly uniting with Christ as the parent of this new spiritual life [and] the head of the new spiritual kingdom. Such an acceptance of the truth of Christ liberates [man] from sin (although not from sins) and forms [moulds] the new spiritual man.

But there can be [also] a merely outward acceptance of Christ, a mere acknowledgement of the miraculous incarnation of the Divine Being for the salvation of men, and the acceptance of His commandments in the letter, as an outward, obligatory law. Such external Christianity contains the danger of falling into the first temptation of the evil beginning. That is to say, the historical appearance of Christianity has divided all mankind into two groups: the Christian Church which possesses the divine truth and represents the will of God upon earth— and the world which remains outside of Christianity, has no knowledge of the true God, lieth in evil. Such external Christians, believing in the truth of Christ but not regenerated by it, can feel the need and even assume it to be their duty, to subjugate to Christ and to His Church all that outside and hostile world; and, since the world lying in evil will not voluntarily submit to the sons of God, [they may resolve] to subjugate it *by force*. Part of the Church, led by the Roman hierarchy, succumbed to that temptation—and dragged with it the majority of Western humanity in the first great period of its historical life, the Middle Ages. The essential falsity of this path [of this type of Christianity] is contained in that hidden unbelief which lies at its root. Indeed, the actual faith in the truth of Christ presupposes that this truth is stronger than the evil which reigns in the world, that it can by its own spiritual [and] moral force subjugate evil, i.e. bring it to [convert it into] the good; [whereas] to assume that the truth of Christ, i.e. the truth of the eternal love and of the unconditional good, for its realization needs alien and even directly opposite means of coercion and deceit, is to profess this truth to be powerless, to profess that evil is stronger than the good; it means not to believe in the good, not to believe in God. And this unbelief, which at first was hidden in Roman Catholicism as an unperceivable embryo was later on clearly revealed. Thus in Jesuitism—that extreme, purest expression of the Catholic principle—the moving force was an outright lust for power, and not the Christian zeal; nations were being brought into subjection not to Christ, but to the Church authority; the people were not asked for a real confession of the Christian faith: the acknowledgement of the Pope [as the head of the Church] and obedience to the Church authorities were sufficient.[1] Here the Christian faith is but a chance form, the essence and the aim is posited in the sovereignty of the hierarchy; but this is a

[1] Several years ago in Paris I heard a French Jesuit give the following reasoning: 'Of course, at present no one can believe the greater part of the Christian dogmas, for example, the Divinity of Christ. But you will agree that civilized human society cannot exist without a strong authority and a firmly organized hierarchy; only the Catholic Church possesses such an authority and such a hierarchy; therefore, every enlightened man who values the interest of mankind must side with the Catholic Church, that is to say, must be a Catholic.'

direct self-conviction and self-annihilation [on the part] of the false principle, for here is lost the very foundation of that authority for which [in the name of which] they act.

The falsity of the Catholic way was early recognized in the West, and finally this realization found its full expression in Protestantism. Protestantism rebels against the Catholic way of salvation [regarded and practised] as an external act, and demands a personal religious relation of man to God, a personal faith without any traditional ecclesiastical mediation. But personal faith, as such, i.e. as a merely subjective fact, does not contain in itself any guarantee of its verity—such faith requires a criterion. In the beginning, the Holy Scriptures, i.e. a book, appeared as such a criterion for Protestantism. But a book requires [proper] understanding; for the establishment of the *correct* understanding, analysis and reasoning are necessary, i.e. the activity of a personal [individual] *reason*, which, thus, becomes the actual source of the religious truth, so that Protestantism naturally passes into rationalism— a transition which is logically inevitable, and which historically, indubitably has been going on. It would be out of place to present here the momenti of this transition; we shall dwell only upon the general result of this path, i.e. on pure rationalism. It consists essentially in the belief that the human mind is not only a law unto itself but gives laws to all that exists in the practical and social spheres. This principle is expressed in the demand that all life, all political and social relations, be organized and directed exclusively on the foundations worked out by the personal [individual] human mind, regardless of any tradition, of any immediate faith—a demand which permeated all of the so-called enlightenment of the eighteenth century and served as the guiding idea of the first French Revolution. Theoretically, the principle of rationalism is expressed in the claim that the whole content of knowledge can be deduced from pure reason (*a priori*) or that all branches of science can be construed apperceptively. This claim formed the essence of German philosophy—it was assumed in a naïve way by Leibniz and Wolf, [later on] consciously (although in a modest form and with limitations) set forth by Kant, [then] resolutely declared by Fichte, and finally, with a complete self-confidence and awareness [of what was being asserted], but resulting in a just as complete a failure, [was fully] carried out by Hegel.

This self-confidence and self-assertion of human reason in life and knowledge is an abnormal phenomenon, it is the pride of the mind: in

Protestantism, and in rationalism which issued from it, Western humanity fell into the second temptation. But the falsity of this path was soon manifested in the sharp contradiction between the excessive claims of the reason and its actual impotence. In the practical domain, reason found itself impotent against the passions and [the lower] interests [of the people], and the kingdom of reason proclaimed by the French Revolution ended in a wild chaos of insanity and violence; in the domain of theory, reason found itself impotent against the empirical fact, and the presention to build a universal science on the principles of pure reason ended in the construction of a system of empty abstract concepts.

Of course, the failures of the French Revolution and of German philosophy would not in themselves prove the insolvency of rationalism. The point is, however, that the historical downfall of rationalism was only the expression of its inner, logical contradiction, of the contradiction between the relative nature of reason and its unconditional [absolute] claims. Reason is a certain relation (*ratio*) of things that gives them a certain form. But relationship presupposes the related parties, the form presupposes content; rationalism, however, positing human reason, as such, as the supreme principle, abstracts it thereby from all content, and [therefore] has in reason only an empty form; but at the same time, by virtue of such an abstraction of reason from all content, from all that is given in life and knowledge, all this datum remains for it unreasonable [irrational]. Therefore, when reason comes forth against the actuality of life and knowledge with a consciousness of its own supreme rights, it finds in life everything strange to itself, dark, impermeable, and cannot do anything with it; for, abstracted from all content, changed into an empty concept, reason naturally cannot have any power over actuality. Thus the self-elevation of human reason, the pride of the mind, at the end inevitably leads to its downfall and abasement.

The falsity of this path, cognated through experience, was acknowledged by Western humanity; but it freed itself from it only to fall into the third and last temptation.

Human reason could master neither the passions and the lower human interests in life, nor the facts of the empirical reality, in science; i.e. in life and in science it found itself opposed by the *material* beginning; was it not right to conclude from this that the material element in life and knowledge—the animal nature of man, the material mechanism of the world—[is precisely what] forms the true essence of all, [and] that the aims of life and science really consist of the maximum possible satisfaction of material needs and the greatest possible knowledge of empirical facts? And, behold, indeed, the dominion of rationalism in European politics and science is replaced with the preponderance of materialism and empiricism. This path has not been traversed to the end as yet, but its falsity has been already recognized by the leading minds in the West itself. Just as the previous path, this one also falls the victim of its inner contradiction. Starting from the material element, the element of discord and chance, they wish to reach unity and integrity, to organize a right human society and a universal science. At the same time the material aspect of existence, the cravings and passions of human nature, the facts of external experience, all these comprise only a general foundation of life and knowledge, the material of which they are formed; but in order that anything might be really created out of this material, a formative, uniting principle and a form of unity are necessary. And if it has already been shown that human reason cannot serve as such a formative principle, and [that] in its abstractness, [it] contains no real form of unity; if it has been shown that the principle of rationalism cannot form either a right commonwealth or a true science: it follows that it is necessary to have recourse to another, more powerful principle of unity—but by no means that it is necessary to be content with the material side of life and knowledge, which by itself cannot form either the human society or science. Therefore, when we see that economic socialism wishes to place the material interests at the foundation of the whole society, and positivism, the empirical knowledge as the basis of all science: then we can foretell in advance the failure of both of these systems with the same certitude with which we should assert that a pile of stones by itself, without an architect and a plan, will not compose itself into a correct[ly built] purposeful building.

An attempt actually to place the material beginning alone at the foundation of life and knowledge, an attempt to realize, in fact and in full, the lie that man shall live by bread alone, such an attempt would perforce lead to the disintegration of mankind, to the destruction of society and science, to a universal chaos. To what extent Western humanity, which has fallen into the last temptation of the evil beginning, is destined to experience all those consequences—cannot be said in advance. In any event, having learned by experience the falsehood of the three 'broad ways', having experienced the deceitfulness of the three great temptations, Western humanity sooner or later must turn to the truth of Godmanhood. From whence, then, and in what form will this truth now appear? And, first of all, is this conscious but involuntary conversion to the truth, through actual experience of every falsehood, the only possible path for mankind?

As a matter of fact, not all Christian humanity has followed that path. It was chosen by Rome and the Germano-Romantic nations which accepted the Roman culture. The East, i.e. Byzantium and the nations (with Russia at their head) which received the Byzantine culture, remained aside.

The East did not fall into the three temptations of the evil beginning —it preserved the truth of Christ; but keeping it in the *soul* of her nations, the Eastern Church has not realized it in external actuality, has not given it expression in factual reality, has not created a *Christian culture* in the same manner as the West has created an anti-Christian culture. And it [the Eastern Church] could not have created it, it could not have realized the Christian truth. For what must we understand under such a realization, what is a truly Christian culture? The establishment in the whole of human society and in all its activities, of such a relationship among the three elements of the human being as was realized individually in the person of Christ. This relationship, as we know, consists of the free co-ordination of the two lower elements (the rational and the material) with the higher, the divine beginning, by their voluntary subjection to it; not as to [a coercive] force but as to the good. For such a *free* subjection of the lower elements to the higher beginning, in order that they may *of themselves* come to the recognition of the higher beginning as the good, it is necessary they be independent. Otherwise the truth would not have anything on which it could manifest its action, in which it could become actualized. But in the Orthodox Church the enormous majority of its members were captivated into obedience to the truth through an immediate [direct] inclination, not through a conscious [reflective] process in their inner lives. The really human element, in consequence, proved in the [Eastern] Christian society to be too weak and insufficient for a free and rational carrying out of the divine beginning into the external actuality—and as a result of this, the latter (i.e. the material actuality) remained outside of the divine beginning, and the Christian consciousness was not free from a certain *dualism* between [its attitude towards] God and [towards] the world. Thus the Christian truth, mutilated and finally repudiated by Western man, remained imperfect in the man of the East. This imperfection, conditioned by the weakness of the human element (reason and personality), could be removed only with the full development of the latter—the task which fell to the lot of the West. Thus, the great Western development, negative in its direct results, indirectly has had a positive value and purpose.

If the true society of Godmanhood, created in the image and likeness of the God-man Himself, ought to represent a free concordance of the divine and human beginnings, then, obviously, it is conditioned by the active force of the first as well as by the co-operative force of the second. Consequently, it is required that society would, first, preserve the divine beginning (the truth of Christ) in all of its purity and, secondly, develop the principle of human initiative in all its fullness. But by the law of the development or of the growth of the body of Christ, a concomitant fulfilment of these two demands—as the highest ideal of society—could not be given all at once, but had to be attained [gradually]. That is to say, before the perfect unity [is reached], appears disunity, the disunity which, with the [general] solidarity of mankind, and the law of the division of historical functions following from it, was expressed as a partition of the Christian world into two halves, in which the East with all the forces of its spirit was attached to the divine [beginning] and preserved it, working out in itself the conservative and ascetic attitude necessary for that [function]; while the West applied its whole energy to the development of the human element, which was necessarily detrimental to the [conservation] of the divine truth, which was at first mutilated and then altogether repudiated. The above makes it clear that the two historical trends, far from excluding each other, have been absolutely necessary to each other and for the 'fullness of the stature of Christ' in all humanity; for if history were limited to the Western development only, if the immovable and unconditional principle of the Christian truth did not stand behind this uninterrupted stream of movements [which were] replacing one another, and of principles [which were] mutually destructive, the whole Western development would have been devoid of any positive sense, and modern history would have ended in decadence and chaos. On the other hand, had history included only the Byzantine Christianity, the truth of Christ (Godmanhood) would have remained imperfect, in the absence of a [developed] human element of free initiative and activity necessary for its perfection. As it is, however, the divine element of Christianity, preserved by the East, can now reach its perfection in mankind, for now it has the material upon which it can act, in which it can manifest its internal force: namely, the human element which has been emancipated and developed in the West. And this has not only a historical, but also a mystical, meaning.

If the overshadowing that descended upon the human Mother with the active power of God, produced the incarnation of Divinity; then the fertilization of the divine Mother (the Church) by the active human beginning must produce a free deification of humanity. Before Christianity, the natural principle in humanity represented the datum (the fact), Divinity represented the unknown (the ideal), and as the unknown, acted (ideally) on man. In Christ the unknown was given, the ideal became a fact, became an event, the active divine beginning became material. The Word became flesh, and this new flesh is the divine substance of the Church. Before Christianity, the immovable basis of life was human nature (the ancient Adam), while the divine was the principle of change, motion, progress; after Christianity, on the contrary, the divine, as incarnate, becomes the immovable foundation, the stratum of the life of humanity, while humanity appears as the unknown —[that part of humanity] which would correspond to the divine, i.e. which is capable of uniting with it of itself, [and] assimilating it. As the sought [the ideal], this ideal humanity appears as the active beginning [force] of history, the element of motion, of progress. And, as in the pre-Christian course of history, human nature or the natural element of mankind represented the basis, matter; the divine mind (in Greek, O logos tu Feu) represented the active and formative principle; and God-man, i.e. God who has adopted human nature, was the result (the offspring): so in the process of Christianity the divine nature or the divine stratum (the Word which became flesh, as well as the body of Christ, the Sophia) appears as the foundation or matter, while human reason appears as the active and formative principle; and the man-God, i.e. man who adopted Divinity, appears as the result. And, since man can receive Divinity only in his absolute totality, i.e. in union with *all*, the man-God is necessarily collective and universal, i.e. [it is] the all-humanity [the whole of mankind] or the Universal Church [that receives Divinity]; the God-man is individual, the man-God is universal. Thus the radius is one and the same for the whole circumference at any one of its points, and consequently it is itself the beginning of a circle; while the points on the periphery form the circle only in their totality. In the history of Christianity, the immovable divine foundation in humanity is represented by the Eastern Church, while the Western world is the representative of the human element. And here also, before reason could become the fertilizing principle of the Church, it had to move away from it in order that it might be at liberty to develop all its powers. After the human element is completely segregated, and then in that separateness becomes aware of its helplessness, it will be able to enter into a free union with the divine foundation of Christianity, which has been preserved in the Eastern Church—and, in consequence of that free union, to give birth to the spiritual mankind.

Lectures on Godmanhood (1878)

PART II

BRITISH AND AMERICAN

CHAPTER I

COLERIDGE

Samuel Taylor Coleridge, poet, philosopher, literary critic and talker, was
born in 1772 at his father's Devonshire vicarage of Ottery St Mary. Schooled
at Christ's Hospital, to which he was sent at the age of 9, he entered Jesus
College, Cambridge, in 1791. There he soon acquired an ardent sympathy
with the principles of both the French Revolution and William Godwin's
philosophy, an application of which latter, in the form of a 'Pantisocracy',
he planned, along with Robert Southey, to realize on the banks of the
Susquehannah. But Coleridge was as constitutionally impractical as his
republicanism was shallow and the venture remained a dream. The great
event of his life was his meeting, in 1795, with Wordsworth—he meantime
had left Cambridge without taking a degree—and with the poet, whose
genius he at once hailed, he formed an intimate friendship destined to spur
both men to their finest poetic efforts. *Lyrical Ballads*, a joint production to
which Coleridge contributed 'The Rime of the Ancient Mariner', appeared
in 1798, the two authors, accompanied by Wordsworth's sister Dorothy,
setting off on a visit to Germany on the very eve of its publication. But
Coleridge, the husband now of Southey's sister-in-law, had also met and
become warmly attached to Wordsworth's own future sister-in-law, Sarah
Hutchinson. Their relationship observed the strictest propriety—Coleridge's
belief in the indissolubility of marriage was entirely sincere—but regrets
on the poet's side were deep and lasting. Emotional frustration combined
with the physical pain—evidently rheumatic—to which he was continually
subject turned him to opium and he became addicted. Alcohol too was not
untried. The Coleridges moved north to join the Wordsworths in the
summer of 1800, but their marriage—four children were born to them, of
whom three survived—did not prosper, and Coleridge's health was not
improved by the climate of the Lakes. In 1804 he left England for Malta,
to take up duty as secretary to the governor, Sir Alexander Ball. Returning
home little bettered, even by absence from his wife, he tried public lecturing,
the success of which was immediate. In 1809 began the publication of *The
Friend*, a periodical to be devoted to the discussion of morals, politics and
allied subjects, which came out at irregular intervals until March 1810. In
that year occurred his lamentable quarrel with Wordsworth and the ending
of his association with Sarah Hutchinson. The years which followed only
increased his misery; he now was chronically sick, homeless, impoverished
and in thrall to his own weaknesses. Yet he was able to deliver further

brilliant lecture-courses and to write his critical masterpiece, the *Biographia Literaria*. In April 1816 he went to stay at the Highgate house of James Gillman, the surgeon who befriended him with the offer of a month's rest that became a sojourn of eighteen years. Regaining, under this gentle discipline, some measure of good health, he brought out a revised edition of *The Friend* in volume form and published the *Biographia* (1817). But his books sold badly, and he was obliged to resort once more to public lecturing. *Aids to Reflection* appeared in 1825 and *The Constitution of Church and State* in 1830, as well as new editions of his verse. He died in July 1834, his *Confessions of an Enquiring Spirit* coming out posthumously, in 1840.

J. S. Mill coupled Coleridge with Bentham as 'one of the two great seminal minds of England in their age', considering—he was writing in 1838—that there was hardly 'an individual of any importance in the world of mind who...did not first learn from one of these two'. F. D. Maurice declared that it was mainly to him that, in his (Maurice's) own day in particular, theology had come to realize that 'the highest truths are those which lie beyond the truths of Experience', and that 'the essential principles of the Reason are those which cannot be proved by syllogisms'. Coleridge, despite his defects of character—though his virtues, on a long view, far outshine them—was certainly among the most original and penetrative thinkers in Europe. His early Godwinian phase was no more than a passing fancy; temperamentally, as by growing conviction, he was wholly opposed to the trite rationalism of the preceding century and to the fruits—utilitarianism, determinism, materialism—which its principles were beginning to bear in his own. The soul of man had been betrayed by a 'mechanical philosophy' that substituted—to cite his well-known distinction—'Understanding' for 'Reason'. The former, which has its entirely appropriate uses, is abstract, reflective and analytical—'the translation of a living word into a dead language'—whereas the latter yields us 'knowledge of the laws of the whole considered as one'. Understanding, the 'science of phenomena', studies means; Reason, the 'organ of the supersensuous', seeks ultimate ends. To suppose that Understanding can dispense with Reason—Coleridge's use of these terms, like his parallel definitions of Fancy and Imagination, is of course peculiarly his own—was the cardinal error of the age. Faith accordingly must be a matter of Reason and is rooted in man's whole moral experience; mere ratiocination has nothing to do with it. Indeed deep thinking was attainable only by a man of deep feeling, all truth being a 'species of revelation'. But if faith is not to be destroyed by abstract argument that does not touch its springs neither can it be defended with the same weapon. Spiritual truth must be spiritually discerned; faith is not the outcome and reward of dialectical skill. Religion, as both 'the corner-stone and the key-stone of morality', must have a moral origin, 'so far at least, that the evidence of its doctrines could not, like the truths of abstract science, be wholly independent of the will'. Its fundamental truth might in fact be denied, 'though only by the fool, and even by the fool from the madness of the heart alone'. Yet the existence of God 'would not be intellectually more evident without being morally less effective', and proof in matters of faith would but sacrifice its life to 'the cold mechanism of a worthless because compulsory assent'.

Nowhere does Coleridge better reveal the prescience of his thinking more than in his discussion—before the coming of the 'Higher Criticism'—of the Bible. He found nothing of true faith in the dry and unconsidering biblicism characteristic of the religion of his time. The real worth of Scripture was such, he held, as to be invulnerable to the assaults of the sceptical critic; but here again useless defences would have to be abandoned. 'Evidences of Christianity!' he exclaims, 'I am weary of the word. Make a man feel the want; rouse him, if you can, to the self-knowledge of his need; and you may safely trust it to its own Evidence.' The inspiration of Scripture self-testifying; its proof is that it *finds* us.

Apart from his early and brief excursion into Unitarianism Coleridge was a devoted son of the Church of England. His idea of a 'National Church' was indeed of something a great deal more inclusive than the established religion of the day. It would promote 'the harmonious development of those qualities and faculties that characterize our humanity' by embodying a 'Clerisy' of all clerkly persons, whatever their beliefs and opinions. Some would be dedicated to learned research and higher academic teaching, others to the general instruction of the young; and the clergy as such would have their place. For this comprehensive 'National Church' the State would make pecuniary provision from the national wealth. Organized Christianity was thus but an aspect of it, though an aspect of unique if accidental purpose—for 'in relation to the national Church, Christianity, or the Church of Christ', so Coleridge explains, 'is a blessed accident'; adding, 'Let not the religious reader be offended with this phrase. I mean only that Christianity is an aid and instrument which no State or realm could have produced out of its own elements, which no State had a right to expect. It was, most awfully, a GOD-SEND.' The Church is distinguished—and the pity was that it has so often shown itself unaware or negligent of its true nature and high calling—by four principal qualities or characters: First, it is not of this world, as a mere estate of the secular realm, but rather the 'appointed opposite of them all collectively—the sustaining, correcting, befriending opposite of the world; the compensating counterforce to the inherent and inevitable evils and defects of the State'. Secondly, it is not invisible and secret, but, as an historic institution, visible, manifest and militant. On the other hand, and thirdly, it has no recognized sovereign or head, nor any local centre of unity, and is not an institution parallel and competitive with the State, of which

Christians would be exemplary citizens. Finally, it is universal, which is to say that no branch of it can claim to be the whole or the alone true.

The theological significance of Coleridge's philosophy lies in its appreciation of the essential subjectivity of religious and moral convictions. 'My metaphysics', he wrote, 'are merely the referring of the mind to its own consciousness for the truth indispensable to its own happiness.' Its postulates —the Kantian echo is clear—of God, the freedom of the will, the authority of conscience and the immortality of the soul derive their origin from man's moral consciousness and any reception of them as objectively true is determined by a practical interest only. Its basis, like that of the rest of our beliefs, is experience. Coleridge never published a philosophical system. Perhaps he never fully devised one: his mind was always growing and changing; but at any given moment his thought, for all the fragmentariness of its expression—in this case an index, for worse rather than better, of his personal character—was ever inwardly consistent and its overall direction did not alter.

Bibliographical note

Aids to Reflection, in Bohn's Library (1904); *Confessions of an Enquiring Spirit*, ed. H. St J. Hart (1956). A first complete edition of the *Works*, under the general editorship of K. Coburn, is in preparation. See also *Inquiring Spirit, a New Presentation from Coleridge's Published and Unpublished Writings*, ed. K. Coburn (1951); E. K. Chambers, *Samuel Taylor Coleridge, a Biographical Study* (1938); J. H. Muirhead, *Coleridge as Philosopher* (1930).

I. REASON AND UNDERSTANDING

Reason is the Power of Universal and necessary Convictions, the Source and Substance of Truths above Sense, and having their evidence in themselves. Its presence is always marked by the *necessity* of the position affirmed: this necessity being *conditional*, when a truth of Reason is applied to Facts of Experience, or to the rules and maxims of the Understanding; but *absolute*, when the subject-matter is itself the growth or offspring of the Reason. Hence arises a distinction in the Reason itself, derived from the different mode of applying it, and from the objects to which it is directed: accordingly as we consider one and the same gift, now as the ground of formal principles, and now as the origin of *ideas*. Contemplated distinctively in reference to *formal* (or abstract) truth, it is the *speculative* reason; but in reference to *actual* (or moral) truth, as the fountain of ideas, and the *light* of the conscience, we name it the *practical* reason. Whenever by self-subjection to this universal light, the will of the individual, the *particular* will, has become a will of reason, the man is regenerate: and reason is then the *spirit* of the regenerated man, whereby the person is capable of a quickening inter-communion with the Divine Spirit. And herein consists the mystery of Redemption, that this has been rendered possible for us. *And so it is written: the first man Adam was made a living soul, the last Adam a quickening Spirit* (1 Cor. xv. 45). We need only compare the passages in the writings of the Apostles Paul and John, concerning the *spirit* and spiritual Gifts, with those in the Proverbs and in the Wisdom of Solomon respecting *reason*, to be convinced that the terms are synonymous.[1] In this at once most comprehensive and most appropriate acceptation of the word, reason is pre-eminently spiritual, and a spirit, even *our* spirit, through an effluence of the same grace by which we are privileged to say Our Father!

On the other hand, the Judgements of the Understanding are binding only in relation to the objects of our Senses, which we *reflect* under the forms of the Understanding. It is, as Leighton[2] rightly defines it, 'the faculty judging according to sense'. Hence we add the epithet *human*, without tautology: and speak of the *human* understanding, in disjunction from that of beings higher or lower than man. But there is, in this sense, no *human* reason. There neither is nor can be but one reason, one and the same: even the light that lighteth every man's individual Understanding (*Discursus*), and thus maketh it a reasonable understanding, *discourse of reason—one only, yet manifold: it goeth through all understanding, and remaining in itself regenerateth all other powers*. The same writer calls it likewise *an influence from the Glory of the Almighty*, this being one of the names of the Messiah, as the *Logos*, or co-eternal Filial Word. And most noticeable for its coincidence is a fragment of Heraclitus, as I have indeed already noticed elsewhere—'To discourse rationally it behoves us to derive strength from that which is common to all men: for all human Understandings are nourished by the one DIVINE WORD.'

Aids to Reflection (1825)

[1] See Wisd. of Sol. vii. 22, 23, 27. [H. N. Coleridge.]
[2] Robert Leighton (1611–84), Archbishop of Glasgow, author of *Rules and Instruction for a Holy Life.—Ed.*

II. FAITH

Faith may be defined as fidelity to our own being—so far as such being is not and cannot become an object of the senses; and hence, by clear inference or implication, to being generally, as far as the same is not the object of the senses: and again to whatever is affirmed or understood as the condition, or concomitant, or consequence of the same. This will be best explained by an instance or example. That I am conscious of something within me peremptorily commanding me to do unto others as I would they should do unto me—in other words, a categorical (that is, primary and unconditional) imperative—that the maxim (*regula maxima*, or supreme rule) of my actions, both inward and outward, should be such as I could, without any contradiction arising therefrom, will to be the law of all moral and rational beings—this, I say, is a fact of which I am no less conscious (though in a different way), nor less assured, than I am of any appearance presented by my outward senses. Nor is this all; but in the very act of being conscious of this in my own nature, I know that it is a fact of which all men either are or ought to be conscious—a fact, the ignorance of which constitutes either the non-personality of the ignorant, or the guilt, in which latter case the ignorance is equivalent to knowledge wilfully darkened. I know that I possess this knowledge as a man, and not as Samuel Taylor Coleridge; hence, knowing that consciousness of this fact is the root of all other consciousness, and the only practical contradistinction of man from the brutes, we name it the conscience; by the natural absence or presumed presence of which, the law, both divine and human, determines whether X Y Z be a thing or a person—the conscience being that which never to have had places the objects in the same order of things as the brutes, for example, idiots; and to have lost which implies either insanity or apostasy. Well, this we have affirmed is a fact of which every honest man is as fully assured as of his seeing, hearing, or smelling. But though the former assurance does not differ from the latter in the degree, it is altogether diverse in the kind; the senses being morally passive, while the conscience is essentially connected with the will, though not always, nor, indeed, in any case, except after frequent attempts and aversions of will, dependent on the choice. Thence we call the presentations of the senses impressions, those of the conscience commands or dictates. In the senses we find our

receptivity, and as far as our personal being is concerned, we are
passive; but in the fact of the conscience we are not only agents, but
it is by this alone that we know ourselves to be such; nay, that our very
passiveness in this latter is an act of passiveness, and that we are patient
(*patientes*)—not, as in the other case, *simply* passive.

The result is, the consciousness of responsibility; and the proof is
afforded by the inward experience of the diversity between regret and
remorse.

If I have sound ears, and my companion speaks to me with a due
proportion of voice, I may persuade him that I did not hear, but cannot
deceive myself. But when my conscience speaks to me, I can, by
repeated efforts, render myself finally insensible; to which add this
other difference, namely, that to make myself deaf is one and the same
thing with making my conscience dumb, till at length I become
unconscious of my conscience. Frequent are the instances in which it
is suspended, and, as it were, drowned in the inundation of the appetites,
passions, and imaginations, to which I have resigned myself, making use
of my will in order to abandon my free-will; and there are not, I fear,
examples wanting of the conscience being utterly destroyed, or of the
passage of wickedness into madness—that species of madness, namely, in
which the reason is lost. For so long as the reason continues, so long must
the conscience exist, either as a good conscience or as a bad conscience.

It appears then, that even the very first step, that the initiation of
the process, the becoming conscious of a conscience, partakes of the
nature of an act. It is an act in and by which we take upon ourselves
an allegiance, and consequently the obligation of fealty; and this fealty
or fidelity implying the power of being unfaithful, it is the first and
fundamental sense of Faith. It is likewise the commencement of experience, and the result of all other experience. In other words, conscience,
in this its simplest form, must be supposed in order to consciousness,
that is, to human consciousness. Brutes may be, and are, scious, but
those beings only, who have an I, *scire possunt hoc vel illud una cum
seipsis*; that is, *conscire vel scire aliquid mecum*, or to know a thing in
relation to myself, and in the act of knowing myself as acted upon by
that something.

Now the third person could never have been distinguished from the
first but by means of the second. There can be no He without a previous
Thou. Much less could an I exist for us, except as it exists during the
suspension of the will, as in dreams; and the nature of brutes may be

best understood by considering them as somnambulists. This is a deep meditation, though the position is capable of the strictest proof—namely, that there can be no I without a Thou, and that a Thou is only possible by an equation in which I is taken as equal to Thou, and yet not the same. And this, again, is only possible by putting them in opposition as correspondent opposites, or correlatives. In order to do this, a something must be affirmed in the one, which is rejected in the other, and this something is the will. I do not will to consider myself as equal to myself, for in the very act of constructing myself I, I take it as the same, and therefore as incapable of comparison, that is, of any application of the will. If then, I *minus* the will be the *thesis*;[1] Thou *plus* will must be the *antithesis*, but the equation of Thou with I, by means of a free act, negativing the sameness in order to establish the equality, is the true definition of conscience. But as without a Thou there can be no You, so without a You no They, These, or Those; and as all these conjointly form the materials and subjects of consciousness, and the conditions of experience, it is evident that conscience is the root of all consciousness—*a fortiori*, the precondition of all experience—and that the conscience cannot have been in its first revelation deduced from experience.

Soon, however, experience comes into play. We learn that there are other impulses beside the dictates of conscience; that there are powers within us and without us ready to usurp the throne of conscience, and busy in tempting us to transfer our allegiance. We learn that there are many things contrary to conscience, and therefore to be rejected and utterly excluded, and many that can co-exist with its supremacy only by being subjugated, as beasts of burthen; and others, again, as, for instance, the social tendernesses and affections, and the faculties and excitations of the intellect, which must be at least subordinated. The preservation of our loyalty and fealty under these trials, and against

---

[1] There are four kinds of *Theses*, θεσεις, puttings or placings.

1. *Prothesis.*

2. *Thesis.*   3. *Antithesis.*

4. *Synthesis.*

A and B are said to be thesis and antithesis, when if A be the *thesis*, B is the *antithesis* to A, and if B be made the *thesis*, then A becomes the *antithesis*. Thus making me the *thesis*, you are thou to me, but making you the *thesis*, I become thou to you. *Synthesis* is a putting together of the two, so that a third something is generated. Thus the *synthesis* of hydrogen and oxygen is water, a third something, neither hydrogen nor oxygen. But the blade of a knife and its handle when put together do not form a *synthesis*, but still remain a blade and a handle. And as a *synthesis* is a unity that results from the union of two things, so a *prothesis* is a primary unity that gives itself forth into two things.

these rivals, constitutes the second sense of Faith; and we shall need but one more point of view to complete its full import. This is the consideration of what is presupposed in the human conscience. The answer is ready. As in the equation of the correlative I and Thou, one of the twin constituents is to be taken as *plus* will, the other as *minus* will, so is it here: and it is obvious that the reason or *super*-individual of each man, whereby he is a man, is the factor we are to take as *minus* will; and that the individual will or personalizing principle of free agency (arbitrement is Milton's word) is the factor marked *plus* will; and, again, that as the identity or coinherence of the absolute will and the reason, is the peculiar character of God; so is the *synthesis* of the individual will and the common reason, by the subordination of the former to the latter, the only possible likeness or image of the *prothesis*, or identity, and therefore the required proper character of man. Conscience, then, is a witness respecting the identity of the will and the reason effected by the self-subordination of the will, or self, to the reason, as equal to, or representing, the will of God. But the personal will is a factor in other moral *syntheses*; for example, appetite *plus* personal will = sensuality; lust of power, *plus* personal will = ambition, and so on, equally as in the *synthesis*, on which the conscience is grounded. Not this, therefore, but the other *synthesis*, must supply the specific character of the conscience; and we must enter into an analysis of reason. Such as the nature and objects of the reason are, such must be the functions and objects of the conscience. And the former we shall best learn by recapitulating those constituents of the total man which are either contrary to, or disparate from, the reason.

I. Reason, and the proper objects of reason, are wholly alien from sensation. Reason is super-sensual, and its antagonist is appetite, and the objects of appetite the lust of the flesh.

II. Reason and its objects do not appertain to the world of the senses, inward or outward; that is, they partake not of sense or fancy. Reason is super-sensuous, and here its antagonist is the lust of the eye.

III. Reason and its objects are not things of reflexion, association, discursion, discourse in the old sense of the word as opposed to intuition; 'discursive or intuitive', as Milton has it. Reason does not indeed necessarily exclude the finite, either in time or in space, but it includes them *eminenter*. Thus the prime mover of the material universe is affirmed to contain all motion as its cause, but not to be, or to suffer, motion in itself.

Reason is not the faculty of the finite. But here I must premise the following. The faculty of the finite is that which reduces the confused impressions of sense to their essential forms—quantity, quality, relation, and in these action and reaction, cause and effect, and the like; thus raises the materials furnished by the senses and sensations into objects of reflexion, and so makes experience possible. Without it, man's representative powers would be a delirium, a chaos, a scudding cloud-age of shapes; and it is therefore most appropriately called the under-standing, or substantiative faculty. Our elder metaphysicians, down to Hobbes inclusively, called this likewise discourse, *discursus*, *discursio*, from its mode of action as not staying at any one object, but running, as it were, to and fro to abstract, generalize, and classify. Now when this faculty is employed in the service of the pure reason, it brings out the necessary and universal truths contained in the infinite into distinct contemplation by the pure act of the sensuous imagination, that is, in the production of the forms of space and time abstracted from all corporeity, and likewise of the inherent forms of the understanding itself abstractedly from the consideration of particulars, as in the case of geometry, numeral mathematics, universal logic, and pure meta-physics. The discursive faculty then becomes what our Shakespeare, with happy precision, calls 'discourse of reason'.

We will now take up our reasoning again from the words 'motion in itself'.

It is evident, then, that the reason as the irradiative power, and the representative of the infinite, judges the understanding as the faculty of the finite, and cannot without error be judged by it. When this is attempted, or when the understanding in its *synthesis* with the personal will, usurps the supremacy of the reason, or affects to supersede the reason, it is then what St Paul calls the mind of the flesh (φρόνημα σαρκός), or the wisdom of this world. The result is, that the reason is super-finite; and in this relation, its antagonist is the insubordinate understanding, or mind of the flesh.

IV. Reason, as one with the absolute will (*In the beginning was the Logos, and the Logos was with God, and the Logos was God*), and there-fore for man the certain representative of the will of God, is above the will of man as an individual will. We have seen in III that it stands in antagonism to all mere particulars; but here it stands in antagonism to all mere individual interests as so many selves, to the personal will as seeking its objects in the manifestation of itself for itself—*sit pro ratione voluntas*—whether this be realized with adjuncts, as in the lust of the flesh, and in the lust of the eye; or without adjuncts, as in the thirst and pride of power, despotism, egostic ambition. The fourth antagonist, then, of reason, is the lust of the will.

Corollary. Unlike a million of tigers, a million of men is very different from a million times one man. Each man in a numerous society is not only coexistent with, but virtually organized into, the multitude of which he is an integral part. His *idem* is modified by the *alter*. And there arise impulses and objects from this *synthesis* of the *alter et idem*, myself and my neighbour. This, again, is strictly analogous to what takes places in the vital organization of the individual man. The cerebral system of the nerves has its correspondent *antithesis* in the abdominal system: but hence arises a *synthesis* of the two in the pectoral system as the intermediate, and, like a drawbridge, at once conductor and boundary. In the latter, as objectized by the former, arise the emotions, affections, and, in one word, the passions, as distinguished from the cognitions and appetites. Now, the reason has been shown to be super-individual, generally, and therefore not less so when the form of an individualization subsists in the *alter*, than when it is confined to the *idem*; not less when the emotions have their conscious or believed object in another, than when their subject is the individual personal self. For though these emotions, affections, attachments, and the like, are the prepared ladder by which the lower nature is taken up into, and made to partake of, the highest room—as we are taught to give a feeling of reality to the higher *per medium commune* with the lower, and thus gradually to see the reality of the higher (namely, the objects of reason), and finally to know that the latter are indeed, and pre-eminently real, as if you love your earthly parents whom you see, by these means you will learn to love your Heavenly Father who is invisible—yet this holds good only so far as the reason is the president, and its objects the ultimate aim; and cases may arise in which the Christ as the Logos, or Redemptive Reason, declares, *He that loves father or mother more than me, is not worthy of me*; nay, he that can permit his emotions to rise to an equality with the universal reason, is in enmity with that reason. Here, then, reason appears as the love of God; and its antagonist is the attachment to individuals wherever it exists in diminution of, or in competition with, the love which is reason.

In these five paragraphs I have enumerated and explained the several powers or forces belonging or incidental to human nature, which in all matters of reason the man is bound either to subjugate or subordinate to reason. The application to Faith follows of its own accord. The first or most indefinite sense of faith is fidelity: then fidelity under previous contract or particular moral obligation. In this sense faith is fealty to a rightful superior: faith is the duty of a faithful subject to a rightful governor. Then it is allegiance in active service; fidelity to the liege lord under circumstances, and amid the temptations of usurpation, rebellion, and intestine discord. Next we seek for that rightful superior on our duties to whom all our duties to all other superiors, on our faithfulness to whom all our bounden relations to all other objects of fidelity, are founded. We must inquire after that duty in which all others find their several degrees and dignities, and from which they derive their obligative force. We are to find a superior, whose rights, including our duties, are presented to the mind in the very idea of that Supreme Being, whose sovereign prerogatives are predicates implied in the subjects, as the essential properties of a circle are co-assumed in the first assumption of a circle, consequently underived, unconditional, and as rationally unsusceptible, so probably prohibitive, of all further question. In this sense, then, faith is fidelity, fealty, allegiance of the moral nature to God, in opposition to all usurpation, and in resistance to all temptation to the placing any other claim above or equal with our fidelity to God.

The will of God is the last ground and final aim of all our duties, and to that the whole man is to be harmonized by subordination, sub-jugation, or suppression alike in commission and omission. But the will of God, which is one with the supreme intelligence, is revealed to man through the conscience. But the conscience, which consists in an inappellable bearing-witness to the truth and reality of our reason, may legitimately be construed with the term reason, so far as the conscience is prescriptive; while as approving or condemning, it is the consciousness of the subordination or insubordination, the harmony or discord, of the personal will of man to and with the representative of the will of God. This brings me to the last and fullest sense of Faith, that is, the obedience of the individual will to the reason, in the lust of the flesh as opposed to the supersensual; in the lust of the eye as opposed to the supersensuous; in the pride of the understanding as opposed to the infinite; in the φρόνημα σαρκός in contrariety to the spiritual truth; in the lust of the personal will as opposed to the absolute and universal; and in the love of the creature, as far as it is opposed to the love which is one with the reason, namely, the love of God.

Thus, then, to conclude. Faith subsists in the *synthesis* of the Reason and the individual Will. By virtue of the latter, therefore, it must be an energy, and, inasmuch as it relates to the whole moral man, it must be exerted in each and all of his constituents or incidents, faculties and tendencies; it must be a total, not a partial—a continuous, not a desultory or occasional—energy. And by virtue of the former, that is, Reason, Faith must be a Light, a form of knowing, a beholding of Truth. In the incomparable words of the Evangelist, therefore, *Faith must be a Light originating in the Logos, or the substantial Reason, which is co-eternal and one with the Holy Will, and which Light is at the same time the Life of men.* Now, as *Life* is here the sum or collective of all moral and spiritual acts, in suffering, doing, and being, so is Faith the source and the sum, the energy and the principle of the fidelity of Man to God, by the subordination of his human Will, in all provinces of his nature, to his Reason, as the sum of spiritual Truth, representing and manifesting the Will Divine.

The 'Essay on Faith', first published in *The Literary Remains* (1836–9), ed. H. N. Coleridge, as possibly being part of an uncompleted 'Supplementary Volume' to *Aids to Reflection*

III. THE AUTHORITY OF SCRIPTURE

The Bible is the appointed conservatory, an indispensable criterion, and a continual source and support of true Belief. But that the Bible is the sole source; that it not only contains, but constitutes, the Christian Religion; that it is, in short, a Creed, consisting wholly of articles of Faith; that consequently we need no rule, help, or guide, spiritual or historical, to teach us what parts are and what are not articles of Faith— all being such—and the difference between the Bible and the Creed being this, that the clauses of the latter are all unconditionally necessary to salvation, but those of the former conditionally so, that is, as soon as the words are known to exist in any one of the canonical Books; and that, under this limitation, the belief is of the same necessity in both, and not at all affected by the greater or lesser importance of the matter to be believed—this scheme differs widely from the preceding, though its adherents often make use of the same words in expressing their belief. And this latter scheme, I assert, was brought into currency by and in favour of those by whom the operation of grace, the aids of the Spirit, the necessity of regeneration, the corruption of our nature, in short, all the peculiar and spiritual mysteries of the Gospel were explained and diluted away.

And how have these men treated this very Bible? I, who indeed prize and reverence this sacred library, as of all outward means and conservatives of Christian faith and practice the surest and the most reflective of the inward Word; I, who hold that the Bible contains the religion of Christians, but who dare not say that whatever is contained in the Bible is the Christian religion, and who shrink from all question respecting the comparative worth and efficacy of the written Word as weighed against the preaching of the Gospel, the discipline of the Churches, the continued succession of the Ministry, and the communion of Saints, lest by comparing I should seem to detach them; I tremble at the processes, which the Grotian divines without scruple carry on in their treatment of the sacred Writers, as soon as any texts declaring the peculiar tenets of our Faith are cited against them, even tenets and mysteries which the believer at his baptism receives as the title-writ and bosom-roll of his adoption; and which, according to my scheme, every Christian born in Church-membership ought to bring with him to the study of the sacred Scriptures as the master-key of interpretation. Whatever the doctrine of infallible dictation may be in itself, in *their* hands it is to the last degree nugatory, and to be paralleled only by the Romish tenet of Infallibility—in the existence of which all agree, but where, and in whom, it exists *stat adhuc sub lite*. Every sentence found in a canonical Book, rightly interpreted, contains the *dictum* of an infallible Mind; but what the right interpretation is—or whether the very words now extant are corrupt or genuine—must be determined by the industry and understanding of fallible, and alas! more or less prejudiced theologians...

*　　*　　*

'Friend! The truth revealed through Christ has its evidence in itself, and the proof of its divine authority in its fitness to our nature and needs—the clearness and cogency of this proof being proportionate to the degree of self-knowledge in each individual hearer. Christianity has likewise its historical evidences, and these as strong as is compatible with the nature of history, and with the aims and objects of a religious dispensation. And to all these Christianity itself, as an existing Power in the world, and Christendom as an existing Fact, with the no less evident fact of a progressive expansion, give a force of moral demonstration that almost supersedes particular testimony. These proofs and evidences would remain unshaken, even though the sum of our religion were to be drawn from the theologians of each successive century, on the principle of receiving that only as divine which should be found in all—*quod semper, quod ubique, quod ab omnibus.* Be only, my Friend! as orthodox a believer as you would have abundant reason to be, though from some accident of birth, country, or education, the precious boon of the Bible, with its additional evidence, had up to this moment been concealed from you—and then read its contents with only the same piety which you freely accord on other occasions to the writings of men, considered the best and wisest of their several ages! What you find therein coincident with your pre-established convictions, you will of course recognize as the Revealed Word, while, as you read the recorded workings of the Word and the Spirit in the minds, lives, and hearts of spiritual men, the influence of the same Spirit on your own being, and the conflicts of grace and infirmity in your own soul, will enable you to discern and to know in and by what spirit they spake and acted—as far at least as shall be needful for you, and in the times of your need.

'Thenceforward, therefore, your doubts will be confined to such parts or passages of the received Canon, as seem to you irreconcilable with known truths, and at variance with the tests given in the Scriptures themselves, and as shall continue so to appear after you have examined each in reference to the circumstances of the Writer or Speaker, the dispensation under which he lived, the purpose of the particular passage, and the intent and object of the Scriptures at large. Respecting these, decide for yourself: and fear not for the result. I venture to tell it you beforehand. The result will be, a confidence in the judgement and fidelity of the compilers of the Canon increased by the apparent exceptions. For they will be found neither more nor greater than may well be supposed requisite, on the one hand, to prevent us from sinking into a habit of slothful, undiscriminating acquiescence, and on the other to provide a check against those presumptuous fanatics, who would rend the *Urim and Thummim from the breastplate of judgement*, and frame oracles by private divination from each letter of each disjointed gem, uninterpreted by the Priest, and deserted by the Spirit, which shines in the parts only as it pervades and irradiates the whole.'

Such is the language in which I have addressed a halting friend—halting, yet with his face toward the right path. If I have erred, enable me to see my error. Correct me, or confirm me. Farewell.

Confessions of an Enquiring Spirit (1840)

F. D. MAURICE

It could well be claimed that no English theologian of the nineteenth century has exercised a more pervasive and persistent influence than Frederick Denison Maurice. Misunderstood in his own day—he was a man difficult to identify with the views and aims of any ecclesiastical party—and with no great gift as a writer—the opacity of his style has always been a hindrance to the direct dissemination of his ideas—Maurice's teaching, alike in its balance and imaginative scope, has been a valuable corrective to one-sided if more ear-catching opinions. J. S. Mill thought 'that there was more intellectual power wasted in Maurice than in any other of my contemporaries', a false judgement which nevertheless contains truth. Yet in October 1853 the Council of King's College, London, scandalized by his refusal to equate 'eternal punishment' with 'everlasting torment', deemed it their painful duty to state that the continuance of Professor Maurice's connexion with the College as one of its professors would be 'seriously detrimental to its usefulness', and dismissed him forthwith.

The son of a Unitarian minister, Maurice was born near Lowestoft in 1805, but was brought up at Frenchay, near Bristol. In 1823 he entered Trinity College, Cambridge, where he attended Julius Hare's lectures, his contemporaries including Alfred Tennyson and John Sterling, the future philosopher, whose sister-in-law, Annie Barton, he eventually married. Later he migrated to Trinity Hall to study law. In days, however, when subscription to the Thirty-Nine Articles of Religion was still a condition of graduation in the ancient universities Maurice's conscience was uncompliant and he left without taking a degree. Yet he had no objection to the test as such and when eventually he himself became an Anglican he warmly defended the right and the propriety of an academic institution to impose it. 'Subscription', he urged, 'is a declaration of the terms on which the University professes to teach its pupils; upon what terms they agree to learn; it is fairer to express those terms than to conceal them, and they are not an unfit introduction to a general education in humanity and physics.' He even saw in them the possibility of contributing to 'the reconciliation of what is positive in all Christian sects'. In 1834 he was ordained a priest in the Church of England, and following a country curacy in Warwickshire was appointed chaplain of Guy's Hospital in London and subsequently (1846) of Lincoln's Inn, as well as professor of theology at King's. In 1866 he was given the chair of moral philosophy at Cambridge, but by then his life-work was over. His second marriage, four years after his first wife's death, was to Julius Hare's half-sister, Georgiana. His many friends were drawn from a wide circle, although Coleridge, by whose work he was profoundly influenced, he never met. Among them was Thomas Carlyle who, whilst (in some moods, at least) greatly admiring and liking Maurice the man, dismissed his doctrine as 'mainly moonshine and *Spitzfindigkeit*'; though Maurice in turn, and despite his genuine reverence for the Scottish oracle, was not taken in by the latter's 'silly rant about the great bosom of the universe'. Maurice died at Cambridge in 1872.

He wrote much, but the best introduction to his thought is to be found less in any book of his own than in the *Life*—which also makes the fullest use of his letters—from the pen of his son, Frederick Maurice (1884). His principal publications were *The Kingdom of Christ* (1838), *Theological Essays* (1853), *What is Revelation?* (1859) (his attack on Mansel's Bampton Lectures), *The Gospel of the Kingdom of Heaven* (1864) and the lectures on casuistry entitled *Conscience* (1868).

The ground of Maurice's thinking is his deep sense of the divine power and presence in life. God is not remote but at hand. Like his master, Coleridge, he had no use for the evidential or inferential method in theology beloved of the eighteenth-century divines, who for the living God tended to substitute if not 'Nature' then a mere Demiurge—nature's 'Author'; although he also saw that the reaction against 'this mischievous dogma' was the deification of human institutions 'or at best the Reason from which they flow'. The truth lay, he believed—the expression is Coleridge's—in 'the Mesothesis of the internal and the external'. The old idea of revelation had been that of an announcement of decrees, imperative laws enacted by God; the new, on the other hand, portrayed the divine as 'an endless flux of which the source is the creative energy of man'; whereas the truth of Christianity lies in its reconciliation of these ideas, each of which, of itself, tends only to 'Atheism and superstition'. But if, in fact as in principle, the revelation of God in Christ is complete there yet is an aspect of it which must be held to be still in process. An impulse towards religion seems to be native to man, but continuous seeking after God is intelligible only if God himself is already and continuously working in man. The latter's spiritual potentiality, therefore, is boundless: the soul lies open to the ever-flowing tide of the divine life. To find God a man has only to look within himself. Hence Maurice's vehement objection to Mansel's *Limits of Religious Thought*,[1] to which he replied in his own *What is Revelation?*, an ungainly compilation consisting partly of sermons (in themselves excellent), partly of a series of supposed 'Letters to a Student of Theology', in which Maurice's defects as a controversialist are evident. But the 'scholasticism' of Mansel's carefully

[1] See ch. 4 below.

contrived argument had incensed him. He answered that God *himself* is known to us, as the ground of a vital experience; revelation, accordingly, is not the mere imparting of symbolical propositions but the 'unveiling of a Person' to 'the very man himself'—conscience, heart, will and reason— whom God has created 'to know Him, and be like Him'. There also can be no religion which is the product simply of reason apart from revelation. Such knowledge of God as man has is God's own act, and comes to him as the inward truth about his own being.

Yet the essential orthodoxy of Maurice's position is not open to doubt. Man's need, he taught, is fully met by Christ and Christ alone; no other religion, whatever its merits, is sufficient in the way that Christianity is sufficient. The Trinitarianism, moreover, that replaced the Unitarian doctrine in which Maurice was brought up became for him far more than the object of a bare intellectual assent. 'I not only', he wrote, 'believe in the Trinity in Unity but I find in it the centre of all my beliefs: the rest of my spirit when I contemplate myself or mankind.' But Trinitarian theology turns upon the conviction of the deity of Christ and here Maurice's thought is at its boldest, though not always at its most lucid. Human life, he holds, has meaning only in relation to Christ, apart from whom there is no true unity, whether in family, nation or Church. For Christ is at once the root and the head of humanity, and as such is 'in every man'. As himself the image of God he is, so to say, the mirror in which we behold our true selves. Here Maurice's doctrine has been criticized as more Platonist than Christian. Yet it is questionable whether he himself went further than the prologue to the Fourth Gospel and certain passages in St Paul. His starting-point was not so much the sin of man as the 'true sinless root' whence our humanity springs. Redemption is an eternal act; let us but recognize this and live accordingly. The characteristic fault of contemporary theology, he judged, was 'that we talk about God and about religion, and do not confess Him as a Living God'. The mere concept had become a substitute for the reality.

The Kingdom of Christ is subtitled 'Hints on the Principles, Ordinances, and Constitution of the Catholic Church', and develops the thesis that the Church is the Kingdom in anticipation. Maurice was certainly no Puseyite, yet he declared that he 'could live and die' for the assertion of the truth 'that the Universal Church is as much a reality as any particular nation', and is a 'witness for the true constitution of man as man, a child of God, an heir of heaven'. Fullness of spiritual life and truth are to be found moreover in the Church of England—not since Hooker had the Established Church known a more convinced apologist. Other denominations might express certain aspects of Christian truth more emphatically, but none taught the whole with such far-seeing wisdom. Maurice rejected any idea that his teaching was 'Broad Church'. He could no more condone indifference to dogma than Newman himself. But his special gift was his ability to discover in dogma a principle not of faction but of unity. Nowhere but in the Church could there be universal communion, 'in one body, by one Spirit'. He would 'hold fast by that which alone stands forth and upholds universal brotherhood, on the only basis in which brotherhood is possible'. On this score too the Church of England satisfied him.

It is easy to see, therefore, how Maurice, along with Charles Kingsley and C. M. Ludlow, should have become a leader of the Christian Social movement of 1848–54. It was in no spirit of reaction that he judged an 'English theological reformation' to be the means of averting an English political revolution. The evil results of *laissez-faire* seemed to him latent in the system. 'Competition', he wrote to Kingsley, 'is put forth as the law of the universe. Yet it is a lie. The time has come for us to declare that it is a lie by word and deed.' Community, the proper condition of social man, would be achieved only by co-operation, of which the Church has the dynamic principle. Adoption of the word 'Socialism' was intended to provoke, to throw down a challenge to 'Unsocial Christians'; but to qualify the effort as Christian was no less to challenge 'Un-Christian Socialists'. The movement did not at the time win the support of any large body of public opinion, but it at least took the first step in a direction which Christian social concern has since generally pursued.

Bibliographical note

Theological Essays, with a biographical foreword by E. Carpenter, was reprinted in 1957, and *The Kingdom of Christ* (ed. A. R. Vidler, 2 vols.) in 1958. See also Sir Frederick Maurice, *The Life of Frederick Denison Maurice* (2 vols., 4th ed., 1885); A. R. Vidler, *The Theology of F. D. Maurice* (1949); H. G. Wood, *Frederick Denison Maurice* (1950); A. M. Ramsey, *F. D. Maurice and the Conflicts of Modern Theology* (1951); M. B. Reckitt, *Maurice to Temple* (1947).

I. WHAT IS REVELATION?

If [the word Revelation] denotes—wherever it is used, to whatever time it is referred—the removal of a veil which had hidden the eternal God from men; if from the hour in which men were created such veils had been removing; if the sin of man, which had seemed to cut him off from God, had been a means of discovering the nature and essential character of God, by His warfare with it and forgiveness of it; if no one step in Jewish history, or in any history, could be regarded by holy men except as the instrument of such a discovery, as setting forth something of the divine power and righteousness; if the one desire of those holy men was for the complete rending asunder of that which had hidden from all nations the light in which they were intended to walk, and in which alone they could see themselves or see each other; if the Son of Man did, while he was on earth, by all His acts, discourses, parables, declare the Kingdom of God to men, did manifest to men the Father; if, when He had overcome the sharpness of death, He opened the Kingdom, and discovered the inner mind of the Father to all who believed in Him, who received Him as the well-beloved Son; if this unveiling of His Kingdom to men was precisely that which the Apostles were appointed to preach, and did preach; if they preached it to a world which contradicted all they said, and treated it as ridiculous; if the spectacle which that world presented seemed to make it ridiculous to themselves, so that to keep the faith that it was not all a dream for which they were giving up the traditions of infancy, old friendships, all that belonged to life, and life itself, was often unspeakably hard, and would have been impossible if the partaking of God's nature had not been the one only refuge from the curse and plague of their own— what encouragement could they hold out but this: 'There will verily be a revelation of the Son of Man and of the Son of God to the Universe; it will be, whether we look for it or not; it will be attested by that doom upon our own holy city and temple of which our Lord spoke when He was upon earth, and which He denoted as a revelation or appearing of the Son of Man; but if you look for it, if you brace up your spirits to the expectation of it, if you resist whatever dulls or stifles that expectation within you—then this unveiling will indeed be to you the satisfaction of all your longings, and of all the longings of past ages. It will be this blessing to you, because it will be not for you, but for the world; because it *will be as the lightning, which lighteneth from one part of heaven, and shineth even to the other.*' You will see how consistent this language was with all their other language; how little the use of it was affected by any ignorance they might have of times and seasons, or of the exact nature of the change which was to take place in the condition of the outward world. If what they expected was not a full unveiling of the Eternal Mind, of that which is the same yesterday and today and for ever, points of chronology would have been of the most vast importance to them; a mistake about such points would have been fatal to their hopes. If what they expected was not the full manifestation of Him of whom the things of time and sense are all testifying, but about whom no conclusion can be deduced from them, their conception of those things would have determined the degree and character of their hopes. As it was, the invisible things were no more limited by the narrowness of their intellects than the vision of sea and sky is limited by the size of the eye which took it in. Faith, not in some notions or communications about God, but in God himself, made them inheritors of His righteousness, capable of entering into His infinite love, and of losing themselves in it...

*   *   *

If there is nothing in the people to whom we deliver our message but a faculty which forms notions, judges of opinions, criticizes documents, we know that we have not a Gospel to the poor—it is monstrous to pretend that we have. That faculty of forming notions, judging opinions, criticizing documents, is a peculiar one; it requires a special cultivation; the degrees in which those possess it in whom it has been cultivated, are more various than it is possible to express. The difference between Bentley and the most ignorant undergraduate who answers a question at an Oxford or Cambridge examination, is an inadequate measure of the variety in one direction. Those in whom the faculty exists in the highest degree, are not always the persons to whom one would appeal with confidence on a moral question. And when one compares their different exercises upon their own ground, e.g. the Discussion on the Epistles of Phalaris with the Commentary on Paradise Lost, one feels how a homely perception of facts is needful even to a critic, how worthless the merely critical power becomes without it. Even therefore if one wanted to bring out this power in its strength, one would have need to educate another first, one which is not special, but human. In a university, if that human faculty is denied or not appealed to, all special studies will be worthless—yes, mischievous and accursed. But for the Minister of the Gospel, *that* is what he has to speak to: I had nearly said *that* only. It is because the Bible addresses that human faculty and not some special faculty, that it can bear to be translated into every tongue of the earth, that it can speak to all tribes and nations. For *us* to deny the existence of such a faculty, is simply to deny our own work. Any one who tells us that it does not exist, is bound also to tell us that if we are honest men we must relinquish that work.

'What,' you say, 'does it depend upon our acceptance of a certain philosophy whether we shall do our work as Evangelists?' Not the least. You need know nothing about philosophy. If you do not, you will take for granted the existence of this faculty to which you can speak. It is the ordinary postulate of an Englishman's life that there is such a one. That is what he means when he says, 'I do not care for your fine notions; I have something in me which tells me when a man is speaking truth or falsehood.' Of course, he may be very much deceived about his own preference for truth over falsehood in any particular case; he may be bribed to like a lie better than the truth. But are you justified in telling him that he has not that faculty? Are you not destroying his soul if you do? Are you not saving his soul alive if you can persuade him to use that faculty, if you can teach him how he may use it, who is helping him to use it, who would deliver him from the falsehoods which are corrupting and enchaining him? This, I say, is the ordinary judgement of a practical man. And the part of Kant's philosophy which Mr Mansel rejects is the part which owns that the philosopher *cannot* interfere with this practical human faith, that it is worth more than all the notions of the understanding, because it takes hold of that which is substantial—worth more than all the conclusions of the understanding, because it converses with premisses.

'Yes,' Mr Mansel will say, 'but I acknowledge a faith which goes beyond these notions; I admit that the realm of existence is not bounded by the realm of thought. What I object to is your speaking of the Reason, as if that had anything to do with this faith, as if that were distinct from the Understanding.' Now observe; about nomenclature I care nothing, or next to nothing. Throw over Kant's nomenclature if you dislike it. There is no sacredness in the names of Understanding or of Reason; one cannot be quite certain whether they are respectively the best equivalents for the words which Kant has used—supposing that were a point of any importance. But we must not be cheated by compliments to our faith, nor yet by the distinction—all-important as it is when rightly apprehended—between thought and existence. Does the faith you speak of take hold of existence, or, as I should say—for I do not like school-terms when I can get plain words—of that which is? If not, it is not what we mean by faith; it is not the faith which is the substance of things hoped for, the evidence of things not seen. It is an act of the mind; therefore I have to ask, Of what mind? It is the belief in something; then I have to ask, What is that something? The mind, according to Mr Mansel, only gives out thoughts, and thoughts are in no connexion with existence or that which is. Whence then comes this faith? Whither does it go? How should it be described? I know how it would be described by some persons; they would call it a faculty or the exercise of a faculty of lies. I do not like such language. Mr Mansel, who does, must vindicate the Faith which he speaks of from the imputation which he has bestowed upon Kant's Reason.

What concerns you and me is that faith should be the act of the man himself, of that which is most truly, radically human in him, call it by what name you please, and that it should be in direct contact with that which is most living and most substantial. Less than this we will not accept from any philosopher, religious or irreligious. Any one who tells us of another faith than this, must begin with erasing the eleventh chapter of the Epistle to the Hebrews out of the Bible, must go on to destroy the whole Gospel which the Bible contains. Remember that that is the issue. We are not now talking about the Finite or the Infinite, the Relative or the Absolute. To those words, and to Mr Mansel's treatment of them, I hope to come in due time; I have not the least wish to avoid the fullest examination of what he says about them. But that is not our business now. I will repeat it even to weariness: the question is concerning that which *is* and that which is not; whether there is any faculty in man that can be brought to perceive that which is, and to reject that which is not, *in any matter whatsoever*; whether that faculty is extinguished when we are called to pay the highest reverence and worship to a certain object or objects; or whether it is this to which God himself appeals. For I must again beseech you not to be deceived by Mr Mansel's rhetoric into the supposition that what he is saying only concerns those who reject the Bible, or fancy that they are wiser than the writers of it. It concerns quite as much every one who accepts the Bible as God's speech to man; it concerns the humblest believer in every cottage, on every hospital pallet. He himself has told us that he is equally at war with those who start from the Divine and reason down to the Human, as with those who start from the Human and reason up to the Divine. He *must* be equally at war with both. On the other hand, those who accept a revelation of God to man, i.e. of the Divine meeting the Human, must be very careful indeed how they trifle with any of those efforts, even if they have been failures, of the Human to meet the Divine, lest haply they should be fighting not merely with the spirit of man, but with the Spirit of God. Mr Mansel has said himself: 'The Philosophy which reasons downwards from the Infinite is but an exaggeration(?) of the true conviction that God's thoughts are not our thoughts, nor His ways our ways: the philosophy which reasons upwards from the human, bears witness, even in its perversion, to the unextinguishable consciousness that man, however fallen, was created in the image of God' (p. 43).

Just so. It is the very point for which I am contending, and therefore it must be your business and mine to recognize the truth of both these opposing principles, quite indifferent who calls us Mystics and who calls us Rationalists, because it is our business to show that God's thoughts are not our thoughts, nor His ways our ways, because it is our business to tell men that they are created in the image of God, and that Christ, the express Image of God, has come to raise them out of their fall, and to renew them after that image. Our preaching is continually encountered by the argument, 'We are fallen creatures; what can we know of God? how can we ever rise to the perception of the Eternal Truth and Goodness?' Must we not answer that argument by appealing to every witness of the heart, the Conscience, the Reason—if you will, to every contradiction of Philosophy—that the spirit of man within us demands the knowledge of God, demands the perception of Eternal Truth and Goodness? If we can say also, 'What the spirit of man seeks, the Spirit of God will give', may we not feel that we have indeed preached good news to our fellows?   *What is Revelation?* (1859)

II. THE CREEDS

There is actually found at this present day, in every Christian country, a certain document called a Creed. It is not necessary to inquire minutely at what time it was formed. Let it be admitted that there is an obscurity over its origin; that we cannot say who put it into that shape in which we now see it. From whatever quarter it may have come, here it is. It has lasted through a great many storms and revolutions. The Roman Empire has passed away; modern European society has risen out of its ruins. Political systems have been established and overthrown; religious systems have been established and overthrown. Even the physical world has undergone mighty alterations, and our conception of its laws is altogether changed. The very languages which were spoken in all parts of the world when the Gospel was first preached, have given place to others; but this 'I believe' remains. It is substantially what it was, to say the very least, sixteen hundred years ago. During that time it has not been lying hid in the closet of some antiquarian. It has been repeated by the peasants and children of the different lands into which it has come. It has been given to them as a record of facts with which they had as much to do as any noble. In most parts of Europe it has been repeated publicly every day in the year; and though it has been thus hawked about, and, as men would say, vulgarized, the most earnest and thoughtful men in different countries, different periods, different stages of civilization, have felt that it connected itself with the most permanent part of their being, that it had to do with each of them personally, and that it was the symbol of that humanity which they shared with their brethren. Reformers who have been engaged in conflict with all the prevailing systems of their age, have gone back to this old form of words, and have said that they lived to reassert the truths which it embodied. Men on sick beds, martyrs at the stake, have said that because they held it fast, they could look death in the face. And, to sink much lower, yet to say what may strike many as far more wonderful, there are many in this day who, having asked the different philosophers of their own and of past times what they could do in helping them to understand the world, to fight against its evils, to love their fellow-men, are ready to declare that in this child's creed they have found the secret which these philosophers could not give them, and which, by God's grace, they shall not take away from them.

Now a man who has noticed these facts, and has settled it in his mind that, whatever they mean, they must mean something, would certainly wish to inquire into the nature of this document which has been diffused so widely, has lasted so long, and has seemed to so many different persons of so much value. He will find, I think, that it differs from all the digests of doctrines, whether religious or philosophical, which he has ever seen. A man is speaking in it. The form of it is, *I believe*. That which is believed in is not a certain scheme of divinity, but a name—a Father, who has made the heaven and the earth: his Son, our Lord, who has been conceived, born, and died, and been buried, and gone down into hell, who has ascended, and is at the right hand of God, who will come to judge the world: a Holy Spirit who has established a holy universal Church, who makes men a communion of saints, who is the witness and power whereby they receive forgiveness of sins, who shall quicken their mortal bodies, who enables them to receive everlasting life. The creed is evidently an act of allegiance or affiance; and since it has ever been connected with baptism, one must suppose that from baptism it derives its interpretation. If by that act we are acknowledged as spiritual creatures, united to a spiritual Being, by this act we claim our spiritual position, we assert our union with that Being. The name into which we are adopted there, is the name we confess here. Those acts which, having been done for all mankind, were the warrant for our particular admission into the covenant, are the acts which we here proclaim to be the warrant of our faith and our fellowship. So far the form is consistent with its apparent object. But is it also consistent with the idea of Christ's kingdom which the Bible develops to us? There we found the primary postulate of such a kingdom to be a condescension of God to man, a cognizance taken of the creature by the Creator; the second, an apprehension of God by men, a recognition of the Creator by the creature. By grace are ye saved; by faith are ye saved. The position is freely given; a position of union and fellowship with another, a position of self-renunciation; the power is given wherewith to claim it: then comes the claim itself. Such seems to be the testimony of Scripture: and the relation in which the creed stands to baptism, and their common relation to that name and that kingdom which Scripture is revealing, surely expounds, in a remarkable way, that testimony.

But there is another creed possessing apparently equal authority with the one of which I have spoken, adopted perhaps into earlier use in the Eastern part of Christendom, and recognized by the Western ever since the age of Constantine. If it should be found that these two creeds clash with each other, or that they are not constructed upon the same principle, or that they do not both connect themselves with the idea of which we have spoken, the evidence from the preservation of either would certainly be weakened. Or if, these differences not appearing, it should seem that one could be conveniently substituted for the other, that there is nothing distinct and peculiar in each, one might be puzzled to account for the existence of both, at least as universal symbols. To see whether any of these objections apply, I would urge the reader to a thoughtful comparison of the two documents. First I would ask him whether in reading that which we call the Apostles' Creed, considering it as a declaration of the name into which he is baptized, he do not feel that it is meant to proclaim the distinct personality of the Father, the Son, and the Spirit, as signified by certain relations in which they have been manifested to men? Then whether another question do not arise in his mind, which he may perceive from history has arisen also in other men's minds: Is there not a more mysterious and awful relation implied and prefigured in these? Does not the name express such a relation? Is not the knowledge of this, as the ground of those relations, part of the revelation which has been vouchsafed to us; one of the deep things which cannot indeed be understood (for who understands the mystery of his own ordinary human relations?) but which lies so immediately beneath those facts which most concern us all, is so needful as the interpretation and reconciliation of those facts, has been so eagerly felt after in all ages, that if it be not disclosed to the heart and reason of man, they will be tormented with such dreams and imaginations concerning it, as must make the acknowledgement of the divine Unity impossible?

Now the Nicene Creed agrees with the Apostles' altogether in its form and principle. It is still *I believe*; it is still belief in a name, and not in notions. It differs in this, that it unites with a declaration of the divine relations to men, a declaration of the relations in the Godhead.

To every peasant and child it speaks of this marvellous subject. Certainly a strange fact, doubly strange when one knows how much it has been the tendency of teachers and priests in all ages to believe that only a few initiated persons are fit to know anything which concerns the name and nature of God; and how much this tendency did actually mingle itself with the awe and reverence of those ages by which these creeds have been transmitted to us. That the doctors of the Church should have allowed the Apostles' Creed to be heard in every cottage is strange; that they should not have said that this deeper creed, though embodying the principles and data of the other, was only for theologians, is scarcely credible: yet so it was. Now if it were the purpose of God that his name should be revealed to men; if his name, which seems to most of us to be connected with the highest and most esoteric abstractions, be really the only ground of a universal society, we can interpret these facts...

*   *   *

The rationalist denies that the creed can be a permanent symbol of human fellowship, because it rests upon the acknowledgement of certain events. 'Now, assuredly,' he says, 'these events could not have met with so much credence, if they had not pointed to certain great principles or ideas which are characteristic of us as members of a race. They do point most clearly to the sense which there is in all men of a something divine; to the possibility that this should overcome evil, sorrow, and death; to the feeling that it must submit to sorrow and death as a way to that victory. This, which is the essence of the creed, is no doubt universal; it may be traced in heathen and Jewish records; it has survived all the fables with which, in both, it is encompassed. There is therefore every probability that it will survive what are called the facts of Christianity likewise. And this is the more likely, because every day the documents in which those facts are recorded are subjected to a more sifting analysis, and because every day the evidence in their favour seems to be less decisive.'

In the former part of this book I have considered the general meaning and effect of this argument. I have endeavoured to show how true the assertion is upon which it is grounded, that the belief of a divine humanity has existed in all ages, that it has taken innumerable forms. I have maintained that all these forms have presumed the existence of some more perfect form; that they never have compassed the end at which they aimed; that they have not revealed THE MAN, the head of the race, while nevertheless they have testified, one and all, with more or less distinctness in proportion as the light which they endeavoured to concentrate was more or less clear, that such a one there must be. When a great man assumed to be this, he became a tyrant and oppressor; in our Lord's words, a thief and a robber, not the assertor of humanity, but the denier of it. You do not therefore advance one step in weakening the authority of this creed, by producing instances of this worship from ancient or modern history, or by dwelling upon the tendency which they so manifestly indicate. The more you can produce of them the better; the more they are examined the better. They prove that there is such an idea in humanity as you speak of; they prove just as strongly that with the idea humanity can never be satisfied; they declare that the idea is the idea of an actual living Being, of a perfect Being; of one who should prove his perfectness by entering entirely into the lowest condition into which man has ever entered, and actually rising into the highest of which man has ever dreamed. If these two elements of the lowest humiliation, of the greatest exaltation, be not combined, if they are not combined in acts, the idea is not fulfilled, it waits to be fulfilled; that is to say, we wait for a person who shall do precisely those acts of which the creed speaks. Any others will not avail; any others will not be universal enough, will not be the testimonies that he who performs them is THE MAN. We are asked then for the evidences of the creed. Our answer is this—You have shown why it has been believed, what heed there was in the deepest heart of mankind that it should be believed. It was believed, not upon the evidence of documents, but upon the simple proclamation of men who had the whole universe against them. They said to men, Christ must be; Christ you have been asking for in every land, through every age: Jesus the crucified is the Christ. The answers were three: The first was: 'There are a thousand Christs; every kingdom and district has its own.' The answer would have been satisfactory, if men had not listened to that other proclamation: 'You are members of one body, and therefore you need one Head.' But they did listen to it; they felt it to be true; therefore the thousand could not prevail against the one. No wonder this answer should be revived now; no wonder that when the sense of being one body has so practically forsaken us, the principle which is its counterpart should be so readily abandoned. But I hope I have shown that there never was so strong a cry for a universal and united fellowship as in this day of division; a cry proceeding from so many opposite corners of the earth, from so many different kinds of men. This reply, then, if it failed once, will not prevail now. The second answer was: 'There is an ideal Christ under these different Christs; and it is this, not they, you are to worship.' The people admitted the doctrine of the philosopher, but they said, 'This is the ideal Christ, and here he is manifested to us.' That this argument should be repeated in a day when abstract notions have been so much substituted for living truths, cannot be surprising. Yet we have seen, I think, that there was never more impatience of these abstractions, or a more vehement demand for realities, than at this very time. If then there be an idea of a universal Prince in men's minds, they will either continue to believe that this idea has been realized in Jesus of Nazareth, or they will seek a realization of it in some other person. And thus we arrive at the third answer which was made to the proclamation of the creed in the first ages, and which has been made so often since: 'This crucified man is not the perfect Being we look for; we want a warrior, a philosopher, a poet, possessing qualities altogether different from those which are brought out in the Gospel narrative, though we may acknowledge that these too have a certain value of their own.' Such has for twelve centuries been the belief of a large portion of the world which was once Christian. Another portion of it has declared that they see in the Cross the symbol of love triumphing through suffering, in the Crescent only of power claiming dominion over weakness; that the first is a bond of mutual fellowship among the members of a suffering race; the other the pledge of a universal slavery. That the spirit of the Cross prevails very little in the nations which still profess to honour it; that self-sacrifice is very generally and very systematically denied to be the law of our being—most of us are ready with shame to confess. And therefore the expectation is surely very reasonable, that the experiment which was so successful in the nations of the East, will be made, under other conditions, in the West. We have had many preparatory Antichrists, many sovereigns reigning by the strength of mind and will, and scorning all other right; why should we doubt that this image will be yet more completely manifested?

May God preserve those who live in the day when it is manifested to the world, and when the world goes wondering after it! In that day when intellect and will shall be utterly crushed under the car of the idol which they have set up; in that day when the poor man shall cry, and there shall be no helper, may God teach his saints to proclaim these words to the sons of men: 'He was born of the Virgin; he suffered under Pontius Pilate; he was crucified, dead, and buried, and went down into hell; he rose again on the third day; he ascended on high; he sitteth on the right hand of God; he shall come to judge the quick and the dead.' May they be able to say, This is our God; we have waited for him.

The Kingdom of Christ (1838)

CHAPTER 3

NEWMAN

John Henry Newman was born in 1801, the eldest child of a London banker.
At first educated at home, he was sent at the age of 7 to a school at Ealing
where he came under Calvinist influence and, as he himself relates, experienced a conversion both deep and lasting. In December 1810 he entered
Trinity College, Oxford, but his academic achievement was undistinguished
until his election to an Oriel fellowship in 1822. Ordained priest a year later,
he became vicar of the university church, St Mary's, in 1828. So began a
period in his life in which his name and fame spread from Oxford throughout
England, but it was in the then narrow confines of the university, and above
all from the pulpit of his parish church, that his influence was most effectively
exerted. His religious outlook had changed from a moderate evangelicalism
to the latitudinarianism characteristic of the Oriel intellectuals. But this
liberal phase was not to last. From his studies in the early Church Fathers the
conviction grew in him that antiquity was 'the true exponent of the doctrines
of Christianity and the basis of the Church of England'. In 1832 he travelled
abroad with his friend Richard Hurrell Froude, also a former Oriel fellow,
touring the Mediterranean and visiting Rome. It was while his ship was
becalmed in the Straits of Bonifacio that he wrote the well-known hymn,
'Lead, kindly Light'. No sooner had he arrived home than John Keble, on
14 July 1833, preached the Oxford assize sermon on 'National Apostasy',
which Newman always afterwards looked back to as the beginning of the
religious movement of which he himself was to become the leader and
inspiring genius. His belief now was that the Church of England, as a true
part of the Church Catholic and Apostolic, offered a *via media* between the
excesses of Rome and the errors of Protestantism. To publicize this view he
and a few associates set about composing a series of *Tracts for the Times*, of
which the greater number came from Newman's own pen. In the last of
them, no. XC, he argued that the Thirty-Nine Articles are in character and
purpose political rather than theological, designed to comprehend a variety
of opinions rather than state the Church's positive doctrine, although basically, he contended, they were Catholic and patient of an interpretation
incompatible only with teachings distinctively Roman. Yet even then (1841)
he was becoming increasingly doubtful of the soundness of his position. In
1842 he withdrew to the village of Littlemore, near Oxford, and in the
following year resigned his benefice. It was at this Littlemore retreat, where
he and a group of followers had adopted a kind of monastic discipline, that

he wrote his *Essay on the Development of Christian Doctrine*, published in 1845, in the October of which year he was received into the Roman Catholic Church, many of his friends and disciples seceding with him.

In 1846 Newman visited Rome and after a brief period of training was ordained to the Roman Catholic priesthood. On his return to England he was granted permission to establish a branch of the Congregation of the Oratory of St Philip Neri, and its Birmingham house became his permanent abode. In 1852 he was appointed rector of the new Catholic university in Dublin, where he delivered his *Discourses on University Education*, later entitled 'The Idea of a University'. Nevertheless, the Dublin post was not, from Newman's own point of view, by any means an unqualified success and from 1858 the life which he had resumed at Birmingham became more and more that of a recluse. His opinions were suspect at Rome, whilst in England, although in 1857 he had been asked by the English hierarchy to prepare a new translation of the Bible—an undertaking that proved abortive —he stood apart from the general course of ecclesiastical life. Even when, in 1860, he took over the editorship of a periodical, *The Rambler*, he found himself obliged to resign within a few months. His fortunes were now indeed at their lowest ebb, and his estrangement from the influential Henry Manning, later Archbishop of Westminster, did nothing to improve them. The tide turned, however, in 1864 with Charles Kingsley's maladroit attack on his veracity. Newman replied in the series of pamphlets which subsequently appeared in volume form as the celebrated *Apologia pro vita sua*, a religious document of unique interest and appeal. At once his position in public estimation altered. His self-vindication was accepted and thereafter his personal prestige steadily grew. With unflagging energy he continued to preach, publish and maintain a voluminous correspondence. In 1877 he received the gratifying distinction of an honorary fellowship at his old college of Trinity and in the ensuing year he visited Oxford for the first time since 1845. Finally, in 1879, Pope Leo XIII created him cardinal with San Georgio in Velatro as his titular church. But the aged prelate did not go to Rome to receive the hat and remained in Birmingham until his death in 1890. In these last years he was revered as the pre-eminent figure in the religious life of his country and respected as a master of English prose style.

As a thinker Newman is difficult to place. His mind was original and subtle and his power of argument formidable. But although he had the qualities of a philosopher, he had no interest in technical philosophy, in which he was little versed. Certainly he offers no system of his own. Writing, almost always, only as the needs of an occasion demanded, his dominating concerns were the nature of faith and the necessity for authority in religion, and his views on both signify his instinctive reaction to the tendencies of an age which he felt to be hostile to all that he most cherished. As he saw it a spirit of disruptive liberalism was abroad which could be countered only by unshaken adherence to that 'dogmatic principle' whose custodian was the Church. 'Man's energy of intellect', he declared, 'must be smitten hard and thrown back by infallible authority, if religion is to be saved at all.' For if religion were to be lost what meaning would life itself have? Newman was ever distrustful of 'reason' as a sufficient guide. In his early university sermons he had questioned 'whether Atheism is not as philosophically consistent with the phenomena of the physical world, taken by themselves, as the doctrine of a creative and governing Power'. More was required in religious belief than bare assent to 'evidences', for which Newman had as little regard as had Coleridge. 'A mutilated and defective evidence', he held, suffices for persuasion 'where the heart is alive', but 'dead evidences', however perfect, can 'but create a dead faith'. Living faith does not depend on inquiry and examination but on a special support of its own, namely the moral conscience, a personal disposition involving temperament, character and volition. 'No analysis', he wrote, 'is subtle and delicate enough to represent adequately the state of mind, under which we believe, or the subjects of belief, as they are presented to our thoughts.' Thus there are reasons for believing which to the religious mind are cogent but which to the irreligious are non-existent. Belief presupposes a fundamental awareness of spiritual values antecedent to all formal processes of rational assent; nay, 'almost all reasons,' he suggests, 'formally adduced in moral inquiries, are rather specimens and symbols of the real grounds than those grounds themselves'.

This attitude to the problem of faith received more systematic statement in a work of Newman's later years, the *Essay in Aid of a Grammar of Assent*, published in 1870. Here the nature of religious belief is scrutinized and the laws of its growth observed. Newman rejects Locke's idea that assent is a matter of degree and insists that it is unconditional. The mind demands not probabilities merely but certainties; at least it must be able to rest in a state of certitude, must *feel* that it possesses the truth. But once in possession of it it repudiates all contrary suggestions by the 'spontaneous action of the intellect'. That the mind, despite its assurance, may actually be in error Newman of course admits, but the guarantee of certitude is, he thinks, its permanence: it should 'stand all trials'. And at bottom, as always, is the testimony of conscience, 'that solemn Monitor, personal, peremptory, unargumentative, irreparable, minatory, definitive', whose witness to God's existence is direct and independent of revelation or dogma. Once this conviction is lodged in the mind others come by means of an 'illative sense'— a sense, Newman argues, of probability or fitness—that enables us to pass from the truths of natural religion to those of revelation and finally to an acknowledgement of that Church which is the one infallible dispenser and guardian of the knowledge of God. But only by his initial obedience to the imperative voice of conscience does the believer reach the 'triumphant repose' of an integral faith.

Newman never indeed tired of urging 'the potent implicit reason of man against the fruitless and formal explicit reason'. His aim in the *Grammar* was to meet the difficulties of the modern sceptic, with whose doubts and reservations he had himself an acute imaginative sympathy. (T. H. Huxley remarked that a 'primer of unbelief' could be compiled from the cardinal's writings.) Yet the long and laborious argument—it is the least accessible of all Newman's works—is more concerned with the psychological state of believing than with the rational justification of belief itself. If assent, however, rests on certitude Newman was satisfied that his purpose would be achieved by treating of the mind's native processes rather than faith's objective grounds. His analysis is undeniably searching. Men's beliefs, he rightly points out, are often better than the reasons they adduce for holding them. It is the strength of the conviction itself that matters: 'No man is certain of a truth who *can endure the thought* of its contrary' (italics ours). But if in the end rational justification may be thrown to the winds what need is there for anything more than a trustworthy *authority*? So of Christianity Newman writes that 'it is a "Revelatio revelata"; it is a definite chosen message from God to man distinctively conveyed by His chosen instruments, and to be received as such a message; and therefore to be positively acknowledged, embraced, and maintained as true, on the ground of its being divine, not as true on intrinsic grounds, nor as probably true, or partially true, but as absolutely certain knowledge, certain in a sense in which nothing else can be certain, because it comes from Him who neither can deceive nor be deceived'. Between the poles of sheer scepticism and unquestioning assent the intellect has no intermediate foothold. The dilemma, we can only infer, was Newman's own.

But the one work of his which has the strongest claim to originality is the *Essay* on Development. Once more it is an *argumentum ad hominem*, with the author himself as its object. For the problem confronting him at the time was that of discovering in the modern Roman Catholic Church an essential identity with the Church of the apostles. The answer he gave was that this identity is preserved under a process of development, and his book is a discussion both of the fact of such development and the conditions under which it can be held to be legitimate. Again it is the necessity of an external and infallible guiding authority that emerges. Although the motive of the essay is polemical it nevertheless marked a concession to the facts of history which was later to be invoked by the Roman Catholic Modernists, although to an end very different from anything Newman himself would have welcomed. For whatever his personal intentions, his apologetic methods were to prove, in more than one instance, a two-edged weapon, as perilous to the wielder as to his foe.

Bibliographical note

Newman's principal works have often been reissued and are readily obtainable. His Letters and Diaries (ed. C. S. Dessain) are in process of publication and are likely to comprise more than twenty volumes. The *Life* by Wilfrid Ward (2 vols., 1912) is supplemented, but not replaced, by M. Trevor, *Newman*. I. *The Pillar of the Cloud*, and II. *Light in Winter* (1962). On Newman's thought see A. J. Boekraad, *The Personal Conquest of Truth according to J. H. Newman* (1954), A. D. Culler, *The Imperial Intellect* (1956), J. H. Walgrave, *Newman the Theologian* (1960), J. Guitton, *La Philosophie de Newman* (1933) and the Preface by M. de Nédoncelle to *Œuvres philosophiques de Newman* (1945). On the Oxford Movement generally see I. Brilioth, *The Anglican Revival* (1925), C. C. J. Webb, *Religious Thought in the Oxford Movement* (1928), and O. Chadwick, *The Mind of the Oxford Movement* (1960).

I. FAITH AND REASON

It is plain in what sense Faith is a moral principle. It is created in the mind, not so much by facts, as by probabilities; and since probabilities have no definite ascertained value, and are reducible to no scientific standard, what are such to each individual, depends on his moral temperament. A good and a bad man will think very different things probable. In the judgement of a rightly disposed mind, objects are desirable and attainable which irreligious men will consider to be but fancies. Such a correct moral judgement and view of things is the very medium in which the argument for Christianity has its constraining influence; a faint proof under circumstances being more availing than a strong one, apart from those circumstances.

This holds good as regards the matter as well as the evidence of the Gospel. It is difficult to say where the evidence, whether for Scripture or the Creed, would be found, if it were deprived of those adventitious illustrations which it extracts and absorbs from the mind of the inquirer, and which a merciful Providence places there for that very purpose. Texts have their illuminating power, from the atmosphere of habit, opinion, usage, tradition, through which we see them. On the other hand, irreligious men are adequate judges of the value of mere evidence, when the decision turns upon it; for evidence is addressed to the Reason, compels the Reason to assent so far as it is strong, and allows the Reason to doubt or disbelieve so far as it is weak. The blood on Joseph's coat of many colours was as perceptible to enemy as to friend; miracles appeal to the senses of all men, good and bad; and, while their supernatural character is learned from that experience of nature which is common to the just and to the unjust, the fact of their occurrence depends on considerations about testimony, enthusiasm, imposture, and the like, in which there is nothing inward, nothing personal. It is a sort of proof which a man does not make for himself, but which is made for him. It exists independently of him, and is apprehended from its own clear and objective character. It is its very boast that it does but require a candid hearing; nay, it especially addresses itself to the unbeliever, and engages to convert him as if against his will. There is no room for choice; there is no merit, no praise or blame, in believing or disbelieving; no test of character in the one or the other. But a man *is* responsible for his faith, because he is responsiblefor his likings and dislikings, his hopes and his opinions, on all of which his faith depends. And whereas unbelievers do not see this distinction, they persist in saying that a man is as little responsible for his faith as for his bodily functions; that both are from nature; that the will cannot make a weak proof a strong one; that if a person thinks a certain reason goes only a certain way, he is dishonest in attempting to make it go farther; that if he is after all wrong in his judgement, it is only his misfortune, not his fault; that he is acted on by certain principles from without, and must obey the laws of evidence, which are necessary and constant. But in truth, though a given evidence does not vary in force, the antecedent probability attending it does vary without limit, according to the temper of the mind surveying it.

University Sermons (1843), Sermon x (1839)

II. BELIEF IN GOD

There is one God, such and such in Nature and Attributes.

I say 'such and such', for, unless I explain what I mean by 'one God', I use words which may mean any thing or nothing. I may mean a mere *anima mundi*; or an initial principle which once was in action and now is not; or collective humanity. I speak then of the God of the Theist and of the Christian: a God who is numerically One, who is Personal; the Author, Sustainer, and Finisher of all things, the Life of Law and Order, the Moral Governor; One who is Supreme and Sole;

like Himself, unlike all things besides Himself, which all are but His creatures; distinct from, independent of them all; One who is self-existing, absolutely infinite, who has ever been and ever will be, to whom nothing is past or future; who is all perfection, and the fullness and archetype of every possible excellence, the Truth Itself, Wisdom, Love, Justice, Holiness; One who is All-powerful, All-knowing, Omnipresent, Incomprehensible. These are some of the distinctive prerogatives which I ascribe unconditionally and unreservedly to the great Being whom I call God.

This being what Theists mean when they speak of God, their assent to this truth admits without difficulty of being what I have called a notional assent. It is an assent following upon acts of inference, and other purely intellectual exercises; and it is an assent to a large development of predicates, correlative to each other, or at least intimately connected together, drawn out as if on paper, as we might map a country which we had never seen, or construct mathematical tables, or master the methods of discovery of Newton or Davy, without being astronomers, mathematicians, or chemists ourselves.

So far is clear; but the question follows, Can I attain to any more vivid assent to the Being of a God, than that which is given merely to notions of the intellect? Can I enter with a personal knowledge into the circle of truths which make up that great thought? Can I rise to what I have called an imaginative apprehension of it? Can I believe as if I saw? Since such a high assent requires a present experience or memory of the fact, at first sight it would seem as if the answer must be in the negative; for how can I assent as if I saw, unless I have seen? but no one in this life can see God. Yet I conceive a real assent is possible, and I proceed to show how.

When it is said that we cannot see God, this is undeniable; but in what sense have we a discernment of His creatures, of the individual beings which surround us? The evidence which we have of their presence lies in the phenomena which address our senses, and our warrant for taking these for evidence is our instinctive certitude that they are evidence. By the law of our nature we associate those sensible phenomena or impressions with certain units, individuals, substances, whatever they are to be called, which are outside and out of the reach of sense, and we picture them to ourselves in those phenomena. The phenomena are as if pictures; but at the same time they give us no exact measure or character of the unknown things beyond them—for who will say there is any uniformity between the impressions which two of us would respectively have of some third thing, supposing one of us had only the sense of touch, and the other only the sense of hearing? Therefore, when we speak of our having a picture of the things which are perceived through the senses, we mean a certain representation, true as far as it goes, but not adequate.

And so of those intellectual objects which are brought home to us through our senses: that they exist, we know by instinct; that they are such and such, we apprehend from the impressions which they leave upon our minds. Thus the life and writings of Cicero or Dr Johnson, of St Jerome or St Chrysostom, leave upon us certain impressions of the intellectual and moral character of each of them, *sui generis*, and unmistakable. We take up a passage of Chrysostom or a passage of Jerome; there is no possibility of confusing the one with the other; in each case we see the man in his language. And so of any great man whom we may have known: that he is not a mere impression on our senses, we know by instinct; that he is such and such, we know by the matter or quality of that impression.

Now certainly the thought of God, as Theists entertain it, is not gained by an instinctive association of His presence with any sensible phenomena; but the office which the senses directly fulfil as regards the external world, that devolves indirectly on certain of our mental phenomena as regards its Maker. Those phenomena are found in the sense of moral obligation. As from a multitude of instinctive perceptions, acting in particular instances, of something beyond the senses, we generalize the notion of an external world, and then picture that world in and according to those particular phenomena from which we started, so from the perceptive power which identifies the intimations of conscience with the reverberations or echoes (so to say) of an external admonition, we proceed on to the notion of a Supreme Ruler and Judge, and then again we image Him and His attributes in those recurring intimations, out of which, as mental phenomena, our recognition of His existence was originally gained. And, if the impressions which His creatures make on us through our senses oblige us to regard those creatures as *sui generis* respectively, it is not wonderful that the notices which He indirectly gives us of His own nature are such as to make us understand that He is like Himself and like nothing else.

I have already said I am not proposing here to prove the Being of a God; yet I have found it impossible to avoid saying where I look for the proof of it. For I would begin to prove it by the same means by which I would commence a proof of His attributes and character; by the same means by which I show how we apprehend Him, not merely as a notion, but as a reality. The last indeed of these three investigations alone concerns me here, but I cannot altogether exclude the two former from my consideration. However, I repeat, what I am directly aiming at, is to explain how we gain an image of God and give a real assent to the proposition that He exists. And next, in order to do this, of course I must start from some first principle—and that first principle, which I assume and shall not attempt to prove, is that we have naturally a conscience.

I assume, then, that Conscience has a legitimate place among our mental acts; as really so, as the action of memory, of reasoning, of imagination, or as the sense of the beautiful; that, as there are objects which, when presented to the mind, cause it to feel grief, regret, joy, or desire, so there are things which excite in us approbation or blame, and which we in consequence call right or wrong; and which, experienced in ourselves, kindle in us that specific sense of pleasure or pain, which goes by the name of a good or bad conscience. This being taken for granted, I shall attempt to show that in this special feeling, which follows on the commission of what we call right and wrong, lie the materials for the real apprehension of a Divine Sovereign and Judge.

The feeling of conscience being, I repeat, a certain keen sensibility, pleasant or painful—self-approval and hope, or compunction and fear—attendant on certain of our actions, which in consequence we call right or wrong, is twofold: it is a moral sense, and a sense of duty; a judgement of the reason and a magisterial dictate. Of course its act is indivisible; still it has these two aspects, distinct from each other, and admitting of a separate consideration. Though I lost my sense of the obligation which I lie under to abstain from acts of dishonesty, I should not in consequence lose my sense that such actions were an outrage offered to my moral nature. Again; though I lost my sense of their moral deformity, I should not therefore lose my sense that they were forbidden to me. Thus conscience has both a critical and a judicial office, and though its promptings, in the breasts of the millions of human beings to whom it is given, are not in all cases correct, that does not necessarily interfere with the force of its testimony and of its sanction: its testimony that there is a right and a wrong, and its sanction to that testimony conveyed in the feelings which attend on right or wrong conduct.

Here I have to speak of conscience in the latter point of view, not as supplying us, by means of its various acts, with the elements of morals, which may be developed by the intellect into an ethical code, but simply as the dictate of an authoritative monitor bearing upon the details of conduct as they come before us, and complete in its several acts, one by one.

Let us thus consider conscience then, not as a rule of right conduct, but as a sanction of right conduct. This is its primary and most authoritative aspect; it is the ordinary sense of the word. Half the world would be puzzled to know what was meant by the moral sense; but every one knows what is meant by a good or bad conscience. Conscience is ever forcing on us by threats and by promises that we must follow the right and avoid the wrong; so far it is one and the same in the mind of every one, whatever be its particular errors in particular minds as to the acts which it orders to be done or to be avoided; and in this respect it corresponds to our perception of the beautiful and deformed. As we have naturally a sense of the beautiful and graceful in nature and art, though tastes proverbially differ, so we have a sense of duty and obligation, whether we all associate it with the same particular actions or not. Here, however, Taste and Conscience part company: for the sense of beautifulness, as indeed the Moral Sense, has no special relations to persons, but contemplates objects in themselves; conscience, on the other hand, is concerned with persons primarily, and with actions mainly as viewed in their doers, or rather with self alone and one's own actions, and with others only indirectly and as if in association with self. And further, taste is its own evidence, appealing to nothing beyond its own sense of the beautiful or the ugly, and enjoying the specimens of the beautiful simply for their own sake; but conscience does not repose on itself, but vaguely reaches forward to something beyond self, and dimly discerns a sanction higher than self for its decisions, as evidenced in that keen sense of obligation and responsibility which informs them. And hence it is that we are accustomed to speak of conscience as a voice, a term which we should never think of applying to the sense of the beautiful; and moreover a voice, or the echo of a voice, imperative and constraining, like no other dictate in the whole of our experience.

And again, in consequence of this prerogative of dictating and commanding, which is of its essence, Conscience has an intimate bearing on our affections and emotions, leading us to reverence and awe, hope and fear, especially fear, a feeling which is foreign for the most part, not only to Taste, but even to the Moral Sense, except in consequence of accidental associations. No fear is felt by any one who recognizes that his conduct has not been beautiful, though he may be mortified at himself, if perhaps he has thereby forfeited some advantage; but, if he has been betrayed into any kind of immorality, he has a lively sense of responsibility and guilt, though the act be no offence against society —of distress and apprehension, even though it may be of present service to him, of compunction and regret, though in itself it be most pleasurable, of confusion of face, though it may have no witnesses. These various perturbations of mind, which are characteristic of a bad conscience, and may be very considerable—self-reproach, poignant shame, haunting remorse, chill dismay at the prospect of the future— and their contraries, when the conscience is good, as real though less forcible, self-approval, inward peace, lightness of heart, and the like— these emotions constitute a generic difference between conscience and our other intellectual senses—common sense, good sense, sense of expedience, taste, sense of honour, and the like—as indeed they would also create between conscience and the moral sense, supposing these two were not aspects of one and the same feeling, exercised upon one and the same subject-matter.

So much for the characteristic phenomena, which conscience presents, nor is it difficult to determine what they imply. I refer once more to our sense of the beautiful. This sense is attended by an intellectual enjoyment, and is free from whatever is of the nature of emotion, except in one case, viz. when it is excited by personal objects; then it is that the tranquil feeling of admiration is exchanged for the excitement of affection and passion. Conscience too, considered as a moral sense, an intellectual sentiment, is a sense of admiration and disgust, of approbation and blame: but it is something more than a moral sense; it is always, what the sense of the beautiful is only in certain cases; it is always emotional. No wonder then that it always implies what that sense only sometimes implies; that it always involves the recognition of a living object, towards which it is directed. Inanimate things cannot stir our affections; these are correlative with persons. If, as is the case, we feel responsibility, are ashamed, are frightened, at transgressing the voice of conscience, this implies that there is One to whom we are responsible, before whom we are ashamed, whose claims upon us we fear. If, on doing wrong, we feel the same tearful, broken-hearted sorrow which overwhelms us on hurting a mother; if, on doing right, we enjoy the same sunny serenity of mind, the same soothing, satisfactory delight which follows on our receiving praise from a father, we certainly have within us the image of some person, to whom our love and veneration look, in whose smile we find our happiness, for whom we yearn, towards whom we direct our pleadings, in whose anger we are troubled and waste away. These feelings in us are such as require for their exciting cause an intelligent being: we are not affectionate towards a stone, nor do we feel shame before a horse or a dog; we have no remorse or compunction on breaking mere human law: yet, so it is, conscience excites all these painful emotions, confusion, foreboding, self-condemnation; and on the other hand it sheds upon us a deep peace, a sense of security, a resignation, and a hope, which there is no sensible, no earthly object to elicit. 'The wicked flees, when no one pursueth'; then why does he flee? whence his terror? Who is it that he sees in solitude, in darkness, in the hidden chambers of his heart? If the cause of these emotions does not belong to this visible world, the Object to which his perception is directed must be Supernatural and Divine; and thus the phenomena of Conscience, as a dictate, avail to impress the imagination with the picture of a Supreme Governor, a Judge, holy, just, powerful, all-seeing, retributive, and is the creative principle of religion, as the Moral Sense is the principle of ethics.

And let me here refer again to the fact, to which I have already drawn attention, that this instinct of the mind recognizing an external Master in the dictate of conscience, and imaging the thought of Him in the definite impressions which conscience creates, is parallel to that other law of, not only human, but of brute nature, by which the presence of unseen individual beings is discerned under the shifting shapes and colours of the visible world. Is it by sense, or by reason, that brutes understand the real unities, material and spiritual, which are signified by the lights and shadows, the brilliant ever-changing kaleidoscope, as it may be called, which plays upon their *retina*? Not by reason, for they have not reason; not by sense, because they are transcending sense; therefore it is an instinct. This faculty on the part of brutes, unless we were used to it, would strike us as a great mystery. It is one peculiarity of animal natures to be susceptible of phenomena through the channels of sense; it is another to have in those sensible phenomena a perception of the individuals to which certain groups of them belong. This perception of individual things is given to brutes in large measures, and that, apparently from the moment of their birth. It is by no mere physical instinct, such as that which leads him to his mother for milk, that the new-dropped lamb recognizes each of his fellow lambkins as a whole, consisting of many parts bound up in one, and, before he is an hour old, makes experience of his and their rival individualities. And much more distinctly do the horse and dog recognize even the personality of their masters. How are we to explain this apprehension of things, which are one and individual, in the midst of a world of pluralities and transmutations, whether in the instance of brutes or of children? But until we account for the knowledge which an infant has of his mother or his nurse, what reason have we to take exception at the doctrine, as strange and difficult, that in the dictate of conscience, without previous experiences or analogical reasoning, he is able gradually to perceive the voice, or the echoes of the voice, of a Master, living, personal, and sovereign?

I grant, of course, that we cannot assign a date, ever so early, before which he had learned nothing at all, and formed no mental associations, from the words and conduct of those who have the care of him. But still, if a child of five or six years old, when reason is at length fully awake, has already mastered and appropriated thoughts and beliefs, in consequence of their teaching, in such sort as to be able to handle and apply them familiarly, according to the occasion, as principles of intellectual action, those beliefs at the very least must be singularly congenial to his mind, if not connatural with its initial action. And that such a spontaneous reception of religious truths is common with children, I shall take for granted, till I am convinced that I am wrong in so doing. The child keenly understands that there is a difference between right and wrong; and when he has done what he believes to be wrong, he is conscious that he is offending One to whom he is amenable, whom he does not see, who sees him. His mind reaches forward with a strong presentiment to the thought of a Moral Governor, sovereign over him, mindful, and just. It comes to him like an impulse of nature to entertain it.

It is my wish to take an ordinary child, but one who is safe from influences destructive of his religious instincts. Supposing he has offended his parents, he will all alone and without effort, as if it were the most natural of acts, place himself in the presence of God, and beg of Him to set him right with them. Let us consider how much is contained in this simple act. First, it involves the impression on his mind of an unseen Being with whom he is in immediate relation, and that relation so familiar that he can address Him whenever he himself chooses; next, of One whose goodwill towards him he is assured of, and can take for granted—nay, who loves him better, and is nearer to him, than his parents; further, of One who can hear him, wherever he happens to be, and who can read his thoughts, for his prayer need not be vocal; lastly, of One who can effect a critical change in the state of feeling of others towards him. That is, we shall not be wrong in holding that this child has in his mind the image of an Invisible Being, who exercises a particular providence among us, who is present everywhere, who is heart-reading, heart-changing, ever-accessible, open to impetration. What a strong and intimate vision of God must he have already attained, if, as I have supposed, an ordinary trouble of mind has the spontaneous effect of leading him for consolation and aid to an Invisible Personal Power!

Moreover, this image brought before his mental vision is the image of One who by implicit threat and promise commands certain things which he, the same child, coincidently, by the same act of his mind, approves; which receive the adhesion of his moral sense and judgement, as right and good. It is the image of One who is good, inasmuch as enjoining and enforcing what is right and good, and who, in consequence, not only excites in the child hope and fear—nay (it may be added), gratitude towards Him, as giving a law and maintaining it by reward and punishment—but kindles in him love towards Him, as giving him a good law, and therefore as being good Himself, for it is the property of goodness to kindle love, or rather the very object of love is goodness; and all those distinct elements of the moral law, which the typical child, whom I am supposing, more or less consciously loves and approves—truth, purity, justice, kindness, and the like—are but shapes and aspects of goodness. And having in his degree a sensibility towards them all, for the sake of them all he is moved to love the Lawgiver, who enjoins them upon him. And, as he can contemplate these qualities and their manifestations under the common name of goodness, he is prepared to think of them as indivisible, correlative, supplementary of each other in one and the same Personality, so that there is no aspect of goodness which God is not; and that the more, because the notion of a perfection embracing all possible excellences, both moral and intellectual, is especially congenial to the mind, and there are in fact intellectual attributes, as well as moral, included in the child's image of God, as above represented.

Such is the apprehension which even a child may have of his Sovereign, Lawgiver, and Judge; which is possible in the case of children, because, at least, some children possess it, whether others possess it or no; and which, when it is found in children, is found to act promptly and keenly, by reason of the paucity of their ideas. It is an image of the good God, good in Himself, good relatively to the child, with whatever incompleteness; an image before it has been reflected on, and before it is recognized by him as a notion. Though he cannot explain or define the word 'God', when told to use it, his acts show that to him it is far more than a word. He listens, indeed, with wonder and interest to fables or tales; he has a dim, shadowy sense of what he hears about persons and matters of this world; but he has that within him which actually vibrates, responds, and gives a deep meaning to the lessons of his first teachers about the will and the providence of God.

How far this initial religious knowledge comes from without, and how much from within, how much is natural, how much implies a special divine aid which is above nature, we have no means of determining, nor is it necessary for my present purpose to determine. I am not engaged in tracing the image of God in the mind of a child or a man to its first origins, but showing that he can become possessed of such an image, over and above all mere notions of God, and in what that image consists. Whether its elements, latent in the mind, would ever be elicited without extrinsic help is very doubtful; but whatever be the actual history of the first formation of the divine image within us, so far is certain, that, by informations external to ourselves, as time goes on, it admits of being strengthened and improved. It is certain too, that, whether it grows brighter and stronger, or, on the other hand, is dimmed, distorted, or obliterated, depends on each of us individually, and on his circumstances. It is more than probable that, in the event, from neglect, from the temptations of life, from bad companions, or from the urgency of secular occupations, the light of the soul will fade away and die out. Men transgress their sense of duty, and gradually lose those sentiments of shame and fear, the natural supplements of transgression, which, as I have said, are the witnesses of the Unseen Judge. And, even were it deemed impossible that those who had in their first youth a genuine apprehension of Him, could ever utterly lose it, yet that apprehension may become almost undistinguishable from an inferential acceptance of the great truth, or may dwindle into a mere notion of their intellect. On the contrary, the image of God, if duly cherished, may expand, deepen, and be completed, with the growth of their powers and in the course of life, under the varied lessons, within and without them, which are brought home to them concerning that same God, One and Personal, by means of education, social intercourse, experience, and literature.

An Essay in Aid of a Grammar of Assent (1870)

III. DEVELOPMENT IN IDEAS

When an idea, whether real or not, is of a nature to interest and possess the mind, it is said to have life, that is, to live in the mind which is the recipient of it. Thus, mathematical ideas, real as they are, cannot be called living, for they have no influence and lead to nothing. But when some great enunciation, whether true or false, about human nature, or present good, or government, or duty, or religion, is carried forward into the public throng and draws attention, then it is not only passively admitted in this or that form into the minds of men, but it becomes a living principle within them, leading them to an ever-new contemplation of itself, an acting upon it and a propagation of it. Such is the doctrine of the natural bondage of the will, or of individual responsibility, or of the immortality of the soul, or of the rights of man, or of the divine right of kings, or of the hypocrisy and tyranny of priestcraft, or of the lawfulness of self-indulgence—doctrines which are of a nature to arrest, attract, or persuade, and have so far the *prima facie* appearance of reality that they may be looked at on many sides and strike various minds very variously. Let one such idea get possession of the popular mind, or the mind of any set of persons, and it is not difficult to understand the effects which will ensue. There will be a general agitation of thought, and an action of mind both upon itself and upon other minds. New lights will be brought to bear upon the original idea, aspects will multiply, and judgements will accumulate. There will be a time of confusion, when conceptions and misconceptions are in conflict; and it is uncertain whether anything is to come of the idea at all, or which view of it is to get the start of the others. After a while some definite form of doctrine emerges; and, as time proceeds, one view of it will be modified or expanded by another, and then,

284

combined with a third, till the idea in which they centre will be to each mind separately what at first it was only to all together. It will be surveyed, too, in its relation to other doctrines or facts, to other natural laws or established rules, to the varying circumstances of times and places, to other religions, polities, philosophies, as the case may be. How it stands affected towards other systems, how it affects them, how far it coalesces with them, how far it tolerates, when it interferes with them, will be gradually wrought out. It will be questioned and criticized by enemies, and explained by well-wishers. The multitude of opinions formed concerning it, in these respects and many others, will be collected, compared, sorted, sifted, selected, or rejected, and gradually attached to it, or separated from it, in the minds of individuals and of the community. It will, in proportion to its native vigour and subtlety, introduce itself into the framework and details of social life, changing public opinion and supporting or undermining the foundations of established order. Thus in time it has grown into an ethical code, or into a system of government, or into a theology, or into a ritual, according to its capabilities; and this system, or body of thought, theoretical and practical, thus laboriously gained, will after all be only the adequate representation of the original idea, being nothing else than what that very idea *meant* from the first—its exact image as seen in a combination of the most diversified aspects, with the suggestions and corrections of many minds, and the illustration of many trials.

This process is called the development of an idea, being the germination, growth, and perfection of some living, that is, influential truth, or apparent truth, in the minds of men during a sufficient period. And it has this necessary characteristic, that, since its province is the busy scene of human life, it cannot develop at all, except either by destroying, or modifying and incorporating with itself, existing modes of thinking and acting. Its development then is not like a mathematical theorem worked out on paper, in which each successive advance is a pure evolution from a foregoing, but it is carried on through individuals and bodies of men; it employs their minds as instruments, and depends upon them while it uses them. And so as regards their existing opinions, principles, measures, and institutions, it develops in establishing relations between them and itself, in giving them a meaning, in creating what may be called a jurisdiction over them, in throwing off from itself what is utterly heterogeneous in them. It grows when it incorporates;

and its purity consists, not in isolation, but in its continuity and sovereignty. This it is which imparts to the history both of states and of religions its especially turbulent or polemical character. Such is the explanation of the wranglings whether of Schools or of Parliaments. It is the warfare of ideas, striving for the mastery, each of them enterprising, engrossing, imperious, more or less incompatible with the rest, and rallying followers or rousing foes according as it acts upon the faith, the prejudices, or the interests of individuals.

Moreover, an idea not only modifies, but, as has been implied, is modified or at least influenced by the state of things in which it is carried out, and depends in various ways on the circumstances around it. Its development proceeds quickly or slowly; the order of succession in its separate stages is irregular; it will show differently in a small sphere of action and in an extended; it may be interrupted, retarded, mutilated, distorted, by external violence; it may be enfeebled by the effort of ridding itself of domestic foes; it may be impeded and swayed or even absorbed by counter energetic ideas; it may be coloured by the received tone of thought into which it comes, or depraved by the intrusion of foreign principles, or at length shattered by the development of some original fault within it.

But, whatever be the risk of corruption from intercourse with the world around it, such a risk must be undergone, if it is duly to be understood, and much more if it is to be fully exhibited. It is elicited by trial, and struggles into perfection. Nor does it escape the collision of opinion even in its earlier years; nor does it remain truer to itself, and more one and the same, though protected from vicissitude and change. It is indeed sometimes said that the stream is clearest near the spring. Whatever use may fairly be made of this image, it does not apply to the history of a philosophy or sect, which, on the contrary, is more equable, and purer, and stronger, when its bed has become deep, and broad, and full. It necessarily rises out of an existing state of things, and, for a time, savours of the soil. Its vital element needs disengaging from what is foreign and temporary, and is employed in efforts after freedom, more vigorous and hopeful as its years increase. Its beginnings are no measure of its capabilities, nor of its scope. At first, no one knows what it is, or what it is worth. It remains perhaps for a time quiescent: it tries, as it were, its limbs, and proves the ground under it, and feels its way. From time to time, it makes essays which fail, and are in consequence abandoned. It seems in suspense which way to go; it wavers, and at length strikes out in one definite direction. In time it enters upon strange territory; points of controversy alter their bearing; parties rise and fall about it; dangers and hopes appear in new relations, and old principles reappear under new forms; it changes with them in order to remain the same. In a higher world it is otherwise; but here below to live is to change, and to be perfect is to have changed often. *An Essay on the Development of Christian Doctrine* (1845)

CHAPTER 4

MANSEL

It occasionally happens that a thinker or artist who in his own day seemed to accord little with the general trend and who in consequence was either ignored or opposed will appear to a later age to convey a more intelligible and relevant message than did most of his contemporaries. Henry Longueville Mansel, it may be claimed, provides an instance of this, particularly in respect of his famous dispute with F. D. Maurice on the nature of divine revelation.[1] Maurice himself was a man not always well understood or approved, but in retrospect at least he seems more representative of his period than Mansel, who in the eyes of his numerous critics was at once a reactionary and a sceptic.

Born in 1820, Mansel was the eldest son of the then rector of Cosgrove, Northants, and was educated at Merchant Taylors' School and St John's College, Oxford, where his intellectual abilities quickly became evident. Appointed a tutor of his college in 1846, he was ordained priest two years later. In 1855 he was elected Waynflete professor of moral and metaphysical Philosophy at Magdalen College, in which capacity he delivered the Bampton Lectures for 1858, greatly puzzling his hearers—one elderly don remarked that he 'never expected to hear atheism preached in the pulpit of the university church'—and giving rise to sharp controversy when, in the following year, the lectures were published under the title, *The Limits of Religious Thought Examined*. Learned, witty and a gifted writer, Mansel was always a keen polemist, whether resisting university reform or the newest fashion in Oxford philosophy. His versatility is suggested by his nomination in 1860 to the university chair of ecclesiastical history, but although his lectures on the Gnostic heresies, published posthumously in 1875, can still offer a useful account of their subject he was by temperament and interest an abstract thinker. In 1868 he left Oxford to become dean of St Paul's, in the hope that his new office might afford him more leisure for writing than had been possible hitherto, but his tenure of it was comparatively brief, for he died whilst on a visit to his old home in Northamptonshire in 1871.

The argument of the Bamptons is indicated by the two quotations printed on the book's title-page. The first, from Bishop Berkeley, states that 'The objections to faith are by no means an effect of knowledge, but proceed rather from an ignorance of what knowledge is'; the other, from Mansel's elder contemporary, the Scottish philosopher, Sir William Hamilton (1788–

[1] See ch. 2 above.

1856), that 'No difficulty emerges in theology which had not previously emerged in philosophy.' Mansel's view is in fact based on Hamilton's 'Philosophy of the Unconscious', according to which 'the Unconditioned is conceived only as the negative of the Conditioned'. The transcendent, Mansel points out, is by definition 'incognizable and inconceivable', so that there can be no speculative knowledge of God attainable by reason alone and independently of a divine revelation. If man is to know God at all revelation is a necessity, and when given is above criticism. Mansel's use of the word 'speculative', however, does not include 'intuitive' certitude, nor does he imply that the religious consciousness is not a deeply significant aspect of man's mental life, carrying with it, as it does, both a feeling of dependence and a conviction of moral obligation. Moreover, if religion is to be identified with a system of intelligible truths the actual disclosure of them must be externally testified; no merely private apprehension would suffice.

Mansel's approach to the problem of religious knowledge is illustrated by some critical reflexions which he had earlier expressed upon Maurice's doctrine of eternity. 'To conceive', he writes, 'an Eternal Being, I must have experienced a consciousness out of time, i.e. a consciousness other than human in its constitution. The term Eternity, in this sense, expresses not a conception but the negation of a conception, the acknowledgement of the possible existence of a Being concerning whose consciousness we can only make the negative assertion that it is not like our consciousness.' In the Bampton Lectures he goes further and attacks the whole project of a philosophical theology as an impossible attempt to 'produce a coincidence between what we believe and what we think', the truth being that there are definite and discernible limits to the province of reason itself. Christian dogma, accordingly, cannot be 'rationalized'. That it is anthropomorphic Mansel freely admits, but he insists that any attempt to conceive God is bound to be so, since all reason and experience are necessarily man's own. Indeed the abstract view of God preferred by philosophy is but an inferior reflexion of our 'marred and mutilated humanity'. Hence if the nature and meaning of religion are to be properly understood, inquiry must begin with the human mind itself and the fact of its limitations securely grasped. An object which transcends terrestrial experience cannot be clearly represented; eternity and infinity—that the words themselves may of course be non-significant Mansel does not discuss—are concepts to which we can assign no positive content inasmuch as the primary function of reason, which is to distinguish one entity from another, immediately becomes inoperative. Beyond the conviction that the infinite is real we can say nothing at all about it. Thus a metaphysical absolute is for the purposes of religion a merely vacuous notion. When we think of God it is as a being *sub specie temporis*, comparable with other such beings.

For this reason, Mansel stresses, a divine revelation cannot be critically judged: we have no prior knowledge of what it represents. Consider, for example, the problem of a personal deity. The belief that God is personal is a necessity of the religious life; without it prayer would be impossible. Further, since personality is the ground of our conceptual thinking we can form no adequate idea of God which omits the personal element. But if personality can be thought of only in terms of relation and succession how, without involving ourselves in contradiction, can we conceive a personality which is *infinite*? The believer finds himself in the paradoxical situation of having to affirm two evidently incompatible truths, since neither of them can be denied without betrayal of a fundamental conviction. Despite, therefore, what critical reason may say he will bow to revelation, though he also will recognize it as 'a duty, enjoined by reason itself', to believe in that which he is unable to comprehend. But, since 'the provinces of Reason and Faith are not co-extensive', the knowledge which revelation provides is 'regulative' only, a series of symbols by which to direct conduct.

Much in this plainly accords with present-day theological thought and Mansel's book is now no longer a mere period-piece. Nevertheless, on its constructive side the argument bears the marks of its age. As Maurice complained, its appeal is simply to the Bible as interpreted by the orthodoxy of the day. Polemically brilliant, it needs to be offset by Maurice's more clumsily expressed but profounder insight.

Bibliographical note

Regrettably there is no modern reprint of *The Limits of Religious Thought Examined*. The 5th edition appeared in 1867. A collection of Mansel's *Letters, Lectures and Reviews*, edited by H. W. Chandler, was published in 1873. See W. R. Matthews, *The Religious Philosophy of Dean Mansel* (Dr Williams Lecture, 1956), M. Nédoncelle, *La Philosophie religieuse en Grande-Bretagne de 1850 à nos jours* (Cahiers de la nouvelle Journée, no. 26, n.d.), ch. 1, and the references in V. F. Storr, *The Development of English Theology in the Nineteenth Century* (1913). There is also a lengthy discussion of Mansel in J. Martineau's *Essays* (1875), vol. 1, pp. 213–43. The article in the *D.N.B.* (vol. xii) is by Sir Leslie Stephen.

THE NATURE AND PURPOSE OF THEOLOGICAL TRUTHS

In religion, in morals, in our daily business, in the care of our lives, in the exercise of our senses, the rules which guide our practice cannot be reduced to principles which satisfy our reason.

The very first Law of Thought, and, through Thought, of all Consciousness, by which alone we are able to discern objects as such, or to distinguish them one from another, involves in its constitution a mystery and a doubt, which no effort of Philosophy has been able to penetrate: How can the One be many, or the Many one? We are compelled to regard ourselves and our fellow-men as *persons*, and the visible world around us as made up of *things*: but what is *personality*, and what is *reality*, are questions which the wisest have tried to answer, and have tried in vain. Man, as a Person, is one, yet composed of many elements—not identical with any one of them, nor yet with the aggregate of them all; and yet not separable from them by any effort of abstraction. Man is one in his thoughts, in his actions, in his feelings, and in the responsibilities which these involve. It is *I* who think, *I* who act, *I* who feel; yet I am not thought, nor action, nor feeling, nor a combination of thoughts and actions and feelings heaped together. Extension, and resistance, and shape, and the various sensible qualities, make up my conception of each individual body as such; yet *the body* is not its extension, nor its shape, nor its hardness, nor its colour, nor its smell, nor its taste; nor yet is it a mere aggregate of all these with no principle of unity among them. If these several parts constitute a single whole, the unity, as well as the plurality, must depend upon some principle which that whole contains: if they do not constitute a whole, the difficulty is removed but a single step; for the same question— what constitutes individuality?—must be asked in relation to each separate part. The actual conception of every object, as such, involves the combination of the One and the Many; and that combination is practically made every time we think at all. But at the same time no effort of reason is able to explain how such a relation is possible; or to satisfy the intellectual doubt which necessarily arises on the contemplation of it.

As it is with the first law of Thought, so it is with the first principle of Action and of Feeling. All action, whether free or constrained, and all passion, implies and rests upon another great mystery of Philosophy —the Commerce between Mind and Matter. The properties and operations of matter are known only by the external senses; the faculties and acts of the mind are known only by the internal apprehension. The energy of the one is motion: the energy of the other is consciousness. What is the middle term which unites these two? and how can their reciprocal action, unquestionable as it is in fact, be conceived as possible in theory? How can a contact between body and body produce consciousness in the immaterial soul? How can a mental self-determination produce the motion of material organs? How can mind, which is neither extended nor figured nor coloured in itself, represent by its ideas the extension and figure and colour of bodies? How can the body be determined to a new position in space by an act of thought, to which space has no relation? How can thought itself be carried on by bodily instruments, and yet itself have nothing in common with bodily affections? What is the relation between the last pulsation of the material brain and the first awakening of the mental perception? How does the spoken word, a merely material vibration of the atmosphere, become echoed, as it were, in the silent voice of thought, and take its part in an operation wholly spiritual? Here again we acknowledge, in our daily practice, a fact which we are unable to represent in theory; and the various hypotheses to which Philosophy has had recourse—the Divine Assistance, the Pre-established Harmony, the Plastic Medium, and others, are but so many confessions of the existence of the mystery, and of the extraordinary, yet wholly insufficient efforts made by human reason to penetrate it.

The very perception of our senses is subject to the same restrictions. 'No priestly dogmas', says Hume, 'ever shocked common sense more than the infinite divisibility of extension, with its consequences.' He should have added, that the antagonist assumption of a finite divisibility is equally incomprehensible; it being as impossible to conceive an ultimate unit, or least possible extension, as it is to conceive the process of division carried on to infinity. Extension is presented to the mind as a relation between parts exterior to each other, whose reality cannot consist merely in their juxtaposition. We are thus compelled to believe that extension itself is dependent upon some higher law—that it is not an original principle of things in themselves, but a derived result of their connexion with each other. But to conceive how this generation of space is possible—how unextended objects can by their conjunction produce extension—baffles the utmost efforts of the wildest imagination or the profoundest reflexion. We cannot conceive how unextended matter can become extended; for of unextended matter we know nothing, either in itself or in its relations; though we are apparently compelled to postulate its existence, as implied in the appearances of which alone we are conscious. The existence of mental succession in time is as inexplicable as that of material extension in space—a first moment and an infinite regress of moments being both equally inconceivable, no less than the corresponding theories of a first atom and an infinite division.

The difficulty which meets us in these problems may help to throw some light on the purposes for which human thought is designed, and the limits within which it may be legitimately exercised. The primary fact of consciousness, which is accepted as regulating our practice, is in itself *inexplicable*, but not *inconceivable*. There is *mystery*; but there is not yet *contradiction*. Thought is baffled, and unable to pursue the track of investigation; but it does not grapple with an idea and destroy itself in the struggle. Contradiction does not begin till we direct our thoughts, not to the fact itself, but to that which it suggests as beyond itself. This difference is precisely that which exists between following the laws of thought, and striving to transcend them—between leaving the mystery of Knowing and Being unsolved, and making unlawful attempts to solve it. The facts—that all objects of thought are conceived as wholes composed of parts; that mind acts upon matter, and matter upon mind; that bodies are extended in space, and thoughts successive in time—do not, in their own statement, severally contain elements repulsive of each other. As mere facts, they are so far from being inconceivable, that they embody the very laws of conception itself, and are experienced at every moment as true: but though we are able, nay, compelled, to conceive them as *facts*, we find it impossible to conceive them as *ultimate facts*. They are made known to us as *relations*; and all relations are in themselves complex, and imply simpler principles—objects to be related, and a ground by which the relation is constituted. The conception of any such relation as a fact thus involves a further inquiry concerning its existence as a consequence; and to this inquiry no satisfactory answer can be given. Thus the highest principles of thought and action, to which we can attain, are *regulative*, not *speculative*: they do not serve to satisfy the reason, but to guide the conduct: they do not tell us what things are in themselves, but how we must conduct ourselves in relation to them.

The conclusion which this condition of human consciousness almost irresistibly forces upon us, is one which equally exhibits the strength and the weakness of the human intellect. We are compelled to admit that the mind, in its contemplation of objects, is not the mere passive recipient of the things presented to it; but has an activity and a law of its own, by virtue of which it reacts upon the materials existing without, and moulds them into that form in which consciousness is capable of apprehending them. The existence of modes of thought, which we are compelled to accept as at the same time relatively ultimate and absolutely derived—as limits beyond which we cannot penetrate, yet which themselves proclaim that there is a further truth behind and above them—suggests, as its obvious explanation, the hypothesis of a mind cramped by its own laws, and bewildered in the contemplation of its own forms. If the mind, in the act of consciousness, were merely blank and inert—if the entire object of its contemplation came from without, and nothing from within—no fact of consciousness would be inexplicable; for everything would present itself as it is. No reality would be suggested, beyond what is actually given: no question would be asked which is not already answered. For how can doubt arise, where there is no innate power in the mind to think beyond what is placed before it, to react upon that which acts upon it? But upon the contrary supposition, all is regular, and the result such as might naturally be expected. If thought has laws of its own, it cannot by its own act go beyond them; yet the recognition of law, as a restraint, implies the existence of a sphere of liberty beyond. If the mind contributes its own element to the objects of consciousness, it must, in its first recognition of those objects, necessarily regard them as something complex, something generated partly from without and partly from within. Yet in that very recognition of the complex, as such, is implied an impossibility of attaining to the simple; for to resolve the composition is to destroy the very act of knowledge, and the relation by which consciousness is constituted. The object of which we are conscious is thus, to adopt the well-known language of the Kantian philosophy, a *phenomenon*, not a *thing in itself*—a product, resulting from the twofold action of the thing apprehended, on the one side, and the faculties apprehending it, on the other. The perceiving subject alone, and the perceived object alone, are two unmeaning elements, which first acquire a significance in and by the act of their conjunction.

It is thus strictly in analogy with the method of God's Providence in the constitution of man's mental faculties, if we believe that, in Religion also, He has given us truths which are designed to be regulative, rather than speculative; intended, not to satisfy our reason, but to guide our practice; not to tell us what God is in His absolute nature, but how He wills that we should think of Him in our present finite state. In my last Lecture I endeavoured to show that our knowledge of God is not a consciousness of the Infinite as such, but that of the relation of a Person to a Person—the conception of personality being, humanly speaking, one of *limitation*. This amounts to the admission that, in natural religion at least, our knowledge of God does not satisfy the conditions of speculative philosophy, and is incapable of reduction to an ultimate and absolute truth. And this, as we now see, is in accordance with the analogy which the character of human philosophy in other provinces would naturally lead us to expect. It is reasonable also that we should expect to find, as part of the same analogy, that the revealed manifestation of the Divine nature and attributes should likewise carry on its face the marks of subordination to some higher truth, of which it indicates the existence, but does not make known the substance. It is to be expected that our apprehension of the revealed Deity should involve mysteries inscrutable and doubts insoluble by our present faculties; while, at the same time, it inculcates the true spirit in which such doubts should be dealt with; by warning us, as plainly as such a warning is possible, that we see a part only, and not the whole; that we behold effects only, and not causes; that our knowledge of God, though revealed by Himself, is revealed in relation to human faculties, and subject to the limitations and imperfections inseparable from the constitution of the human mind. We may neglect this warning if we please: we may endeavour to supply the imperfection and thereby make it more imperfect still: we may twist and torture the divine image on the rack of human philosophy, and call its mangled relics by the high-sounding titles of the Absolute and the Infinite; but these ambitious conceptions, the instant we attempt to employ them in any act of thought, manifest at once, by their inherent absurdities, that they are not that which they pretend to be—that, in the place of the Absolute and Infinite manifested in its own nature, we have merely the Relative and Finite contradicting itself.

We may indeed believe, and ought to believe, that the knowledge which our Creator has permitted us to attain to, whether by Revelation or by our natural faculties, is not given to us as an instrument of deception. We may believe, and ought to believe, that, intellectually as well as morally, our present life is a state of discipline and preparation for another; and that the conceptions which we are compelled to adopt, as the guides of our thoughts and actions now, may indeed, in the sight of a higher Intelligence, be but partial truth, but cannot be total falsehood. But in thus believing, we desert the evidence of Reason, to rest on that of Faith; and of the principles on which Reason itself depends, it is obviously impossible to have any other guarantee. But such a Faith, however well founded, has itself only a regulative and practical, not a speculative and theoretical application. It bids us rest content within the limits which have been assigned to us; but it cannot enable us to overleap those limits, nor exalt to a more absolute character the conclusions obtained by finite thinkers under the conditions of finite thought. But on the other hand, we must beware of the opposite extreme—that of mistaking the inability to affirm for the ability to deny. We cannot say that our conception of the Divine Nature exactly resembles that Nature in its absolute existence; for we know not what that absolute existence is. But, for the same reason, we are equally unable to say that it does not resemble; for, if we know not the Absolute and Infinite at all, we cannot say how far it is or is not capable of likeness or unlikeness to the Relative and Finite. We must remain content with the belief that we have that knowledge of God which is best adapted to our wants and training. How far that knowledge represents God as He is, we know not, and we have no need to know.

The Limits of Religious Thought Examined (1859)

CHAPTER 5

J. S. MILL

John Stuart Mill, philosopher and economist, and eldest son of James Mill, was born in London in 1806. Details of his early education, conducted by his father on rigorously doctrinaire lines, are familiar from his *Autobiography*. He started Greek at the age of 3, Latin at 7, and by the time he was 12, with a considerable first-hand knowledge of the classical authors already at his disposal, he had embarked, with Aristotle's *Logic*, on the study of philosophy. And much else had also to be mastered—mathematics as far as the differential calculus, natural science, history. At 14 came Ricardo's *Political Economy*. 'Anything', Mill wrote, 'which could be found out by thinking I was never told, until I had exhausted my efforts to find it out for myself.' A year in France provided further intellectual stimulus, but the climax was reached with the works of Jeremy Bentham. 'I now', he records, 'had opinions, a creed, a doctrine, a philosophy; in one among the best senses of the word, a religion; the inculcation and diffusion of which could be made the principal outward purpose of my life.' At the age of 17 he was appointed to a clerk-ship in the office of the East India Company's examiner of India correspon-dence, and here he remained for the ensuing thirty-five years, retiring, as head of his department, when the company's governmental powers were transferred to the Crown. His spare time, however, had been given to literary work. A frequent contributor to the radical *Westminster Review*, founded in 1823, he became in 1834 editor of the *London Review*, later to be combined with the *Westminster*. But the year 1826–7 had brought on a mental crisis the result of which was a considerable modification of the out-look imposed by his previous training. The basic truth of 'philosophical radicalism', his Benthamite inheritance, he was never disposed to deny, but its influence had, he feared, made of him a mere 'reasoning machine'. Imagination and feeling—'poetical culture'—were lacking; the solvent power of unremitting rational analysis had been applied too far. He had started, as he thought, with 'a well-equipped ship and a rudder, but no sail'. Yet the crisis itself was strongly emotional and Mill was very nearly prostrated by it. In his subsequent restoration the poetry of Wordsworth, as he warmly acknowledged, was no small factor, since it offered precisely that 'culture of the feelings' which he was in quest of. But other influences were also pressing upon him: Coleridge, Sterling, Maurice, Goethe, Comte, Carlyle—the last in the form of an astringent personal friendship. The brash and narrow Benthamite self-confidence gave way to a deep and often disturbing sense of the manifold variety and complexity of human existence. In addition, Mrs Taylor was to enter his life. This lady he met in 1830 and twenty years afterwards, on the death of her husband, he married her. His attachment was profound and almost as heady as Auguste Comte's to Madame de Vaux, and doubtless her regard was of great comfort to him; but his encomiums upon her inexhaustible wisdom and acumen are absurdly fulsome. She died in 1858. In 1865 Mill was elected member of Parliament for Westminster and in the debates on the 1867 Reform Bill he zealously advocated female suffrage. His own death, in 1873, occurred, like his wife's, at Avignon, where he is buried. At the time he was esteemed as the foremost philosophical thinker in England.

His chief publications include *A System of Logic* (1843), *The Principles of Political Economy* (1848), the celebrated *Essay on Liberty* (1859), *Considerations on Representative Government* (1861), *Utilitarianism* (1863), *An Examination of Sir William Hamilton's Philosophy* (1865), *Auguste Comte and Positivism* (1865), *The Subjection of Women* (1869) and the *Autobiography* (1873). A volume containing his *Three Essays on Religion* appeared posthumously, in 1874.

Mill's outlook, although perceptive of contemporary tendencies, was fundamentally that of the eighteenth century. He was a life-long campaigner in the cause of what he conceived to be 'reason' and a tireless enemy of tyranny and injustice in any shape. This militancy gives an edge to all he wrote, but with it goes a certain intellectual cecity, a defect of sympathy and insight, which somewhat offsets his unquestionable virtues. Carlyle saw in the *Autobiography* nothing but 'the life of a logic-chopping engine'— itself, however, an unfair opinion. Yet most would agree with R. H. Hutton in finding in Mill's work 'a monotonous joylessness', for all 'the hectic sanguineness of its author's theoretic creed'. This last of course was his utilitarianism, the fount of which was Bentham's doctrine of the pleasure-principle. 'Nature', declares Mill, 'has placed mankind under the governance of two sovereign masters, pain and pleasure. It is for them alone to point to what we ought to do, as well as determine what we shall do.' Mill is well aware of the distaste which this view arouses in many minds and so endeavours to give it a more conventional moral aura by distinguishing between 'sorts' of pleasure, insisting that some are more desirable and valuable than others. 'Higher' pleasures will be pursued at the cost of 'lower' ones by those who realize what both involve. Thus is it better to be 'a human being dissatisfied than a pig satisfied'. The more desirable pleasures —the true goods—are, in other words, those actually desired by the best judges. These true goods society will seek to promote by the progressive amelioration of the people's condition, since the major causes of human suffering are in great degree, if not indeed entirely, conquerable by human care and effort. The process may be slow, but it is feasible and an inspiration, such as no mere impulse to selfish indulgence can rival, to any who dedicates himself to its furtherance. But Mill's rhetoric, impressive though it is, will hardly dispel the suspicion that the plain man feels no powerful urge to seek some dimly apprehended general good rather than the specific advantages of his own. If all men are in fact naturally selfish, as Bentham and Mill contend, the problem of how to turn selfishness into altruism, even were we to grant that right actions are but an elevated form of selfishness, suggests no ready solution; and all that Mill himself says betrays his basic uncertainty on the matter. What is needed, he believes, is the compelling force of religion; a religion, however, not of deity but of humanity, the substance of which will be 'a feeling of unity with our fellow-creatures' so deeply rooted in men's characters as to be virtually instinctive. Such a feeling of unity is in truth, Mill points out, what Christ himself intended. Nevertheless, can he, on his own principles, establish the necessity of altruism—the 'higher humanitarianism'—except by claiming it as 'pleasurable'—by arguing that the surest way to one's own satisfaction is in discharging one's 'duty' to one's fellows? Mill's trust in the power of education to produce uniformly desirable sentiments seems, in the light of experience, not a little naïve; yet there are many who still share his conviction.

Mill's views on religion, expounded in the *Three Essays* with the pains-taking dryness of manner he seldom abandoned, are characteristic of the Age of Reason rather than of the century that gave birth to the Romantic move-ment. Hume is evident on every page, but of Schleiermacher or Hegel, of Coleridge (here at least) or Newman, there is no trace. Christianity would appear to the author to consist of nothing but propositional *credenda* that no reasonable man could now regard as tenable. The first of the essays is con-cerned with the meaning of Nature, which may be so defined as either to include man or to exclude him. Taken in the former sense it is seen to have within it the power of self-improvement, whereas the 'nature' with which man contrasts himself—'that which takes place without the agency, or without the voluntary and intentional agency, of man'—is wholly non-moral. 'Nearly all the things which men are hanged or imprisoned for doing to one another, are nature's everyday performances.' That it cannot be the work of a being 'at once good and omnipotent' is manifest. Man's vocation therefore is to bring morality to bear on the world he inhabits, and whatever tendencies of a beneficent kind that nature may chance to disclose must be made the most of. But the idea of a Power behind nature controlling it for good is one that has to be dismissed. The second essay discusses the Utility of Religion. The question arises: What is there which might impel man to exert moral effort? Mill contends that nowadays it is the 'usefulness' of religion rather than its alleged truth which is commonly stressed and concedes that religion may be morally useful without being 'intellectually sustainable'. But this is far from saying that morality is dependent on religion. No doubt it once was, but it is so no longer. The inspiration we look for is to be found not in incredible religious dogmas but in man himself, whose noblest representatives—a 'Socrates, or Howard, or Washington, or Antoninus, or Christ'—provide the patterns we should set before ourselves. For what is the essence of religion but 'the strong and earnest direction of the emotions and desires towards an ideal object, recognized as one of the highest excellence, and as rightfully paramount over all selfish objects of desire'? And this condition, Mill urges, is fulfilled by the 'Religion of Humanity' in as eminent a degree, and in as high a sense, as by the supernatural religions 'even in their best manifestations'. What, however, of the life of the world to come? When—so he answers—men 'cease to need a future existence as a consolation for the sufferings of the present, it will lose its chief value to them'.

The last of the essays is entitled 'Theism' and is the maturest statement of Mill's opinions on the religious question. Again he sees religious beliefs merely as 'scientific theorems' and asks what basis in reason they can have. He reviews the traditional theistic arguments and of course finds them wanting. At any rate only the argument from design is worth more than a moment's consideration, since the theory of evolution—Darwin's *Origin of Species* had appeared in 1859—calls attention to 'adaptations' in nature such as 'afford a large balance of probability in favour of creation by intelligence'. Marks of beneficence in nature, that is, are more evident than might at first seem, but they at most can point to a Being of great but not unlimited power. Miracles certainly are not to be adduced as testimony that this Being is also self-revealing in any specific way. Yet the example of Christ, 'a unique figure', remains profoundly impressive. 'Religion', Mill even concludes, 'cannot be said to have made a bad choice in pitching on (*sic*) this man as the ideal representative and guide of humanity'. In the end, however, the rationalist's faith stands unshaken, for the only religion which Christ's example serves to validate is that of man in his own natural constitution and terrestrial vocation.

Bibliographical note

Mill's *System of Logic* has often been reprinted. Of the *Three Essays on Religion*, however, there is no recent edition. On Mill generally see J. Plamenatz, *The English Utilitarians* (1949), R. P. Anschutz, *The Philosophy of J. S. Mill* (1953) and K. Britton, *John Stuart Mill* (1953). See also B. Willey, *Nineteenth Century Studies* (1949), ch. VI.

THEISM

From the result of the preceding examination of the evidences of Theism, and (Theism being presupposed) of the evidences of any Revelation, it follows that the rational attitude of a thinking mind towards the supernatural, whether in natural or in revealed religion, is that of scepticism as distinguished from belief on the one hand, and from atheism on the other: including, in the present case, under atheism, the negative as well as the positive form of disbelief in a God, viz. not only the dogmatic denial of his existence, but the denial that there is any evidence on either side, which for most practical purposes amounts to the same thing as if the existence of a God had been disproved. If we are right in the conclusions to which we have been led by the preceding inquiry there is evidence, but insufficient for proof, and amounting only to one of the lower degrees of probability. The indication given by such evidence as there is, points to the creation, not indeed of the universe, but of the present order of it by an Intelligent Mind, whose power over the materials was not absolute, whose love for his creatures was not his sole actuating inducement, but who nevertheless desired their good. The notion of a providential government by an omnipotent Being for the good of his creatures must be entirely dismissed. Even of the continued existence of the Creator we have no other guarantee than that he cannot be subject to the law of death which affects terrestrial beings, since the conditions that produce this liability wherever it is known to exist are of his creating. That this Being, not being omnipotent, may have produced a machinery falling short of his intentions, and which may require the occasional interposition of the Maker's hand, is a supposition not in itself absurd nor impossible, though in none of the cases in which such interposition is believed to have occurred is the evidence such as could possibly prove it; it remains a simple possibility, which those may dwell on to whom it yields comfort to suppose that blessings which ordinary human power is inadequate to attain, may come not from extraordinary human power, but from the bounty of an intelligence beyond the human, and which continuously cares for man. The possibility of a life after death rests on the same footing—of a boon which this powerful Being who wishes well to man, may have the power to grant, and which if the message alleged to have been sent by him was really sent, he has actually promised. The whole domain of the supernatural is thus removed from the region of Belief into that of simple Hope; and in that, for anything we can see, it is likely always to remain; for we can hardly anticipate either that any positive evidence will be acquired of the direct agency of Divine Benevolence in human destiny, or that any reason will be discovered for considering the realization of human hopes on that subject as beyond the pale of possibility.

It is now to be considered whether the indulgence of hope, in a region of imagination merely, in which there is no prospect that any probable grounds of expectation will ever be obtained, is irrational, and ought to be discouraged as a departure from the rational principle of regulating our feelings as well as opinions strictly by evidence.

This is a point which different thinkers are likely, for a long time at least, to decide differently, according to their individual temperament. The principles which ought to govern the cultivation and the regulation of the imagination—with a view on the one hand of preventing it from disturbing the rectitude of the intellect and the right direction of the actions and will, and on the other hand of employing it as a power for increasing the happiness of life and giving elevation to the character —are a subject which has never yet engaged the serious consideration of philosophers, though some opinion on it is implied in almost all modes of thinking on human character and education. And, I expect, that this will hereafter be regarded as a very important branch of study for practical purposes, and the more, in proportion as the weakening of positive beliefs respecting states of existence superior to the human, leaves the imagination of higher things less provided with material from the domain of supposed reality. To me it seems that human life, small and confined as it is, and as, considered merely in the present, it is likely to remain even when the progress of material and moral improvement may have freed it from the greater part of its present calamities, stands greatly in need of any wider range and greater height of aspiration for itself and its destination, which the exercise of imagination can yield to it without running counter to the evidence of fact; and that it is a part of wisdom to make the most of any, even small, probabilities on this subject, which furnish imagination with any footing to support itself upon. And I am satisfied that the cultivation of such a tendency in the imagination, provided it goes on *pari passu* with the cultivation of severe reason, has no necessary tendency to pervert the judgement; but that it is possible to form a perfectly sober estimate of the evidences on both sides of a question and yet to let the imagination dwell by preference on those possibilities, which are at once the most comforting and the most improving, without in the least degree overrating the solidity of the grounds for expecting that these rather than any others will be the possibilities actually realized.

Though this is not in the number of the practical maxims handed down by tradition and recognized as rules for the conduct of life, a great part of the happiness of life depends upon the tacit observance of it. What, for instance, is the meaning of that which is always accounted one of the chief blessings of life, a cheerful disposition? What but the tendency, either from constitution or habit, to dwell chiefly on the brighter side both of the present and of the future? If every aspect, whether agreeable or odious of every thing, ought to occupy exactly the same place in our imagination which it fills in fact, and therefore ought to fill in our deliberate reason, what we call a cheerful disposition would be but one of the forms of folly, on a par except in agreeableness with the opposite disposition in which the gloomy and painful view of all things is habitually predominant. But it is not found in practice that those who take life cheerfully are less alive to rational prospects of evil or danger and more careless of making due provision against them, than other people. The tendency is rather the other way, for a hopeful disposition gives a spur to the faculties and keeps all the active energies in good working order. When imagination and reason receive each its appropriate culture they do not succeed in usurping each other's prerogatives. It is not necessary for keeping up our conviction that we must die, that we should be always brooding over death. It is far better that we should think no further about what we cannot possibly avert, than is required for observing the rules of prudence in regard to our own life and that of others, and fulfilling whatever duties devolve upon us in contemplation of the inevitable event. The way to secure this is not to think perpetually of death, but to think perpetually of our duties, and of the rule of life. The true rule of practical wisdom is not that of making all the aspects of things equally prominent in our habitual contemplations, but of giving the greatest prominence to those of their aspects which depend on, or can be modified by, our own conduct. In things which do not depend on us, it is not solely for the sake of a more enjoyable life that the habit is desirable of looking at things and at mankind by preference on their pleasant side; it is also in order that we may be able to love them better and work with more heart for their improvement. To what purpose, indeed, should we feed our imagination with the unlovely aspect of persons and things? All *unnecessary* dwelling upon the evils of life is at best a useless expenditure of nervous force: and when I say unnecessary I mean all that is not necessary either in the sense of being unavoidable, or in that of being needed for the performance of our duties and for preventing our sense of the reality of those evils from becoming speculative and dim. But if it is often waste of strength to dwell on the evils of life, it is worse than waste to dwell habitually on its meannesses and basenesses. It is necessary to be aware of them; but to live in their contemplation makes it scarcely possible to keep up in oneself a high tone of mind. The imagination and feelings become tuned to a lower pitch; degrading instead of elevating associations become connected with the daily objects and incidents of life, and give their colour to the thoughts, just as associations of sensuality do in those who indulge freely in that sort of contemplations. Men have often felt what it is to have had their imaginations corrupted by one class of ideas, and I think they must have felt with the same kind of pain how the poetry is taken out of the things fullest of it, by mean associations, as when a beautiful air that had been associated with highly poetical words is heard sung with trivial and vulgar ones. All these things are said in mere illustration of the principle that in the regulation of the imagination literal truth of facts is not the only thing to be considered. Truth is the province of reason, and it is by the cultivation of the rational faculty that provision is made for its being known always, and thought of as often as is required by duty and the circumstances of human life. But when the reason is strongly cultivated, the imagination may safely follow its own end, and do its best to make life pleasant and lovely inside the castle, in reliance on the fortifications raised and maintained by Reason round the outward bounds.

On these principles it appears to me that the indulgence of hope with regard to the government of the universe and the destiny of man after death, while we recognize as a clear truth that we have no ground for more than a hope, is legitimate and philosophically defensible. The beneficial effect of such a hope is far from trifling. It makes life and human nature a far greater thing to the feelings, and gives greater strength as well as greater solemnity to all the sentiments which are awakened in us by our fellow-creatures and by mankind at large. It allays the sense of that irony of Nature which is so painfully felt when we see the exertions and sacrifices of a life culminating in the formation of a wise and noble mind, only to disappear from the world when the time has just arrived at which the world seems about to begin reaping the benefit of it. The truth that life is short and art is long is from of old one of the most discouraging parts of our condition; this hope admits the possibility that the art employed in improving and beautifying the soul itself may avail for good in some other life, even when seemingly useless for this. But the benefit consists less in the presence of any specific hope than in the enlargement of the general scale of the feelings; the loftier aspirations being no longer in the same degree checked and kept down by a sense of the insignificance of human life—by the disastrous feeling of 'not worth while'. The gain obtained in the increased inducement to cultivate the improvement of character up to the end of life, is obvious without being specified.

There is another and a most important exercise of imagination which, in the past and present, has been kept up principally by means of religious belief and which is infinitely precious to mankind, so much so that human excellence greatly depends upon the sufficiency of the provision made for it. This consists of the familiarity of the imagination with the conception of a morally perfect Being, and the habit of taking the approbation of such a Being as the *norma* or standard to which to refer and by which to regulate our own characters and lives. This idealization of our standard of excellence in a Person is quite possible, even when that Person is conceived as merely imaginary. But religion, since the birth of Christianity, has inculcated the belief that our highest conceptions of combined wisdom and goodness exist in the concrete in a living Being who has his eyes on us and cares for our good. Through the darkest and most corrupt periods Christianity has raised this torch on high—has kept this object of veneration and imitation before the eyes of man. True, the image of perfection has been a most imperfect, and, in many respects a perverting and corrupting one, not only from the low moral ideas of the times, but from the mass of moral contradictions which the deluded worshipper was compelled to swallow by the supposed necessity of complimenting the Good Principle with the possession of infinite power. But it is one of the most universal as well as of the most surprising characteristics of human nature, and one of the most speaking proofs of the low stage to which the reason of mankind at large has ever yet advanced, that they are capable of overlooking any amount of either moral or intellectual contradictions and receiving into their minds propositions utterly inconsistent with one another, not only without being shocked by the contradiction, but without preventing both the contradictory beliefs from producing a part at least of their natural consequences in the mind. Pious men and women have gone on ascribing to God particular acts and a general course of will and conduct incompatible with even the most ordinary and limited conception of moral goodness, and have had their own ideas of morality, in many important particulars, totally warped and distorted, and notwithstanding this have continued to conceive their God as clothed with all the attributes of the highest ideal goodness which their state of mind enabled them to conceive, and have had their aspirations towards goodness stimulated and encouraged by that conception. And, it cannot be questioned that the undoubting belief of the real existence of a Being who realizes our own best ideas of perfection, and of our being in the hands of that Being as the ruler of the universe, gives an increase of force to these feelings beyond what they can receive from reference to a merely ideal conception.

This particular advantage it is not possible for those to enjoy, who take a rational view of the nature and amount of the evidence for the existence and attributes of the Creator. On the other hand, they are not encumbered with the moral contradictions which beset every form of religion which aims at justifying in a moral point of view the whole government of the world. They are, therefore, enabled to form a far truer and more consistent conception of Ideal Goodness, than is possible to any one who thinks it necessary to find ideal goodness in an omnipotent ruler of the world. The power of the Creator once recognized as limited, there is nothing to disprove the supposition that his goodness is complete and that the ideally perfect character in whose likeness we should wish to form ourselves and to whose supposed approbation we refer our actions, may have a real existence in a Being to whom we owe all such good as we enjoy.

Above all, the most valuable part of the effect on the character which Christianity has produced by holding up in a Divine Person a standard of excellence and model for imitation, is available even to the absolute unbeliever and can never more be lost to humanity. For it is Christ, rather than God, whom Christianity has held up to believers as the pattern of perfection for humanity. It is the God incarnate, more than the God of the Jews or of Nature, who being idealized has taken so great and salutary a hold on the modern mind. And whatever else may be taken away from us by rational criticism, Christ is still left; a unique figure, not more unlike all his precursors than all his followers, even those who had the direct benefit of his personal teaching. It is of no use to say that Christ as exhibited in the Gospels is not historical and that we know not how much of what is admirable has been superadded by the tradition of his followers. The tradition of followers suffices to insert any number of marvels, and may have inserted all the miracles which he is reputed to have wrought. But who among his disciples or among their proselytes was capable of inventing the sayings ascribed to Jesus or of imagining the life and character revealed in the Gospels? Certainly not the fishermen of Galilee; as certainly not St Paul, whose character and idiosyncrasies were of a totally different sort; still less the early Christian writers in whom nothing is more evident than that the good which was in them was all derived, as they always professed that it was derived, from the higher source. What *could* be added and interpolated by a disciple we may see in the mystical parts of the Gospel of St John, matter imported from Philo and the Alexandrian Platonists and put into the mouth of the Saviour in long speeches about himself such as the other Gospels contain not the slightest vestige of, though pretended to have been delivered on occasions of the deepest interest and when his principal followers were all present; most prominently at the last supper. The East was full of men who could have stolen any quantity of this poor stuff, as the multitudinous Oriental sects of Gnostics afterwards did. But about the life and sayings of Jesus there is a stamp of personal originality combined with profundity of insight, which if we abandon the idle expectation of finding scientific precision where something very different was aimed at, must place the Prophet of Nazareth, even in the estimation of those who have no belief in his inspiration, in the very first rank of the men of sublime genius of whom our species can boast. When this pre-eminent genius is combined with the qualities of probably the greatest moral reformer, and martyr to that mission, who ever existed upon earth, religion cannot be said to have made a bad choice in pitching on this man as the ideal representative and guide of humanity; nor, even now, would it be easy, even for an unbeliever, to find a better translation of the rule of virtue from the abstract into the concrete, than to endeavour so to live that Christ would approve our life. When to this we add that, to the conception of the rational sceptic, it remains a possibility that Christ actually was what he supposed himself to be—not God, for he never made the smallest pretension to that character and would probably have thought such a pretension as blasphemous as it seemed to the men who condemned him—but a man charged with a special, express and unique commission from God to lead mankind to truth and virtue; we may well conclude that the influences of religion on the character which will remain after rational criticism has done its utmost against the evidences of religion, are well worth preserving, and that what they lack in direct strength as compared with those of a firmer belief, is more than compensated by the greater truth and rectitude of the morality they sanction.

Impressions such as these, though not in themselves amounting to what can properly be called a religion, seem to me excellently fitted to aid and fortify that real, though purely human religion, which sometimes calls itself the Religion of Humanity and sometimes that of Duty. To the other inducements for cultivating a religious devotion to the welfare of our fellow-creatures as an obligatory limit to every selfish aim, and an end for the direct promotion of which no sacrifice can be too great, it superadds the feeling that in making this the rule of our life, we may be co-operating with the unseen Being to whom we owe all that is enjoyable in life. One elevated feeling this form of religious idea admits of, which is not open to those who believe in the omnipotence of the good principle in the universe, the feeling of helping God—of requiting the good he has given by a voluntary co-operation which he, not being omnipotent, really needs, and by which a somewhat nearer approach may be made to the fulfilment of his purposes. The conditions of human existence are highly favourable to the growth of such a feeling inasmuch as a battle is constantly going on, in which the humblest human creature is not incapable of taking some part, between the powers of good and those of evil, and in which every, even the smallest, help to the right side has its value in promoting the very slow and often almost insensible progress by which good is gradually gaining ground from evil, yet gaining it so visibly at considerable intervals as to promise the very distant but not uncertain final victory of Good. To do something during life, on even the humblest scale if nothing more is within reach, towards bringing this consummation ever so little nearer, is the most animating and invigorating thought which can inspire a human creature; and that it is destined, with or without supernatural sanctions, to be the religion of the Future I cannot entertain a doubt. But it appears to me that supernatural hopes, in the degree and kind in which what I have called rational scepticism does not refuse to sanction them, may still contribute not a little to give to this religion its due ascendancy over the human mind. *Three Essays on Religion* (1874)

CHAPTER 6

BENJAMIN JOWETT AND
'ESSAYS AND REVIEWS'

The most sensational theological event in England in the mid-nineteenth century—apart from the appearance a year earlier of Darwin's epoch-making treatise in the realm of biology—was the publication in 1860 of *Essays and Reviews*. The studiously non-committal title of the volume belied the nature of its contents. To us today these seem harmless enough, but at the time—and the Darwinian controversy was already inflaming partisan feeling—its effect in ecclesiastical circles—far more representative of the general opinion than now—was explosive. It was the joint effort of seven friends, mostly Oxford men and all of them liberal churchmen, who included Frederick Temple, headmaster of Rugby and subsequently Archbishop of Canterbury, Rowland Williams, fellow of King's College, Cambridge, Mark Pattison, tutor, afterwards Rector, of Lincoln College, Oxford, and Benjamin Jowett, professor of Greek in the same university. Their confessed aim was to promote the free discussion of controversial subjects in theology; such in fact as were 'particularly liable', in the writers' judgement, 'to suffer by the repetition of conventional language, and from traditional methods of treatment'. Reticence in these matters, they felt, could do no good and would in the end prove mischievous. Jowett was especially outspoken. 'We do not wish', he wrote to a friend, 'to do anything rash or irritating to the public or the University, but we are determined not to submit to this abominable system of terrorism, which prevents the statement of the plainest facts, and makes true theology or theological education impossible.' That the reception likely to be accorded to their views would be hostile they could hardly therefore have doubted.

Temple's essay, 'On the Education of the World', was an appeal to the witness of conscience, not least in the interpretation of the Bible. Williams discoursed on divine revelation, Baden Powell, Savilian professor of geometry at Oxford, on Christian evidences, discounting the value of miracles in this respect as all but useless. Other contributors discussed the 'National Church' and the 'Mosaic Cosmogony'. Mark Pattison, in reviewing the 'Tendencies of Religious Thought in England, 1688–1720'—a notably rationalistic period—seemed on the face of it to aim at historical impartiality, but he concluded with the mordant observation that 'whoever would take the religious literature of the present day as a whole, and endeavour to make out clearly on what basis Revelation is supposed by it to rest, whether on Authority, on the Inward Light, self-evidencing Scripture, or on the combination of the four, or some of them, and in what proportions, would probably find that he had undertaken a perplexing but not altogether profitless inquiry'. The last and most substantial essay in the book was Jowett's 'On the Interpretation of Scripture', and it is from this that an extract is given below.

The author, one of the most eminent classical scholars of the century, was born in London in 1817 and educated at St Paul's School and Balliol College, Oxford, of which he became a fellow in 1838 and tutor in 1840. Two years later he was ordained. In 1855 he was appointed to the Regius professorship of Greek and in the same year published a commentary on the epistles of St Paul. For the offence of his contribution to *Essays and Reviews*, however, he was ordered, at the instigation of Dr Pusey and others, to appear before the Vice-Chancellor's Court, although the prosecution was dropped. In 1870 he became Master of Balliol and in the following year brought out his most important work, a translation in four volumes of the *Dialogues of Plato*. He later published versions of Thucydides (1881) and the *Politics* of Aristotle (1885). All were effective as renderings of the original into the English of Jowett's day, but do not conceal the translator's lack of exact scholarship. He died in 1893.

Jowett was known to his contemporaries for a declared liberal in religion as in politics. His religious opinions may indeed have been difficult to define, even by himself. Pusey—no favourable witness—doubted whether he himself and Professor Jowett held any single truth 'in common, except that somehow Jesus came from God, which the Mohammedans believe too'. The Master of Balliol was a Broad Churchman, rather too easily assured that faith and reason could be reconciled in a manner salutary to faith itself no matter how 'negative' the rational representation of it might appear. But the argument of his *Essays and Reviews* dissertation, though provocative at the time, has by now become commonplace. 'Nevertheless it remains', in the judgement of a recent biographer, 'one of those few topical masterpieces as easy and profitable to read after a hundred years as when they were first written. No matter what advances in the art of interpreting the scriptures have been made since Jowett's time, or how the various parties in the various churches have accommodated themselves to these advances, or where they all variously stand today, Jowett's essay has the lasting quality of a classic statement.' Many of its leading ideas had already been stated in the commentary on the Pauline epistles. Thus between 'natural' and 'revealed' religion, he there had argued, no clear separation is possible, to oppose them being to deal merely in abstractions, and he regards it as preferable 'to lay aside the two modes of expression and think only of that "increasing purpose which through the ages ran"'. God is never left without witness, his self-revelation to mankind is universal and continuous. Judaism and Christianity are not therefore its sole vehicle. But even with regard to scripture Jowett had stressed the importance of letting the biblical writers speak for themselves and not smothering their meaning with interpretations appropriate only to a later age. Moreover, though dogma has its uses it can obscure the very truths it seeks to preserve. 'In theology the less we define the better.' So, when he comes to the 1860 essay—originally intended as one of the dissertations appended to the second edition of the *Commentary*—Jowett can sum up his position thus:

'That Scripture, like other books, has one meaning, which is to be gathered from itself without reference to the adaptations of Fathers or Divines; and without regard to *a priori* notions about its nature and origin. It is to be interpreted like other books, with attention to the character of its authors, and the prevailing state of civilization and knowledge, with allowance for peculiarities of style and language, and modes of thought and figures of speech. Yet not without a sense that as we read there grows upon us the witness of God in the world, anticipating in a rude and primitive age the truth that was to be, shining more and more unto the perfect day in the life of Christ, which again is reflected from different points of view in the teaching of His Apostles.'

Essays and Reviews was bitterly attacked in conservative quarters. Frederick Harrison, from the rationalist standpoint, mocked it as a mere compromising and intellectually paltering 'Neo-Christianity', fit possibly for a few university professors and the like, but useless to the man who wanted a religion to live by. Bishop Wilberforce, the most influential prelate of the day, denounced it in a widely read article in the *Quarterly Review*. Eventually suits were brought against two of the contributors, Williams and H. B. Wilson, and heard in the ecclesiastical Court of Arches, the adverse decision of which was, however, reversed by the Judicial Committee of the Privy Council, which declined to hold it as penal for a cleric to maintain that 'the Bible is the expression of devout reason, and therefore to be read with reason in freedom', or deny its verbal inspiration, or—in the case of Wilson—to voice a hope of the ultimate pardon of sinners condemned in the Day of Judgement. The Judicial Committee's ruling was a victory for theological liberalism, even if the strong feelings which *Essays and Reviews* provoked did not quickly abate. The book was condemned by Convocation in 1864 and the repercussions of the controversy continued throughout the decade.

Bibliographical note

On the *Essays and Reviews* controversy see F. Warre Cornish, *The English Church in the Nineteenth Century* (1910), vol. II, ch. XI, and Basil Willey, *More Nineteenth Century Studies* (1956), ch. IV. On Jowett see Geoffrey Faber, *Jowett: a Portrait with Background* (1957).

THE INTERPRETATION OF SCRIPTURE

As the time has come when it is no longer possible to ignore the results of criticism, it is of importance that Christianity should be seen to be in harmony with them. That objections to some received views should be valid, and yet that they should be always held up as the objections of infidels, is a mischief to the Christian cause. It is a mischief that critical observations which any intelligent man can make for himself, should be ascribed to atheism or unbelief. It would be a strange and almost incredible thing that the Gospel, which at first made war only on the vices of mankind, should now be opposed to one of the highest and rarest of human virtues—the love of truth. And that in the present day the great object of Christianity should be, not to change the lives of men, but to prevent them from changing their opinions; that would be a singular inversion of the purposes for which Christ came into the world. The Christian religion is in a false position when all the tendencies of knowledge are opposed to it. Such a position cannot be long maintained, or can only end in the withdrawal of the educated classes from the influences of religion. It is a grave consideration whether we ourselves may not be in an earlier stage of the same religious dissolution, which seems to have gone further in Italy and France. The reason for thinking so is not to be sought in the external circumstances of our own or any other religious communion, but in the progress of ideas with which Christian teachers seem to be ill at ease. Time was when the Gospel was before the age; when it breathed a new life into a decaying world—when the difficulties of Christianity were difficulties of the heart only, and the highest minds found in its truths not only the rule of their lives, but a well-spring of intellectual delight. Is it to be held a thing impossible that the Christian religion, instead of shrinking into itself, may again embrace the thoughts of men upon the earth? Or is it true that since the Reformation 'all intellect has gone the other way?' and that in Protestant countries reconciliation is as hopeless as Protestants commonly believe to be the case in Catholic.

Those who hold the possibility of such a reconcilement or restoration of belief, are anxious to disengage Christianity from all suspicion of disguise or unfairness. They wish to preserve the historical use of Scripture as the continuous witness in all ages of the higher things in the heart of man, as the inspired source of truth and the way to the better life. They are willing to take away some of the external supports, because they are not needed and do harm; also, because they interfere with the meaning. They have a faith, not that after a period of transition all things will remain just as they were before, but that they will all come round again to the use of man and to the glory of God. When interpreted like any other book, by the same rules of evidence and the same canons of criticism, the Bible will still remain unlike any other book; its beauty will be freshly seen, as of a picture which is restored after many ages to its original state; it will create a new interest and make for itself a new kind of authority by the life which is in it. It will be a spirit and not a letter; as it was in the beginning, having an influence like that of the spoken word, or the book newly found. The purer the light in the human heart, the more it will have an expression of itself in the mind of Christ; the greater the knowledge of the development of man, the truer will be the insight gained into the 'increasing purpose' of revelation. In which also the individual soul has a practical part, finding a sympathy with its own imperfect feelings, in the broken utterance of the Psalmist or the Prophet as well as in the fullness of Christ. The harmony between Scripture and the life of man, in all its stages, may be far greater than appears at present. No one can form any notion from what we see around us, of the power which Christianity might have if it were at one with the conscience of man, and not at variance with his intellectual convictions. There, a world weary of the heat and dust of controversy—of speculations about God and man—weary too of the rapidity of its own motion, would return home and find rest.

But for the faith that the Gospel might win again the minds of intellectual men, it would be better to leave religion to itself, instead of attempting to draw them together. Other walks in literature have peace and pleasure and profit; the path of the critical Interpreter of Scripture is almost always a thorny one in England. It is not worth while for any one to enter upon it who is not supported by a sense that he has a Christian and moral object. For although an Interpreter of Scripture in modern times will hardly say with the emphasis of the Apostle, 'Woe is me, if I speak not the truth without regard to consequences', yet he too may feel it a matter of duty not to conceal the things which he knows. He does not hide the discrepancies of Scripture, because the acknowledgement of them is the first step towards agreement among interpreters. He would restore the original meaning, because 'seven other' meanings take the place of it; the book is made the sport of opinion and the instrument of perversion of life. He would take the excuses of the head out of the way of the heart; there is hope too that by drawing Christians together on the ground of Scripture, he may also draw them nearer to one another. He is not afraid that inquiries, which have for their object the truth, can ever be displeasing to the God of truth; or that the Word of God is in any such sense a word as to be hurt by investigations into its human origin and conception.

It may be thought another ungracious aspect of the preceding remarks, that they cast a slight upon the interpreters of Scripture in former ages. The early Fathers, the Roman Catholic mystical writers, the Swiss and German Reformers, the Nonconformist divines, have qualities for which we look in vain among ourselves; they throw an intensity of light upon the page of Scripture which we nowhere find in modern commentaries. But it is not the light of interpretation. They have a faith which seems indeed to have grown dim nowadays, but that faith is not drawn from the study of Scripture; it is the element in which their own mind moves which overflows on the meaning of the text. The words of Scripture suggest to them their own thoughts or feelings. They are preachers, or in the New Testament sense of the word, prophets rather than interpreters. There is nothing in such a view derogatory to the saints and doctors of former ages. That Aquinas or Bernard did not shake themselves free from the mystical method of the Patristic times, or the Scholastic one which was more peculiarly their own; that Luther and Calvin read the Scriptures in connexion with the ideas which were kindling in the mind of their age, and the events which were passing before their eyes, these and similar remarks are not to be construed as depreciatory of the genius or learning of famous men of old; they relate only to their interpretation of Scripture, in which it is no slight upon them to maintain that they were not before their day.

What remains may be comprised in a few precepts, or rather is the expansion of a single one. *Interpret the Scripture like any other book.* There are many respects in which Scripture is unlike any other book; these will appear in the results of such an interpretation. The first step is to know the meaning, and this can only be done in the same careful and impartial way that we ascertain the meaning of Sophocles or of Plato. The subordinate principles which flow out of this general one will also be gathered from the observation of Scripture. No other science of Hermeneutics is possible but an inductive one, that is to say, one based on the language and thoughts and narrations of the sacred writers. And it would be well to carry the theory of interpretation no further than in the case of other works. Excessive system tends to create an impression that the meaning of Scripture is out of our reach, or is to be attained in some other way than by the exercise of manly sense and industry. Who would write a bulky treatise about the method to be pursued in interpreting Plato or Sophocles? Let us not set out on our journey so heavily equipped that there is little chance of our arriving at the end of it. The method creates itself as we go on, beginning only with a few reflexions directed against plain errors. Such reflexions are the rules of common sense, which we acknowledge with respect to other works written in dead languages: without pretending to novelty they may help us to 'return to nature' in the study of the sacred writings.

First, it may be laid down that Scripture has one meaning—the meaning which it had to the mind of the prophet or evangelist who first uttered or wrote, to the hearers or readers who first received it. Another view may be easier or more familiar to us, seeming to receive a light and interest from the circumstances of our own age. But such accommodation of the text must be laid aside by the interpreter, whose business is to place himself as nearly as possible in the position of the sacred writer. That is no easy task—to call up the inner and outer life of the contemporaries of our Saviour; to follow the abrupt and involved utterance of St Paul or one of the old Prophets; to trace the meaning of words when language first became Christian. He will often have to choose the more difficult interpretation (Gal. ii. 20; Rom. iii. 15, etc.), and to refuse one more in agreement with received opinions, because the latter is less true to the style and time of the author. He may incur the charge of singularity, or confusion of ideas, or ignorance of Greek, from a misunderstanding of the peculiarity of the subject in the person who makes the charge. For if it be said that the translation of some Greek words is contrary to the usages of grammar (Gal. iv. 13), that is not in every instance to be denied; the point is whether the usages of grammar are always observed. Or if it be objected to some interpretation of Scripture that it is difficult and perplexing, the answer is—'that may very well be—it is the fact', arising out of differences in the modes of thought of other times, or irregularities in the use of language which no art of the interpreter can evade. One consideration should be borne in mind, that the Bible is the only book in the world written in different styles and at many different times, which is in the hands of persons of all degrees of know-ledge and education. The benefit of this outweighs the evil, yet the evil should be admitted—namely, that it leads to a hasty and partial interpretation of Scripture, which often obscures the true one. A sort of conflict arises between scientific criticism and popular opinion. The indiscriminate use of Scripture has a further tendency to maintain erroneous readings or translations; some which are allowed to be such by scholars have been stereotyped in the mind of the English reader; and it becomes almost a political question how far we can venture to disturb them.

There are difficulties of another kind in many parts of Scripture, the depth and inwardness of which require a measure of the same qualities in the interpreter himself. There are notes struck in places, which like some discoveries of science have sounded before their time; and only after many days have been caught up and found a response on the earth. There are germs of truth which after thousands of years have never yet taken root in the world. There are lessons in the Pro-phets which, however simple, mankind have not yet learned even in theory; and which the complexity of society rather tends to hide; aspects of human life in Job and Ecclesiastes which have a truth of desolation about them which we faintly realize in ordinary circum-stances. It is, perhaps, the greatest difficulty of all to enter into the meaning of the words of Christ—so gentle, so human, so divine, neither adding to them nor marring their simplicity. The attempt to illustrate or draw them out in detail, even to guard against their abuse, is apt to disturb the balance of truth. The interpreter needs nothing short of 'fashioning' in himself the image of the mind of Christ. He has to be born again into a new spiritual or intellectual world, from which the thoughts of this world are shut out. It is one of the highest tasks on which the labour of a life can be spent, to bring the words of Christ a little nearer the heart of man.

But while acknowledging this inexhaustible or infinite character of the sacred writings, it does not, therefore, follow that we are willing to admit of hidden or mysterious meanings in them (in the same way we recognize the wonders and complexity of the laws of nature to be far beyond what eye has seen or knowledge reached, yet it is not therefore to be supposed that we acknowledge the existence of some other laws different in kind from those we know which are incapable of philosophical analysis). In like manner we have no reason to attribute to the Prophet or Evangelist any second or hidden sense different from that which appears on the surface. All that the Prophet meant may not have been consciously present to his mind; there were depths which to himself also were but half revealed. He beheld the fortunes of Israel passing into the heavens; the temporal kingdom was fading into an eternal one. It is not to be supposed that what he saw at a distance only was clearly defined to him; or that the universal truth which was appearing and reappearing in the history of the surrounding world took a purely spiritual or abstract form in his mind. There is a sense in which we may still say with Lord Bacon, that the words of prophecy are to be interpreted as the words of one 'with whom a thousand years are as one day, and one day as a thousand years'. But that is no reason for turning days into years, or for interpreting the things 'that must shortly come to pass' in the book of Revelation, as the events of modern history, or for separating the day of judgement from the destruction of Jerusalem in the Gospels. The double meaning which is given to our Saviour's discourse respecting the last things is not that 'form of eternity' of which Lord Bacon speaks; it resembles rather the doubling of an object when seen through glasses placed at different angles. It is true also that there are types in Scripture which were regarded as such by the Jews themselves, as for example, the scapegoat, or the paschal lamb. But that is no proof of all outward ceremonies being types when Scripture is silent (if we assume the New Testament as a tradition running parallel with the Old, may not the Roman Catholic assume with equal reason a tradition running parallel with the New?). Prophetic symbols, again, have often the same meaning in different places (e.g. the four beasts or living creatures, the colours white or red); the reason is that this meaning is derived from some natural association (as of fruitfulness, purity, or the like); or again, they are borrowed in some of the later prophecies from earlier ones; we are not, therefore, justified in supposing any hidden connexion in the prophecies where they occur. Neither is there any ground for assuming design of any other kind in Scripture any more than in Plato or Homer. Wherever there is beauty and order, there is design; but there is no proof of any artificial design, such as is often traced by the Fathers, in the relation of the several parts of a book, or of the several books to each other. That is one of those mischievous notions which enables us, under the disguise of reverence, to make Scripture mean what we please. Nothing that can be said of the greatness or sublimity, or truth, or depth, or tenderness, of many passages, is too much. But that greatness is of a simple kind; it is not increased by double senses, or systems of types, or elaborate structure, or design. If every sentence was a mystery, every word a riddle, every letter a symbol, that would not make the Scriptures more worthy of a Divine author; it is a heathenish or Rabbinical fancy which reads them in this way. Such complexity would not place them above but below human compositions in general; for it would deprive them of the ordinary intelligibleness of human language. It is not for a Christian theologian to say that words were given to mankind to conceal their thoughts, neither was revelation given them to conceal the Divine.

The second rule is an application of the general principle; 'interpret Scripture from itself' as in other respects, like any other book written in an age and country of which little or no other literature survives, and about which we know almost nothing except what is derived from its pages. Not that all the parts of Scripture are to be regarded as an indistinguishable mass. The Old Testament is not to be identified with the New, nor the Law with the Prophets, nor the Gospels with the Epistles, nor the Epistles of St Paul to be violently harmonized with the Epistle of St James. Each writer, each successive age, has characteristics of its own, as strongly marked, or more strongly, than those which are found in the authors or periods of classical literature. These differences are not to be lost in the idea of a Spirit from whom they proceed or by which they were overruled. And therefore, illustration of one part of Scripture by another should be confined to writings of the same age and the same authors, except where the writings of different ages or persons offer obvious similarities. It may be said further that illustration should be chiefly derived, not only from the same author, but from the same writing, or from one of the same period of his life.

For example, the comparison of St John and the 'synoptic' Gospels, or of the Gospel of St John with the Revelation of St John, will tend rather to confuse than to elucidate the meaning of either; while, on the other hand, the comparison of the Prophets with one another, and with the Psalms, offers many valuable helps and lights to the interpreter. Again, the connexion between the Epistles written by the Apostle St Paul about the same time (e.g. Romans, 1 and 2 Corinthians, Galatians —Colossians, Philippians, Ephesians—compared with Romans, Colossians—Ephesians, Galatians, etc.) is far closer than of Epistles which are separated by an interval of only a few years.

But supposing all this to be understood, and that by the interpretation of Scripture from itself is meant a real interpretation of like by like, it may be asked, what is it that we gain from a minute comparison of a particular author or writing? The indiscriminate use of parallel passages taken from one end of Scripture and applied to the other (except so far as earlier compositions may have afforded the material or the form of later ones) is useless and uncritical. The uneducated, or imperfectly educated person who looks out the marginal references of the English Bible, imagining himself in this way to gain a clearer insight into the Divine meaning, is really following the religious associations of his own mind. Even the critical use of parallel passages is not without danger. For are we to conclude that an author meant in one place what he says in another? Shall we venture to mend a corrupt phrase on the model of some other phrase, which memory, prevailing over judgement, calls up and thrusts into the text? It is this fallacy which has filled the pages of classical writers with useless and unfounded emendations.

The meaning of the Canon 'Non nisi ex Scriptura Scripturam potes interpretari', is only this, 'That we cannot understand Scripture without becoming familiar with it.' Scripture is a world by itself, from which we must exclude foreign influences, whether theological or classical. To get inside that world is an effort of thought and imagination, requiring the sense of a poet as well as a critic—demanding much more than learning a degree of original power and intensity of mind. Any one who, instead of burying himself in the pages of the commentators, would learn the sacred writings by heart, and paraphrase them in English, will probably make a nearer approach to their true meaning than he would gather from any commentary. The intelligent mind will ask its own questions, and find for the most part its own answers. The true use of interpretation is to get rid of interpretation, and leave us alone in company with the author. When the meaning of Greek words is once known, the young student has almost all the real materials which are possessed by the greatest Biblical scholar, in the book itself. For almost our whole knowledge of the history of the Jews is derived from the Old Testament and the Apocryphal books, and almost our whole knowledge of the life of Christ and of the Apostolical age is derived from the New; whatever is added to them is either conjecture, or very slight topographical or chronological illustration. For this reason the rule given above, which is applicable to all books, is applicable to the New Testament more than any other.

Yet in this consideration of the separate books of Scripture it is not to be forgotten that they have also a sort of continuity. We make a separate study of the subject, the mode of thought, in some degree also of the language of each book. And at length the idea arises in our minds of a common literature, a pervading life, an overruling law. It may be compared to the effect of some natural scene in which we suddenly perceive a harmony or picture, or to the imperfect appearance of design which suggests itself in looking at the surface of the globe. That is to say, there is nothing miraculous or artificial in the arrangement of the books of Scripture; it is the result, not the design, which appears in them when bound in the same volume. Or if we like so to say, there *is* design, but a natural design which is revealed to after ages. Such continuity or design is best expressed under some notion of progress or growth, not regular, however, but with broken and imperfect stages, which the want of knowledge prevents our minutely defining. The great truth of the unity of God was there from the first; slowly as the morning broke in the heavens, like some central light, it filled and afterwards dispersed the mists of human passion in which it was itself enveloped. A change passes over the Jewish religion from fear to love, from power to wisdom, from the justice of God to the mercy of God, from the nation to the individual, from this world to another; from the visitation of the sins of the fathers upon the children, to 'every soul shall bear its own iniquity'; from the fire, the earthquake, and the storm, to the still small voice. There never was a time after the deliverance from Egypt, in which the Jewish people did not bear a kind of witness against the cruelty and licentiousness of the surrounding tribes. In the decline of the monarchy, as the kingdom itself was sinking under foreign conquerors, whether springing from contact with the outer world, or from some reaction within, the undergrowth of morality gathers strength; first, in the anticipation of prophecy, secondly, like a green plant in the hollow rind of Pharisaism—and individuals pray and commune with God each one for himself. At length the tree of life blossoms; the faith in immortality which had hitherto slumbered in the heart of man, intimated only in doubtful words (2 Sam. xii. 23; Ps. xvii. 15), or beaming for an instant in dark places (Job xix. 25), has become the prevailing belief.

There is an interval in the Jewish annals which we often exclude from our thoughts, because it has no record in the canonical writings— extending over about four hundred years, from the last of the prophets of the Old Testament to the forerunner of Christ in the New. This interval, about which we know so little, which is regarded by many as a portion of secular rather than of sacred history, was nevertheless as fruitful in religious changes as any similar period which preceded. The establishment of the Jewish sects, and the wars of the Maccabees, probably exercised as great an influence on Judaism as the captivity itself. A third influence was that of the Alexandrian literature, which was attracting the Jewish intellect, at the same time that the Galilean zealot was tearing the nation in pieces with the doctrine that it was lawful to call 'no man master but God'. In contrast with that wild fanaticism as well as with the proud Pharisee, came One most unlike all that had been before, as the kings or rulers of mankind. In an age which was the victim of its own passions, the creature of its own circumstances, the slave of its own degenerate religion, our Saviour taught a lesson absolutely free from all the influences of a surrounding world. He made the last perfect revelation of God to man; a revelation not indeed immediately applicable to the state of society or the world, but in its truth and purity inexhaustible by the after generations of men. And of the first application of the truth which he taught as a counsel of perfection to the actual circumstances of mankind, we have the example in the Epistles.

Such a general conception of growth or development in Scripture, beginning with the truth of the Unity of God in the earliest books and ending with the perfection of Christ, naturally springs up in our minds in the perusal of the sacred writings. It is a notion of value to the inter-preter, for it enables him at the same time to grasp the whole and distinguish the parts. It saves him from the necessity of maintaining that the Old Testament is one and the same everywhere; that the books of Moses contain truths or precepts, such as the duty of prayer or the faith in immortality, or the spiritual interpretation of sacrifice, which no one has ever seen there. It leaves him room enough to admit all the facts of the case. No longer is he required to defend or to explain away David's imprecations against his enemies, or his injunctions to Solomon, any more than his sin in the matter of Uriah. Nor is he hampered with a theory of accommodation. Still the sense of 'the increasing purpose which through the ages ran' is present to him, nowhere else continuously discernible or ending in a divine perfection. Nowhere else is there found the same interpenetration of the political and religious element— a whole nation, 'though never good for much at any time,' possessed with the conviction that it was living in the face of God—in whom the Sun of righteousness shone upon the corruption of an Eastern nature—the 'fewest of all people', yet bearing the greatest part in the education of the world. Nowhere else among the teachers and bene- factors of mankind is there any form like His, in whom the desire of the nation is fulfilled, and 'not of that nation only', but of all mankind, whom He restores to His Father and their Father, to His God and their God.

Such a growth or development may be regarded as a kind of progress from childhood to manhood. In the child there is an anticipation of truth; his reason is latent in the form of feeling; many words are used by him which he imperfectly understands; he is led by temporal promises, believing that to be good is to be happy always; he is pleased by marvels and has vague terrors. He is confined to a spot of earth, and lives in a sort of prison of sense, yet is bursting also with a fullness of childish life: he imagines God to be like a human father, only greater and more awful; he is easily impressed with solemn thoughts, but soon 'rises up to play' with other children. It is observable that his ideas of right and wrong are very simple, hardly extending to another life; they consist chiefly in obedience to his parents, whose word is his law. As he grows older he mixes more and more with others; first with one or two who have a great influence in the direction of his mind. At length the world opens upon him; another work of education begins; and he learns to discern more truly the meaning of things and his rela- tion to men in general. (You may complete the image, by supposing that there was a time in his early days when he was a helpless outcast 'in the land of Egypt and the house of bondage'.) And as he arrives at manhood he reflects on his former years, the progress of his education, the hardships of his infancy, the home of his youth (the thought of which is ineffaceable in after life), and he now understands that all this was but a preparation for another state of being, in which he is to play a part for himself. And once more in age you may imagine him like the patriarch looking back on the entire past, which he reads anew, perceiving that the events of life had a purpose or result which was not seen at the time; they seem to him bound 'each to each by natural piety'.

'Which things are an allegory', the particulars of which any one may interpret for himself. For the child born after the flesh is the symbol of the child born after the Spirit. 'The law was a schoolmaster to bring men to Christ', and now 'we are under a schoolmaster' no longer. The anticipation of truth which came from without to the childhood or youth of the human race is witnessed to within; the revelation of God is not lost but renewed in the heart and understanding of the man. Experience has taught us the application of the lesson in a wider sphere. And many influences have combined to form the 'after life' of the world. When at the close (shall we say) of a great period in the history of man, we cast our eyes back on the course of events, from the 'angel of his presence in the wilderness' to the multitude of peoples, nations, languages, who are being drawn together by His Providence—from the simplicity of the pastoral state in the dawn of the world's day, to all the elements of civilization and knowledge which are beginning to meet and mingle in a common life, we also understand that we are no longer in our early home, to which, nevertheless, we fondly look; and that the end is yet unseen, and the purposes of God towards the human race only half revealed. And to turn once more to the Interpreter of Scripture, he too feels that the continuous growth of revelation which he traces in the Old and New Testament is a part of a larger whole extending over the earth and reaching to another world.

Essays and Reviews (1860), Essay 'On the Interpretation of Scripture', by Benjamin Jowett

CHAPTER 7

MATTHEW ARNOLD

In the context of his age Matthew Arnold is a key-figure. He fully shared
its moral concern, if not all its moral attitudes. He was a man with a mission,
who could not be content with the role solely of poet or literary critic,
dedicated as these callings might be. He became an apostle of 'culture', a
word not to be taken in any merely aesthetic sense—despite the necessity,
for the critic, of a truly critical 'detachment'—but as implying a force for
moral good. That he was conscious of this missionary purpose is—save for
his verse, in which he appears in a different light—clear in all he wrote. A
statement in a private letter of 1863 reveals not only a sense of duty to be
done but of fervour in doing it: 'It is very animating to think that one at
last has a chance of getting at the English public. Such a public as it is and
such a work as one wants to do with it.' As a poet, however, and occasionally
even as a literary critic, it is the 'other' self that speaks—introverted, self-
doubting, nostalgic:

> Ah! two desires toss about
> The poet's feverish blood.
> One drives him to the world without,
> And one to solitude.

So acutely aware of this was he that he could describe himself as 'fragments'.
But here too he is a key-figure: his age, for all its apparent certitudes, was
fragmented. His own incertitude especially betrays itself in his attitude to
religion, with which alone we are concerned.

Matthew Arnold, son of Dr Thomas Arnold of Rugby, was born at
Laleham-on-Thames in December 1822 and was educated at Winchester,
Rugby and Balliol College, Oxford, gaining an Oriel fellowship in 1845.
On his marriage in 1851 he obtained through Lord Lansdowne, whose
private secretary he had been, the post of school inspector which he held
continuously, and to which he devoted the most conscientious effort, until
his retirement in 1886. A more conspicuous or congenial office was never
to be found for him, and he undoubtedly felt some resentment at this prolonged lack of opportunity for the deployment of talents the reality of which
none could question. The only alleviation to the monotony of official life
came in the shape of the Oxford professorship of poetry, which he held
from 1857 to 1867, occasional missions, as well as holiday trips, to the
continent, and a six-month lecture-tour in the U.S.A. in 1883-4. But per-

haps a regular routine, a happy family life and an omnivorous reading gave him greater satisfaction than would more spectacular activities, for which he probably had little aptitude. He may have realized this himself. At least, in 1853, he could write to Arthur Hugh Clough: 'I catch myself desiring now at times political life, and this and that; and I say to myself you do not desire these things because you are really adapted to them, and therefore the desire for them is merely contemptible—and it is so.'

Arnold's earliest volumes of verse, *The Strayed Reveller* and *Empedocles on Etna*, appeared—anonymously—in 1849 and 1852 respectively. A new edition of these (1853) included some fresh poems, among them 'Sohrab and Rustum' and 'The Scholar Gypsy', and further editions, in various ways altered or enlarged, followed in 1854, 1855 (with 'Balder Dead' added) and 1857. *Merope: a Tragedy*, came out in 1858. His lectures *On Translating Homer* (1861–2), the *Essays in Criticism* (1865), *On the Study of Celtic Literature* (1867), *Culture and Anarchy* (1869) and the *Essays in Criticism, Second Series* (1888), comprise his main ventures in the field of literary and social criticism. His strong and persistent interest in religion and theology is evidenced by *St Paul and Protestantism* (1870), *Literature and Dogma* (1873), *God and the Bible* (1875) and *Last Essays on Church and Religion* (1877). His numerous publications on educational matters, especially *Schools and Universities on the Continent* (1868) should also not be overlooked. Arnold died suddenly at Liverpool in 1888.

Matthew Arnold's work must be viewed as a whole if the man himself is to be understood. He is a poet and critic of letters who also, in his own right, is a critic of ideas and institutions, religious as well as social. In this he was perhaps the first of his kind. He believed passionately in the beneficent influence of 'culture', urgently needful in an age whose civilization had become increasingly 'mechanical and external' and whose religious traditions were in decline. In fact the role of culture was itself religious. For the perfection which it envisages is not 'a having and a resting, but a growing and a becoming', and in this respect 'it coincides with religion'. 'Culture indefatigably tries, not to make what each raw person may like, the rule by which he fashions himself: but to draw ever nearer to a sense of what is indeed beautiful, graceful, and becoming, and to get the raw person to like that.' It appeals from 'our ordinary self'—'our old, untransformed self'— to 'our best self'. In England in particular, so Arnold was convinced, culture would serve to supplement an ingrained 'Hebraism', the principle of conduct, with a no less necessary 'Hellenism', the principle of 'sweetness and light'.

With the problem of religion Arnold was intensely concerned, especially in later life. 'At the present moment', he declared, 'two things about the Christian religion must surely be clear to anybody with eyes in his head.

One is, that men cannot do without it; the other, that they cannot do with it as it is.' His words exactly characterized his own position. It thus became for him a personal vocation to do what he could to discover a middle way of enlightened belief between a rigid orthodoxy and sceptical free-thought neither of which was acceptable, the one being insufficient, the other unintelligible. Man could not dispense with religion, since it is a necessary factor in his spiritual development; but for the most part he now could make nothing of the creed inherited from antiquity. What was required was a Christianity renewed and transformed. Arnold's fellow-countrymen might be behind their continental neighbours in realizing the changes which the age had brought, but these time would manifest and the resulting disillusion had now to be anticipated and prepared for by all who stood near enough to Christianity 'to feel the attraction which a thing so very great, when one stands really near to it, cannot but exercise'.

To describe Arnold as a Victorian Broadchurchman would be untrue, although his own influence on English liberal or 'modernist' theology has been marked. Far more radical than this, he was ahead of his time in foreshadowing trends in philosophical and theological thinking characteristic of our own day. For what he offers is a Christianity reduced to its essential values—and so rendered credible—by the elimination of an obsolete and incredible supernaturalism. He appeals to the basic fact of Christian experience, discounting the dogmatic formulae and pseudo-historical 'evidences' which the modern mind either cannot grasp or will not entertain. Moreover, his approach is that, not of the theological or biblical specialist whose professional interest may well obscure his vision, but of the literary critic, content to judge language as men normally use it. For the classic error, constantly repeated, is to take the language of the Bible in a *dogmatic* sense, as though its expression were something 'rigid, fixed and scientific' instead of 'fluid, passing and literary'. The very word *God* is a case in point. What it conveys is not a 'scientific', a philosophical or logical, idea. For 'scientific' purposes God may usefully perhaps be described as 'the stream of tendency by which all things seek to fulfil the law of their being'. But once the attempt is made to correlate such an idea with the imagery of religion, and notably its picture of a 'magnified and non-natural man', every kind of contradiction results. Yet for Israel 'the monotheistic idea' was simply '*seriousness*'; it was not a concept rationally deduced. Israel's essential faith, as a sympathetic but candid student of the Bible at once perceives, was in 'the Eternal not ourselves that makes for righteousness'. The substance of the biblical religion is conduct, which indeed is 'three-fourths of life', religion itself being but 'morality touched by emotion'. Yet to this simple but fundamental apprehension men persist in adding *Aberglaube*, far beyond what is certain, verifiable or even intelligible. It may have poetic quality, but it is not science, although 'it tends always to imagine itself science, to substitute itself for science'. An instance is the Messianic ideas 'which were the poetry of life in the age when Jesus Christ came', whereas the distinctiveness of Jesus' own teaching lay in its new conception of righteousness. He made his followers first look within and examine themselves: a man's true destiny was 'to find his own soul'—his best, his permanent, self. Jesus not only recommended but exemplified in his actual life the two qualities by which 'our ordinary self' is counteracted, viz. 'self-renouncement and mildness'. To attain them was in the highest degree 'requisite and natural', and a man's 'whole happiness' depended on it. Jesus' abiding significance lies therefore, not in the metaphysical notions by which his historic personality became enshrined but in his being the living embodiment of the selflessness, the mildness and 'sweet reasonableness' which are the essential marks of a true humanity. Yet he was 'the last sort of Messiah whom the Jews expected'.

In *St Paul and Protestantism* Arnold complains of the traditional misrepresentation of the apostle, especially by Calvinism with its 'covenants, conditions, bargains and party-contractors', the classical English statement of which, the Westminster Confession, 'could have proceeded from no one but the born Anglo-Saxon man of business, British or American'. Paul's own, naturally Hebraic, concern was for righteousness; but mere obedience to divine law failed to satisfy him. It was his discovery of Christ that yielded him the necessary transforming experience. 'The struggling stream of duty, which had not volume enough to bear him to his goal, was suddenly reinforced by the immense tidal wave of sympathy and emotion.' This new and potent influence he called by the name of *faith*. But, once more, it is the *Aberglaube* by which this same faith has been corroded that now discredits it and prompts men to turn from religion to science, although religion itself, in the proper sense of the word, is scientific. It arises, not from speculation but from experience—experience of salvation through a righteousness whose pattern and exemplar is Jesus Christ.

Bibliographical note

A new edition of Arnold's complete prose works, by R. H. Super, is in process of publication. There is also an edition of *Culture and Anarchy* by J. Dover Wilson (1932; corrected reprint, 1935). *Literature and Dogma* has not been reprinted in recent years. See L. Trilling, *Matthew Arnold* (2nd ed., 1949) and J. D. Jump, *Matthew Arnold* (1955).

CHRISTIANITY

The *mystery* hidden from ages and generations, which none of the rulers of this world knew, the mystery revealed finally by Christ and rejected by the Jews, was not the doctrine of the Trinity, nor anything speculative; it was the method and the secret of Jesus. Jesus did not change the object for men—righteousness; he made clear what it was, and that it was this: his *method* and his *secret*.

This was the *mystery*, and the Apostles had still the consciousness that it was. To 'learn Christ', to 'be taught the truth as it is in Jesus', was not, with them, to acquire certain tenets about One God in Trinity and Trinity in Unity; it was, to '*be renewed in the spirit of your mind, and to put on the new man which after God is created in righteousness and true holiness*'. And this exactly amounts to the method and secret of Jesus.

For Catholic and for Protestant theology alike, this consciousness, which the Apostles had still preserved, was lost. For Catholic and Protestant theology alike, the truth as it is in Jesus, the mystery revealed in Christ, meant something totally different from his method and secret. But they recognized, and indeed the thing was so plain that they could not well miss it, they recognized that on all Christians the method and secret of Jesus were enjoined. So to this extent the method and secret of Jesus were preached and had their effect. To this extent true Christianity has been known, and to the extent before stated it has been neglected. Now, as we say that the truth and grandeur of the Old Testament most comes out *experimentally*—that is, by the whole course of the world establishing it, and confuting what is opposed to it—so it is with Christianity. Its grandeur and truth are for most brought out *experimentally*; and the thing is, to make people see this.

But there is this difference between the religion of the Old Testament and Christianity. Of the religion of the Old Testament we can pretty well see to the end, we can trace fully enough the experimental proof of it in history. But of Christianity the future is as yet almost unknown. For that the world cannot get on without righteousness we have the clear experience, and a grand and admirable experience it is. But what the world will become by the thorough use of that which is really righteousness, the method and the secret and the sweet reasonableness of Jesus, we have as yet hardly any experience at all.

Therefore we, who in this essay limit ourselves to experience, shall speak here of Christianity and its greatness very soberly. Yet Christianity is really all the grander for that very reason which makes us speak about it in this sober manner—that it has such an immense development still before it, and that it has as yet so little shown all it contains, all it can do. Indeed, that Christianity has already done so much as it has, is a witness to it; and that it has not yet done more, is a witness to it too. Let us observe how this is so.

2

Few things are more melancholy than to observe Christian apologists taunting the Jews with the failure of Hebraism to fulfil the splendid promises of prophecy, and Jewish apologists taunting Christendom with the failure of Christianity to fulfil these. Neither has yet fulfilled them, or could yet have fulfilled them. Certainly the restoration by Cyrus, the Second Temple, the Maccabean victories, are hardly more than the shadows of a fulfilment of the magnificent words: 'The sons of them that afflicted thee shall come bending unto thee, and all they that despised thee shall bow themselves down at the soles of thy feet; thy gates shall not be shut day nor night, that men may bring unto thee the treasures of the Gentiles and that their kings may be brought.' The Christianization of all the leading nations of the world is, it is said, a much better fulfilment of that promise. Be it so. Yet does Christendom, let us ask, offer more than a shadow of the fulfilment of *this*: 'Violence shall no more be heard in thy land; the vile person shall no more be called liberal, nor the churl bountiful; thy people shall be *all* righteous; they shall *all* know me, from the least to the greatest; I will put my law in their inward parts, and write it in their hearts; the Eternal shall be thine everlasting light and the days of thy mourning shall be ended'? Manifestly it does not; yet the two promises hang together, one of them is not truly fulfilled unless the other is.

The promises were made to *righteousness*, with all which the idea of righteousness involves; and it involves Christianity. They were made on the immediate prospect of a small triumph for righteousness, the restoration of the Jews after the captivity in Babylon; but they are not satisfied by that triumph. The prevalence of the profession of Christianity is a larger triumph; yet in itself it hardly satisfies them any better. What satisfies them is the prevailing of that which righteousness really is, and nothing else satisfies them. Now Christianity is that which righteousness really is. Therefore, if something called Christianity prevails, and yet the promises are not satisfied, the inference is that this *something* is not that which righteousness really is, and therefore not really Christianity. And as the course of the world is perpetually establishing the pre-eminence of righteousness, and confounding whatever denies this pre-eminence, so, too, the course of the world is for ever establishing what righteousness really is—that is to say, true Christianity—and confounding whatever pretends to be true Christianity and is not.

Now, just as the constitution of things turned out to be against the great unrighteous kingdoms of the heathen world, and against all the brilliant Ishmaels we have seen since, so the constitution of things turns out to be against all false presentations of Christianity, such as the theology of the Fathers or Protestant theology. They do not work successfully, they do not reach the aim, they do not bring the world to the fruition of the promises made to righteousness. And the reason is, because they substitute for what is really righteousness something else. Catholic dogma or Lutheran justification by faith they substitute for the method and secret of Jesus.

Nevertheless, as all Christian Churches do recommend the method and the secret of Jesus, though not in the right way or in the right eminency, still the world is made acquainted with what righteousness really is, and the doctrine produces some effect, although the full effect is much thwarted and deadened by the false way in which the doctrine is presented. Still the effect produced is great; for instance, the sum of individual happiness that has been caused by Christianity is, anyone can see, enormous. But let us take the effect of Christianity on the world. And if we look at the thing closely, we shall find that its effect has been this: Christianity has brought the world, or at any rate all the leading part of the world, *to regard righteousness as only the Jews regarded it before the coming of Christ*. The world has accepted, so far as profession goes, that original revelation made to Israel: the pre-eminence of righteousness. The infinite truth and attractiveness of the method and secret and character of Jesus, however falsely surrounded, have prevailed with the world so far as this. And this is an immense gain, and a signal witness to Christianity. The world does homage to the pre-eminence of righteousness; and here we have one of those fulfilments of prophecy which are so true and so glorious. 'Glorious things are spoken of thee, O City of God! I will make mention of

Rahab and Babylon as of them that know me! behold, the Philistines also, and Tyre, with the Ethiopians—these were born *there*! And of Zion it shall be reported: This and that man was born in *her*!—and the Most High shall stablish her. The Eternal shall count, when he writeth up the people: This man was born *there*!' That prophecy is at this present day abundantly fulfilled. The world's chief nations have now all come, we see, to reckon and profess themselves adherents of the religion of Zion, the city of *righteousness*.

But there remains the question: *what* righteousness really is. The method and secret and sweet reasonableness of Jesus. But the world does not see this; for it puts, as righteousness, something else first and this second. So that here, too, as to seeing what righteousness really is, the world now is just in the same position in which the Jews, when Christ came, were. It is often said: If Christ came now, his religion would be rejected. And this is only another way of saying that the world now, as the Jewish people formerly, has something which thwarts and confuses its perception of what righteousness really is. It is so; and the thwarting cause is the same now as then—the dogmatic system current, the so-called orthodox theology. This prevents now, as it did then, that which righteousness really is, the method and secret of Jesus, from being rightly received, from operating fully, and from accomplishing its due effect.

So true is this, that we have only to look at our own community to see the almost precise parallel, so far as religion is concerned, to the state of things presented in Judaea when Christ came. The multitudes are the same everywhere. The chief priests and elders of the people and the scribes, are our bishops and dogmatists, with their pseudo-science of learned theology blinding their eyes, and always—whenever simple souls are disposed to think that the method and secret of Jesus is true religion, and that the great Personal First Cause and the Godhead of the Eternal Son have nothing to do with it—eager to cry out: *This people that knoweth not the law are cursed!* The Pharisees, with their genuine concern for religion, but total want of perception of what religion really is, and by their temper, attitude, and aims doing their best to make religion impossible, are the Protestant Dissenters. The Sadducees are our friends the philosophical Liberals, who believe neither in angel nor spirit but in Mr Herbert Spencer. Even the Roman governor has his close parallel in our celebrated aristocracy, with its superficial good sense and good nature, its thorough inaptitude for ideas, its profound helplessness in presence of all great spiritual move-ments. And the result is, that the splendid promises to righteousness made by the Hebrew prophets, claimed by the Jews as the property of Judaism, claimed by us as the property of Christianity, are almost as ludicrously inapplicable to our religious state now, as to theirs then.

And this, we say, is again a signal witness to Christianity. Christ came to reveal what righteousness, to which the promises belong, really is; and so long as this, though shown by Christ, is not seen by us, we may call ourselves Christendom as much as we please, the true character of a Christendom will be wanting to us, because the great promises of prophecy will be still without their fulfilment. Nothing will do, except righteousness; and no other conception of righteousness will do, except Christ's conception of it—his *method* and his *secret*.

3

Yes, the grandeur of Christianity and the imposing and impressive attestation of it, if we could but worthily bring the thing out, is here: in that immense experimental proof of the necessity of it, which the whole course of the world has steadily accumulated, and indicates to us as still continuing and extending. Men will not admit assumptions, the popular legend they call a fairy-tale the metaphysical demonstra-tions do not demonstrate, nothing but experimental proof will go down and here is an experimental proof which never fails, and which at the same time is infinitely grander, by the vastness of its scale, the scope of its duration, the gravity of its results, than the machinery of the popular fairy-tale. Walking on the water, multiplying loaves, raising corpses, a heavenly judge appearing with trumpets in the clouds while we are yet alive—what is this compared to the real experience offered as wit-ness to us by Christianity? It is like the difference between the grandeur of an extravaganza and the grandeur of the sea or the sky—immense objects which dwarf us, but where we are in contact with reality, and a reality of which we can slowly trace the laws.

The more we trace the real law of Christianity's action, the grander it will seem. Certainly in the Gospels there is plenty of matter to call out our feelings, but perhaps this has been somewhat over-used and mis-used, applied, as it has been, chiefly so as to be subservient to what we call the fairy-tale of the three Lord Shaftesburys[1]—a story which

---

[1] Arnold's figurative representation of the Trinity. It gave offence to many of his readers.

we do not deny to have, like other products of the popular imagination, its pathos and power, but which we have seen to be no solid foundation to rest our faith in the Bible on. And perhaps, too, we do wrong, and inevitably fall into what is artificial and unnatural, in labouring so much to produce in ourselves, as the one impulse determining us to use the method and secret of Jesus, that conscious ardent sensation of personal love to him, which we find the first generation of Christians feeling and professing, and which was the natural motor for those who were with him or near him, and, so to speak, touched him; and in making this our first object. At any rate, misemployed as this motor has often been, it might be well to forego or at least suspend its use for ourselves and others for a time, and to fix our minds exclusively on the recommendation given to the method and secret of Jesus by their being *true*, and by the whole course of things proving this.

Now, just as the best recommendation of the oracle committed to Israel, *Righteousness is salvation*, is found in our more and more discovering, in our own history and in the whole history of the world, that it *is* so, so we shall find it to be with the method and secret of Jesus. That this *is* the righteousness which is salvation, that the method and secret of Jesus, that is to say, conscience and self-renouncement, *are* righteousness, bring about the kingdom of God or the reign of righteousness—this, which is the Christian revelation and what Jesus came to establish, is best impressed, for the present at any rate, by experiencing and showing again and again, in ourselves and in the course of the world, that it *is* so; that this is the righteousness which is saving, and that there is none other. Let us but well observe what comes, in ourselves or the world, of trying any other, of not being convinced that this is righteousness, and this only; and we shall find ourselves more and more, as by irresistible viewless hands, caught and drawn towards the Christian revelation, and made to desire more and more to serve it. No proof can be so solid as this experimental proof; and none again, can be so grand, so fitted to fill us with awe, admiration, and gratitude; so that feeling and emotion will now well come in after it, though not before it. For the whole course of human things is really, according to this experience, leading up to the fulfilment of Christ's promise to his disciples: *Fear not, little flock! for it is your Father's good pleasure to give you the kingdom*. And thus that comes after all to be true, which St Paul announced prematurely to the first generation of Christians: *When Christ, who is our life, shall appear, then shall ye also appear with him in glory.* And the author of the Apocalypse, in like manner, foretold: *The kingdom of the world is become the kingdom of our Lord and his Christ.* The kingdom of the Eternal the world is already become, by its chief nations professing the religion of righteousness. The kingdom of Christ the world will have to become, it is on its way to become, because the profession of righteousness, except as Christ interpreted righteousness, is vain. We can see the process, we are ourselves part of it, and can in our measure forward or keep back its completion.

When the prophet, indeed, says to Israel, on the point of being restored by Cyrus: ' *The nation and kingdom that will not serve thee shall perish!*' the promise, applied literally, fails. But extended to that idea of righteousness, of which Israel was the depositary and in which the real life of Israel lay, the promise is true, and we can see it steadily fulfilling itself. In like manner, when the Apostle says to the Colossians, instructed that the second advent would come in their own generation: ' *When Christ, who is our life, shall appear, then shall ye also appear with him in glory!*' the promise, applied literally, as the Apostle meant it and the Colossians understood it, fails. But divested of this *Aberglaube* or extra-belief, it is true; if indeed the world can be shown— and it can—to be moving necessarily towards the triumph of that Christ in whom the Colossian disciples lived, and whose triumph is the triumph of all his disciples also.

4

Let us keep hold of this same experimental process in dealing with the promise of immortality; although here, if anywhere, *Aberglaube*, extra-belief, hope, anticipation, may well be permitted to come in. Still, what we need for our foundation is not *Aberglaube*, but *Glaube*; not extra-belief in what is beyond the range of possible experience, but belief in what can and should be known to be true.

By what futilities the demonstration of our immortality may be attempted is to be seen in Plato's *Phaedo.* Man's natural desire for continuance, however little it may be worth as a scientific proof of our immortality, is at least a proof a thousand times stronger than any such demonstration. The want of solidity in such argument is so palpable, that one scarcely cares to turn a steady regard upon it at all. But of the common Christian conception of immortality the want of solidity is perhaps most conclusively shown by the impossibility of so framing it, as that it will at all support a steady regard turned upon it.

In our English popular religion, for instance, the common conception of a future state of bliss is that of the Vision of Mirza: 'Persons dressed in glorious habits with garlands on their heads, passing among the trees, lying down by the fountains, or resting on beds of flowers, amid a confused harmony of singing birds, falling waters, human voices, and musical instruments.' Or, even, with many, it is that of a kind of perfected middle-class home, with labour ended, the table spread, goodness all around, the lost ones restored, hymnody incessant. '*Poor fragments all of this low earth!*' Keble might well say. That this conception of immortality cannot possibly be true we feel, the moment we consider it seriously; and yet who can devise any conception of a future state of bliss which shall bear close examination better?

Here, again, it is far best to take what is experimentally true, and nothing else, as our foundation, and afterwards to let hope and aspiration grow, if so it may be, out of this. Israel had said: 'In the way of righteousness is life, and in the pathway thereof there is no death.' And by a kind of short cut to the conclusion thus laid down, the Jews constructed their fairy-tale of an advent, judgement, and resurrection, as we find it in the Book of Daniel. Jesus had said: 'If a man keep my word, he shall never see death'; and by a kind of short cut to the conclusion thus laid down, Christians constructed their fairy-tale of the second advent, the resurrection of the body, the New Jerusalem. But instead of fairy-tales, let us begin, at least, with certainties.

And a certainty is the sense of *life*, of being truly *alive*, which accompanies righteousness. If this experimental sense does not rise to be stronger in us, does not rise to the sense of being inextinguishable, that is probably because our experience of righteousness is really so very small; and here we may well permit ourselves to trust Jesus, whose practice and intuition both of them went, in these matters, so far deeper than ours. At any rate, we have in our experience this strong sense of *life from righteousness* to start with; capable of being developed, apparently, by progress in righteousness into something immeasurably stronger. Here is the true basis for all religious aspiration after immortality. And it is an experimental basis; and therefore, as to grandeur, it is again, when compared with the popular *Aberglaube*, grand with all the superior grandeur, on a subject of the highest seriousness, of reality over fantasy.

At present, the fantasy hides the grandeur of the reality. But when all the *Aberglaube* of the second advent, with its signs in the sky, sounding trumpets and opening graves, is cleared away, then and not till then will come out the profound truth and grandeur of words of Jesus like these: 'The hour is coming, when they that are in the graves shall hear the voice of the Son of Man; and they that hear shall *live*.'

5

Finally, and above all. As, for the right inculcation of righteousness, we need the inspiring words of Israel's love for it, that is, we need the Bible; so, for the right inculcation of the method and secret of Jesus, we need the *epieikeia*, the sweet reasonableness, of Jesus. That is, in other words again, we need the *Bible*; for only through the Bible-records of Jesus can we get at his *epieikeia*. Even in these records, it is and can be presented but imperfectly; but only by reading and re-reading the Bible can we get at it at all.

Now, greatly as the failure, from the stress laid upon the pseudo-science of Church dogma, to lay enough stress upon the method and secret of Jesus, has kept Christianity back from showing itself in its full power, it is probable that the failure to apply to the method and secret of Jesus, so far as these have at any rate been used, his sweet reasonableness or *epieikeia*, has kept it back even more. And the *infinite* of the religion of Jesus—its immense capacity for ceaseless progress and farther development—lies principally, perhaps, in the line of extricating more and more his sweet reasonableness, and applying it to his method and secret. For it is obvious from experience how much our use of Christ's method and secret requires to be guided and governed by his *epieikeia*; indeed, without this, his method and secret seem often of no use at all. The Flagellants imagined that they were employing his secret; and the Dissenters, with their 'spirit of watchful jealousy', imagine that they are employing his method. To be sure, Mr Bradlaugh[1] imagines that the method and the secret of Jesus, nay and Jesus himself too, are all baneful, and that the sooner we get rid of them all, the better. So far, then, the Flagellants and the Dissenters are in advance of Mr Bradlaugh; they value Christianity, and they profess the method and secret of Jesus. But they employ them so ill, that one is tempted to say they might nearly as well be without them. And this is because they are wholly without his sweet reasonableness, or *epieikeia*. Now this can only be got, first, by knowing that it is in the Bible, and looking

---

[1] Charles Bradlaugh (1833–1901), in his day a well-known freethinker.—*Ed.*

for it there; and then, by reading and re-reading the Gospels continually, until we catch something of it.

This, again, is an experimental process. That the *epieikeia* or sweet reasonableness of Jesus may be brought to govern our use of his method and secret, and that it can and will make our use of his method and secret quite a different thing, is proved by our actually finding this to be so when we try. So that the culmination of Christian righteousness in the applying, to guide our use of the method and secret of Jesus, his sweet reasonableness or *epieikeia*, is proved from experience. We end, therefore, as we began. For the whole series of experiences, of which the survey is thus completed, rests, primarily, upon one fundamental fact—itself, also, a fact of experience: *the necessity of righteousness.*

Literature and Dogma (1873)

CHAPTER 8

SCOTT HOLLAND AND 'LUX MUNDI'

The Oxford Movement, in outlook and in aim, was unyieldingly conservative. Its enemy had been 'liberalism', its palladium 'the dogmatic principle'. But even in Oxford, as certainly elsewhere, the foe had continued to advance and traditional religious belief was thrown more and more upon the defensive. *Essays and Reviews* had been an attempt on the part of a group of liberal churchmen to mediate between new knowledge and progressive ideals on the one hand and the Church's historic creed on the other. A new generation was to witness how this same spirit of mediation was to imbue the heirs of the Oxford revival itself. Its manifesto was a second volume of essays, *Lux Mundi*, published in 1889, the editor of which was the young Charles Gore (1853–1932), then Principal of Pusey House, Oxford, but afterwards bishop successively of Worcester, Birmingham and Oxford, and probably the most forceful and influential figure in the Church of England. The book's contributors, who included, besides Gore himself, E. S. Talbot, R. C. Moberly, J. R. Illingworth and H. S. Holland, had all been influenced to a greater or lesser degree, by both F. D. Maurice and the leader of the new school of English idealist philosophers, T. H. Green. Talbot, later Bishop of Winchester, envisaged 'a Catholic theology utterly fixed in its great central principles and in many of their corollaries, yet ever yielding up new meanings, even from its central depths, in the light of other knowledge and human development', and in the Preface to the volume—it was subtitled 'A series of studies in the Religion of the Incarnation', the 'incarnationalist' emphasis prevailing throughout—Gore made it clear that the authors, whilst not mere 'guessers at truth' but 'servants of the Catholic Creed and Church', had also written 'with the conviction that the epoch in which we live is one of profound transformation, intellectual and social...and certain therefore to involve great changes in the outlying departments of theology, where it is linked to other sciences, and to necessitate some general restatement of its claim and meaning'. The most striking of the several papers was indeed the editor's own, on 'The Holy Spirit and Inspiration', which caused H. P. Liddon, whom the whole enterprise offended, especial distress. But although older men might regard the book with misgiving, the High Church or 'Anglo-Catholic' movement, in its intellectual and social aspects, was henceforth to become increasingly receptive of new ideas. Anglican 'Liberal

338

Catholicism', a somewhat chameleon-like phenomenon, was born of it. The extract which follows is from the first essay in the volume, Henry Scott Holland's on 'Faith'.

Holland was born near Ledbury in 1847 and educated at Eton and Balliol College, Oxford. Elected to a senior studentship at Christ Church in 1870, he remained at Oxford—he was ordained priest in 1874—until his appointment in 1884 to a canonry of St Paul's Cathedral, where R. W. Church was already dean. These London years became the heart and substance of Holland's whole career and when, twenty-six years later, he left the cathedral to return to Oxford and Christ Church as Regius professor of divinity it was with regret and misgiving. He had become known as an eloquent preacher, a 'personality' and a man energetic in the cause of social reform. His founding in 1889 of the Christian Social Union, with Bishop Westcott of Durham as its president, was a landmark in the history of Christian social effort in this country. He died in the early spring of 1918, a natural optimist made despondent by the course which the events of the day had taken.

Holland had grave doubts about his own qualifications for the Regius professorship. Certainly he was not a scholar, or a theologian of the more academic type. Yet his view of life was essentially theological, his special vocation that of a preacher seeking to interpret Christian belief in a way relevant to the experience of his hearers. Most of Holland's published work consists of collections of sermons, *Logic and Life* (1882), *Creed and Character* (1887), *On Behalf of Belief* (1889) and *Pleas and Claims for Christ* (1892) being probably the best, although a great deal of arresting comment from his pen appeared in *The Commonwealth*, the C.S.U. organ, of which he was for many years the editor. In 1908 he delivered at Oxford a notable Romanes Lecture on 'The Optimism of Butler's "Analogy"'.

The aim of Holland's teaching was, in general, to exhibit the rationality of faith. In endeavouring to commend the gospel he attempted also to defend it by demonstrating its applicability to the moral and social life of the age. He was convinced that the Christian's faith finds its due expression and fulfilment only in a social context, Christ being the Head not only of the Church but ideally, as F. D. Maurice had taught, of all humanity. The key to the meaning of human existence is, therefore, the Incarnation, for Jesus Christ is 'the Man' and so must be 'the solution of all human problems'. But Holland was not content merely to state the broad theological principles and moral axioms on which reform should proceed: concrete situations had to be met and specific action taken. Hence the formation of the Union. He himself had no scruple about using the language of socialism, which 'challenged "the political Economists" (i.e. the Manchester school) with a social philosophy as scientific as their own'. The question was simply that of determining how socialism might 'claim the sanction of Jesus Christ'.

Philosophically Scott Holland owed much to Green. His conception of reason is not that of a prefabricated instrument which man acquires whole and intact for such use he may wish to make of it, but a 'living and pliable' process by which he brings himself into a rational and intelligible relation with his surroundings. It is dependent upon experience, upon facts, thought being the 'power of allying ourselves to facts'. To separate and juxtapose 'reason' and 'experience' as if reason could subsist *in vacuo* and apart from experience is an absurdity. Man reveals and develops his rationality only in contact with and by means of the manifold data of experience. Reason cannot, accordingly, be opposed to faith. As the former has its roots in the unconsciousness so the latter also rests on an 'underworld' of thought and emotion that is never more than half recognized. The spring of man's being is his *will* and to departmentalize reason and faith is to lose sight of the fundamental impulse by which human life is actuated. Either could, with equal justice, be described as an 'elemental energy of the soul'.

Religion, it follows, can be profitably discussed only when seen as a function of the life of the 'whole man'. But although faith as an act of the 'basal personality' is not a distinctive faculty by whose exercise religion acquires its place beside other human activities, yet it is in religion that the faith-content of all human endeavour is proclaimed. Life in its entire range is God-given and has God as its end; 'but the *fact* of this being so is one thing: the recognition of it is another; and it is this recognition of God in things which is the core and essence of religion'. The heart, however, of the Christian experience is the experience of Christ, of whose historical existence the gospels, Holland never doubts, are the reliable witnesses; and the experience of Christ is not merely knowledge about him but life *in* him: he is a 'new power of life' whereby those who believe in him are together constituted to be his 'Body'. The Catholic Church is the 'organic expression' of a universal experience, from which creed, rite and formula draw their life and authority. They convey the 'common heritage' and must be 'weighed and considered and explained in their relation to this overwhelming context'. Thus the Church cannot be an exclusive sect; as the Christian experience is potentially universal—open to all mankind—so too is the Church; which is why society itself calls for redemption, to be reconstituted in the light of Christ's person and teaching.

Bibliographical note

Lux Mundi has frequently been reprinted. See also B. M. G. Reardon, *Henry Scott Holland: a Selection from his Writings* (1962), and Holland's *Fibres of Faith*, reprinted with an introduction by the same editor (1962). A volume of Holland's occasional papers was published in 1918 under the title *Creeds and Critics* (ed. C. Cheshire). For his life consult Stephen Paget, *Henry Scott Holland: Memoir and Letters* (1922). On *Lux Mundi* itself see A. M. Ramsey, *From Gore to Temple* (1960), ch. 1. On Charles Gore, J. Carpenter, *Gore. A Study in Liberal Catholic Thought* (1960) is of value.

I. WHAT IS FAITH?

In proposing to consider the origin and growth of faith, we have a practical, and not a merely theoretical, aim. We are thinking of the actual problems which are, at this moment, encompassing and hindering faith: and it is because of their urgency and their pressure, that we find it worth while to go back upon our earliest beginnings, in order to ask what Faith itself means. For only through an examination of its nature, its origin, and its structure, will it be possible for us to sift the questions which beset us, and to distinguish those to which Faith is bound to give an answer from those which it can afford to let alone.

'What is it to believe? Do I know what it is to believe? Have I, or have I not, that which can be called "faith"? How can I be sure? What can I say of myself?' Such questions as these are haunting and harassing many among us who find themselves facing the Catholic Creed, with its ring of undaunted assurance, with its unhesitating claim to unique and universal supremacy, and contrast with this their own faint and tentative apprehension of the strong truths, which are so confidently asserted. Such men and women are anxious and eager to number themselves among those that believe: but can they call this temper 'belief', which is so far below the level of the genuine response which the Creeds obviously expect?

The urgency, the peril of the hour, lies, not so much in the novelty, or force, of the pressure that is brought to bear against faith, as in the behaviour of faith itself under the pressure. What has happened is, not that faith has been confounded, but that it has been challenged. It has been challenged by new social needs, by strange developments of civilization, by hungers that it had not yet taken into account, by thirsts that it had not prepared itself to satisfy. It has been challenged by new scientific methods, wholly unlike its familiar intellectual equipment; by new worlds of facts opened to its astonishment through discoveries which have changed the entire look of the earth; by immense masses of novel material, which it has been suddenly and violently required to assimilate; by strange fashions of speech in science and history; by a babel of 'unknown tongues' in all departments of learning and literature.

Faith is under the pressure of this challenge: and the primary question is, how will it behave? Will it prove itself adequate to the crisis?

For the peculiarity of the disturbance which we have got to encounter lies in this, that it has removed from us the very weapons by which we might hope to encounter it. Faith's evidential material is all corroborative and accumulative; it draws it from out of an external world, which can never wholly justify, or account for the internal reality, yet which can so group itself, that from a hundred differing lines, it offers indirect and parenthetic and convergent witness of that which is, itself, beyond the reach of external proof. When once the grouping is achieved, so that the outer world, known under certain scientific principles, tallies harmoniously with its inner convictions, faith feels secure. The external life offers it pictures, analogies, metaphors—all echoing and repeating the internal world. Faith beholds itself mirrored: and, so echoed, so mirrored, it feels itself in possession of corroborating evidences. But the present scientific confusion seems to have shattered the mirror—to have broken up the perspective—to have dissolved the well-known groupings. The habitual ways of argument, the accepted assumptions have been withdrawn—have become obsolete. [Modern man] is bitterly sensitive to the sharp contrast between the triumphant solidity with which scientific facts bear down upon him, certified, undeniable, substantial, and the vague, shifty, indistinct phantom, into which his conviction vanishes as soon as he attempts to observe it in itself, or draw it out for public inspection.

Yet, if we consider what faith signifies, we shall see at once that this contrast ought to carry with it no alarm. It is a contrast which follows on the very nature of faith. If we had understood its nature, we could never have expected it to disclose itself under the same conditions as those which govern the observation of scientific facts. Faith is an elemental energy of the soul, and the surprise that we are undergoing at not being able to bring it under direct observation, is only an echo of the familiar shock with which we learn that science has ransacked the entire bodily fabric of man, and has nowhere come across his soul; or has searched the heavens through and through with its telescope, and has seen no God.

How can an act of will, or of love, be submitted to observation?

Its outward result is there to be examined; but it, itself, is incapable of transportation. If anyone were to ask 'What is it you mean by thinking, or loving, or willing?' who could tell him? It would be obviously impossible to explain, except to a being who could think, will, and love. You could give him illustrations of what you mean—signs—instances—evidences; but they can only be intelligible, as evidences, to one who already possesses the faculties. No one can do a piece of thinking for another, and hand it over to him in a parcel. Only by thinking, can it be known what thought is: only by feeling can it be understood what is meant by a feeling: only by seeing, willing, loving, can we have the least conception of sight, or of will, or of love.

And faith stands with these primary intuitions. It is deeper and more elemental than them all: and, therefore, still less than they can it admit of translation into other conditions than its own—can still less submit itself to public observation. It can never be looked at from without. It can be known only from within itself. Belief is only intelligible by believing. Faith, [now] robbed of its habitual aids to expression, is summoned to show itself on the field, in its own inner character. And this is just what it never can or may do. It can only reiterate, in response to the demand for definition, 'Faith is faith'. 'Believing is—just believing.' Why, then, let ourselves be distressed, or bewildered, by finding ourselves reduced to this impotence of explanation? Far from it being an incrimination of our faith, to find ourselves caught in such a difficulty of utterance, it is just what must happen if faith be a profound and radical act of the inner soul. It is, essentially, an active principle, a source of energy, a spring of movement: and, as such, its verification can never take place through passive introspection. It verifies itself only in actions: its reality can only be made evident through experience of its living work.

No wonder that, under the pressure of a hostile challenge, we often lose ourselves in a confused babble, as we struggle to make plain to others, or even to ourselves, these innermost convictions of our souls. Indeed, such things can never be made plain: no one ought to expect that they should.

Surely, this truth clears us from many clamorous demands, which ask of us an impossible verification. For if once we saw that we were employed in verifying the nature of that which, if it be real, can, confessedly, present us, on this side of the grave, only with the most fragmentary evidence of its character, we should put lightly aside the taunting challenge to produce such proof of our motive principle as will stand comparison with the adequate and precise evidences of a scientific fact, or which will submit to the rigid tests of a legal examination. If faith be faith, it could not, for that very reason, fulfil the conditions so proposed to it. For what is faith? It is no steady force, existing under certified and unvarying conditions which receive their final determination in the world about us. Faith is, while it is here on earth, only a tentative probation: it is a struggling and fluctuating effort in man to win for himself a valid hold upon things that exist under the conditions of eternity. Its significance, its interpretation, its future possibilities, its secret of development—all these lie elsewhere, beyond death, beyond vision: we can but dimly guess, from its action here, what powers feed it, on what resources it can rely, what capacity of growth is open to it, what final issue determines the measure and value of its efforts and achievements. Where, then, must we dig to unearth the roots of faith? What are the conditions of its rise and exercise? Wherein lie its grounds, and the justification of its claim?

Faith grounds itself, solely and wholly, on an inner and vital relation of the soul to its source. This source is most certainly elsewhere; it is not within the compass of the soul's own activity. In some mode, inconceivable and mysterious, our life issues out of an impenetrable background: and as our life includes spiritual elements, that background has spiritual factors: and as our life is personal, within that background exists personality. This supply of life in which we begin, from out of which our being opens, can never cease, so long as we exist, to sustain us by one continuous act. Ever its resources flow in: ever its vital support is unwithdrawn. In some fashion or other, we all know that this must be so: and the Christian Creed only lifts into clear daylight, and endows with perfect expression, this elementary and universal verity, when it asserts that at the very core of each man's being lies, and lives, and moves, and works, the creative energy of the Divine Will—'the Will of our Father Which is in Heaven'.

We stand, by the necessities of our existence, in the relationship of sons to a Father, who has poured out into us, and still pours, the vigour of His own life. This is the one basis of all faith. Unless this relationship actually exists, there could be no faith: if it exists, then faith is its essential corollary: it is bound to appear. Our faith is simply the witness to this inner bond of being. That bond, which is the secret of our entire existence, accounting for all that we are, or do, or feel, or think, or say, must become capable of recognition by a being that is, in any sense, free, intelligent, conscious: and this recognition by us of the source from whence we derive, is what we mean by faith. Faith is the sense in us that we are Another's creature, Another's making.

And its entire office and use lies in realizing the secret fact. For the bond is spiritual; and it can only realize itself in a spirit that has become aware of its own laws. Faith opens an entirely new career for creaturely existence; and the novelty of this career is expressed in the word 'supernatural'. The 'supernatural' world opens upon us as soon as faith is in being.[1] The history of faith is the history of this gradual disclosure, this growing capacity to recognize and receive, until the rudimentary omen of God's fatherhood in the rudest savage who draws, by clumsy fetich, or weird incantation, upon a power outside himself, closes its long story in the absolute recognition, the perfect and entire receptivity, of that Son of man, who can do nothing of Himself, 'but what He seeth the Father do', and, for that very reason, can do everything: for whatsoever 'the Father doeth, the Son doeth also'.

Faith [thus] is not only the recognition by man of the secret source of his being, but it is itself, also, the condition under which the powers, that issue from that source, make their arrival within him. The sonship, already germinal, completes itself, realizes itself in man, through his faith. Faith is that temper of sympathetic and immediate response to Another's will which belongs to a recognized relationship of vital communion. It is the spirit of confident surrender, which can only be justified by an inner identification of life. Its primary note, therefore, will be *trust*—that trust of Another, which needs no ulterior grounds on which to base itself, beyond what is involved in the inherent law of this life. Faith will ever discover, when its reason for action, or belief, are traced to their last source, that it arrives at a point where its only and all-sufficient plea will be 'God is my Father: I am His child'. Our manhood lies in this essential sonship: and, if so, then to be without faith, without the conscious realization of the sonship, is to be without the fullness of a man's proper nature. It is to be inhuman: to be curtailed of the natural development: to be maimed and thwarted. It means that the vital outcome of the inner verity has been arrested.

[1] The word 'super-natural' is obviously misleading, since it seems to imply that the higher spiritual levels of life are *not* 'natural'. Of course, the higher the life, the more intensely 'natural' it is; and the nature of God must be the supreme expression of the natural. But the word 'supernatural' is, in reality, only concerned with the partial and conventional use of 'nature', as a term under which we sum up all that constitutes this present and visible system of things.

If faith, then, be the witness and the exercise of our sonship in God, we can recognize at once the place it will hold among the other powers and capacities of our nature. We are so unfortunately apt to rank it as one among many faculties, and then to find ourselves engaged in agitating controversies concerning its limits and its claims. We have to secure for it, against the rest, a field for free dominion; and that field is hard to define; and rival powers beset it; and there are raids and skirmishes on every frontier; and reason is ever making violent incursions on the one side, and feeling is actively besieging it on the other: and the scientific frontiers, which we are ever on the point of fixing, shift, and change, and vanish, as soon as we determine them; and the whole force of Christian apologetics is spent in aimless and barren border-warfare.

But, if what we have been saying be true, the whole trouble turns on a mistake. Faith is not to be ranked by the side of the other faculties in a federation of rival powers, but is behind them all. It goes back to a deeper root; it springs from a more primitive and radical act of the central self than they. It belongs to that original spot of our being, where it adheres in God, and draws on divine resources. Out from that spot our powers divide, radiating into separate gifts—will, memory, feeling, reason, imagination, affection; but all of them are but varying expressions of that essential sonship, which is their base. And all, therefore, run back into that home where faith abides, and works, and rises, and expands. By adherence in God, we put out our gifts, we exercise our functions, we develop our faculties; and faith, therefore, far from being their rival, whom they are interested in suspecting, and curbing, and confining within its limits, is the secret spring of their force, and the inspiration of their growth, and the assurance of their success. All our knowledge, for instance, relies upon our sonship; it starts with an act of faith. We throw ourselves, with the confidence of children, upon an external world, which offers itself to our vision, to our touch, to our review, to our calculation, to our handling, to our use. Who can assure us of its reality, of its truth? We must measure it by those faculties under the manipulation of which it falls: but how can the faculties guarantee to us their own accuracy? How can we justify an extension of our own inner necessities to the world of outward things? How can we attribute to nature that rational and causative existence which we find ourselves forced to assume in it? Our justification, our confidence, all issue, in the last resort, from our sonship.

Our powers have, in them, some likeness to those of God. If He be our Father, if we be made in His image, then, in our measure, we can rely upon it that we close with Nature in its reality; that our touch, our sight, our reason, have some hold on the actual life of things; that we see and know in some such manner, after our degree, as God Himself sees and knows.

New knowledge, new experience, far from expunging the elements of faith, make ever fresh demands upon it; they constitute perpetual appeals to it to enlarge its trust, to expand its original audacity. And yet the very vastness of those demands serves to obscure and conceal their true character. This is the key to much of our present bewilderment. The worlds of knowledge and of action have assumed such huge proportions, have accumulated such immense and complicated resources, have gained such supreme confidence in their own stability, have pushed forward their successes with such startling power and rapidity, that we have lost count of their primal assumption. Our secular and scientific life is an immense experiment in faith—an experiment which verifies itself by success, but which justifies itself only if it remembers to attribute all its success to the reality of that hidden relationship to God, which is the key to all its capacities, the justification of all its confidence, and the security of all its advance.

Such a remembrance is not easy for it: for the exercise of the capacities is instinctive and spontaneous, and it requires an effort of reflexion to question the validity of such exercise. Faith lies *behind* our secular life, secreted within it: and the secular life, therefore, can go on as if no faith was wanted; it need not trouble its head with perplexing questions, whether its base be verifiable by the same standards and measures as its superstructure. Its own practical activity is complete and free, whether it discover its hidden principle or not.

But, in religion, this hidden activity is evoked by a direct appeal: it is unearthed; it is summoned to come forward on its own account. God demands of this secret and innermost vitality that it should no longer lie incased within the other capacities, but that it should throw off its sheltering covers, and should emerge into positive action, and should disclose its peculiar and native character. This definite and direct contact between the God Who is the hidden source of all life, and the faith which is the hidden spring of all human activity—this disclosure by the Father, met by this discovery by the son—this is Religion: and the history of Religion is the story of its slow and gradual advance in sanity and clearness, until it culminates in that special disclosure which we call Revelation.

Now here we have reached a parting of ways. For we have touched the point at which the distinctions start out between what is secular and what is sacred—between virtue and godliness—between the world and the Church. If 'Religion' means this coming forward into the foreground of that which is the universal background of all existence, then we cut ourselves free from the perplexity which benumbs us when we hear of the 'Gospel of the Secular Life'; of the 'Religion of Humanity'; of doctors and scientific professors being 'Ministers of Religion'; of the 'Natural Religion' which is contained within the borders of science with its sense of wonder, or of art with its vision of beauty. All this is so obviously true in one sense that it sinks to the level of an amiable commonplace; but if this be the sense intended, why is all this emphasis laid upon it? Yet if more than this is meant, we are caught in a juggling maze of words, and are losing hold on vital distinctions, and feel ourselves to be rapidly collapsing into the condition of the unhappy Ninevites, who knew not their right hands from their left.

The word 'Religion', after all, has a meaning: and we do not get forward by labouring to disguise from ourselves this awkward fact. This positive meaning allows everything that can be asked in the way of sanctity and worth, for nature and the natural life. All of it is God-given, God-inspired, God-directed; all of it is holy. But the *fact* of this being so is one thing: the *recognition* of it is another; and it is this recognition of God in things which is the core and essence of religion. Religion, in this sense, is perfectly distinct from what is secular: yet, in making this distinction, it brings no reproach: it pronounces nothing common or unclean. It only asks us not to play with words: and it reminds us that, in blurring this radical distinction, we are undoing all the work which it has been the aim of the religious movement to achieve. For the history of this movement is the record of the gradual advance man has made in disentangling 'the Name of God' from all its manifestations. Religion is the effort to arrive at that Name, in its separable identity, in its personal and distinct significance. It is the fulfilment of the unceasing cry 'Tell me Thy name!'

Abridged from *Lux Mundi* (1889)

II. DOGMA

The supreme act of personal surrender, for which Christ unhesitatingly asks, cannot conceivably pass beyond its child-stage without forming a direct and urgent challenge to the intellect to say how, and why, such an act can be justified, or such a claim interpreted. No faith can reach to such an absolute condition without finding itself involved in anxieties, perils, problems, complications. Its very absoluteness is a provocation to the questioning and disputing mind—to the hesitating and scrupulous will. And the result, the inevitable result, of such a faith—proposed, as it was, to a world no longer young and childlike, but matured, old, thoughtful, experienced—is the Dogmatic Creeds. We clamour against these intellectual complications: we cry out for the simple primitive faith. But, once again, it is a mistake of dates. We cannot ask to be as if eighteen centuries had dropped out, unnoticed—as if the mind had slumbered since the days of Christ, and had never asked a question. We cannot hope to be in the same condition after a question has been asked, as we were before it had ever occurred to us to ask it. The Creeds only record that certain questions have, as a fact, been asked. Could our world be what it is, and not have asked them? These difficulties of a complicated faith are only the reflexion of the difficulties of a complicated life. If, as a fact, we are engaged in living a life which is intricate, subtle, anxious, then any faith which hopes to cover and embrace that life, cannot escape the necessity of being intricate, subtle, and anxious also. No child's creed can satisfy a man's needs, hunger, hopes, anxieties. If we are asked to throw over the complications of our Creeds, we must beg those that ask us, to begin by throwing over the complications of this social and moral life.

But still, with the Creeds as with the Bible, it is the personal intimacy with God in Christ which alone is our concern. We do not, in the strict sense, believe *in* the Bible, or *in* the Creeds: we believe solely and absolutely in Christ Jesus. Faith is our living act of adherence in Him, of cohesion with God. But still, once more, we must recognize that this act of adhesion has a history: it has gradually been trained and perfected: and this has been accomplished through the long and perilous experiences recorded in the Old Testament; and it has been consummated in the final sealing of the perfected intimacy attained in Him, in Whose person it was realized and made possible for us: and it has been guarded and secured to us in the face of the overwhelming pressure of eighteen strong, stormy, and distracted centuries. And therefore it is that we now must attain our cohesion with God, subject to all the necessities laid upon us by the fact that we enter on the world's stage at a late hour, when the drama has already developed its plot and complicated its situations. This is why we cannot now, in full view of the facts, believe in Christ, without finding that our belief includes the Bible and the Creeds.

Dogmas of faith do not the least correspond to the classifications and laws of physical science; and for this reason, that the matter to which they relate is wholly different in kind. Dogmas represent reason in its application to a personal life: scientific generalizations represent reason as applied to matter, from which the conditions of personality have been rigorously and rightly excluded. The difference is vital; and it affects the entire character of the working of reason.

The dogmatic definitions of Christian theology can never be divorced from their contact in the personality of Christ. They are statements concerning a living character. As such, and only as such, do they come within the lines of faith. We do not, in the strict sense, believe in them: for belief is never a purely intellectual act; it is a movement of the living man drawn towards a living person. Belief can only be in Jesus Christ. To Him alone do we ever commit ourselves, surrender ourselves, for ever and aye. But a personality, though its roots lie deeper than reason, yet includes reason within its compass: a personality cannot but be rational, though it be more than merely rational; it has in it a rational ground, a rational construction; it could not be what it is without being of such and such a fixed and organic character. And a personality, therefore, is intelligible; it lays itself open to rational treatment; its characteristics can be stated in terms of thought. The Will of God is the Word of God; the Life is also the Light. That which is loved can be apprehended; that which is felt can be named. So the Personality of the Word admits of being rationally expressed in the sense that reason can name and distinguish those elements in it, which constitute its enduring and essential conditions. The dogmas, now in question, are simply careful rehearsals of those inherent necessities which, inevitably, are involved in the rational construction of Christ's living character. They are statements of what He must be, if He is what our hearts assure us; if He can do that for which our wills tender Him their life-long self-surrender. Unless these rational conditions stand, then, no act of faith is justifiable, unless His personality correspond to these assertions, we can never be authorized in worshipping Him.

But, if so, then we can commit ourselves to these dogmas in the same way, and degree, as we commit ourselves to Him. We can do so, in the absolute assurance that He cannot but abide for ever, that which we know Him to be today. We know Him indeed, but 'in part': but it is part of a fixed and integral character, which is whole in every part, and can never falsify, in the future, the revelation which it has already made of itself.

The real question, as to Christian dogma, lies in the prior question— Is Christianity justified in claiming to have reached a *final* position? If the position is rightly final, then the intellectual expression of its inherent elements is final also. Here is the deep contrast between it and science. The scientific man is forbidden, by the very nature of his studies, to assume finality for his propositions. For he is not yet in command of his material. Far, very far, from it. He is touching it on its very edge. He is engaged in slowly pushing tentative advances into an unknown world, looming, vast, dim, manifold, beyond his frontier of light. The coherence of his known matter with that huge mass beyond his ken, can be but faintly imaged and suspected. Wholly unreckoned forces are in operation. At any moment he may be called upon to throw over the classification which sums up his hitherto experience, he may have to adopt a new centre, to bring his facts into a novel focus; and this involves at once a novel principle of arrangement. In such conditions dogma is, of course, an absurdity. But, if we are in a position to have any faith in Jesus Christ, then we must suppose that we have arrived at the one centre to all possible experiences, the one focus, under which all sights must fall. To believe in Him at all is to believe that, by and in 'this Man, will God judge the world'. In His personality, in His character, we are in possession of the ultimate principle, under which the final estimate of all things will be taken. We have given us, in His sacrifice and mission, the absolute rule, standard, test, right to the very end. Nothing can fall outside it. In Him, God has summed up creation. We have touched, in Him, the 'last days', the ultimate stage of all development. We cannot believe in Him at all, and not believe that His message is final.

And it is this finality which justifies dogma. If Christianity is final, it can afford to be dogmatic; and we, who give our adhesion to it, must, in so doing, profess our adhesion to the irreversible nature of its inherent principles: for, in so doing, we are but reasserting our belief in the absolute and final sufficiency of His person.

Abridged from *Lux Mundi* (1889)

CHAPTER 9

THE BRITISH HEGELIANS

The influence of German idealism upon British thought was tardy. In spite of Coleridge and Carlyle there was in this country little systematic knowledge of post-Kantian tendencies. Mansel was a notable exception, but he himself had no sympathy with the movement and deplored any attempt to interpret Christian theology in terms of a speculative metaphysic. The leading figure in British philosophy was J. S. Mill, whilst Comte's positivism was being enthusiastically introduced to English readers by G. H. Lewes and Harriet Martineau. The appearance of an idealist school, therefore, in the persons of James Ferrier, whose *Institutes of Metaphysics* was published in 1854, Benjamin Jowett—an essentially eclectic thinker, however—and finally of T. H. Green and his disciples, was in strong contrast with the prevailing philosophical outlook, although, somewhat ironically, the doctrines it espoused were already losing favour in the land of their origin. It was a reaction in no small part explicable, in a nation at the time more consistently traditionalist in its religious attitudes than any other in western Europe, by growing distaste for both a dry empiricism and the religious agnosticism which was its usual concomitant, and the naturalism which the new evolutionary hypothesis seemed, in the name of science, to wish to impose upon all thought. The spirit of man, it was felt, needed the concept of God, and of God not as a merely residual or marginal existence but as the soul and substance of all reality. Thus British idealism at once acquired a religious impulse, a fact which lent added momentum to its attack upon empiricism. But this tone of spiritual elevation also encouraged a rhetorical style of language which, when at the beginning of the present century the eclipse of idealism had already started, made it an object not only of disapproval but of derision. Empiricism regained control of English philosophy and keeps it still.

Green's opposition to utilitarianism was in large measure ethical; the idea of pleasure being the end of moral action was repugnant to him. The *summum bonum* must lie, rather, in 'some perfection of human life, some realization of human capacities'. Though not himself an orthodox believer, his attitude to Christianity was conservative. With his contemporaries, John and Edward Caird, the theological direction of the idealism became overt and dominant. The Scottish brothers were, moreover, better writers and teachers than was Green, and more forceful personalities. Edward especially had rare expository gifts. Born at Greenock in 1835, he became professor of moral philosophy at Glasgow in 1866 and Master of Balliol College, Oxford, in 1893, which post he held until a year before his death in 1908. In both capacities he exercised a powerful influence over successive generations of students. His principal publications include *A Critical Account of the Philosophy of Kant* (1877), later revised and enlarged as *The Critical Philosophy of Kant* (1889), *The Evolution of Religion* (1893) and *The Evolution of Theology in the Greek Philosophers* (1904). Small in bulk but admirable in its clarity and penetration is his short study of Hegel in 'Blackwood's Philosophical Classics', which remains one of the best introductions to its subject in English. Always reserved, temperate yet live in the manner in which he deals with the problems he is discussing, Caird realized that dogmatic religious orthodoxy—and Scottish Calvinism especially—had become more and more of an anachronism in a rapidly changing world, and would have to be modified if the Christian expression of the religious spirit were to survive. Materialism, he was convinced, required the antidote of the idealist metaphysic, to which Christian doctrine could very properly be adapted.

For Edward Caird, whose Hegelianism is more pronounced than that of any other thinker standing in the central orthodox tradition, God is the principle and end of all knowledge, the synthesis of which the self and the not-self are respectively the thesis and antithesis. He is not, therefore, a Hamiltonian or Spencerian Unknowable, a remote Transcendence of whom or of which nothing positive can be said, but the Soul of our souls, the unique Spirit who is at once eternally realized yet progressively revealed in all spirits. So far is he from being a *Deus absconditus*, that if he appear to us obscure it is only by the very excess of his light, not because of any concealing darkness. In him we transcend our own limitations, for the finite is not suppressed by the Infinite but sustained and integrated by it in an all-comprehending unity. Apart indeed from God nothing whatever can be understood: the merest sensation is inexplicable without him. *Intra cuncta, nec inclusus; extra cunctus, nec exclusus.* Further, as all history is the articulation of an immanent Idea, so religion, in the historic life of man, at first assumes forms that are 'objective', approximating to nature and feeling; later it is interiorized, reflexion and conscience being awakened and imagination subdued to the demands of logic. The final stage in the evolution of the religious consciousness is represented by Christianity, in which alone is man's full spiritual development attained. And of Christianity the essence is contained in the gospel saying, that 'He that saveth his life shall lose it, and he that loseth his life shall save it'; words, however, which do not mean 'that this world should be sacrificed that the next day be won', since anything of the kind would be no more than gratification of individual desires, hereafter instead of here. The true interpretation is that 'the individual must die to an isolated life, in order that he may live the spiritual life, the universal life'.

The basic values for which Christianity stands are thus, in Caird's view, *immanent* values, to be realized in the world we know. What appears as the progress of the race is not a series of chance occurrences but the self-revelation of the Eternal within us. Much the same view was held by Caird's elder brother, John (1820–98), at first professor of theology, and then, from 1873, Principal, of Glasgow University, and author of an Hegelianizing *Introduction to the Philosophy of Religion* (1880) and a series of Gifford lectures entitled *Fundamental Ideas of Christianity* (1899). For him too the Infinite contains and determines all finite consciousness. The ultimate unity of thought and reality, which in the religion of even the simple soul is already vaguely apprehended, becomes, for the reflecting mind, articulate in a religious philosophy. God can therefore be truly known by us, for although religion contains a necessary element of mystery, 'a religion all mystery is an absurd and impossible notion'. What may now in fact lie beyond knowledge should not be thought of as in its nature unknowable. 'The grandeur that surrounds the absolute, the infinite reality beyond the finite, can only arise from this, not that it is something utterly inconceivable and unthinkable, but that it is for thought or self-consciousness the realization of its highest ideal of spiritual excellence.' In the final resort the idea of God would seem to be the projection of man's ever-deepening intuitive self-understanding.

With F. H. Bradley (1846–1924), Bernard Bosanquet (1848–1923) and J. McT. E. McTaggart (1866–1925) the Hegelian influence intensifies and in regard to religion all three writers assume positions away from the general current even of liberal theological thinking. To conceptualize the Absolute they found it necessary to sacrifice one after another of the convictions which personal idealists took to be fundamental. Bradley, a fellow, from 1870 until his death, of Merton College, Oxford, and author of *Appearance and Reality* (1893), the outstanding British contribution to metaphysics in its century, grounds reality in 'experience', a paradoxical-sounding doctrine for a pro-fessed idealist until we learn his use of the word *real* excludes all finite individuals and all personal relations. The very idea of a 'self', he argues, is so riddled with contradictions that it can tell us nothing concerning the ultimate nature of reality. The unity of existence hence must lie beyond anything which personal thought can affirm. In the later chapters of *Appearance and Reality* Bradley seeks to reconstitute the world of integral experience and so carry over the qualities presented to us in appearance into a reality where nothing finally is lost. But to do so he must suppress the existence not only of individual consciousnesses but the divine also, since to attribute personality to God is to confuse two diverse orders of thought and to speak of the Absolute in terms which are appropriate only to what is infinitely inferior to it. Centres of consciousness are merely personal and artificial perspectives having no more reality than, say, the relations of mathematical space. This position Bradley has of course already established by his theory of internal relations, according to which truth tends both to realize and lose itself in unity. Every isolated truth is an error, for every relation intrinsically modifies the terms as between which it subsists. The result is that there can be no particular truths or multiple realities, but only, as it were, a single *bloc* of ideal becoming in which being and knowledge alike have their ground and in which the islets of mere individual consciousness are necessarily submerged. In a word, all relationship is *appearance*, and in the Absolute appearance ceases. We are left with a pure monism which, although with Pater we may feel it to be, in its way, 'an echo, a haunting recurrent voice of the human soul itself, and as such sealed with a natural truth', and hence to have an undeniable religious quality, is nevertheless wholly incompatible with anything normally identified as Christian thinking.

Bibliographical note

On the British idealist movement generally see J. H. Muirhead, *The Platonic Tradition in Anglo-Saxon Philosophy* (1931) and G. Watts Cunningham, *The Idealistic Argument in Recent British and American Philosophy* (New York, 1933). More recent is J. Pucelle, *L'Idéalisme en Angleterre* (1955). On Edward Caird see H. Jones and J. H. Muirhead, *The Life and Philosophy of Edward Caird* (1923), the obituary notice in B. Bosanquet in the *Proceedings of the British Academy* (1907–8), pp. 379–86, and the entry in *D.N.B. 1901–1911*, I, 291–5. There is a Memoir of John Caird by his brother prefixed to the first volume of the latter's *Fundamental Ideas of Christianity* (1899), I, ix–cxli. On F. H. Bradley see in particular the study by Richard Wollheim (Penguin Books, 1959).

I. JOHN CAIRD: RELIGION AND PHILOSOPHY

We have seen that the history of religions or of the progressive religious experience of mankind constitutes a necessary element of the science of religion; that it is not religion only, but the history of religion which the philosophy of religion has to explain, and that, in one point of view, the history of religion might even be said to be itself the philosophy of religion. But if so much must be credited to experience, what function is left for philosophy? If the contribution of history to philosophy be what we have just represented it to be, what in its turn is the contribution which philosophy renders to history in a philosophy of religion?

It has been implied in what has been said that a true philosophy is not open to the reproach of disdaining experience—of attempting by any *a priori* method to construct a system of religious ideas—or even of approaching experience with its own presuppositions and forcing the facts which it finds into a ready-made mould. Yet it is easy to exaggerate the place and value of experience; or rather, to put the matter more exactly, it is easy to misconceive what experience really is. To the uncritical mind there is great plausibility in the contrast sometimes drawn between the empirical and the speculative methods. 'Make your mind the mirror of experience, abjure all preconception, take the humble place of the minister and interpreter of nature, and let the facts speak for themselves'—nothing surely can be more wholesome or unexceptionable than such counsels as these? Why should we attempt to excogitate from our minds a theory of the nature of religion, when we can go to the history of the world and see what religion actually has been? Metaphysical theories and systems are notoriously uncertain, but the solid results of modern research into the religious notions and practices of primitive races, the facts which have been elicited by the recovery and critical examination of the Vedas and other sacred books, by the deciphering of inscriptions and monuments, by the investigations of Comparative Philology, etc., as to the religious beliefs and rites of the ancient nations of the East, and the still more abundant resources accessible to the student of other religions—these fruits of modern inquiry have created a Science of Religions resting on the same sure basis with the other sciences of experience. In this science there is no place for mere subjective theories and speculations. The humbler but safer function to which scientific investigators in this field have had to restrict themselves is the same as in the other inductive sciences. They have endeavoured to reduce the vast store of facts to some clearly defined groups and classes, and to elicit from a comparative study of the various religions of the world some general principles as to the nature of religious ideas and the conditions of their rise and development. In this way the subject of religion has been transferred from the domain of metaphysical or theological speculation to the sure ground of science.

Now, it is no doubt true that a science of religion must be based on experience, and that we can no more create such a science by *a priori* methods than we can create out of our own consciousness a science of Astronomy or Chemistry or Biology. Nevertheless, in this as in other cases, it is possible to make good the claim of philosophy to be something more than a reproduction of experience or a classification and generalization of facts. Let us endeavour to see what that 'something more' is.

1. When we are told to 'observe facts', to make our minds simply 'the mirror of experience', we must, at least, know in a more or less definite way, what sort of facts we are in search of—what, amidst the manifold varieties of human experience, is *the particular kind of experience* we are to observe. It is not any or every fact or class of facts that are relevant to this special inquiry, and we must start with, at least, so much preliminary knowledge of the object of investigation as will enable us to pronounce whether the facts which present themselves have or have not any bearing upon it. It is not Astronomy or Botany or Physiology —not the phenomena and laws of Nature, which we intend to study, neither is it Art or Politics, or Ethnology or Comparative Philology; it is that special department of human experience, those facts and phenomena of man's nature and life, which, as distinguished from all others, belong to the province of what we call 'Religion'. What then *is* Religion? What do we mean when we speak of a particular attitude of the human spirit and its outward manifestations and expressions as 'religious'? It is not the facts themselves or the history of them which can furnish the answer to these questions; for it is our presupposed knowledge of the answer that lends special interest to the facts. Facts pertaining to other provinces of experience may be in various ways related to this particular subject. The phenomena of Nature, the productions of Art, may have been either themselves the objects of religious worship or inseparably connected with these objects in the mind of the worshipper; the religious sentiment may have expressed itself through the medium of poetic fiction or of mythical personification; but it is not *as* natural phenomena or works of art, or mythological explanations of nature, that the science of religion has to do with them. In order to be contemplated in this special point of view, these and other objects of observation or products of human activity must become related to each other and to our minds as manifestations of that attitude or activity of the human spirit which we term 'Religion'. And to discover what that is, it is not to experience we can betake ourselves, for that which we are in quest of, though indivisible from positive experience, is presupposed in experience and logically prior to it.

It is true indeed, that when we ask what is the general idea or principle of religion, the answer must, in one sense, come from experience; for the general idea of religion is not a thing which has any existence or reality apart from experience. There is no such thing as religion in general apart from all particular or positive religions; it is only in and through particular or positive religious experience that we have come to know anything about religion. But neither, in like manner, is there any such thing as an abstract cause which is no particular cause or force, or an abstract principle of life which exists outside of all particular living beings, or an abstract beauty and morality separate from beautiful objects and from the actions of rational or moral agents. In all these cases the universal, the idea or principle, is not a thing in the air, a metaphysical entity, with an independent being of its own, but it is that which exists and is known in and through the particular or the multiplicity of particulars which express it. On the other hand, there is present in all particular experience an ideal or universal element which is not due to experience, inasmuch as no experience would be possible without it—an element, therefore, which experience itself cannot explain or interpret. It is, for instance, from observation and experiment that we learn what are the sequences and co-existences of phenomena in nature—what particular causes are connected with what particular effects. But the idea or category of causality itself is not given by experience, inasmuch as no science of nature would be possible save on the presupposition that the order of nature is constant, that its sequences are not arbitrary but invariable. When therefore we desire to know what is the nature and significance of that idea which every scientific observation or experiment pre-supposes—that hidden ideal element which constitutes the impulse to all scientific investigation, and gives to outward experience its reality and rationality—it is not to outward experience itself, nor even to the sciences which record and generalize experience, but to that which is the science of sciences, which deals with those principles of thought on which all science rests, in short, it is to philosophy, that we must have recourse.

In the same way, whilst religion has no existence as a mere abstract notion apart from the positive religions or the religious experience of the world, yet that experience would have no meaning or interest for us *as* religious, but for the fact that, consciously or unconsciously in all our observation of it, the idea of religion is presupposed. Here, as elsewhere, the universal or ideal element does not exist apart from, but realizes and expresses itself in the particular. And here, as else-where, it is not experience or a so-called science of experience, but philosophy, which is the highest interpreter of experience, that must examine into the nature of that ideal element and determine its import. It is this function of philosophy which in the foregoing pages we have attempted to fulfil. There is involved, as we have seen, in man's spiritual nature a consciousness which goes beyond his consciousness of himself and of things without—an absolute self-consciousness which is the unity of all thought and being. It is of the very essence of man as a spiritual, self-conscious being to transcend the finite, to rise above the world of inner and outer experience, seeing that neither would have any meaning or reality if they did not rest on and imply a consciousness deeper than the consciousness of the individual self, deeper than the consciousness of Nature, a universal Mind or Intelligence which is the *prius* and the unity of both. It is this capacity of transcending the finite, this affinity to that which is universal and Infinite, which constitutes the latent grandeur of man's nature and has been the secret impulse to all that is great and noble in the individual life and in the history of the race. It is this relation to the Infinite which, above all, gives meaning to the outward history of religion. Man's spiritual nature is the form of an infinite content, and morality and religion are the practical, as philosophy is the speculative, effort to realize it. When we contemplate the religious experience of man as the endeavour to make himself one with that Infinite life which his spiritual nature presupposes, to renounce himself and all finite ends, and to become the organ of the Infinite Mind—or, in briefer terms, when we conceive of religion as the self-surrender of the human spirit to the Divine—we have the key to the religious experience of mankind. In this idea we find the answer to the question, why we isolate certain facts of human history as belonging to *religious* experience in distinction from all other experiences. It is in recognizing them as the progressive manifestations of this idea, the attempts, more or less imperfect, to give expression and realization to it, that we discern the true significance of the various positive religions as stages in the religious history of the world.

2. It is, then, one function of philosophy to apprehend and define the fundamental idea of religion, that idea which determines what special phenomena of human experience are relevant to an inquiry into the history of religions. But the colligation of appropriate facts is something far short of a science or philosophy of religion. When that task has

been accomplished we are as yet in possession only of the materials out of which such a science is to be constructed. It is the function of science not merely to observe and register facts, but to interpret them— to give them rational significance and systematic coherence and order. What we want to know is not merely the historical fact that the religious principle has at various times and amongst various nations and races manifested itself in certain rites, observances, notions, institutions—at one time apparently running riot in a mere indiscriminating and arbitrary consecration of material objects; at another expressing itself in a more regulated nature-worship, by offerings, sacrifices, words and acts of adoration addressed to the sun, the moon, the bright heavens, the dawn, the winds and storms; at another, embodying its conception of the Divine, not in the powers of nature, but in a multiplicity of humanized divinities—individualities invested with human qualities and relations, and represented in the idealized forms of Art; or, once more, transcending all material and finite things and beings, and finding its object either in a mysterious essence which is the negation of the finite world, or in a living all-controlling power or personality to whose absolute will the whole finite world is subjected. What we are in search of is not simply these and other facts of man's religious history, but the clue to the spiritual meaning and relations of these facts—some principle by which we can discern why at one time and place religion took this form, at another that; what is the characteristic genius and spirit of each religion, and what is meant by its particular notions and observances. Finally, we ask of a science of religions that it shall enable us to estimate the measure of truth which the various positive religions contain, and to determine what is the place and value of each religion, and its relation to the other religions, not merely as respects the time of its appearance in history, but as respects its inner, ideal character. We ask that it shall tell us whether we are to regard the religious history of the world as a series of accidental phenomena, i.e. of phenomena determined or modified only by external conditions, or whether we are to regard it as the organic evolution of one spiritual principle advancing through definite stages to a predetermined end and goal.

Now it is obvious that, if the 'science of religions' is to meet these demands, it can only be by viewing the materials which history supplies, that is, the facts of the religious experience of man, in the light of the fundamental idea of religion itself. It is this idea which furnishes the only adequate criterion of the value of each religion and the only adequate means of determining the relation of the various religions to each other. Even if the only function of science were the comparison and classification of facts, it would be impossible for it to fulfil this function without some *principle* of comparison and classification. But the only adequate principle is that which carries us beyond accidental resemblances and differences, and enables us to penetrate to the essential nature of the thing itself. Apart from such a principle, the mere outward form of fact may easily mislead us. Superficial resemblances may lead us to connect religions which are essentially different, apparent differences to dissociate those between which there is the closest affinity. A common but inadequate classification, for example, is that by which religions are divided into Monotheistic and Polytheistic. In this classification the various religions are arranged and graduated by the application of a mere numerical criterion to the object of worship. But, from a point of view so external and superficial, we can learn nothing as to the essential relations of religions to each other. It would not be difficult to show that all religions alike are, in one sense, monotheistic, in another, polytheistic—that they ascribe to the object of worship at once unity and plurality. The early religion of India, the religion of Greece, are polytheistic religions. But the most eminent English authority on the Science of Religions has shown that the Gods of the Vedic Pantheon lose, on close examination, their separate individuality, and that each for the time becomes to the mind of the worshipper the representative of all that is Divine. 'Each God is felt at the time as supreme and absolute, in spite of the necessary limitation which, to our minds, a plurality of Gods must entail on every single God.'[1] Greek polytheism, again, can be understood only by one who looks not merely to the many Gods—'the fair humanities of old religion', with which the religion of Beauty filled the earth and the heavens—but also to the dark unity of Fate or Necessity hidden behind, yet enthroned above all, and in the presence of which the Gods of Olympus sink into finite and transitory forms. Nor is the mere numerical principle of distinction less fallacious when applied to those religions which are usually classed as monotheistic. The God of Christianity is not a numerical unit. In whatever way we conceive of the doctrine of the Trinity, it forces us to ascribe distinctions to the Divine nature, to include plurality as well as unity in our conception of the

---

[1] Prof. Max Müller's *Hibbert Lectures*, p. 283.

Godhead. And even in the abstract monotheism of the Jewish religion the idea of God is not a bare unit; for Jehovah is a Spiritual Being who manifests Himself in a diversity of attributes or names, and therefore His nature can only be apprehended as that which involves diversity as well as unity.

In contrast with this and other arbitrary and inadequate classifications, the true classification of religions must turn, not on accidental differences, but on those that have reference to the essential idea of religion itself, and to the measure in which that idea is expressed or realized in the various positive religions. In other words, it is the idea of religion which gives us the key to the significance of each of the particular religions and the principle which determines their relative place and worth. For all religions may be regarded as the unconscious effort of the human spirit in various forms to express that elevation above ourselves and the world, that aspiration after and rest in an infinite unity of thought and being, in which the essence of religion has been shown to lie. To distinguish therefore one religion from another, to apprehend their reciprocal relations, to pronounce what religions belong to the same group or class, and whether one religion or group of religions is higher or lower than another, is possible only when, passing by external and arbitrary resemblances and differences, we ask in what manner and to what extent each religion fulfils or realizes the fundamental idea of all religion. Moreover it is in the light of this idea, if at all, that we shall be able to perceive whether the various religions of the world and the successive stages in the history of individual religions, rise out of each other, not arbitrarily or in obedience to merely external conditions, but by a natural transition, as the stages of one organic process. For whatever in the history of religion we may ascribe to accident and the force of circumstances, it is only when we approach the facts and phenomena of religion with a clear apprehension of the principle which underlies them that we can hope to discern in their apparently arbitrary succession the steps of a rational order, the inherent, all-dominating activity of an ideal and spiritual development.

John Caird, *An Introduction to the Philosophy of Religion* (1880)

II. EDWARD CAIRD: RELIGION AND THE HUMAN CONSCIOUSNESS

The most general and superficial view of history is sufficient to show that, while all religion involves a conscious relation to a being called God, this Divine Being is in different religions conceived in the most different ways; as one and as many, as natural and as spiritual, as like to, and manifested in, almost every object in the heavens above or earth beneath, in mountains and trees, in animals and men; or, on the contrary, as incapable of being represented by any finite image whatsoever; and, again, as the God of a family, of a nation, or of humanity. But, further, when we regard the history of religion as a process of evolution, we do not need to go beyond the most general facts to discover that, in the development of the idea of God, there is a certain trend or direction of progress from multiplicity to unity, from the natural to the spiritual, from the particular to the universal. We are, therefore, able to say that *now*, as the result of the long process, the only God whom it is possible to worship is one who manifests Himself both in nature and in spirit, but more clearly in spirit than in nature, and most clearly of all in the highest developments of the intellectual and moral life of man. Farther, we can say that all ideas of a family or national god have disappeared from the minds of civilized men, or that they exist only as survivals from an earlier stage of human culture. It is universally acknowledged that, if there be a God, he can be no 'respecter of persons', but must be a 'God of the whole earth', manifested in and to the spirit of man in all times and places alike. Sentiment and aesthetic feeling may at times make us throw ourselves back into the spirit of an earlier faith, and wish, like Wordsworth, that we could

> Have sight of Proteus rising from the sea,
> Or hear old Triton blow his wreathed horn.

But we cannot really worship such divinities. The only Deity we can believe in, nay, we might say, the only Deity we can disbelieve in, or seriously deny is a universal God, a spiritual principle manifested in all nature and history.

Now, regarding the historical development of religion as a whole, up to its culmination in a universal religion, we may reasonably ask how we are to explain its possibility. An element of human life which has had such a history, whose influence has been steadily widening and deepening with the general advance of civilization through age after age, must be closely, if not indissolubly, bound up with the nature of man. And it must be so, whether ultimately we are to regard it as a fundamental truth or a fundamental error. It may be an illusion, but it is not at least a superficial illusion, produced by the accidental circumstances of our environment, or, as was at one time supposed, by the intrigues of interested impostors. It is a belief which, whether true or false, has a psychological necessity as an important phase in the development of the human spirit, a belief which has a deep root in the spirit of man, even if it is not a permanent element of his life. And the only way to find a rational criterion, by which we may ascertain the nature and extent of its validity, and determine the truth or falsity of its claims, is by asking ourselves what that root is.

What, then, I ask, is the root or basis of religion in the nature of our intelligence? Why is not man content with the experience of the finite, and why does he seek after an infinite Being, if haply he may find Him? Can it be said that the idea of God is bound up with the other elements of our general consciousness of the world and of ourselves? And if so, what place does it hold in relation to the other elements of that consciousness?

I answer that, when we consider the general nature of our conscious life—our life as rational beings endowed with the powers of thinking and willing—we find that it is defined and, so to speak, circumscribed by three ideas, which are closely, and even indissolubly, connected with each other.

These are the idea of the object or not-self, the idea of the subject or self, and the idea of the unity which is presupposed in the difference of the self and the not-self, and within which they act and react on each other: in other words, the idea of God. Let me explain these terms more fully. The object is the general name under which we include the external world and all the things and beings in it, all that we know and all that we act on, the whole environment, which conditions the activity of the ego and furnishes the means and the sphere in which it realizes itself. All this we call object, in order to indicate its distinction from and its relation to the subject for which it exists. We call it by this name also to indicate that we are obliged to think of it as one whole, one world, all of whose parts are embraced in one connexion of space and all whose changes take place in one connexion of time. All these parts and changes, therefore, form elements in one system, and modern science teaches us to regard them all as connected together by links of causation. There is only one thing which stands over against this complex whole of existence, and refuses to be regarded *simply* as a part of the system; and that is the ego, the self, the *subject* for which it exists. For the primary condition of the existence of this subject is that it should distinguish itself from the object as such—from each object, and from the whole system of objects. Hence, strictly speaking, there is but one object and one subject for each of us; for, in opposition to the subject, the totality of objects constitute one world, and in opposition to the object all the experiences of the subject, all its thought and action, are merged in the unity of one self. All our life, then, moves between these two terms which are essentially distinct from, and even opposed to, each other. Yet, though thus set in an antagonism which can never cease, because with its ceasing the whole nature of both would be subverted, they are also essentially related, nor could either of them be conceived to exist without the other. The consciousness of the one, we might even say, is inseparably the consciousness of its relation to the other. We know the *object* only as we bring it back to the unity of the self; we know the *subject* only as we realize it in the object.

But, lastly, these two ideas, between which our whole life of thought and action is contained, and from one to the other of which it is continually moving, point back to a third idea which embraces them both, and which in turn constitutes their limit and ultimate condition. For where we have two terms, which are thus at once essentially distinguished and essentially related, which we are obliged to *contrast and oppose* to each other, seeing that they have neither of them any meaning except as opposite counterparts of each other, and which we are equally obliged to *unite*, seeing that the whole content of each is just its movement towards the other, we are necessarily driven to think of these two terms as the manifestation or realization of a third term, which is higher than either. Recognizing that the object only exists in distinction from, and relation to, the subject, we find it impossible to reduce the subject to a *mere* object among other objects. Recognizing that the subject exists only as it returns upon itself from or realizes itself in the object, we find it impossible to reduce the object to a *mere* phase in the life of the subject. But, recognizing them as indivisible yet necessarily opposed, as incapable of identification yet necessarily related, we are forced to seek the secret of their being in a higher principle, of whose unity they in their action and reaction are the manifestation, which they presuppose as their beginning and to which they point as their end. How otherwise can we do justice at once to their distinction and their relation, to their independence and their essential connexion with each other? The two, subject and object, are the extreme terms in the difference which is essential to our rational life. Each of them presupposes the other, and therefore neither can be regarded as producing the other. Hence, we are compelled to think of them both as rooted in a still higher principle, which is at once the source of their relatively independent existence and the all-embracing unity that limits their independence. This principle, therefore, may be imaged as a crystal sphere that holds them together, and which, through its very transparency, is apt to escape our notice, yet which must always be there as the condition and limit of their operation. To put it more directly, the idea of an absolute unity, which transcends all the oppositions of finitude, and especially the last opposition which includes all others—the opposition of subject and object—*is the ultimate presupposition of our consciousness*. Hence we cannot understand the real character of our rational life or appreciate the full compass of its movement, unless we recognize as its necessary constituents or guiding ideas, not only the ideas of object and subject, but also the idea of God. The idea of God, therefore—meaning by that, in the first instance, only the idea of an absolute principle of unity which binds in one 'all thinking things, all objects of all thought', which is at once the source of being to all things that are, and of knowing to all beings that know—is an essential principle, or rather the ultimate essential principle of our intelligence, a principle which must manifest itself in the life of every rational creature. Every creature, who is capable of the consciousness of an objective world and of the consciousness of a self, is capable also of the consciousness of God. Or, to sum up the whole matter in one word, every rational being as such is a religious being.[1]

While we say this, however, we must at once guard against a misunderstanding which is very apt to arise. If all men are religious, and if religion involves the idea of an absolute principle of unity in our lives, it might seem to follow that the belief in such a principle must be found in connexion with every form of religion. But, as a matter

---

[1] The above, of course, is only a very abstract statement of an idea which requires much illustration and explanation. It was necessary, however, to make it at once, in order to indicate the point of view from which the subject is to be treated. This and several of the following lectures will be devoted to the further exposition of it.

of fact, this is far from being the case. Indeed, it would be hard to discover in any pre-Christian religion a thought that fully answers to the account of religion just given. Yet, in development, the earliest stages always point for their explanation and completion to the later stage; and the germ of the idea of God as the ultimate unity of being and knowing, subject and object, must in some way be present in every rational consciousness. For such a consciousness necessarily involves the idea of the self and the not-self, the ego and the world, as distinct yet in relation, i.e. as opposed within a unity. The clear reflective consciousness of the object without, of the subject within, and of God as the absolute reality which is beyond and beneath both— as one complete rational consciousness in which each of these terms is clearly distinguished and definitely related to the others—is, in the nature of the case, a late acquisition of man's spirit, one that can come to him only as the result of a long process of development. But the three elements are there in the mind of the simplest human being who opens his eyes upon the world, who distinguishes himself from it yet relates himself to it. And the difficulty and perplexity which is occasioned by the unity and the difference of these elements is the moving principle of development from the very dawn of intelligence.

Let it not, therefore, be thought that we are supposing primitive man to possess developed philosophical ideas of the relations of the self and the not-self. We can no more expect him to attain to such ideas than we can expect him to analyse grammatically or logically any sentence which he utters. We assume that he is conscious of an external world, but not that he knows anything of the conditions under which knowledge of that world is possible—anything of the nature of an object as such, or of the relations of objects in general. We assume that he is conscious of a self, but not that he has ever considered what is meant by a self, or that he has distinguished between the self—as the centre of unity in all his thinking and feeling and willing—and the particular thoughts and feelings and acts which he refers to it. Finally, we assume that he *does* relate self and not-self to each other, and that, therefore, in some way he rises in thought above his own individual existence and the individual existence of the objects he knows; we assume, in other words, that, as a rational being, he is not limited to a purely objective consciousness of things, nor imprisoned in a subjective consciousness of his own ideas, but that he takes up a point of view above this opposition. And this necessity of his rational nature, the necessity which places him at a universal point of view, cannot but modify his consciousness both of the object and of himself; it cannot but lead him in some way to raise his thoughts from the world and from himself to that which is beyond both, or to see in them something which is greater than their immediate existence as finite things. But this does not mean that the savage or the child is able to analyse the idea of God or to give any intelligible account of the infinite and the universal, of that something, higher than the immediate objects of his consciousness, which so persistently haunts him and disturbs his life 'with thoughts beyond the reaches of his soul'. In fact, we only assume that he is a self-conscious being, and that, as such, he cannot but oppose himself to objects and relate himself to them; for this already involves that these three elements are present, if not *to*, yet *in* his consciousness, stimulating it to development, and therefore to the differentiation and integration of the confused unity of sense. But this, as will be shown more fully in the sequel, is quite consistent with the fullest recognition of the crudeness, the materialism, the almost brutal sensuousness and coarseness, of the ideas of uncivilized man, who has never distinctly realized, nay, who scarce can be said to have realized at all, the existence of anything that is not given in the particular impressions of sense. Whether realized or not, the universal principle is there, ruling over man's consciousness of the particular. But at this early stage he cannot make it an object of reflexion. It cannot, therefore, present itself to him *as* a universal principle, but only in the guise of a particular and finite object; and his consciousness, if he has any consciousness of it, must be in the utmost degree incoherent and confused. Man is always man; but in this stage he is least of all conscious what it is to be a man; and, in spite of the immense formal difference which separates him from a pure animal or sensitive being, from beings who are not self-conscious, the difference of the content of his thought and feeling from theirs seems almost infinitesimal. Nay, we might even say that, in a moral point of view, it is a difference for the worse. God has given him a glimpse of heaven's light, and, as Mephistopheles says in the *Faust*,

> Er braucht's allein
> Nur thierischer als jedes Thier zu seyn.

'He makes use of it only to be more brutal than any brute.' He distinguishes himself from the animals mainly by the fact that he has lost the simplicity, the innocence, the contentment with the present, which characterizes the animal. The balance of sense has been disturbed or destroyed in him, but the balance of spirit has not been attained. He is the most greedy and fierce and sensual of beasts, because he cannot fully satisfy himself with the diet of the beast, and has as yet acquired no idea of any other diet. And his religion, therefore, seems, in our first view of it, to contain little more than a terror of something more powerful than himself, the haunting consciousness of his weakness before the mighty forces of the universe, and the dream that, by some incantation or propitiation, he may bring them to his side. On a closer view, however, when we regard the growth of savage superstition not merely in itself, but in the light of that which springs out of it, we begin to see that under the unsightliness and horror of his superstition, there is germinating a consciousness of that which is greater than himself and greater than any object, and yet which is so close to him that he cannot neglect or evade it. We cannot, indeed, say in this case that *corruptio optimi pessima*; for what we have here is not corruption and decay, but rather the error and defect of imperfect development: not the babblings of senility but the lispings of infancy. But we *can* say that it is what is best in him—his highest consciousness and that which is most distinctive of him as a man—which is troubling and perplexing him. It is 'heaven's light that is leading him astray'. And his wanderings, terrible as they sometimes are, give proof, nevertheless, of something far higher than the dull complacency and innocence of animal life: they are the indication of a nature that cannot be satisfied with the finite.

Edward Caird, The Evolution of Religion (1893)

III. F. H. BRADLEY: FAITH, GOD AND THE ABSOLUTE

The central point of religion lies in what is called faith. The whole and the individual are perfect and good for faith only. Now faith is not mere holding a general truth, which in detail is not verified; for that attitude, of course, also belongs to theory. Faith is practical, and it is, in short, a making believe; but, *because* it is practical, it is at the same time a making, none the less, as if one did *not* believe. Its maxim is, Be sure that opposition to the good is overcome, and nevertheless act as if it were there; or, Because it is *not* really there, have more courage to attack it. And such a maxim, most assuredly, is not consistent with itself; for either of its sides, if taken too seriously, is fatal to the other side. This inner discrepancy, however, pervades the whole field of religion. We are tempted to exemplify it, once again, by the sexual passion. A man may believe in his mistress, may feel that without that faith he could not live, and may find it natural, at the same time, unceasingly to watch her. Or, again, when he does not believe in her or perhaps even in himself, then he may desire all the more to utter, and to listen to, repeated professions. The same form of self-deception plays its part in the ceremonies of religion.

This criticism might naturally be pursued into indefinite detail, but it is sufficient for us here to have established the main principle. The religious consciousness rests on the felt unity of unreduced opposites; and either to combine these consistently, or upon the other hand to transform them is impossible for religion. And hence self-contradiction in theory, and oscillation in sentiment, is inseparable from its essence. Its dogmas must end in one-sided error, or else in senseless compromise. And, even in its practice, it is beset with two imminent dangers, and it has without clear vision to balance itself between rival abysses. Religion may dwell too intently on the discord in the world or in the self. In the former case it forgoes its perfection and peace, while, at the same time, it may none the less forget the difference between its private will and the Good. And, on the other side, if it emphasizes this latter difference, it is then threatened with a lapse into bare morality. But again if, flying from the discord, religion keeps its thought fixed on harmony, it tends to suffer once more. For, finding that all is already good both in the self and in the world, it may cease to be moral at all, and becomes at once, therefore, irreligious. The truth that devotion even to a finite object may lift us above moral laws, seduces religion into false and immoral perversions. Because, for it, all reality is, in one sense, good alike, every action may become completely indifferent. It idly dreams its life away in the quiet world of divine inanity, or, forced into action by chance desire, it may hallow every practice, however corrupt, by its empty spirit of devotion. And here we find reproduced in a direr form the monstrous births of moral hypocrisy. But we need not enter into the pathology of the religious consciousness. The man who has passed, however little, behind the scenes of the religious life, must have had his moments of revolt. He must have been forced to doubt if the bloody source of so many open crimes, the parent of such inward pollution, can possibly be good.

But if religion is, as we have seen, a necessity, such a doubt may be dismissed. There would be in the end, perhaps, no sense in the inquiry if religion has, on the whole, done more harm than good. My object has been to point out that, like morality, religion is not ultimate. It is a mere appearance, and is therefore inconsistent with itself. And it is hence liable on every side to shift beyond its own limits. But when religion, balancing itself between extremes, has lost its balance on either hand, it becomes irreligious. If it was a moral duty to find more than morality in religion, it is, even more emphatically, a religious duty still to be moral. But each of these is a mode and an expression at a different stage of the good; and the good, as we have found, is a self-contradictory appearance of the Absolute.

It may be instructive to bring out the same inconsistency from another point of view. Religion naturally implies a relation between Man and God. Now a relation always (we have seen throughout) is self-contra-dictory. It implies always two terms which are finite and which claim independence. On the other hand a relation is unmeaning, unless both itself and the relateds are the adjectives of a whole. And to find a solution of this discrepancy would be to pass entirely beyond the relational point of view. This general conclusion may at once be veri-fied in the sphere of religion.

Man is on the one hand a finite subject, who is over against God, and merely 'standing in relation'. And yet, upon the other hand, apart from God man is merely an abstraction. And religion perceives this truth, and it affirms that man is good and real only through grace, or that again, attempting to be independent, he perishes through wrath. He does not merely 'stand in relation', but is moved only by his opposite, and indeed, apart from that inward working, could not stand at all. God again is a finite object, standing above and apart from man, and is something independent of all relation to his will and intelligence. Hence God, if taken as a thinking and feeling being, has a private personality. But, sundered from those relations which qualify him, God is inconsistent emptiness; and, qualified by his relation to an Other, he is distracted finitude. God is therefore taken, again, as transcending this external relation. He wills and knows himself, and he finds his reality and self-consciousness, in union with man. Religion is therefore a process with inseparable factors, each appearing on either side. It is the unity of man and God, which, in various stages and forms,

371

wills and knows itself throughout. It parts itself into opposite terms with a relation between them; but in the same breath it denies this provisional sundering, and it asserts and feels in either term the inward presence of the other. And so religion consists in a practical oscillation, and expresses itself only by the means of theoretical compromise. It would shrink perhaps from the statement that God loves and enjoys himself in human emotion, and it would recoil once more from the assertion that love can be where God is not, and, striving to hug both shores at once, it wavers bewildered. And sin is the hostility of a rebel against a wrathful Ruler. And yet this whole relation too must feel and hate itself in the sinner's heart, while the Ruler also is torn and troubled by conflicting emotions. But to say that sin is a necessary element in the Divine self-consciousness—an element, however, emerging but to be forthwith absorbed, and never liberated as such— this would probably appear to be either nonsense or blasphemy. Religion prefers to put forth statements which it feels are untenable, and to correct them at once by counter-statements which it finds are no better. It is then driven forwards and back between both, like a dog which seeks to follow two masters. A discrepancy worth our notice is the position of God in the universe. We may say that in religion God tends always to pass beyond himself. He is necessarily led to end in the Absolute, which for religion is not God. God, whether a 'person' or not, is, on the one hand, a finite being and an object to man. On the other hand, the consummation, sought by the religious consciousness, is the perfect unity of these terms. And, if so, nothing would in the end fall outside God. But to take God as the ceaseless oscillation and changing movement of the process, is out of the question. On the other side the harmony of all these discords demands, as we have shown, the alteration of their finite character. The unity implies a complete suppression of the relation, as such; but, with that suppression, religion and the good have altogether, as such, disappeared. If you identify the Absolute with God, that is not the God of religion. If again you separate them, God becomes a finite factor in the Whole. And the effort of religion is to put an end to, and break down, this relation—a relation which, none the less, it essentially pre-supposes. Hence, short of the Absolute, God cannot rest, and, having reached that goal, he is lost and religion with him. It is this difficulty which appears in the problem of the religious self-consciousness. God must certainly be conscious of himself in religion, but such self-con-

sciousness is most imperfect.[1] For if the external relation between God
and man were entirely absorbed, the separation of subject and object
would, as such, have gone with it. But if again the self, which is
conscious, still contains in its essence a relation between two unreduced
terms, where is the unity of its selfness? In short, God, as the highest
expression of the realized good, shows the contradiction which we
found to be inherent in that principle. The falling apart of idea and
existence is at once essential to goodness and negated by Reality. And
the process, which moves within Reality, is not Reality itself. We may
say that God is not God, till he has become all in all, and that a God
which is all in all is not the God of religion. God is but an aspect, and
that must mean but an appearance, of the Absolute.

F. H. Bradley, *Appearance and Reality* (1893)

[1] The two extremes in the human–divine self-consciousness cannot wholly unite in one
concordant self. It is interesting to compare such expressions as:

> I am the eye with which the Universe
> Beholds itself and knows itself divine,

and

> They reckon ill who leave me out;
> When me they fly, I am the wings;
> I am the doubter and the doubt,
> And I the hymn the Brahmin sings,

and

> Die Sehnsucht du, und was sie stillt,

with

> Ne suis-je pas un faux accord
> Dans la divine symphonie,
> Grâce à la vorace Ironie
> Qui me secoue et qui me mord?
>
> Elle est dans ma voix, la criarde!
> C'est tout mon sang, ce poison noir!
> Je suis le sinistre miroir
> Où la mégère se regarde!
>
> Je suis la plaie et le couteau!
> Je suis le soufflet et la joue!
> Je suis les membres et la roue,
> Et la victime et le bourreau!

CHAPTER 10

EMERSON

Emerson, said Matthew Arnold, addressing an American audience, 'was your Newman, your man of soul and genius, speaking to your bodily ears, a present object for your heart and imagination'. Any close resemblance between the two is not, however, easy to establish and need not be attempted. But Emerson compares with the great ecclesiastical leader at least in his power to command a devoted following. He also was an eloquent prose writer, although his poeticizing rhetoric is harder to appreciate in our day than it was in his own. Like Carlyle, moreover, whom he greatly admired, he is a prophet whose message no longer stirs us. But no American religious thinker of his time had anything like his influence or enjoyed such general esteem.

Born, in 1803, the son of a Unitarian minister, Ralph Waldo Emerson was educated at the Boston Latin School and at Harvard University. At first, though an omnivorous reader, he showed no special intellectual promise. In 1819 he began to keep a journal whose entries testify at once a youthful romanticist ardour and a New England conscience. He himself entered the Unitarian ministry, but doubts and mental depression, accentuated if not brought on by the deaths of his young wife and his two favourite brothers, Charles and Edward, combined with his own none too robust physical health to cause him to abandon it in 1832. Free now of professional responsibilities he was able to visit Europe, and whilst in Britain he met Landor, Coleridge, Wordsworth and Carlyle, the last of whom alone seriously impressed him. A second marriage in 1835 brought him happiness and he settled permanently in Concord, New Hampshire, lecturing at the Boston masonic temple on a variety of topics. He now felt a new sense of security and his interests revived. To date his only writings had been his numerous sermons, but in 1836 he published what was to be his best book, *Nature*, in which the essentials of his doctrine are to be found. At first it attracted little attention—a second edition did not appear until 1849—but its value was recognized by many, including Hawthorne, Thoreau and Carlyle. Its publication may indeed be said to mark the beginning of the so-called transcendentalist movement, a somewhat vaguely defined philosophical and moral idealism shared by a group of personal friends at Concord, Boston and other New England towns. Transcendentalism had its own organ, *The Dial*, which ran from 1840 to 1844, the general standpoint and editorial policy of which were inspired and largely determined by Emerson himself. The temper of mind which transcendentalism helped to create did much also to shape public opinion on the issues of the Civil War. Emerson's Phi Beta Kappa address at Harvard in 1837 on 'The American Scholar' and his Divinity School oration in the following year came as a sharp challenge to current ideas and beliefs. The former, described by Lowell as 'an event without parallel in our literary annals', was in the nature (as it was said) of 'an intellectual declaration of American independence'. 'We have too long listened', its author stated, 'to the courtly muses of Europe...we will walk on our own feet; we will work with our own hands; we will speak our own minds.' The Divinity School address called for a revision of traditional theology and was not well received. In fact Emerson's unorthodox religious views, combined with his championship of the cause of Negro emancipation and sympathy with Alcott's advanced educational theories, long impeded the nationwide recognition which eventually he gained. As a writer his reputation now rests mainly on his *Essays*, the first series of which was published in 1841 and the second two years later, both being based on lecture-notes. Though their literary merit is undeniable, they may best be described as secular sermons. Certainly the moral truth to be imparted is never left obscure. Emerson was not a systematic thinker and he clearly preferred this 'occasional' mode of communication to more formal exposition. His manner of expression had, besides, a personal quality which precluded successful imitation by others. *Representative Men*, founded on lectures given in England, appeared in 1850. To the question, What is human greatness? he replied in terms of a strongly felt moral and democratic conviction. His American lectures on *English Traits*, published in 1855, ventures an appraisal of English achievement both material and spiritual. *The Conduct of Life* (1860) is a restatement in more studied and less attractive guise of the views already outlined in *Nature*. But it is true of all Emerson's later writings that they are much less spontaneous and betray, through a diminution of emotional warmth, the somewhat disparate elements of which his doctrine was composed. His acceptance of the facts of experience is not allowed to impair his optimistic faith in the ultimacy of the good and the converging pattern of all human idealism, but this assurance is affirmed rather than argued. His final work is represented by a miscellaneous collection of pieces edited by his friend J. E. Cabot, comprising 'Society and Solitude', 'Letters and Social Aims' and a 'Natural History of the Intellect'. They are the fruits of a period of decline. His death occurred in 1882.

The essence of Emerson's religious position is his belief in the divinity of man. This the individual will realize through self-reliance, by which alone he will be able to possess his soul. Mere conventionalism must be thrown off, originality, in thought and experience, cultivated. 'The foregoing generations,' he wrote in *Nature*, 'beheld God and Nature face to face; we, through their eyes. Why should not we also enjoy an original relation to the

Universe?' And again, 'In the soul let redemption be sought. Refuse the good models, even those which are sacred in the imagination of men. Cast conformity behind you. Acquaint men at first hand with deity.' Let a man, then, but trust the deepest voices of his being and obey them. Yet Emerson is not unaware of possible misinterpretations of his neo-Stoicism and of the dangers of reliance wholly upon instinct and impulse. His all-pervading moral sense never deserts him. When a man, he tells us, can say: 'Virtue, I am thine, save me, use me...then is the end of creation answered and God well pleased.' God himself Emerson conceives pantheistically as—to employ his own expression—the 'Oversoul', rather than as personal deity; at any rate the idea is left without precise content. Immortality, too, never rises above a tentative surmise ('All the comfort I have found teaches me to confide that I shall not have less in times and places that I do not yet know'). Traditional teaching, he thinks, over-emphasizes the historical element in Christianity: Jesus is best honoured by men themselves living as he lived, by intuition, the guidance of conscience and faith in the worth of the human soul. Knowledge of the past is but the starting-point of the life of the future. The young, he believed, were 'all religious' but hated religious institutional-ism. As early as 1832 he wrote: 'I have sometimes thought that, in order to be a good minister, it was necessary to leave the ministry. The profession is antiquated. In an altered age we worship in the dead forms of our fathers.' Nevertheless he saw the futility of mere negation in theology, which could only induce 'a cold, denying, unreligious state of mind', and in his own utter-ance of what he believed to be religious truth he avoided the negative attitude.

We look to Emerson in vain, however, for a comprehensive and articulated doctrine. His poems—and he published verse from time to time, often in the *Atlantic Monthly*—were a congenial medium for communicating his religious musings. What he gives us are thoughts, observations, aphorisms, seldom very closely connected. He was perhaps too prone to think of himself as inspired. His strength lay in his unwavering assurance, puritan in spirit, of the primacy of morals in human life, and in the individual life rather than the collective ('God enters by a private door into every individual'). The qualities to be generated and fostered are discipline, thoroughness and con-centration of effort. With these in abundance man has every reason to hope, and sound religion is an indispensable instrument for promoting them.

Bibliographical note

The *Essays* and *The Conduct of Life and Other Essays*, with new introductions by S. Paul, are available in the Everyman Library. See K. W. Cameron, *Emerson the Essayist* (1945), R. I. Rush, *Life of Ralph Waldo Emerson* (1949) and S. Paul, *Emerson's Angle of Vision* (1952).

THE SOUL AND REVELATION

There is a difference between one and another hour of life in their authority and subsequent effect. Our faith comes in moments; our vice is habitual. Yet is there a depth in those brief moments, which constrains us to ascribe more reality to them than to all other experiences. For this reason, the argument, which is always forthcoming to silence those who conceive extraordinary hopes of man, namely, the appeal to experience, is forever invalid and vain. A mightier hope abolishes despair. We give up the past to the objector, and yet we hope. He must explain this hope. We grant that human life is mean; but how did we find out that it was mean? What is the ground of this uneasiness of ours, of this old discontent? What is the universal sense of want and ignorance, but the fine innuendo by which the great soul makes its enormous claim? Why do men feel that the natural history of man has never been written, but always he is leaving behind what you have said of him, and it becomes old, and books of metaphysics worthless? The philosophy of six thousand years has not searched the chambers and magazines of the soul. In its experiments there has always remained in the last analysis a residuum it could not resolve. Man is a stream whose source is hidden. Always our being is descending into us from we know not whence. The most exact calculator has no prescience that somewhat incalculable may not baulk the very next moment. I am constrained every moment to acknowledge a higher origin for events than the will I call mine.

As with events, so is it with thoughts. When I watch that flowing river, which, out of regions I see not, pours for a season its streams into me—I see that I am a pensioner—not a cause, but a surprised spectator of this ethereal water; that I desire and look up, and put myself in the attitude of reception, but from some alien energy the visions come.

The Supreme Critic on all the errors of the past and the present, and the only prophet of that which must be, is that great nature in which we rest, as the earth lies in the soft arms of the atmosphere; that Unity, that Over-Soul, within which every man's particular being is contained and made one with all other; that common heart, of which all sincere conversation is the worship, to which all right action is submission; that overpowering reality which confutes our tricks and talents, and constrains every one to pass for what he is, and to speak from his character and not from his tongue; and which evermore tends and aims to pass into our thought and hand, and become wisdom, and virtue, and power, and beauty. We live in succession, in division, in parts, in particles. Meantime, within man is the soul of the whole; the wise silence; the universal beauty, to which every part and particle is equally related; the eternal ONE. And this deep power in which we exist, and whose beatitude is all accessible to us, is not only self-sufficing and perfect in every hour, but the act of seeing and the thing seen, the seer and the spectacle, the subject and the object, are one. We see the world piece by piece, as the sun, the moon, the animal, the tree; but the whole, of which these are the shining parts, is the soul. It is only by the vision of that Wisdom, that the horoscope of the ages can be read, and it is only by falling back on our better thoughts, by yielding to the spirit of prophecy which is innate in every man, that we can know what it saith. Every man's words, who speaks from that life, must sound vain to those who do not dwell in the same thought on their own part. I dare not speak for it. My words do not carry its august sense; they fall short and cold. Only itself can inspire whom it will, and, behold, their speech shall be lyrical, and sweet, and universal as the rising of the wind. Yet I desire, even by profane words, if sacred I may not use, to indicate the heaven of this deity, and to report what hints I have collected of the transcendent simplicity and energy of the Highest Law.

If we consider what happens in conversation, in reveries, in remorse, in times of passion, in surprises, in the instructions of dreams, wherein often we see ourselves in masquerade—the droll disguises only magnifying and enhancing a real element, and forcing it on our distinct notice—we shall catch many hints that will broaden and lighten into knowledge of the secret of nature. All goes to show that the soul in man is not an organ, but animates and exercises all the organs; is not a function, like the power of memory, of calculation, of comparison—but uses these as hands and feet; is not a faculty, but a light; is not the intellect or the will, but the master of the intellect and the will; is the vast background of our being, in which they lie—an immensity not possessed and that cannot be possessed. From within or from behind, a light shines through us upon things, and makes us aware that we are nothing, but the light is all. A man is the façade of a temple, wherein all wisdom and all good abide. What we commonly call man—the eating, drinking, planting, counting man—does not, as we know him, represent himself, but misrepresents himself. Him we do not respect; but the soul, whose organ he is, would he let it appear through his action, would make our knees bend. When it breathes through his intellect, it is genius; when it breathes through his will, it is virtue; when it flows through his affection, it is love. And the blindness of the intellect begins, when it would be something of itself. The weakness of the will begins, when the individual would be something of himself. All reform aims, in some one particular, to let the great soul have its way through us; in other words, to engage us to obey.

Of this pure nature every man is at some time sensible. Language cannot paint it with his colours. It is too subtle. It is undefinable, unmeasurable; but we know that it pervades and contains us. We know that all spiritual being is in man. A wise old proverb says, 'God comes to see us without bell': that is, as there is no screen or ceiling between our heads and the infinite heavens, so is there no bar or wall in the soul where man, the effect, ceases, and God, the cause, begins. The walls are taken away. We lie open on one side to the deeps of spiritual nature, to all the attributes of God. Justice we see and know, Love, Freedom, Power. These natures no man ever got above, but always they tower over us, and most in the moment when our interests tempt us to wound them.

The sovereignty of this nature whereof we speak is made known by its independency of those limitations which circumscribe us on every hand. The soul circumscribeth all things. As I have said, it contradicts all experience. In like manner it abolishes time and space. The influence of the senses has, in most men, overpowered the mind to that degree, that the walls of time and space have come to look solid, real, and insurmountable; and to speak with levity of these limits is, in the world, the sign of insanity. Yet time and space are but inverse measures of the force of the soul. A man is capable of abolishing them both. The spirit sports with time—

Can crowd eternity into an hour,
Or stretch an hour to eternity.

We are often made to feel that there is another youth and age than that which is measured from the year of our natural birth. Some thoughts always find us young, and keep us so. Such a thought is the love of the universal and eternal beauty. Every man parts from that contemplation with the feeling that it rather belongs to ages than to

379

mortal life. The least activity of the intellectual powers redeems us in a degree from the influences of time. In sickness, in languor, give us a strain of poetry or a profound sentence, and we are refreshed; or produce a volume of Plato or Shakespeare, or remind us of their names, and instantly we come into a feeling of longevity. See how the deep, divine thought demolishes centuries and millenniums, and makes itself present through all ages. Is the teaching of Christ less effective now than it was when first his mouth was opened? The emphasis of facts and persons to my soul has nothing to do with time. And so, always, the soul's scale is one; the scale of the senses and the understanding is another. Before the great revelations of the soul, Time, Space, and Nature shrink away. In common speech, we refer all things to time, as we habitually refer the immensely sundered stars to one concave sphere. And so we say that the Judgement is distant or near; that the Millennium approaches; that a day of certain political, moral, social reforms is at hand; and the like; when we mean, that in the nature of things, one of the facts we contemplate is external and fugitive, and the other is permanent and connate with the soul. The things we now esteem fixed shall, one by one, detach themselves, like ripe fruit, from our experience, and fall. The wind shall blow them none knows whither. The landscape, the figures, Boston, London, are facts as fugitive as any institution past, or any whiff of mist or smoke, and so is society, and so is the world. The soul looketh steadily forwards, creating a world alway before her, and leaving worlds alway behind her. She has no dates, nor rites, nor persons, nor specialties, nor men. The soul knows only the soul. All else is idle weeds for her wearing.

Essays (First Series) 'The Over-soul' (1841)

CHAPTER II

JOSIAH ROYCE

The outstanding representative of the Hegelian influence in American thought is Josiah Royce, the originality of whose contributions to modern philosophy, especially in the field of logic, have lately won further recognition. Born at Grass Valley, Nevada County, California, in 1855, he graduated at the University of California. After a stay in Germany, at Leipzig and Göttingen, he returned to the U.S.A. to complete his studies at the Johns Hopkins University, where his contemporaries included William James and C. S. Peirce. From 1878 to 1882 he taught English at California, and from the latter year until 1885, philosophy at Harvard. In 1892 he was appointed to the professorship there which he held until his death in 1916. His best-known publications include *The Religious Aspect of Philosophy* (1885), *The Spirit of Modern Philosophy* (1892), *The Concept of God* (1897), the Gifford Lectures for 1899–1900 on *The World and the Individual* (1900–1), *The Philosophy of Loyalty* (1908) and *The Problem of Christianity* (1913). Both as a teacher and writer Royce was widely influential, combining solid learning with great versatility, and in his lifetime won for himself an international reputation. Endowed with a restless and searching intelligence, and master of a remarkable dialectical skill, he wrote not only on metaphysics and logic (including mathematical logic), but on history, literature and social ethics. His early volume on *The Religious Aspect of Philosophy*, which deeply impressed William James, so far from being the merely tentative essay of a young author, is striking at once for its maturity of approach and for the extent to which Royce anticipates twentieth-century attitudes. (Gabriel Marcel has said of him that he marks a transition between absolute idealism and existentialist thought.)

Royce did not embark on the career of philosopher from a dilettante taste for abstract speculation but from the pressure of his own doubts and perplexities. He was conscious of a need, in the midst of the apparent meaninglessness of life, to discover a ground of assurance that could be commended as such to others. Hence his principle, in the matter of all philosophical thinking, of 'universalizability': that a philosophy must be self-applicable in the sense of showing sufficient reason why it should itself ever have been devised. A second principle is his distinction between the 'that' and the 'what' of existence: we have no title to affirm *that* a thing is unless at the same time we can specify *what* it is by stating its meaning. An essential requirement of any philosophy, therefore, is that it should be clear as to what it means by *meaning*, of which there are two kinds or types, internal and external. The latter connotes the relation in which a thing stands to other things; but this in turn depends on the former, upon what a thing is in itself. And that which gives internal meaning to anything is its 'embodiment of purpose'. But what is purpose if not the evidence and criterion of 'mentality'? The internal essence of a thing is, accordingly, mental; whence indeed the necessity of idealism. Nevertheless, truth must be distinguishable from error, reality from illusion, and the test thereof is whether any given purpose conforms with the 'ideal community' of the purposes of humanity, as a whole past, present and future. This ideal community was, in fact, for Royce the 'ultimate Real' or Absolute. So the idea of *loyalty* becomes a key-principle: 'the willing and practical and thoroughgoing devotion of a person to a cause'. And to achieve this moral quality is to free oneself from the 'well-known inner sources of dissatisfaction', and so to give unity, fixity and stability to life.

On the place and importance of religion Royce is emphatic. 'Whatever the truth of religion may be,' he writes, 'the office, the task, the need of religion are the most important of the needs, the tasks, the offices of humanity.' The function of a philosophy of religion, if there is to be one, must include 'the office of a positive, and of a deeply sympathetic, interpretation of the spirit of Christianity, and must be just to the fact that the Christian religion is, thus far at least, man's most impressive view of salvation, and his principal glimpse of the homeland of the spirit'. Royce's conception of Christianity is itself founded upon his idea of loyalty: Christianity is a religion of loyalty, loyalty to the 'Beloved Community'—ideally the Church—as in turn the community of the loyal. Herein lies the principle and power of reconciliation or atonement whereby the impossible becomes possible. The Church came into existence through a deed of salvation, original, satisfying and perfectly adapted to the social need, the disruption of sin being attributable to the inherent contrast between the impulse of self-assertion and the demands of the social standard. Atonement therefore is the supreme expression of creative love. But what is the object which calls forth this loyalty? Not, it appears, either Christ or, more remotely, God himself, but the community. Or rather, Royce identifies the spirit of Christ with the spirit of the community and both with the spirit of God. By Christ, then, Royce means primarily the 'Christ of faith', not the 'Jesus of history'. 'The Christian religion always has been and, historically speaking, must be, not simply a religion taught by any man to any company of disciples, but always also a religion whose sense has consisted, at least in part, in the interpretation which later generations gave to the mission and nature of the founder.' This accords with his consistently maintained view that it is 'the higher social religious consciousness of mankind' which exhibits the 'central idea' of religion, more than the experience of individual religious geniuses, however eminent. It is the Church, that is, not the historic Jesus, which is Christianity's central concern. It may even be said—and here Royce's sympathies with Loisy among the contemporary Roman Catholic modernists are obvious—that the true founder of Christianity was not the Nazarene but the primitive community which saw in him that divine 'Christ' who at the same time was the immanent law of its own inner life. The essence of Christianity depends on regarding the being which the primitive Church believed itself to represent—the Beloved Community, that is—as the true source, through loyalty, of the salvation of men. God, we may say, is himself realized in a perfect community. A philosophical appreciation of Christianity will seek to translate the symbolism in which the divine idea has taken shape into modern rational speech, although the original must at the same time be preserved. To ascertain the nature and inner significance of this symbolism will be the work of historical criticism and psychology. Only so can philosophy offer a reasoned evaluation of what the past has handed down to us.

That these opinions are a radical simplification of the historic Christian belief needs no stressing. The identification of God, Christ and the Church can be proffered as an interpretation of Christian experience only at the price of refusing distinctions which the dogmatic expression of that experience has always insisted on drawing. Further, Royce's conception of loyalty itself raises serious doubts, for the object of such loyalty would seem to be only too easily capable of being forgotten in consideration of the attitudes which it is supposed to evoke. Is loyalty a good *per se*, irrespective of what it fastens on? Or to be validated does it not require an object valuable in its, or his, own right? The idea of loyalty simply as such may well appear so vague as to sanction each and any experience that can claim to create it.

Bibliographical note

A new edition of Royce's *The Religious Aspect of Philosophy* appeared in 1958. See J. H. Muirhead, *The Platonic Tradition in Anglo-Saxon Philosophy* (1931), J. E. Smith, *Royce's Social Infinite* (1950), J. H. Cotton, *Royce on the Human Self* (1954), the special Josiah Royce issue, in 1956, of *The Journal of Philosophy*, and *Josiah Royce's Seminar, 1913–1914*, ed. Grover Smith (1963). Gabriel Marcel, *La métaphysique de Royce* (1945) is particularly valuable.

RELIGION AS A MORAL CODE AND
AS A THEORY

We speak commonly of religious feelings and of religious beliefs; but we find difficulty in agreeing about what makes either beliefs or feelings religious. A feeling is not religious merely because it is strong, nor yet because it is also morally valuable, nor yet because it is elevated. If the strength and the moral value of a feeling made it religious, patriotism would be religion. If elevation of feeling were enough, all higher artistic emotion would be religious. But such views would seem to most persons very inadequate. As for belief, it is not religious merely because it is a belief in the supernatural. Not merely is superstition as such very different from religion, but even a belief in God as the highest of beings need not be a religious belief. If La Place had needed what he called 'that hypothesis', the Deity, when introduced into his celestial mechanics, would have been but a mathematical symbol, or a formula like Taylor's theorem—no true object of religious veneration. On the other hand, Spinoza's impersonal Substance, or the Nirvâna of the Buddhists, or any one of many like notions, may have, either as doctrines about the world or as ideals of human conduct, immense religious value. Very much that we associate with religion is therefore non-essential to religion. Yet religion is something unique in human belief and emotion, and must not be dissolved into any lower or more commonplace elements. What then is religion?

I

So much at all events seems sure about religion. It has to do with action. It is impossible without some appearance of moral purpose. A totally immoral religion may exist; but it is like a totally unseaworthy ship at sea, or like a rotten bank, or like a wild-cat mine. It deceives its followers. It pretends to guide them into morality of some sort. If it is blind or wicked, not its error makes it religious, but the faith of its followers in its worth. A religion may teach the men of one tribe to torture and kill men of another tribe. But even such a religion would pretend to teach right conduct. Religion, however, gives us more than a moral code. A moral code alone, with its 'Thou shalt', would be no more religious than is the civil code. A religion adds something to the moral code. And what it adds is, first, enthusiasm. Somehow it makes the faithful regard the moral law with devotion, reverence, love. By history, by parable, by myth, by ceremony, by song, by whatever means you will, the religion gives to the mere code life and warmth. A religion not only commands the faithful, but gives them something that they are glad to live for, and if need be to die for.

But not yet have we mentioned the element of religion that makes it especially interesting to a student of theoretical philosophy. So far as we have gone, ethical philosophy would criticize the codes of various religions, while theoretical philosophy would have no part in the work. But, in fact, religion always adds another element. Not only does religion teach devotion to a moral code, but the means that it uses to this end include a more or less complete theory of things. Religion says not merely *do and feel*, but also *believe*. A religion tells us about the things that it declares to exist, and most especially it tells us about their relations to the moral code and to the religious feeling. There may be a religion without a supernatural, but there cannot be a religion without a theoretical element, without a statement of some supposed matter of fact, as part of the religious doctrine.

These three elements, then, go to constitute any religion. A religion must teach some moral code, must in some way inspire a strong feeling of devotion to that code, and in so doing must show something in the nature of things that answers to the code or that serves to reinforce the feeling. A religion is therefore practical, emotional, and theoretical; it teaches us to do, to feel, and to believe, and it teaches the belief as a means to its teaching of the action and of the feeling.

II

We may now see how philosophy is related to religion. Philosophy is not directly concerned with feeling, but both action and belief are direct objects of philosophical criticism. And on the other hand, in so far as philosophy suggests general rules for conduct, or discusses the theories about the world, philosophy must have a religious aspect. Religion invites the scrutiny of philosophy, and philosophy may not neglect the problems of religion. Kant's fundamental problems: *What do I know?* and *What ought I to do?* are of religious interest no less than of philosophic interest. They ask how the highest thought of man stands related to his highest needs, and what in things answers to our best ideals. Surely no one ought to fear such questions, nor ought any philosophic student to hesitate to suggest in answer to them whatever after due reflexion he honestly can suggest, poor and tentative though it may be. In fact there is no defense for one as sincere thinker if, undertaking to pay attention to philosophy as such, he wilfully or thoughtlessly neglects such problems on the ground that he has no time for them. Surely he has time to be not merely a student of philosophy, but also a man, and these things are among the essentials of humanity, which the non-philosophic treat in their way, and which philosophic students must treat in theirs.

When, however, we say that the thinker must study and revere these questions, we must not fancy that because of their importance he may prejudge them. Assumptions, postulates, *a priori* demands, these indeed are in all thinking, and no thinker is without such. But prejudice, i.e. foregone conclusions in questionable matters, deliberate unwillingness to let the light shine upon our beliefs, all this is foreign to true thought. Thinking is for us just the clarifying of our minds, and because clearness is necessary to the unity of thought, necessary to lessen the strife of sects and the bitterness of doubt, necessary to save our minds from hopeless, everlasting wandering, therefore to resist the clarifying process, even while we undertake it, is to sin against what is best in us, and is also to sin against humanity. Deliberately insincere, dishonest thinking is downright blasphemy. And so, if we take any interest in these things, our duty is plain. Here are questions of tremendous importance to us and to the world. We are sluggards or cowards if, pretending to be philosophic students and genuine seekers of truth, we do not attempt to do something with these questions. We are worse than cowards if, attempting to consider them, we do so otherwise than reverently, fearlessly, and honestly.

III

The religious thought of our time has reached a position that arouses the anxiety of all serious thinkers, and the interest of many who are not serious. We are not content with what we learned from our fathers; we want to correct their dogmas, to prove what they held fast without proof, to work out our own salvation by our own efforts. But we know not yet what form our coming faith will take. We are not yet agreed even about the kind of question that we shall put to ourselves when we begin any specific religious inquiry. People suggest very various facts or aspects of facts in the world as having a religious value. The variety of the suggestions shows the vagueness of the questions that people have in mind when they talk of religion. One man wants to worship Natural Law, or even Nature in general. Another finds Humanity to be his ideal object of religious veneration. Yet another gravely insists that the Unknowable satisfies his religious longings. Now it is something to be plain in expressing a question, even if you cannot give an answer. We shall do something if we only find out what it is that we ought to seek. And the foregoing considerations may help us in this way, even if what follows should be wholly ineffective. For we have tried to give a definition that shall express, not merely what a Buddhist or a Catholic or a Comtist or an Hegelian means by his religion, but what all men everywhere mean by religion. They all want religion to define for them their duty, to give them the heart to do it, and to point out to them such things in the real world as shall help them to be steadfast in their devotion to duty. When people pray that they may be made happy, they still desire to learn what they are to do in order to become happy. When saints of any creed look up to their God as their only good, they are seeking for guidance in the right way. The savages of whom we hear so much nowadays have indeed low forms of religion, but these religions of theirs still require them to do something, and tell them why it is worth while to do this, and make them more or less enthusiastic in doing it. Among ourselves, the poor and the lonely, the desolate and the afflicted, when they demand religious comfort, want something that shall tell them what to do with life, and how to take up once more the burdens of their broken existence. And the religious philosophers must submit to the same test that humanity everywhere proposes to its religions. If one tries to regulate our diet by his theories, he must have the one object, whatever his theory, since he wants to tell us what is healthful for us. If he tells us to eat nothing but snow, that is his fault. The true object of the theory of diet remains the same. And so if men have expressed all sorts of one-sided, disheartening, inadequate views of religion, that does not make the object of religious theory less catholic, less comprehensive, less definitely human. A man who propounds a religious system must have a moral code, an emotional life, and some theory of things to offer us. With less we cannot be content. He need not, indeed, know or pretend to know very much about our wonderful world, but he must know something, and that something must be of definite value.

To state the whole otherwise. Purely theoretic philosophy tries to find out what it can about the real world. When it makes this effort, it has to be perfectly indifferent to consequences. It may not shudder or murmur if it comes upon unspeakably dreadful truths. If it finds nothing in the world but evil, it must still accept the truth, and must calmly state it without praise and without condemnation. Theoretic philosophy knows no passion save the passion for truth, has no fear save the fear of error, cherishes no hope save the hope of theoretic success. But religious philosophy has other objects in addition to these. Religious philosophy is indeed neither the foe nor the mistress of theoretic philosophy. Religious philosophy dare not be in opposition to the truths that theory may have established. But over and above these truths it seeks something else. It seeks to know their value. It comes to the world with other interests, in addition to the purely theoretic ones. It wants to know what in the world is worthy of worship as the good. It seeks not merely the truth, but the inspiring truth. It defines for itself goodness, moral worth, and then it asks, *What in this world is worth anything?* Its demands in this regard are boundless. It will be content only with the best it can find. Having formulated for itself its ideal of worth, it asks at the outset: *Is there then, anywhere in the universe, any real thing of Infinite Worth?* If this cannot be found, then and then only will religious philosophy be content with less. Then it will still ask: *What in this world is worth most?* It cannot make realities, but it is determined to judge them. It cannot be content with blind faith, and demands the actual truth as much as theoretic philosophy demands it; but religious philosophy treats this truth only as the material for its ideal judgements. It seeks the ideal among the realities...

★   ★   ★

IV

People come to such questions as these with certain prejudices about the method and spirit of inquiry; and all their work may be hampered by these prejudices. Let us say yet a little more of what we think as to this matter. There are two extremes to fear in religious philosophy: indifference that arises from a dogmatic disposition to deny, and timidity that arises from an excessive show of reverence for the objects of religious faith. Both of these extreme moods have their defective methods in dealing with religious philosophy. The over-skeptical man looks with impatience on all lengthy discussions of these topics. There can be nothing in it all, he says; nothing but what Hume, in an eloquent passage, called sophistry and delusion. Why spend time to puzzle over these insoluble mysteries? Hence his method is: swift work, clear statement of known difficulties, keen ridicule of hasty assumptions, and then a burning of the old deserted Moscow of theology, and a bewildering flight into the inaccessible wintry wastes, where no army of religious philosophers shall follow him. Now for our part we want to be as skeptical as anybody; and we personally always admire the freedom of motion that pure skepticism gives. Our trouble with it all, however, is that, after we have enjoyed the freedom and the frosty air of pure philosophic skepticism for a while, we find ourselves unexpectedly in the midst of philosophic truth that needs closer examination. The short and easy agnostic method is not enough. You must supplement skepticism by philosophy; and when you do so, you find yourself forced to accept, not indeed the old theology of your childhood, but something that satisfies, oddly enough, certain religious longings, that, as skeptic, you had carefully tried to forget. Then you find yourself with what you may have to call a religious doctrine; and then you may have to state it as we are here going to do, not in an easy or fascinating way, such as the pure skeptic can so well follow, but at all events with some approach to a serious and sustained effort to consider hard questions from many sides. The skeptical method is not only a good, but also a necessary beginning of religious philosophy. But we are bound to go deeper than mere superficial agnosticism. If, however, any reader is already sure that we cannot go deeper, and that modern popular agnosticism has exhausted all that can be said on religious questions, then we bid him an immediate and joyous farewell. If we had not something to say in this book that seems to us both foreign to the popular modern agnostic range of discussion, and deeper than the insight of popular modern skepticism, we should say nothing. The undertaking of this book is not to wrangle in the old way over the well-known ordinary debates of today, but to turn the flank of the common popular thought on these topics altogether, by going back to a type of philosophic investigation, that is nowadays familiar indeed to a certain school of specialists, but forgotten by the general public. In this type of investigation, we have furthermore something to offer that seems to us no mere repetition of the views of other thinkers, but an effort to make at least one little step in advance of the thoughts that the great masters of philosophy have given to us. Yet we know indeed that the range of any useful independent thought in philosophy must be, in the case of any one individual, very narrow.

The other mood and its method remain. It is the mood of excessive reverence. It wastes capital letters on all the pronouns and adjectives that have to do with the objects of religious faith; but it fears to do these objects the honor to get clear ideas about them. Now we respect this mood when it appears in men who do well their life-work, who need their religious faith for their work, and who do not feel any calling as truth-seekers. No man has any business to set up his vocation as the highest one; and the man for whom truth is useful in his actual life-work as an inspiration, revealed to him only in feeling, is welcome to his feelings, is worthy of all regard from those whose vocation is philosophy, and shall not be tormented by our speculations. He is careful and troubled about many things; the world needs him, and philosophy does not. We only lay claim to our own rights, and do not want to interfere with his. Our right to clear thought, we must insist upon. For looked at philosophically, and apart from the necessary limitations of the hard worker, all this dumb reverence, this vague use of vague names, has its serious dangers. You are reverent, we may say to the man who regards philosophic criticism as a dangerous trifling with stupendous truths; you are reverent, but what do you reverence? Have a care lest what you reverence shall turn out to be your own vague and confused notions, and not the real divine Truth at all. Take heed lest your object of worship be only your own little pet infinite, that is sublime to you mainly because it is yours, and that is in truth about as divine and infinite as your hat. For this is the danger that besets these vague and lofty sentiments. Unreflected upon, uncriticized, dumbly experienced, dumbly dreaded, these, your religious objects, may become mere feelings, mere visceral sensations of yours, that you have on Sunday mornings, or when you pray. Of course, if you are a worker, you may actually realize these vague ideas, in so far as they inspire you to work. If they do, they shall be judged by their fruits. Otherwise, do not trust too confidently their religious value. You, individually regarded, are but a mass of thought and feeling. What is only yours and in you, is not divine at all. Unless you lift it up into the light of thought and examine it often, how do you know into what your cherished religious ideal may not have rotted in the darkness of your emotions? Once in a while, there does come to a man some terrible revelation of himself in a great sorrow. Then in the tumult of anguish he looks for his religious faith to clothe his nakedness against the tempest; and he finds perhaps some moth-eaten old garment that profits him nothing, so that his soul miserably perishes in the frost of doubt. Such a man has expected God to come to his help in every time of need; but the only god he has actually and consciously had, has been his own little contemptible, private notion and dim feeling of a god, which he has never dared fairly to look at. Any respectable wooden idol would have done him better service; for then a man could know where and what his idol is. Such is only too apt to be the real state of the man who regards it as profanity to think clearly and sensibly on religious topics.

We claim, then, the right to criticize as fearlessly, as thoroughly, and as skeptically as may be, the foundations of conduct and faith. For what we criticize are, at the outset, our own notions, which we want to have conform to the truth, if so be that there is any truth. As for doubt on religious questions, that is for a truth-seeker not only a privilege, but a duty; and, as we shall experience all through this study, doubt has a curious and very valuable place in philosophy. Philosophic truth, as such, comes to us first under the form of doubt; and we never can be very near it in our search unless, for a longer or shorter time, we have come to despair of it altogether. First, then, the despair of a thorough-going doubt, and then the discovery that this doubt contains in its bosom the truth that we are sworn to discover, however we can— this is the typical philosophic experience.

Josiah Royce, *The Religious Aspect of Philosophy* (1885)

CHAPTER 12

WILLIAM JAMES

Best known and most widely read of American thinkers at the turn of the last century was unquestionably William James, elder brother of Henry James, the novelist. Born in New York in 1842, he attended a series of private schools both there and, later, in France, England and Switzerland. He returned to the U.S.A. at the age of 18 to study art under W. M. Hunt of Boston, but after a year he abandoned this for science and entered Harvard University, where his teachers included Charles W. Eliot and the naturalist, Louis Agassiz. In 1863 he began the study of medicine and two years later joined an expedition led by Agassiz to the Amazon. Recrossing the Atlantic, he settled for a time in Germany, to continue his medical training under, among others, Helmholtz. But his own ill-health—he was to suffer much from neurasthenia—prevented him from taking up medical practice. Moreover, his interest was already turning to psychology and philosophy. In 1872 he commenced his teaching career at Harvard, lecturing on physiology and anatomy, and in 1876 was appointed assistant professor of physiology. It was largely through his efforts that the first laboratory for psychological research in the U.S.A. was established. In 1878 he married. From 1880 to 1885 he was assistant professor of philosophy, and then, until 1889, full professor. In the latter year he changed to the chair of psychology, but resumed that of philosophy in 1897 and occupied it till his retirement in 1907. He died in 1910. His chief publications include *The Principles of Psychology* (1890), a work which, more perhaps than any other single study in its field, gained for psychology an independent scientific status; *The Will to Believe* (1897); *Human Immortality* (1899); his Edinburgh Gifford Lectures (1901–2) on *The Varieties of Religious Experience* (1902), a classic of its subject; *Pragmatism: a New Name for Some Old Ways of Thinking* (1907); *The Meaning of Truth* (1909), a sequel to the foregoing; and the Oxford Hibbert Lectures (1908) entitled *A Pluralistic Universe* (1909).

Original and challenging in his views, James possessed commensurate literary gifts, so that his books continue to attract readers. He is never heavy or involved or platitudinous. His philosophy has been condemned as a patchwork of discordant tendencies and a mixture of opinions both serious and extravagant. But the judgement is unfair. He was not a system-builder; he preferred to examine concrete problems as issues in themselves and was cautious in his conclusions. Above all his thinking was an integral part of his life and not merely an academic role. The upshot was that the development of his mind followed a consistent course of three easily distinguishable stages, represented respectively by his pioneer work in psychology, his defence of pragmatism and the form of philosophic realism to which he gave the name of 'neutral monism'. The pragmatic principle was not of his own inventing. He derived it from his compatriot, C. S. Peirce, but he accorded it a wider, more thorough-going application. For Peirce the 'pragmatic maxim' was a device for achieving clarity of meaning: the question to be asked relative to the truth of a proposition was what difference it would make if it were not true. But he held firmly to the 'correspondence' theory and urged that no clarified hypothesis can ever be identified with the *final* truth upon a given matter, though he disliked metaphysics as a subject more curious than useful. James, however, expanded the maxim into a general principle: ideas should be treated in terms of their function; they are tools whose worth lies in their utility. 'It is astonishing to see', he wrote, 'how many philosophical disputes collapse into insignificance the moment you subject them to the test of tracing a concrete consequence. There can *be* no difference anywhere that does not *make* a difference elsewhere—no difference in abstract truth that does not express itself in a difference in concrete fact and in conduct consequent upon that fact.' Theories were instruments, not answers to enigmas, so that the task of philosophy, so far from being a meagre traffic in first principles, categories and the like, was to seek for 'fruits, consequences, facts'. Indeed the measure of truth itself must be sought in practice. The test of an idea is whether, or to what extent, it 'works'. 'Any idea upon which we can ride, so to speak; any idea that will carry us prosperously from any one part of our experience to any other part, linking things satisfactorily, working securely, simplifying, saving labor, is true for just so much.' Such is the view which James characterizes, suitably enough, as 'radical empiricism'. Truth is not a purely intellectual value, but a directive, rather, for conduct; nor does it possess any quality of absoluteness: it is relative and mutable, according to the conditions and demands of human experience.

In *The Will to Believe* James argues that there are certain 'forced options' in a man's life—questions, that is, about which he must needs make up his mind, for or against, with no *tertium quid*. An example of these is the question of freedom, another that of the existence of God. On such issues one cannot remain neutral, since *not* to decide is itself to opt negatively. Where decision goes beyond the evidence the only genuinely empirical approach is in recognizing that the evidence simply has to be transcended, or at any rate new evidence must be looked for at second remove, by considering the effect of the option upon one's life. Further, the very act of believing itself contributes to the truth of the belief by demonstrating that it does work. The more surely, for instance, I believe in my freedom as an agent the more certainly am I likely to act as one. On the particular issue of religious belief James holds that an attitude of intellectual agnosticism is equivalent to rejecting the religious hypothesis as false. In matters of faith suspension of belief from merely theoretical considerations is impossible. As James forthrightly puts it: 'When I look at the religious question, then the command that we shall put a stopper on our heart, instincts and courage, and *wait*—acting of course meanwhile as if religion were *not* true—till doomsday, or till such time as our intellect and senses working together may have raked in evidence enough—this command, I say, seems to me the queerest idol ever manufactured in the philosophic cave.'

For James the significance of religion is not therefore to be measured by the extent to which its teachings can be justified in terms of metaphysical argument. What we must learn to understand is the function it exercises in life. The deduction of God's metaphysical attributes is but 'a shuffling and matching of pedantic dictionary-adjectives, aloof from morals, aloof from human minds'. Let us turn, then, to the concrete facts of the religious life itself to discover what religion truly is; for what we find there are not proofs of abstractions but changed lives. Not indeed that all the manifest effects of religious conviction can be attributed to a supernatural cause—there is much that psychology can account for on its own principles—and religion in the course of time acquires 'over-beliefs', as James calls them, which have no direct bearing on the experience itself; yet the consequences of religious faith for human conduct are such as to suggest that the religious interpretation of life is a legitimate one. The conscious person, he concludes, is continuous with a wider self through which 'saving experiences' come. The empirical evidence renders this 'literally and objectively true as far as it goes'. We reach out, that is, to the further limits of our being, to an 'altogether other dimension of our existence' from the merely sensible and 'understandable' world. It would be incorrect to describe this region as merely ideal since it produces effects in the world we know, and 'that which produces effects within another reality must be termed a reality itself'. To this reality we fitly give the name of God. 'We and God have business with each other; and in opening ourselves to his influence our deepest destiny is fulfilled.' But in using the word God James does not think it necessary to refer to an absolute or infinite Being. Uniqueness and infinity may be the attributes usually applied to deity, yet he questions whether religious experience can be cited unequivocally as supporting the 'infinitist' belief. The only thing it certainly testifies is that we can experience union with *something* larger than ourselves and in that union find our surest peace. Philosophy and mysticism will seek to go farther, but the 'practical needs and experiences' of religion are sufficiently met by the belief that beyond each man 'and in a fashion continuous with him' there exists a larger power which is friendly to him and to his ideals. Why not content ourselves with the idea of a pluralistic universe and a finite God as most consistent with the facts of the spiritual life?

Bibliographical note

William James' principal publications have been many times reprinted and are easily obtainable. See R. B. Perry, 'William James', in *Dictionary of American Biography*, IX (1932), 590–600, and the same author's *The Thought and Character of William James* (1935). Also L. T. Hobhouse, 'Faith and the Will to Believe', in *Proceedings of the Aristotelian Society* (1903), J. Royce, *William James and Other Essays on the Philosophy of Life* (1912), F. C. S. Schiller, 'William James and Empiricism', in *Journal of Philosophy* (1928), and Margaret Knight, *William James* (1950).

THE WILL TO BELIEVE

Believe truth! Shun error!—these, we see, are two materially different laws; and by choosing between them we may end, coloring differently our whole intellectual life. We may regard the chase for truth as paramount, and the avoidance of error as secondary; or we may, on the other hand, treat the avoidance of error as more imperative, and let truth take its chance. [W. K.] Clifford[1]...exhorts us to the latter course. Believe nothing, he tells us, keep your mind in suspense forever, rather than by closing it on insufficient evidence incur the awful risk of believing lies. You, on the other hand, may think that the risk of being in error is a very small matter when compared with the blessings of real knowledge, and be ready to be duped many times in your investigation rather than postpone indefinitely the chance of guessing true. I myself find it impossible to go with Clifford. We must remember that these feelings of our duty about either truth or error are in any case only expressions of our passional life. Biologically considered, our minds are as ready to grind out falsehood as veracity, and he who says, 'Better go without belief forever than believe a lie!' merely shows his own preponderant private horror of becoming a dupe. He may be critical of many of his desires and fears, but this fear he slavishly obeys. He cannot imagine any one questioning its binding force. For my own part, I have also a horror of being duped; but I can

---

[1] W. K. Clifford (1845–79), mathematician and philosopher. James is referring to the essay on 'The Ethics of Belief', reprinted in Clifford's *Lectures and Essays* (1879).—*Ed.*

believe that worse things than being duped may happen to a man in this world: so Clifford's exhortation has to my ears a thoroughly fantastic sound. It is like a general informing his soldiers that it is better to keep out of battle forever than to risk a single wound. Not so are victories either over enemies or over nature gained. Our errors are surely not such awfully solemn things. In a world where we are so certain to incur them in spite of all our caution, a certain lightness of heart seems healthier than this excessive nervousness on their behalf. At any rate, it seems the fittest thing for the empiricist philosopher.

*　　*　　*

And now...let us go straight at our question. I have said, and now repeat it, that not only as a matter of fact do we find our passional nature influencing us in our opinions, but that there are some options between opinions in which this influence must be regarded both as an inevitable and as a lawful determinant of our choice.

I fear here that some of you my hearers will begin to scent danger, and lend an inhospitable ear. Two first steps of passion you have indeed had to admit as necessary—we must think so as to avoid dupery, and we must think so as to gain truth; but the surest path to those ideal consummations, you will probably consider, is from now onwards to take no further passional step.

Well, of course, I agree as far as the facts will allow. Wherever the option between losing truth and gaining it is not momentous, we can throw the chance of *gaining truth* away, and at any rate save ourselves from any chance of *believing falsehood*, by not making up our minds at all till objective evidence has come. In scientific questions, this is almost always the case; and even in human affairs in general, the need of acting is seldom so urgent that a false belief to act on is better than no belief at all. Law courts, indeed, have to decide on the best evidence attainable for the moment, because a judge's duty is to make law as well as to ascertain it, and (as a learned judge once said to me) few cases are worth spending much time over: the great thing is to have them decided on *any* acceptable principle, and got out of the way. But in our dealings with objective nature we obviously are recorders, not makers, of the truth; and decisions for the mere sake of deciding promptly and getting on to the next business would be wholly out of place. Throughout the breadth of physical nature facts are what they are quite independently of us, and seldom is there any such hurry about them that the risks of being duped by believing a premature theory need be faced. The questions here are always trivial options, the hypotheses are hardly living (at any rate not living for us spectators), the choice between believing truth or falsehood is seldom forced. The attitude of sceptical balance is therefore the absolutely wise one if we would escape mistakes. What difference, indeed, does it make to most of us whether we have or have not a theory of the Röntgen rays, whether we believe or not in mind-stuff, or have a conviction about the causality of conscious states? It makes no difference. Such options are not forced on us. On every account it is better not to make them, but still keep weighing reasons *pro et contra* with an indifferent hand.

I speak, of course, here of the purely judging mind. For purposes of discovery such indifference is to be less highly recommended, and science would be far less advanced than she is if the passionate desires of individuals to get their own faiths confirmed had been kept out of the game. See, for example, the sagacity which [Herbert] Spencer and [August] Weismann[1] now display. On the other hand, if you want an absolute duffer in an investigation, you must, after all, take the man who has no interest whatever in its results: he is the warranted incapable, the positive fool. The most useful investigator, because the most sensitive observer, is always he whose eager interest in one side of the question is balanced by an equally keen nervousness lest he become deceived.[2] Science has organized this nervousness into a regular *technique*, her so-called method of verification; and she has fallen so deeply in love with the method that one may even say she has ceased to care for truth by itself at all. It is only truth as technically verified that interests her. The truth of truths might come in merely affirmative form, and she would decline to touch it. Such truth as that, she might repeat with Clifford, would be stolen in defiance of her duty to mankind. Human passions, however, are stronger than technical rules. 'Le cœur a ses raisons', as Pascal says, 'que la raison ne connaît pas'; and however indifferent to all but the bare rules of the game the umpire, the abstract intellect, may be, the concrete players who furnish him the materials to judge of are usually, each one of them, in love with some pet 'live hypothesis' of his own. Let us agree, however, that

---

[1] August Weismann (1834–1914) a biologist and adherent to the Darwinian theory.—*Ed.*

[2] Compare Wilfrid Ward's Essay, 'The Wish to Believe', in his *Witnesses to the Unseen* (Macmillan and Co., 1893).

wherever there is no forced option, the dispassionately judicial intellect with no pet hypothesis, saving us, as it does, from dupery at any rate, ought to be our ideal.

The question next arises: Are there not somewhere forced options in our speculative questions, and can we (as men who may be interested at least as much in positively gaining truth as in merely escaping dupery) always wait with impunity till the coercive evidence shall have arrived? It seems *a priori* improbable that the truth should be so nicely adjusted to our needs and powers as that. In the great boarding-house of nature, the cakes and the butter and the syrup seldom come out so even and leave the plates so clean. Indeed, we should view them with scientific suspicion if they did.

*   *   *

Moral questions immediately present themselves as questions whose solution cannot wait for sensible proof. A moral question is a question not of what sensibly exists, but of what is good, or would be good if it did exist. Science can tell us what exists; but to compare the *worths*, both of what exists and of what does not exist, we must consult not science, but what Pascal calls our heart. Science herself consults her heart when she lays it down that the infinite ascertainment of fact and correction of false belief are the supreme goods for man. Challenge the statement, and science can only repeat it oracularly, or else prove it by showing that such ascertainment and correction bring man all sorts of other goods which man's heart in turn declares. The question of having moral beliefs at all or not having them is decided by our will. Are our moral preferences true or false, or are they only odd biological phenomena, making things good or bad for *us*, but in themselves indifferent? How can your pure intellect decide? If your heart does not *want* a world of moral reality, your head will assuredly never make you believe in one. Mephistophelian scepticism, indeed, will satisfy the head's play-instincts much better than any rigorous idealism can. Some men (even at the student age) are so naturally cool-hearted that the moralistic hypothesis never has for them any pungent life, and in their supercilious presence the hot young moralist always feels strangely ill at ease. The appearance of knowingness is on their side, of *naïveté* and gullibility on his. Yet, in the inarticulate heart of him, he clings to it that he is not a dupe, and that there is a realm in which (as Emerson says) all their wit and intellectual superiority is no better than the cunning of a fox. Moral scepticism can no more be refuted or proved by logic than intellectual scepticism can. When we stick to it that there *is* truth (be it of either kind), we do so with our whole nature, and resolve to stand or fall by the results. The sceptic with his whole nature adopts the doubting attitude; but which of us is the wiser, Omniscience only knows.

Turn now from these wide questions of good to a certain class of questions of fact, questions concerning personal relations, states of mind between one man and another. *Do you like me or not?*—for example. Whether you do or not depends, in countless instances, on whether I meet you half-way, am willing to assume that you must like me, and show you trust and expectation. The previous faith on my part in your liking's existence is in such cases what makes your liking come. But if I stand aloof, and refuse to budge an inch until I have objective evidence, until you shall have done something apt, as the absolutists say, *ad extorquendum assensum meum*, ten to one your liking never comes. How many women's hearts are vanquished by the mere sanguine insistence of some man that they *must* love him! he will not consent to the hypothesis that they cannot. The desire for a certain kind of truth here brings about that special truth's existence; and so it is in innumerable cases of other sorts. Who gains promotions, boons, appointments, but the man in whose life they are seen to play the part of live hypotheses, who discounts them, sacrifices other things for their sake before they have come, and takes risks for them in advance? His faith acts on the powers above him as a claim, and creates its own verification.

A social organism of any sort whatever, large or small, is what it is because each member proceeds to his own duty with a trust that the other members will simultaneously do theirs. Wherever a desired result is achieved by the co-operation of many independent persons, its existence as a fact is a pure consequence of the precursive faith in one another of those immediately concerned. A government, an army, a commercial system, a ship, a college, an athletic team, all exist on this condition, without which not only is nothing achieved, but nothing is even attempted. A whole train of passengers (individually brave enough) will be looted by a few highwaymen, simply because the latter can count on one another, while each passenger fears that if he makes a movement of resistance, he will be shot before any one else backs him up. If we believed that the whole car-full would rise at once with us, we should each severally rise, and train-robbing would never even be attempted. There are, then, cases where a fact cannot come at all unless a preliminary faith exists in its coming. *And where faith in a fact can help create the fact*, that would be an insane logic which should say that faith running ahead of scientific evidence is the 'lowest kind of immorality' into which a thinking being can fall. Yet such is the logic by which our scientific absolutists pretend to regulate our lives!

*   *   *

In truths dependent on our personal action, then, faith based on desire is certainly a lawful and possibly an indispensable thing.

But now, it will be said, these are all childish human cases, and have nothing to do with great cosmical matters, like the question of religious faith. Let us then pass on to that. Religions differ so much in their accidents that in discussing the religious question we must make it very generic and broad. What then do we now mean by the religious hypothesis? Science says things are; morality says some things are better than other things; and religion says essentially two things.

First, she says that the best things are the more eternal things, the overlapping things, the things in the universe that throw the last stone, so to speak, and say the final word. 'Perfection is eternal'—this phrase of Charles Secrétan[1] seems a good way of putting this first affirmation of religion, an affirmation which obviously cannot yet be verified scientifically at all.

The second affirmation of religion is that we are better off even now if we believe her first affirmation to be true.

Now, let us consider what the logical elements of this situation are *in case the religious hypothesis in both its branches be really true*. (Of course, we must admit that possibility at the outset. If we are to discuss the question at all, it must involve a living option. If for any of you religion be a hypothesis that cannot, by any living possibility be true, then you need go no farther. I speak to the 'saving remnant' alone.) So proceeding, we see, first, that religion offers itself as a *momentous* option. We are supposed to gain, even now, by our belief, and to lose by our non-belief, a certain vital good. Secondly, religion is a *forced* option, so far as that good goes. We cannot escape the issue by remaining sceptical

[1] Charles Secrétan (1815–95), a Swiss theologian whose voluntaristic philosophy of faith showed strong Kantian influence.—*Ed.*

and waiting for more light, because, although we do avoid error in that way *if religion be untrue*, we lose the good, *if it be true*, just as certainly as if we positively chose to disbelieve. It is as if a man should hesitate indefinitely to ask a certain woman to marry him because he was not perfectly sure that she would prove an angel after he brought her home. Would he not cut himself off from that particular angel-possibility as decisively as if he went and married some one else? Scepticism, then, is not avoidance of option; it is option of a certain particular kind of risk. *Better risk loss of truth than chance of error*—that is your faith-vetoer's exact position. He is actively playing his stake as much as the believer is; he is backing the field against the religious hypothesis, just as the believer is backing the religious hypothesis against the field. To preach scepticism to us as a duty until 'sufficient evidence' for religion be found, is tantamount therefore to telling us, when in presence of the religious hypothesis, that to yield to our fear of its being error is wiser and better than to yield to our hope that it may be true. It is not intellect against all passions, then; it is only intellect with one passion laying down its law. And by what, forsooth, is the supreme wisdom of this passion warranted? Dupery for dupery, what proof is there that dupery through hope is so much worse than dupery through fear? I, for one, can see no proof; and I simply refuse obedience to the scientist's command to imitate his kind of option, in a case where my own stake is important enough to give me the right to choose my own form of risk. If religion be true and the evidence for it be still insufficient, I do not wish, by putting your extinguisher upon my nature (which feels to me as if it had after all some business in this matter), to forfeit my sole chance in life of getting upon the winning side— that chance depending, of course, on my willingness to run the risk of acting as if my passional need of taking the world religiously might be prophetic and right.

All this is on the supposition that it really may be prophetic and right, and that, even to us who are discussing the matter, religion is a live hypothesis which may be true. Now, to most of us religion comes in a still further way that makes a veto on our active faith even more illogical. The more perfect and more eternal aspect of the universe is represented in our religions as having personal form. The universe is no longer a mere *It* to us, but a *Thou*, if we are religious; and any relation that may be possible from person to person might be possible here. For instance, although in one sense we are passive portions of the universe, in another we show a curious autonomy, as if we were small active centres on our own account. We feel, too, as if the appeal of religion to us were made to our own active good-will, as if evidence might be forever withheld from us unless we met the hypothesis half-way. To take a trivial illustration: just as a man who in a company of gentlemen made no advances, asked a warrant for every concession, and believed no one's word without proof, would cut himself off by such churlishness from all the social rewards that a more trusting spirit would earn—so here, one who should shut himself up in snarling logicality and try to make the gods extort his recognition willy-nilly, or not get it at all, might cut himself off forever from his only opportunity of making the gods' acquaintance. This feeling, forced on us we know not whence, that by obstinately believing that there are gods (although not to do so would be so easy both for our logic and our life) we are doing the universe the deepest service we can, seems part of the living essence of the religious hypothesis. If the hypothesis *were* true in all its parts, including this one, then pure intellectualism, with its veto on our making willing advances, would be an absurdity; and some participation of our sympathetic nature would be logically required. I, therefore, for one, cannot see my way to accepting the agnostic rules for truth-seeking, or wilfully agree to keep my willing nature out of the game. I cannot do so for this plain reason, that *a rule of thinking which would absolutely prevent me from acknowledging certain kinds of truth if those kinds of truth were really there, would be an irrational rule*. That for me is the long and short of the formal logic of the situation, no matter what the kinds of truth might materially be.

I confess I do not see how this logic can be escaped. But sad experience makes me fear that some of you may still shrink from radically saying with me, *in abstracto*, that we have the right to believe at our own risk any hypothesis that is live enough to tempt our will. I suspect, however, that if this is so, it is because you have got away from the abstract logical point of view altogether, and are thinking (perhaps without realizing it) of some particular religious hypothesis which for you is dead. The freedom to 'believe what we will' you apply to the case of some patent superstition; and the faith you think of is the faith defined by the schoolboy when he said, 'Faith is when you believe something that you know ain't true'. I can only repeat that this is misapprehension. *In concreto*, the freedom to believe can only cover living options which the intellect of the individual cannot by itself resolve; and living options never seem absurdities to him who has them to consider. When I look at the religious question as it really puts itself to concrete men, and when I think of all the possibilities which both practically and theoretically it involves, then this command that we shall put a stopper on our heart, instincts, and courage, and *wait*—acting of course meanwhile more or less as if religion were *not* true[1]—till doomsday, or till such time as our intellect and senses working together may have raked in evidence enough—this command, I say, seems to me the queerest idol ever manufactured in the philosophic cave. Were we scholastic absolutists, there might be more excuse. If we had an infallible intellect with its objective certitudes, we might feel ourselves disloyal to such a perfect organ of knowledge in not trusting to it exclusively, in not waiting for its releasing word. But if we are empiricists, if we believe that no bell in us tolls to let us know for certain when truth is in our grasp, then it seems a piece of idle fantasticality to preach so solemnly our duty of waiting for the bell. Indeed we *may* wait if we will—I hope you do not think that I am denying that—but if we do so, we do so at our peril as much as if we believed. In either case we *act*, taking our life in our hands. No one of us ought to issue vetoes to the other, nor should we bandy words of abuse. We ought, on the contrary, delicately and profoundly to respect one another's mental freedom: then only shall we bring about the intellectual republic; then only shall we have that spirit of inner tolerance without which all our outer tolerance is soulless, and which is empiricism's glory; then only shall we live and let live, in speculative as well as in practical things.

The Will to Believe (1897)

[1] Since belief is measured by action, he who forbids us to believe religion to be true, necessarily also forbids us to act as we should if we did believe it to be true. The whole defence of religious faith hinges upon action. If the action required or inspired by the religious hypothesis is in no way different from that dictated by the naturalistic hypothesis, then religious faith is a pure superfluity, better pruned away, and controversy about its legitimacy is a piece of idle trifling, unworthy of serious minds. I myself believe, of course, that the religious hypothesis gives to the world an expression which specifically determines our reactions, and makes them in a large part unlike what they might be on a purely naturalistic scheme of belief.

INDEX OF WORKS CITED

Arnold, Matthew (1822–88), *Literature and Dogma* (1873), 328–37

Bradley, Francis Herbert (1846–1924), *Appearance and Reality* (1893), 369–73

Caird, Edward (1835–1908), *The Evolution of Religion* (1893), 363–9

Caird, John (1820–98), *An Introduction to the Philosophy of Religion* (1880), 355–62

Coleridge, Samuel Taylor (1772–1834)
Aids to Reflection (1825), 242 f.
Confessions of an Enquiring Spirit (1840), 25 ff.
Literary Remains (ed. H. N. Coleridge) (1836–9), 244–51

Comte, Auguste (1798–1857), *A Discourse on the Positive Spirit* (1844), 199–207

Emerson, Ralph Waldo (1803–82), *Essays* (First Series) (1841), 377–80

Feuerbach, Ludwig (1804–72), *The Essence of Christianity* (1841), 85–112

Harnack, Adolf (1851–1930), *What is Christianity?* (1900), 152–65

Hegel, George Wilhelm Friedrich (1770–1831), *The Philosophy of Religion* (1832), 65–81

Holland, Henry Scott (1847–1918), 'Faith', in *Lux Mundi* (1889), 341–51

James, William (1842–1910), *The Will to Believe* (1897), 395–403

Jowett, Benjamin (1817–93), 'The Interpretation of Scripture', in *Essays and Reviews* (1860), 312–23

Kierkegaard, Søren (1813–55), *Philosophical Fragments* (1844), 170–83

Lamennais, Félicité de (1782–1854), *Essay on Indifference in the Matter of Religion* (1817–24), 187–95

Lotze, Hermann (1817–81), *Mikrokosmus* (1854–6), 127–37

Mansel, Henry Longueville (1820–71), *The Limits of Religious Thought Examined* (1859), 290–6

Maurice, Frederick Denison (1805–72)
The Kingdom of Christ (1838), 262–8
What is Revelation? (1859), 257–62

Mill, John Stuart (1806–73), *Three Essays on Religion* (1874), 300–8

Newman, John Henry (1801–90)
University Sermons (1839), 273 f.
An Essay on the Development of Christian Doctrine (1845), 284–7
An Essay in Aid of a Grammar of Assent (1870), 274–84

Ritschl, Albrecht (1822–89), *The Christian Doctrine of Justification and Reconciliation* (1870–4), 141–8

Royce, Josiah (1853–1916), *The Religious Aspect of Philosophy* (1885), 384–91

INDEX OF WORKS CITED

Sabatier, Auguste (1839–1901), *Outlines of a Philosophy of Religion based on Psychology and History* (1897), 211–17

Schleiermacher, Friedrich Ernst Daniel (1768–1834)
    Speeches on Religion (1799), 42–5
    The Christian Faith (1821–2), 51–64

Solovyov, Vladimir (1853–1900), *Lectures on Godmanhood* (1878), 221–36

Strauss, David Friedrich (1808–74), *The Life of Jesus* (1835), 116–24